SOCIAL JUSTICE

SOCIAL JUSTICE

by David Miller

CLARENDON PRESS · OXFORD
1976

Oxford University Press, Ely House, London W. 1

GLASGOW   NEW YORK   TORONTO   MELBOURNE   WELLINGTON
CAPE TOWN   IBADAN   NAIROBI   DAR ES SALAAM   LUSAKA   ADDIS ABABA
DELHI   BOMBAY   CALCUTTA   MADRAS   KARACHI   LAHORE   DACCA
KUALA LUMPUR   SINGAPORE   HONG KONG   TOKYO

ISBN 0 19 824556 4

Printed in Great Britain by
Billing & Sons Limited, Guildford and London

PREFACE

The purpose of this book is to give an account of an idea which is often voiced but rarely understood: social justice. Many readers will doubtless suspect that this idea is nothing more than a useful ornament for rounding off party manifestos or reformers' tracts, fine-sounding but with no real meaning. I hope to show that the idea has rather more substance than this, but the reader should be warned that he will not be told what social justice is. He may, however, find that the lines of thought contained in this book assist him to make up his own mind.

At an early stage in my research I decided that the idea of social justice could only be understood properly by approaching it from several angles, and this explains the plan of the book. The first part is devoted to conceptual analysis, through which I first identify three criteria for applying the idea of justice, and then examine the meaning and significance of each criterion in turn. The main points which emerge from this analysis are that the three criteria are conceptually distinct, that they give rise to conflicting prescriptions for action, and that there is no logical or conceptual way of choosing between them. These points lead on to the second part of the book, where I compare the writings of three political theorists in order to discover what kind of justification can be given for a criterion of justice. The choice of writers was made partly on the grounds that each held one of the three views of justice I had earlier distinguished, and partly on the grounds that they were worth examining for their own sake—Hume because his political theory had often been misunderstood, Spencer and Kropotkin because they had suffered from undeserved neglect. I hope that even a reader out of sympathy with the general project may find the interpretations offered in these chapters of some interest.

The final part of the book could be described as an exercise in interpretative sociology. I compare the social thinking of

several types of society in order to show that there are quite
radical differences of outlook on matters of social justice
between societies, and that these differences can be explained
by reference to features of the social structure. To make these
comparisons, I have drawn upon the established body of literature dealing with each social type, but I am painfully aware of
the extent of controversy within each field, and specialists in
these areas will no doubt find my analysis oversimplified in
many respects. I can only plead that some oversimplification is
inevitable if the kind of comparative analysis attempted here
is to be carried out; and I believe that comparative analysis is
the only way to avoid the parochialism which has infected so
much recent political theory.

An earlier version of this work was submitted as a doctoral
dissertation, and my first acknowledgement must be to my
supervisor, Professor John Plamenatz, for the constant encouragement which he gave to me during the period of preparation and for the scrupulous attention with which he read
everything I produced. His comments, verbal and written,
were invaluable. I should also like to thank my D.Phil. ex-
aminers, Brian Barry and Professor D. D. Raphael, for their
helpful criticism at the viva voce examination, and Professor
Raphael for kindly allowing me to consult his extensive written notes. Geoffrey Smith has read and commented upon the
entire manuscript, and John Urry has given me valuable
advice on the final chapter. I have also benefited greatly from
discussions at various times with Nicholas Abercrombie, John
Benson, Adrian Cunningham, Peter Hacker, Russell Keat,
Steven Lukes, and Stewart Miller. All of these people will be
disappointed to find that I have sometimes stuck to positions
which they have soundly criticized, and for this perversity I
take sole responsibility.

DAVID MILLER

Lancaster,
January 1975

CONTENTS

page

INTRODUCTION
THE ANALYSIS OF POLITICAL IDEAS

Political theorists are notorious for their disagreement about the proper object of their inquiry. To some, political theory is concerned with certain perennial questions, particularly with the nature of the state, and with the citizen's obligation towards it. To others, the nature of political theory changes as society and government change. New circumstances create fresh problems requiring theoretical attention, while traditional concerns may become less pressing. For those, like the present writer, who take the latter view, a leading characteristic of contemporary political theory is its concern with a range of concepts and principles specifying the ends of government, while questions about the origin, form, and justification of government have become less central. The modern political theorist has to deal with ideas like liberty, equality, welfare, and social justice in terms of which government policies can be evaluated. He may also address himself to the problem of political obligation, but this will not be an overriding concern.

If this point of view is accepted, we can express the problems of method which the political theorist faces in terms of the set of concepts to which he must give his attention—concepts such as liberty and social justice. Given that the meaning of these concepts is problematic, how should he set about analysing and interpreting them? And having given his interpretation, should he also attempt to prescribe that some ends be pursued in preference to others? Would his prescriptions have a different status from those which the man in the street might offer? It is obvious that these questions must be answered before we can begin our analysis of the concept which primarily concerns us, social justice. This section gives such an answer, in setting out a methodological position for political theory. Although the discussion is fairly brief, it should not be thought that I regard these questions of method as unimportant. On the contrary, the remainder of the book is not only an account of social justice but also an attempt to vindicate a certain view of political theory. I hope to show both that the methods advocated here can be implemented in practice, and that they give a fuller understanding of political ideas than any alternative method.

One approach to political ideas which has found favour recently is linguistic analysis. Although it is hard to find a definitive work in which this method is either expounded or defended (Weldon's *The Vocabulary of Politics*, which is often referred to in this connection, was influenced more heavily by logical positivism than by the later analytical movement), it is certainly true that much important work in political theory of recent years has made substantial use of the linguistic method. (Particular mention might be made here of the work of H. L. A. Hart and Brian Barry.) Linguistic analysis was of course first developed as a general programme for philosophy, and only later applied to political ideas in particular. The central thesis of the linguistic school is that the concepts which give rise to philosophical problems should be analysed and clarified by noting their use in everyday life—i.e. by observing how they are used by ordinary men to pass information, get other people to do things, express emotions, and so on. Linguistic philosophers deny that there are any specifically philosophical concepts, and believe that concepts have only acquired a special philosophical sense because earlier philosophers engaged in abstract speculation on ideas like perception, existence, and causation, instead of paying attention to the ordinary use of words such as 'perceives', 'exists', and 'causes' in human intercourse. They also urge us to pay attention to the *variety* of uses which a word such as 'perceives' may have, and argue that a potent source of philosophical error is the assumption that every word has just a single meaning. The implication of this view for political ideas is of course that we should stop asking questions such as 'What does freedom really consist in?' or 'What does "justice" really mean?', and look instead at the actual uses of these concepts in everyday life. To understand what 'freedom' means, for instance, we should look at statements such as 'You are perfectly free to leave', asking when they might be made and what the purpose of making them might be.

Although linguistic analysis as a general method in philosophy has lately attracted criticism from inside the discipline itself, it is not my intention to enter the debate on either side at this level. I want instead to point out some peculiar features of political ideas which imply that the linguistic method has only a limited use in enabling us to understand them. Linguistic analysis is certainly indispensable as a starting-point, but it can only give us a partial understanding of concepts such as justice and freedom. I shall explain shortly what additional help is required.

The first feature of political ideas to which I wish to draw attention is the historical change which these ideas often undergo. If we compare, for instance, the conceptual apparatus available to Greek political thinkers with that which we possess, we shall find important differences. The Greeks, for example, lacked our concept of a moral or legal right; the term 'democracy' carried for them a very different meaning from that which it bears for us; and so on. While such change doubtless occurs with concepts other than political ones, it appears that in the case of political ideas the transformation is both more rapid and more far-reaching—certainly this holds if one compares these ideas with the basic concepts of epistemology such as 'perception' and 'belief'. The linguistic analyst therefore runs the risk of temporal parochialism to a much greater extent in approaching political concepts than in approaching concepts in other areas of philosophy. Because he examines the way in which his contemporaries use certain terms, he loses sight of the historical changes to which those terms have been subject, and thus presents an unduly narrow account of the related concepts. Instead of explaining what a concept such as 'freedom' means, it will rightly be said that he has explained what the concept means for the members of a particular society at a certain moment in time. And not only is this manifestly incomplete as an account of the concept, but it also carries the further risk that concepts currently undergoing a change of meaning will be ossified by the analyst's method, so that he will either overlook the change altogether or else actively intervene on the side of linguistic conservatism by describing the new applications of a particular concept as misapplications. The fact that political concepts change over time, then, limits the usefulness of the linguistic method in understanding them.

A second feature of political ideas which has similar implications is the often acute disagreement over the use of some of these ideas which arises within societies such as our own. The meaning of key political terms such as 'democracy', 'justice', and 'freedom' is contested between different groups, each group attaching its own peculiar significance to a particular term, and trying to get its interpretation generally accepted. These differences over the meaning of words arise largely from more basic political differences. Thus Burkean conservatives and guild socialists can hardly be expected to agree on the meaning of 'democracy'; nor would it surprise us to find that a Marxist and an economic liberal differed over the meaning they attached to 'social justice'. The existence of such disagreement has often been observed, but its implications for the programme of linguistic analysis have not been fully grasped. In the face of sharp divergences in the use of the terms he is studying, how should the linguistic analyst proceed? He can either look for a common element of meaning in all uses of the term he is studying—but this common meaning may be so vague that it masks the significance which the term has for any of the groups who use it; or he can catalogue the variety of uses which he discovers—but a mere listing of uses without any explanation of why a particular group should interpret the term as it does would be most unilluminating. He needs above all to account for the divergence in use which he has found; but to do that he must go beyond the use of language itself, in ways which will be discussed shortly.

Finally, a third characteristic of political ideas must be mentioned, which again is manifest when pointed out, but whose implications for political theory have once more not been properly understood. The concepts which the political theorist studies have an important role to play in justifying policies and institutional arrangements. It is therefore to be expected that they will be incorporated into the systematic ideologies which have been developed to explain and justify the workings of modern societies. Thus, nineteenth-century capitalism and twentieth-century socialism both produced their own distinctive ideologies, and within each was contained a different view of what justice, freedom, etc., really meant. These ideologies,

and others like them, served to protect the classes who benefited from each system from critical attack, and did so by
gaining widespread acceptance among the members of society,
despite the existence of counter-ideologies and of groups wishing to promote them. Where such a dominant ideology exists,
we may observe a further weakness in the linguistic method of
analysing political ideas. This weakness is perhaps best brought
out through an example. Suppose that X says to Y, 'I think
that 75p per hour is a fair rate for that job.' What is X's statement being used to do? A linguistic philosopher will correctly
say that it is probably being used by X to persuade Y to accept
the arrangement referred to—X giving him a particular kind of
reason for accepting it. On the level of the two individuals in
question, X and Y, this is perfectly in order. The analysis fails,
however, to bring out that on another level the statement, by
employing the concept of fairness in the way that it does, may
serve to reinforce a particular ideology, and thus indirectly a
social system. Although it directly only justifies paying a specified sum of money as a reward for one particular job, the
statement indirectly endorses a view of fairness as, roughly,
getting the appropriate reward for the work one does, and this
view in turn plays a part in several social ideologies. This
'use' of the statement cannot be discovered by conventional
techniques of linguistic analysis, since it is not the use which the
statement has for any particular individual. (There is no reason
to suppose that X intends his statement to serve the further
purpose which it does.) To uncover the full range of uses which
a concept such as 'fairness' has, it is therefore not enough to
examine verbal transactions between individuals; it is necessary in addition to look at the concept's place within the whole
set of beliefs which compose an ideology, and at the functions
which that ideology serves.

The three characteristics of political ideas to which I have
referred—their historical variation, their contested character,
and their ideological functions—all suggest that these ideas
cannot be fully understood by examining the use of language
which expresses them. None the less linguistic analysis remains
an indispensable starting-point for two reasons. First, if we
want to explain the variety of uses to which a certain concept is
put, it is necessary at the outset to establish, as accurately as

possible, the range and limits of the concept's use. Linguistic analysis is helpful here precisely because it prevents us from taking too narrow a view of the uses to which the concept we are studying may legitimately be put (or, on the other hand, from supposing that the concept may be used in any way one pleases). Even though the range of uses we discover may be specific to our historical situation, it is only possible to chart historical changes in use by reference to a contemporary conceptual map. Second, linguistic analysis is needed to enable us to distinguish one concept from another. How, for instance, can we show that the principle which states 'A man should not be prevented from doing what he wants except when his actions are harmful to others' is a principle of freedom rather than, say, a principle of democracy, except by pointing out that this simply *is* how the concepts in question are used? 'Freedom' is used to talk about areas of unconstrained action and similar problems, whereas 'democracy' is used when we are discussing ways of making collective decisions, and so on. Thus careful attention to the use of language is an essential part of political theorizing; the question before us now, however, is whether it is the whole of political theorizing, and if not, what else has to be done. My argument has been that something more *is* needed, and I want now to try to say what this 'something more' is.

Let us take it that we have explored the variety of uses to which a political concept such as freedom is put in a society like our own. The next step, I suggest, is to see whether this variety cannot be reduced to manageable proportions by locating a fairly small number of basic meanings which the concept bears. Whether or not this can be done is of course an open question, but it seems a matter of fact that the contested concepts central to political theory—justice, democracy, freedom, and so forth—have at most three or four well-established uses, and that the contest over their meaning takes place between this small number of interpretations. Thus political philosophers have isolated two concepts of liberty,[1] and two concepts of democracy;[2] in this book, I shall distinguish between three

[1] See I. Berlin, 'Two Concepts of Liberty' in his *Four Essays on Liberty* (Oxford, 1969).
[2] See J. Schumpeter, *Capitalism, Socialism and Democracy* (London, 1954), esp. chs. 21 and 22.

concepts of social justice. Whether or not these classifications are wholly correct, they point to a common view that the concepts in question possess, not an irreducibly large number of meanings, but rather a small number of basic meanings which may sensibly be isolated. Assuming, then, that this reduction can be carried out, we must ask whether the political theorist's task is complete, when two or three concepts of freedom, and so on, have been distinguished. In my view his task has only just begun. For if we ask *why* the concepts in question should display such a diversity of meaning, the answer is that each version of a particular concept finds its natural home in a different way of looking at society; and because there are several such ways of looking at society, it is quite understandable that our political concepts should display the diversity that they do.

'A way of looking at society' is an unpleasantly vague phrase, but it seems to be necessary at this point to refer both to the well-articulated, coherent models of society which we find in the writings of the major political thinkers and to the much less coherent world-views upheld by ordinary men who are not theorists, but who require some way of making sense of their social existence. Some of these ways of looking at society will be appropriately described as ideologies, but, since when we so describe them we imply that they embody certain forms of distortion,[3] a neutral description is also required—and 'way of looking at society' or 'view of society' (I shall use these phrases interchangeably) satisfies this requirement. It may also justly be remarked that to speak of concepts 'finding their natural home' in views of society is less than pellucid. The relationship between concept and way of looking at society is hard to state concisely, and is probably best elucidated by considering an example in some detail, which I shall do in Part II. The general point may be put as follows. The concepts of political theory usually carry evaluative overtones; to describe a state of affairs as just or democratic is to pass a favourable judgement upon it. Thus debates about the meaning of these concepts are normally also debates about the desirability of certain arrange-

---

[3] I have attempted to defend this interpretation of 'ideology', and to elucidate the sense in which ideologies embody distortion, in 'Ideology and the Problem of False Consciousness', *Political Studies*, xx (1972).

ments—of, say, a certain distribution of wealth or power.
Now such evaluative judgements themselves depend upon
broader views about the nature of men and societies, which
show, for instance, how these arrangements may be brought
into being, and what human benefits they may be expected to
produce. Thus the argument over whether the term 'democracy' should be used only of a political system with a high
degree of mass participation is closely linked to the questions
whether such mass participation is possible, and what benefits
are likely to flow from it. The answer to these questions in turn
depends upon a view of the political capacities of the ordinary
citizen, of the manner in which political systems function, and
so on. A view of society justifies a certain evaluative stance, and
thus an interpretation of the political concepts in terms of which
this stance is expressed.

Now it seems possible in the abstract to divorce interpretation of concepts from evaluation. For instance, one might
recommend a certain distribution of benefits in society but
decline to call that distribution just, reserving the concept
instead for some alternative distribution which was not regarded as desirable. This would presumably mean expressing
one's favourable evaluation in terms of some other concept or
concepts. But in this case no positive view of justice has been
given. If the person who took this line were asked to justify his
manner of interpreting the concept, he would either be unable
to give any justification, or he would have to point out that
other people used the concept to refer to a mode of distribution
of which he disapproved. In other words, if a person wants to
give a positive defence of one interpretation of a concept, he
must be prepared to defend the evaluative stance which is
normally linked to that interpretation, which in turn means
adopting the appropriate way of looking at society. In this
book, at any rate, I shall only be examining theories which
assume that just arrangements are prima facie desirable, and
which therefore combine the enterprise of understanding justice
with the defence of a certain mode of distributing benefits.

Granted that different interpretations of concepts such as
justice and democracy can be associated with different views of
society, two further questions demand an answer. The first is
why there should be this multiplicity of ways of looking at

society; and the second is whether any one of them can be shown to be correct. As regards the first question, it can hardly escape one's attention that the different views of society have emerged in separate historical periods, often in response to deeply felt political experiences such as revolutions and civil wars; to some extent, too, they have become associated with particular social classes, functioning as ideologies to defend privileged classes or as utopias to encourage exploited groups to struggle for power. So although one cannot deny that there are ways of looking at society which seem to be perennially attractive to certain temperaments,[4] the most fruitful way of explaining the diversity of social perspectives will probably be sociological. The political theorist has at this point to enter (or borrow from) the field of sociology of knowledge. Having related different interpretations of the concept he is studying to different ways of looking at society, he will then place both the interpretation and the view of society in a social context, asking about the type of society which fostered these ideas, about the classes which adopted them, and so on. This will of course show nothing about the validity of interpreting the concept in one way rather than another, but it will allow the theorist to explain why particular interpretations emerged at the time they did—a type of explanation which would never be reached by linguistic analysis alone.

This completes the political theorist's analytical task. He has now, it seems to me, provided as full an account of the meaning of a given concept as can possibly be given. The different interpretations have been isolated, placed in their intellectual context, and finally in their social context. The final question is whether the political theorist can legitimately pass from analysis to prescription—whether he can endorse one version of a concept at the expense of the others, or whether he must confine himself to presenting the range of possible interpretations. This is perhaps the most controversial question of all.

The 'official' view of linguistic philosophy, if it can be said to have one, is that the philosopher cannot prescribe how a

---

[4] The view that the major models of society will find new adherents in every generation is ably expounded by Isaiah Berlin in 'Does Political Theory still exist?' in P. Laslett and W. G. Runciman (eds.), *Philosophy, Politics and Society*, 2nd Ser. (Oxford, 1962).

term shall be used, at least in cases where its use or uses are already well defined (despite Wittgenstein's aphoristic remark 'It is clear that every sentence in our language "is in order as it is" ', it has generally been accepted that terms which are so vague or ambiguous that they lead inevitably to philosophical confusion may be 'tidied up' by the philosopher). This, however, has not prevented some linguistic philosophers from attempting prescriptive definitions of political terms on the grounds that their definitions are the only ones that really correspond to ordinary uses of the terms in question.[5] In the light of what has been said so far, this seems to be a serious mistake. If the dispute over different interpretations of a term is ultimately political in character, then to suppose that it can be settled on linguistic grounds is obviously an error. The linguistic philosopher deceives himself (and perhaps his audience) because he aligns himself on one side of a political argument while believing that he is giving the 'correct' solution to a question of linguistic use.

From our point of view, the question whether any one interpretation of a concept can be prescribed by the political theorist must be immediately related to a second question, whether any one of the conflicting ways of looking at society can be shown to be correct. Arguments about the proper interpretation of a political idea cannot fruitfully remain as arguments about language, but must become more general debates about the relative merits of different ways of conceiving society. But we have still to see how, if at all, such debates can be concluded. Is the choice between different ways of looking at society in the last resort a matter of mere personal preference, or can objective reasons be given for adopting one view rather than another? If the latter is true, what kind of reasons might these be?

A view of society will characteristically include an understanding of how society functions in its current form, and beliefs about desirable alternative social systems. It is therefore open to empirical verification and falsification, both with respect to the correctness of its account of current society, and with respect to the feasibility of the alternative proposed.

---

[5] For an example, see W. Parent, 'Some Recent Work on the Concept of Liberty', *American Philosophical Quarterly*, xi (1974).

Since falsification is generally easier than verification, defending a view of society usually means attempting to falsify competing views while rebutting attempts to falsify your own. To construct such a defence, appeal will be made to sociological evidence. Thus, to take a well-known example,[6] élite theorists such as Schumpeter tried to falsify the Rousseauian model of a democratic society in which power was equally shared among all the people by bringing forward evidence in favour of the élite model—evidence concerning the psychology of leaders and masses, etc. There was not merely a conflict between two incompatible models, but an attempt to resolve the conflict in favour of élitism by appeal to the empirical findings of sociology.

Although empirical evidence can in this way help us to choose between different views of society, we should not press the point too far. To begin with, in order to show that a proposed state of affairs (such as Rousseauian democracy) is strictly impossible, we should have to produce a sociological law of contrary import—and such laws have been notoriously difficult to establish. Moreover, judgements about the possibility or impossibility of a certain state of affairs are often value-impregnated; that is to say, whether a proposal is regarded as possible may depend on whether we are prepared to accept certain features which necessarily accompany it. Thus someone who says that equality is impossible may not mean that the ideal cannot be achieved in any circumstances, but only that it cannot be achieved without consequences that are plainly unacceptable. Finally, two people may agree about the feasibility of some arrangement contained in a view of society, yet disagree about its desirability because their ordering of values is different—one, say, giving a higher priority to liberty than the other. Thus while we should not underestimate the amount that can be done to resolve political arguments by appealing to empirical evidence, we should also recognize that this appeal has its limits. A view of society cannot be *completely* vindicated by empirical methods; at some point the value-assumptions which it contains must be accepted or rejected.

---

[6] This example and the general inspiration of the argument are derived from W. G. Runciman; see 'Sociological Evidence and Political Theory' in P. Laslett and W. G. Runciman (eds.), *Philosophy, Politics and Society*; and *Social Science and Political Theory* (Cambridge, 1969), esp. ch. 8.

My account of the role of empirical evidence in deciding between views of society also faces a more fundamental difficulty.
In order for sociological evidence to falsify a view of society,
it must be acceptable both to the supporters and to the opponents of that view. It must, in other words, be 'theory-neutral',
i.e. not affected by the presuppositions contained in any
particular way of looking at society. Suppose, however, that
this were not the case; then the evidence taken by one party to
justify his own theory will simply be dismissed by the other
parties as not being evidence at all, and a rational argument
between them will no longer be possible. Some philosophers
have argued that it is precisely the nature of empirical evidence
to be theory-dependent in this sense rather than to be theory-
neutral; there are no 'brute facts' accepted by all the parties
which can be used as an external check on each theory.[7]
Clearly these arguments must be rebutted if my position is to
stand secure. However, it is impossible to resolve this difficulty
in the present context; I note it merely to indicate the direction
which a full defence of the methodology advanced here must
take.

If we set this problem to one side, we obtain a reasonably
optimistic prospectus for political theory. Although the political
theorist cannot conclusively justify one of the available views of
society, he can at least provide a rational defence for such a
view, by bringing up empirical evidence in its support, and by
making clear the value-assumptions upon which it rests.
Having done this, he is in a position to offer political prescriptions, both of a substantive nature and concerning the meaning
which is to be attached to key political concepts such as justice
and freedom. His prescriptions will be grounded in his view
of society and will thus have a distinctively philosophical
character. They will differ from the ordinary man's political
opinions in being based upon a more carefully elaborated
view of society, which in turn is justified by its correspondence
with the available sociological evidence. In short, we have seen
how a political theory may be prescriptive without ceasing to be
philosophical.

[7] For positions of this type, see N. R. Hanson, *Patterns of Discovery* (Cambridge,
1958); P. K. Feyerabend, 'Problems of Empiricism' in R. Colodny (ed.), *Beyond
the Edge of Certainty* (New York, 1965); C. Taylor, 'Interpretation and the Sciences
of Man', *Review of Metaphysics*, xxv (1971–2).

In this book, however, I shall have little to say of a prescriptive nature, because all of the available space is needed to complete my analysis of the concept of justice. In giving this analysis I hope both to exemplify and, so far as this may be done with a single example, to justify the approach to political theory advocated in this introduction. I begin, therefore, by offering in the first chapter an analysis of the concept of social justice; in the course of this analysis I distinguish between three basic ways in which the concept may be used, giving rise to three conflicting principles of social justice. The three principles are examined separately and in detail in the subsequent three chapters. The method in this part of the book is analytical, and frequent reference is made to the use of language. I have given reasons for thinking that such linguistic analysis is an indispensable preliminary to a fuller understanding of a concept such as justice. In order to carry it out I have deliberately adopted the fiction that there is general agreement about the three ways of using the concept which I identify, even though this is almost certainly not the case. My procedure will be vindicated provided that everyone can *recognize* the conceptual map which I present, even though some might prefer only to use parts of it themselves.

In Part II, I give serious consideration to the claim that men disagree about the meaning of 'justice', and that the political theorist's task is to understand this disagreement by relating each interpretation of the concept to the view of society with which it is naturally associated. My method here has been to select three political theorists, each of whom clearly endorses one of the three interpretations of justice distinguished in Part I, and to examine the views of society which they respectively hold. I hope in each case to show that the interpretation of justice fits naturally into the corresponding way of looking at society. The advantages to be gained by taking political theorists, rather than the ideas of men at large, are plain; in their writings we find views of society which are more clearly articulated, and this makes the task of relating interpretation of justice to view of society a good deal simpler.

Finally, I attempt to place the idea of social justice in sociological perspective by comparing the conceptions of justice found in several different social contexts. After considering three radically different types of society—primitive, hierarchical, and market—I examine contemporary capitalist societies as a modified form of market society, and conclude by looking at the social circumstances which generate a belief in egalitarian justice. My efforts here fall far short of a complete 'sociology of social justice'. I hope at least that I have demonstrated the value of looking at a concept such as justice in this way, and that the theses advanced may provide a starting-point for more extensive inquiry in the future.

PART I

I

THE CONCEPT OF SOCIAL JUSTICE

---

1 *The Concept of Justice*

The concept of social justice is best understood as forming one part of the broader concept of justice in general. To comprehend it properly, we should begin by looking at justice as a whole, and then attempt to mark off that division of justice which we call social justice.

It takes only a little reflection to realize that the terms 'just' and 'justice' have a broad use. We are perhaps fortunate that we have lost one of the senses which the term had for the Greeks, the sense in which justice was equivalent to virtue in general;[1] nevertheless we use the concept in many different contexts to make a variety of moral and political points. Such breadth of use has led some commentators to think that the idea of justice has no substantive content, but is used rather as a general term of approval which can be applied at will to whatever phenomena one chooses.[2] Such a negative conclusion can, I believe, be avoided by looking carefully at the ways and contexts in which the concept is used; if we do this, we shall discover that it is always applied on the basis of a certain general criterion, and it is only used to advance a limited range of moral considerations.

We talk of just men, just actions, and just states of affairs. But the last of these uses must be regarded as the primary one, for when we describe a man as just we mean that he usually attempts to act in such a way that a just state of affairs results (or at least, that a state of affairs results which is no less just than the state of affairs which obtained before his action). If we did not have independent criteria for assessing the justice of

---

[1] See Aristotle, *Ethica Nichomachea*, Book v, chs. 1 and 2, in *The Works of Aristotle*, ed. W. D. Ross, vol. ix (Oxford, 1915).

[2] See, for instance, Hans Kelsen, 'What is Justice?' in his *What is Justice?* (Berkeley and Los Angeles, 1957).

states of affairs, we could not describe men as just or unjust. In a similar way, we describe actions as just either when we believe that they were undertaken in a serious attempt to bring about a just state of affairs or when we find that they actually have this desirable result. It is, therefore, impossible to assess the justice of actions without a prior identification of just states of affairs.

Not every state of affairs can properly be described as just or unjust. It must, first of all, involve sentient beings, and paradigmatically it involves beings who are both sentient and rational (I shall not discuss whether talk of the just treatment of animals is literal or merely metaphorical). It must also be a state of affairs in which at least one of the sentient beings is enjoying a benefit or suffering a burden; if no one is affected in either of these ways, questions of justice cannot arise. It must, thirdly, be a state of affairs which has resulted from the actions of sentient beings, or is at least capable of being changed by such actions. Thus although we generally regard rain as burdensome and sunshine as beneficial, a state of affairs in which half of England is drenched by rain while the other half is bathed in sunshine cannot be discussed (except metaphorically) in terms of justice—unless we happen to believe that Divine intervention has caused this state of affairs, or that meteorologists could alter it. As long as a state of affairs is regarded simply as a product of natural causes, questions about its justice or injustice do not arise.

Furthermore, to make judgements of justice it is necessary to examine the relationships in which these beings stand to one another—for instance, by looking at the transactions in which they have engaged, or by comparing the amount of some attribute which each possesses. This can be shown in the following way. Suppose that the only piece of information which I have about a state of affairs is that it includes a man who is suffering pain. This single piece of information allows me to make the judgement that the state of affairs in question is prima facie bad—bad unless further information comes to light which shows that other good elements in the situation outweigh the pain which the man is suffering. I cannot, however, either make the judgement that the state of affairs is prima facie just, or make the judgement that it is prima facie unjust. To make these judgements, I would have to know, for instance, whether the pain was naturally caused or inflicted by another man; if the latter, whether the man who inflicted the pain was entitled to do so or not; how the amount of pain suffered by the first man stood in comparison to the amounts suffered by other men in similar circumstances; and so on. I would have, in short, to examine the circumstances of a number of men, consider the relations in which they stood to one another, and compare the relative amounts of benefit enjoyed, and burden suffered by each man. We may therefore state, as a first step towards an analysis, that the *subject-matter* of justice is the manner in which benefits and burdens are distributed among men (strictly, sentient beings) whose qualities and relationships can be investigated.

To bring out the full significance of this statement, I want to introduce and clarify a distinction, due originally to Barry,[3] between *aggregative* and *distributive* political principles. An aggregative principle is one which refers only to the total amount of good enjoyed by a particular group, whereas a distributive principle refers to the share of that good which different members of the group have for themselves. For instance, the principle that the sum total of happiness enjoyed by the group should be maximized is aggregative, while the principle that each member of the group should enjoy an equal amount of happiness is distributive. This distinction picks out two important types of political principle without being exhaustive. The principle that society should be organized in such a way that great works of art are created is (as it stands) neither aggregative nor distributive.

Distributive principles may be formulated in several different ways. The good whose distribution is referred to may consist either of valued individual states (happiness, want-satisfaction, etc.) or of resources external to the individual (wealth, education, etc.). The distributive principle itself may either state simply how the good is to be divided (equal division is the most straightforward example), or it may specify some property of the individual which will determine what his share of the good shall be (for instance, the allocation of medicine according to need). Finally, the principle may either

[3] B. Barry, *Political Argument* (London, 1965), esp. ch. 3.

be formulated in such a way that it specifies a *complete* distribution of all the resources available, or in such a way that it specifies only a *partial* distribution, leaving certain resources to be allocated on another basis.

Two further comments may serve to ward off misunderstanding. First, in order to implement a distributive principle, it is not necessary that there should be a physical act of distribution. A possible distributive principle, for example, is that everyone should retain what he currently possesses. Nor does it follow, in cases where redistribution *is* necessary to satisfy a principle, that some one person or agency must act as a distributor; a distributive ideal may be implemented by the concurrence of a large number of people or institutions. One must avoid taking 'distribute' and its derivatives too literally here. Second, to avoid trivializing the distinction between aggregative and distributive principles, principles whose verbal form is distributive but whose substance is aggregative must be placed in the aggregative category. For instance, the principle 'Distribute resources in such a way that the greatest total amount of happiness is produced' is distributive only in superficial appearance. A certain distribution of resources is being recommended only as a means to an aggregative goal, not as an end in itself. A genuine distributive principle must either simply recommend a division of goods, or else it must specify some property of the individual which will determine what his share shall be.

In terms of this distinction, principles of justice are distributive principles, though we have yet to discover what kind of distributive principle they are. Indeed, the most valuable general definition of justice is that which brings out its distributive character most plainly: justice is *suum cuique*, to each his due. The just state of affairs is that in which each individual has exactly those benefits and burdens which are due to him by virtue of his personal characteristics and circumstances. We have yet to inquire what those characteristics and circumstances may consist in, but the general definition conveniently leaves this question open.

Our definition of justice has two important corollaries. First, it implies that where two men are equal in the relevant respects (so that their 'dues' are the same) they should be treated in the same way. This principle ('Treat equals equally' or 'Treat men equally except where there are relevant differences between them') has often been proposed as a general characterization of justice, but it seems to me inferior to the one I have given. This is mainly because it presents the relation between the concepts of justice and equality in a misleading way. The principle embodies only a weak sense of equality, whose connection with our general definition of justice is obviously close; but it may also encourage the false belief that justice is conceptually tied to a stronger notion of equality. I shall argue later that, rather than justice necessarily being egalitarian, equality in the strong sense constitutes *one* way of interpreting justice which may either be accepted or rejected. It is therefore better to regard 'treat equals equally' simply as a corollary of the more fundamental principle 'render to each his due'. The second corollary of this principle is perhaps only a corollary in a loose sense, but it does appear to be suggested by the original formula: this is the principle of proportion. Such a principle applies in cases where a person's due depends upon an attribute which can be quantified. We then have the principle that the amount of benefit he enjoys or the amount of burden he suffers should be proportional to the quantity of the relevant attribute which he possesses. Thus if the relevant attribute were 'gravity of crime committed' (calculated, let us suppose, on the basis of the total amount of pain produced), we would have the principle that the amount of punishment inflicted on each man should be proportional to the gravity of the crime which he has committed. The principle of proportion allows us to deal not only with cases in which 'dues' are identical, but with cases in which 'dues' are different, and yet can be expressed as quantities of the same attribute.

Before we turn to look at the ways in which a man's due might be determined, something must be said about the relation between justice in general and social justice. The idea that justice might display a number of subdivisions is an old one, being found in both Greek[4] and Christian[5] thought. For our pur-

[4] See Aristotle, op. cit.; D. G. Ritchie, 'On Aristotle's Subdivisions of Particular Justice', *Classical Review*. viii (1894); W. F. R. Hardie, *Aristotle's Ethical Theory* (Oxford, 1968), ch. 10.

[5] See Thomas Aquinas, *Summa Theologica*, ii–ii, Question 58, in D. Bigongiari (ed.), *The Political Ideas of St. Thomas Aquinas* (New York, 1953), pp. 105–26; G. Del Vecchio, *Justice* (Edinburgh, 1952), ch. 6; J. Y. Calvez and J. Perrin, *The Church and Social Justice* (London, 1961), ch. 6.

poses the most important contrast is between legal and social justice. Legal justice concerns the punishment of wrongdoing and the compensation of injury through the creation and enforcement of a public set of rules (the law). It deals mainly with two types of issue. First of all, it stipulates the conditions under which punishment may be inflicted, adjusts the scale of punishment to fit the nature of different crimes, and, in the sphere of civil law, regulates the amount of restitution which must be made for injuries. Secondly, it lays down procedures for applying the law—the principles of a fair trial, rights of appeal, etc., form part of legal justice. Social justice, on the other hand, concerns the distribution of benefits and burdens throughout a society, as it results from the major social institutions—property systems, public organizations, etc. It deals with such matters as the regulation of wages and (where they exist) profits, the protection of persons' rights through the legal system, the allocation of housing, medicine, welfare benefits, etc. Since punishments have been included in the scope of legal justice, 'burdens' should be read to mean 'disadvantages other than punishments'—i.e. such things as unpleasant or onerous work, bad housing conditions, etc.[6] I also wish to exclude power from among the benefits to be considered under social justice, since we use other concepts to discuss and evaluate the distribution of power in society—concepts such as democracy and authority. This is not to say of course that the distribution of power is irrelevant to social justice, since the allocation of other benefits may in practice depend upon the shape of the power structure, but all this means is that the distribution of power is *causally* rather than *conceptually* relevant to social justice. 'Benefits' should, however, be taken to include intangible benefits such as prestige and self-respect, although we shall mainly consider material goods, especially wealth, which most people would consider the most important concern of social justice.

This separation of legal from social justice is important because the criteria of justice are not necessarily the same in the

---

[6] From the point of view of social justice, burdens may simply be regarded as 'negative benefits', and do not give rise to independent theoretical problems. Thus in assessing how much a particular person is benefiting from an institution, one should balance the various benefits he receives against the burdens he suffers, and arrive at an over-all amount. I have tried to justify this approach in one important area—the benefits and costs of work—in chapter 3, section 4.

two areas. Our understanding of social justice is better served by treating it as a topic in its own right than by attempting a general analysis of justice which is meant to be adequate for all of its subdivisions. It should also be said, however, that certain moral considerations will be common to legal and social justice. For instance, the rights which a person possesses are relevant both to the question of when and how he may be punished, and to the question of what social benefits he ought to be given. Again, it is important that the law as an institution falls within the scope of both subdivisions of justice, although they are concerned with different aspects of it: legal justice with the treatment of offenders, etc., social justice with the benefits to the individual of having legal rights, etc. Thus the separation of the two ideas is made for purposes of analysis, rather than from a conviction that legal and social justice have nothing to do with one another.

Other, less important, subdivisions of justice may also be distinguished. There appears to be a category of 'private justice' which concerns the dealings of a man with his fellows when he is not acting as a participant in one of the major social institutions. The division of goods within a family or among a group of friends would be matters of private justice. This sense of 'justice' raises no new problems on its own account, since the same criteria are relevant here as are relevant to cases of social justice. I shall occasionally refer to instances of private justice to illustrate points about the social idea. Problems do arise, however, when private and social justice come into conflict. For example, an employer may try to deal justly with his work force, by paying each man a wage which is thought to correspond to his contribution at work. Assuming that the assessment is correctly made, private justice between employer and workers has been realized—but the wages received may be out of line with the wages paid in other places for the same work, in which case the employer has unwittingly perpetrated a social injustice. The resolution of such dilemmas falls outside the scope of this book.

We have so far identified the most general sense which the concept of justice bears, and have examined the relationship between its various subdivisions. We must now turn to the more specific criteria which are used to give the general formula ('to each his due') a concrete application.

2 *Three Principles of Justice*

If we leave aside those writers who believe that the concept
of justice is wholly indeterminate, we find that the remaining
commentators on justice fall roughly into two camps: those who
believe that there is a single concept of justice—i.e. that the
same criterion is always used when the concept is applied—and
those who believe that there are several concepts, each en-
capsulating a different way of distinguishing between just and
unjust states of affairs. On the whole, those who take the former
view are the more likely to fall into serious confusion. This
happens in the following way: a criterion of just distribution is
proposed which appears to have a definite content—i.e. it
seems that by using it one could actually distinguish between
just and unjust states of affairs. The proposer, however, sensitive to the variety of ways in which the concept of justice is
actually used, is obliged to stretch the criterion to cover
cases outside of its normal range of application. Tacitly, he has
substituted a formal account of justice for a substantive one,
but he retains the original term to express his view of justice,
thereby suggesting that he has accomplished more than he has.
Common examples are the claim that justice means equality,
or the claim that justice means giving each man what he deserves. Writers who put these claims forward as analyses of the
concept (rather than as substantive moral positions) will
almost certainly turn out to be using the defining term ('equality' or 'desert') in a weak or extended sense.[7]

In giving my general account of justice in the preceding
section, I stressed that the formula offered ('to each his due')
was non-substantive, even though it helped to bring out the
distributive character of justice. The *important* questions about
justice emerge when we try to settle what a person's 'due'
actually means, and here I agree with those who believe that
several different (and conflicting) meanings are possible. This
position is sometimes set out in the form of a list of principles of
justice, but in such cases it is difficult at first to see whether all
the principles offered are really fundamental alternatives, or
whether some at least cannot be grouped together as variants

[7] For an example of such a use of 'desert', see J. Hospers, *Human Conduct* (New
York, 1961), ch. 13.

of a single principle.[8] While one wishes to mark the basic contrasts between different conceptions of justice, there is no point in proliferating formulae in a haphazard fashion. Thus the contrasts made must be carefully justified.

The first contrast to be introduced was drawn by Sidgwick[9] and has more recently formed the theme of a discussion by Raphael;[10] it also has something in common with Aristotle's division of justice mentioned earlier. Sidgwick believed that in our thinking about justice we were inevitably led to contrast conservative justice, consisting in the recognition and protection of legal and other customary rights, with ideal justice, consisting of principles for changing these rights in accordance with some ideal standard.

For, from one point of view, we are disposed to think that the *customary* distribution of rights, goods, and privileges, as well as burdens and pains, is natural and just, and that this ought to be maintained by law, as it usually is: while, from another point of view, we seem to recognise an ideal system of rules of distribution which ought to exist, but perhaps have never yet existed, and we consider laws to be just in proportion as they conform to this ideal.[11]

Raphael analogously contrasts conservative justice, whose 'object is to preserve an existing order of rights and possessions, or to restore it when any breaches have been made', with prosthetic justice, which 'aims at modifying the *status quo*'.[12]

The notion of conservative justice can be derived from the general formula by interpreting a man's due as that to which he has a right or is entitled. It may thus be expressed in the form 'to each according to his rights'. In order to put such a conception of justice into practice, it is of course necessary to know

[8] The reader who wishes to sample such lists of principles should consult one or more of the following: J. A. Ryan, *Distributive Justice* (New York, 1916); C. Perelman, *The Idea of Justice and the Problem of Argument* (London, 1963); A. M. Honoré, 'Social Justice' in R. S. Summers (ed.), *Essays in Legal Philosophy* (Oxford, 1968); N. Rescher, *Distributive Justice* (New York, 1966); J. Hospers, *Human Conduct*, ch. 9. Hospers distinguishes the largest number of principles—eight in all. I have satisfied myself that all the principles offered can either be reduced to one of the three distinguished in this section, or be shown not to be genuine principles of justice.

[9] H. Sidgwick, *The Methods of Ethics* (London, 1907), Book iii, ch. 5.

[10] D. D. Raphael, 'Conservative and Prosthetic Justice', *Political Studies*, xii (1964).

[11] Sidgwick, op. cit., p. 273.   [12] Raphael, op. cit., pp. 154–5.

what each man's rights are. The rights in question may be legal rights, institutional rights, or certain types of moral right, such as the rights one derives from a promise or other non-legal agreement. Rights generally derive from publicly acknowledged rules, established practices, or past transactions: they do not depend upon a person's current behaviour or other individual qualities. For this reason it is appropriate to describe this conception of justice as 'conservative'. It is concerned with the continuity of a social order over time, and with ensuring that men's expectations of one another are not disappointed. I shall say nothing more at this point about the nature of rights, or about the conception of justice which they generate, since both topics are examined at length in the second chapter.

Although we generally think that the protection of individuals' rights is an important matter of justice, we do not usually believe that it exhausts that concept, for the distribution of rights can itself be assessed from the point of view of justice, as Sidgwick saw. To do this we must switch to a different interpretation of justice, termed by Sidgwick 'ideal' and by Raphael 'prosthetic' justice. What is the principle of ideal justice? In Sidgwick's view it was the principle of desert: men ought to be rewarded according to their deserts. This is evidently another way in which the general formula of justice can be filled out, a man's due here being taken to mean his deserts. 'Desert' in turn may be interpreted in a number of ways, although it always depends upon the actions and personal qualities of the person said to be deserving. Thus a man's deserts may be measured by his moral virtue, his productive efforts, his capacities, and so on. There is no one principle of justice as desert, though the various principles offered show a family resemblance to one another. The third chapter contains an attempt to disentangle these principles of desert, and to establish which is the most appropriate as an interpretation of social justice.

It is fairly clear that justice as the protection of rights, and justice as desert are conflicting values. We have no reason to believe in general that individuals' rights, which are to be protected by conservative justice, correspond to their deserts. To take one obvious example from our own society, an individual has a right to inherit wealth, that is to say a right to whatever amount of money another may leave him, once taxes have been deducted; yet he can hardly be said to deserve money so received, unless he has actually earned his benefactor's gratitude through services performed prior to his death. There is a conflict here between conservative justice, which insists that an individual's right to inherit be protected, and justice as desert, which demands that a man should earn whatever benefits he receives. This conflict recurs in many other cases.

Does the principle of desert exhaust ideal justice? Sidgwick believed so—but Raphael, writing nearly a century later, argues that the criterion of need is more central to prosthetic (ideal) justice than the notion of desert. If we take up Raphael's suggestion, we have a third interpretation of justice to contend with, a third rendering of the general formula 'to each his due'. The concept of need must be distinguished from the concept of desert, for when we speak of a man deserving something we have in mind some favourable attribute which we think ought to bring him a benefit, whereas when we speak of him needing something we are thinking of a lack or deficiency on his part— for instance we may say that a man needs food, meaning that it is necessary to him, that it will be injurious to him not to have it. The precise meaning of the concept will be discussed later. It is also clear that justice as distribution according to need comes into conflict with justice as distribution according to desert. We should not expect the most deserving man (for instance the hardest-working man, or the man who contributes most to some common project—depending on our interpretation of desert) also to be the man with the greatest needs. At best it would be a happy accident if desert and need coincided, and if both principles could be satisfied by the same distribution of goods. Such accidents apart, we must reconcile ourselves to a conflict between the two principles.

We have, then, three conflicting interpretations of justice which may be summarized in the three principles: to each according to his rights; to each according to his deserts; to each according to his needs. We should note, however, that the conflict between these principles is not symmetrical, and here the simpler division between conservative and ideal justice should be borne in mind. 'Rights' and 'deserts', and 'rights' and 'needs' are *contingently* in conflict, since we may strive for a social order in which each man has a right to that (and only that) which he deserves, or to that (and only that) which he needs. If such perfectly just societies could be created, the contrast between conservative and ideal justice would vanish, since the actual distribution of rights would correspond to the ideal distribution. On the other hand, 'deserts' and 'needs' are *necessarily* in conflict since (accidents apart) no society can distribute its goods both according to desert and according to need (it can of course distribute part of its goods according to desert and part according to need). The conflict between the two different specifications of ideal justice seems to be ineradicable.

Given that justice bears these diverse interpretations, how should the concept be used? Most people, I suggest, give some weight to each of the three principles of justice, and decide how to act in concrete situations by weighing up the various considerations and allowing the just action to emerge as a resultant. Consider the following case: I engage two small boys to clean the windows of my house, and promise them £1 each for doing the job. After the task is completed, they each have a right to £1, and at first sight the just action on my part will be to give them that sum. Suppose, however, that I notice that one boy has cleaned his share of the windows excellently, while the other boy has done a poor job. I may then judge that the first boy deserves a higher reward than the second, and that from this point of view the just thing to do would be to give the first boy, say, £1·25 and the second boy 75p. I am now in a dilemma, with different considerations of justice pointing in opposite directions. The dilemma can be resolved either by allowing considerations of rights to override considerations of desert, and paying each boy £1; or by allowing deserts to override rights and paying the boys £1·25 and 75p respectively; or by taking both sets of considerations into account, reaching a compromise, and paying, say, the first boy £1·25 and the second boy £1. The case may be further complicated if we suppose in addition that one boy comes from a well-to-do home, always has ample pocket money, and so on, while the other boy comes from a poverty-stricken home. Considerations of need must then be taken into account alongside considerations of rights and desert, and the dilemma I face becomes correspondingly more difficult, as the range of possible solutions expands.

This case is trivial enough in itself, but it illustrates quite well the difficulties we face if we allow our concept of justice to give weight to each of the three principles I have distinguished. Under these circumstances the reflective man is bound to ask whether a simpler theory of justice cannot be found, which would avoid the dilemmas engendered by the threefold concept used by most people. There are two main ways in which such a theory might be developed. First, one might simply endorse *one* of the three competing interpretations of justice, and resolve to ignore considerations of the other two types in arriving at one's judgements of justice. Second, one might look for an alternative principle, or consistent set of principles, which would give some weight to considerations of each of the three types, but would give clear guidance in cases of conflict—i.e. cases in which the three interpretations would, when taken separately, indicate incompatible actions.

The first alternative is the simpler, but it may seem intolerably severe in its demands. If we believe that each of the three principles represents an important aspect of justice in at least some contexts, we may feel that the proposed concept of justice departs too far from firmly held moral convictions to be acceptable. I shall argue later that such a choice has to be made because the different principles of justice find their natural home in conflicting ways of looking at society, and, although one may wish to avoid making a clear choice at this level as well, this makes it hard to combine the different principles in a theoretically satisfactory way. Nevertheless, a sense that each principle embodies an important moral value is undoubtedly one reason why people are deterred from straightforwardly endorsing one interpretation out of the three. A second reason is that such an endorsement *appears* to be arbitrary—it seems to be entirely a matter of preference that one chooses to interpret justice as, say, distribution according to desert, rather than as distribution according to rights or needs. Again, I shall argue later that such a choice is not arbitrary at all, but can be justified in terms of the view of society with which each interpretation is linked. Such a conclusion, however, is unlikely to be evident to the person who has to make the choice.

For these reasons, the second way of constructing a theory of justice looks initially more attractive. One looks for a principle or consistent set of principles which gives some weight to considerations of each of the three types, but which provides guidance in cases of conflict. One hopes that such a principle (or set of principles) will turn out to be consistent with intuitive judgements of justice in cases where these are firmly held and felt to be important. There are currently two theories which make some claim to satisfy both these conditions—utilitarianism, and the contractual theory of justice developed by John Rawls. I shall subject these theories to detailed scrutiny in the two sections that follow. At this point it is worth noting that contemporary proponents of both theories see themselves as undertaking a task of the kind described—introducing system into ordinary judgement, yet without overriding firmly held moral convictions. Utilitarians, of course, claim that theirs is a general moral theory, not merely a theory of justice, but they regard the relationship between the principle of utility and intuitive moral judgements in roughly the way outlined above. Thus Sprigge writes:

For one inclined to the utilitarian point of view . . . the principle [of utility] is accepted partly because it seems to supply a unitary basis to the existing moral sentiments, or to most of them, and is to some extent to be tested by its compatibility with these moral sentiments, but the moral sentiments are themselves under trial by the principle of utility. In cases of conflict, if such should arise, moral sentiments which are not too deeply felt will give way to the principle, but if they *are* deeply felt, then his utilitarian position comes up for review and a choice must be made.[13]

[13] T. L. S. Sprigge, 'A Utilitarian Reply to Dr. McCloskey', *Inquiry*, viii (1965), p. 271. Although I believe that Sprigge speaks for the consensus of opinion, not every modern utilitarian shares his views. Compare the following by J. J. C. Smart:

'I wish to repudiate at the outset that milk and water approach which describes itself sometimes as "investigating what is implicit in the common moral consciousness" and sometimes as "investigating how people ordinarily talk about morality". We have only to read the newspaper correspondence about capital punishment or about what should be done with Formosa to realize that the common moral consciousness is in part made up of superstitious elements, of morally bad elements, and of logically confused elements. I address myself to good hearted and benevolent people and so I hope that if we rid ourselves of the logical confusion the superstitious and morally bad elements will largely fall away.' J. J. C. Smart, 'Extreme and Restricted Utilitarianism' in P. Foot (ed.), *Theories of Ethics* (Oxford, 1967), pp. 173–4.

This is the true spirit of Benthamite utilitarianism. Bentham himself had no time for intuitive notions of justice, and openly displayed his scorn for the concept in passages such as the following:

Rawls puts forward a similar point of view in introducing the notion of 'reflective equilibrium'—a condition in which a person's intuitive moral judgements have been examined in the light of several systematic moral theories, and have been confirmed, modified, or rejected as the case may be.

When a person is presented with an intuitively appealing account of his sense of justice (one, say, which embodies various reasonable and natural presumptions), he may well revise his judgments to conform to its principles even though the theory does not fit his existing judgments exactly. He is especially likely to do this if he can find an explanation for the deviations which undermines his confidence in his original judgments and if the conception presented yields a judgment which he finds he can now accept. From the standpoint of moral philosophy, the best account of a persons' sense of justice is not the one which fits his judgments prior to his examining any conception of justice, but rather the one which matches his judgments in reflective equilibrium. As we have seen, this state is one reached after a person has weighed various proposed conceptions and he has either revised his judgments to accord with one of them or held fast to his initial convictions (and the corresponding conception).[14]

If, therefore, either theory—utilitarian or contractual—deviates sharply from intuitive judgements of justice which we feel no inclination to give up, we are justified in rejecting that theory. On this basis, I shall examine each theory in turn.

3 *Utilitarianism*

The notion of justice probably creates more difficulties for the would-be utilitarian than any other of our moral or political concepts. To understand this, we should return to the distinction between aggregative and distributive political principles.

'Sometimes, in order the better to conceal the cheat (from their own eyes doubtless as well as from others) they set up a phantom of their own, which they call Justice: whose dictates are to modify (which being explained, means to oppose) the dictates of benevolence. But justice, in the only sense in which it has a meaning, is an imaginary personage, feigned for the convenience of discourse, whose dictates are the dictates of utility, applied to certain particular cases.' (J. Bentham, *An Introduction to the Principles of Morals and Legislation* in *A Fragment on Government and An Introduction to the Principles of Morals and Legislation* (Oxford, 1948), p. 240).

The views of utilitarians of this kind fall outside the scope of my discussion.

[14] J. Rawls, *A Theory of Justice* (Oxford, 1972), p. 48.

In its basic form, utilitarianism is an aggregative theory. It tells us to perform whichever action among the options available will produce the greatest sum of happiness for all. Justice, as we have seen, is a distributive idea. The three principles of social justice distinguished in the last section all demand that a person's share of good should be proportioned to some quality he possesses. The principle of rights requires that each person should be given those goods to which he is entitled by virtue of some rule, past agreement, etc.; and similarly for the other two principles.[15] It therefore seems unlikely that utilitarianism will be able to accommodate principles whose form contrasts directly with that of the greatest happiness principle. Why should someone committed to aggregating good care how that good is distributed among different people?

If the conflict were between aggregating happiness and distributing it in certain ways, the utilitarian would have nowhere from which to begin an argument, since these principles obviously cannot be assimilated to one another. But the principles of justice do not in fact prescribe a particular distribution of happiness; they prescribe a distribution of external resources. For example, what a person has a right to is typically a piece of property; what he deserves is a certain income; and so on. This gives the utilitarian the foothold which he needs, for he can now argue that a given distribution of *resources* is justified by the total amount of *happiness* which it produces. From the utilitarian point of view, the principles of justice become rules for distributing resources which are vindicated by the beneficial results of their application.

In order to assess this view, we need to distinguish between different forms of utilitarianism. I take utilitarianism to be the doctrine that the rightness of actions is to be judged (directly or indirectly) by the over-all amount of happiness which they produce. 'Happiness' here may be interpreted as

[15] We may observe that the principle of rights is generally a *partial* distributive principle, since people have rights to specific quantities of resources, and it is not normally the case that every resource is owed to someone in this way. The principle of desert is potentially a *complete* distributive principle, since what each person deserves is a certain share of resources, and it is therefore possible to distribute all resources in proportion to desert. As to the principle of need, to decide whether it is complete or partial we have first to discover whether needs will always outrun available resources or whether more resources can be created than are actually needed. An answer to this question is given in chapter 4.

broadly as one wishes, provided it is understood that happiness is an individual state, and that the general happiness is therefore assessed by summing up individual amounts of happiness. This excludes certain doctrines sometimes referred to as 'ideal utilitarian', according to which the rightness of actions is to be judged by the goodness of their consequences, but the goodness of a set of consequences is not necessarily reducible to a sum of individual goods; it may depend upon the properties of states of affairs, for instance on the way in which benefits or burdens are distributed among a number of people.[16] Such theories are better described as 'consequentialist' than as 'utilitarian'. Theories of this type can obviously incorporate the notion of justice, since the goodness of consequences can be made to depend, in part, upon their justice; but of course no explanation is being given here of why a certain distribution should be regarded as just, and if our problem is to discover what justice really consists in, such a theory will do nothing to enlighten us. I therefore propose to disregard 'ideal utilitarian' theories altogether.

Among utilitarian theories proper, four types may usefully be distinguished:[17]

(1) Act utilitarianism: an act is right if, and only if, it produces a greater amount of happiness than any alternative.

(2) Utilitarian generalization: an act is right if, and only if, the effect of everyone's performing it would be to produce a greater amount of happiness than (everyone's performing) any alternative.

(3) Actual-rule utilitarianism: an act is right if, and only if, it conforms to a rule which is currently recognized. A rule is right if, and only if, its general acceptance produces a greater amount of happiness than (the general acceptance of) any alternative.

(4) Ideal-rule utilitarianism: an act is right if, and only if, it conforms to a rule whose general acceptance would produce a greater amount of happiness than (the general acceptance of) any alternative.

[16] For a position of this type, see G. E. Moore, *Principia Ethica* (Cambridge, 1903).
[17] In compiling this list, and throughout this section, I have been much helped by David Lyons's excellent book *The Forms and Limits of Utilitarianism* (Oxford, 1965).

Fortunately we may discard two of these four forms of utilitarianism fairly swiftly. Although utilitarian generalization appears at first sight to be distinct from act utilitarianism (i.e. it appears that the use of the generalized criterion will produce a different set of prescriptions from the use of the simple utilitarian criterion), Lyons has shown that the two forms are extensionally equivalent.[18] Every act pronounced right by act utilitarianism will also be pronounced right by utilitarian generalization, and vice versa. The apparent discrepancy arises only when an insufficiently complete description is given of the act to which the generalization test is to be applied. We may therefore ignore utilitarian generalization, and consider only act utilitarianism.

We may also disregard actual-rule utilitarianism, not because it is theoretically redundant, but because it is implausible. Utilitarians of this type want to draw a sharp distinction between two questions: 'What makes individual acts right?' and 'What makes general rules right?' The first question is answered in terms of conformity to accepted rules, and only the second in terms of utility. However, this has the consequence that, while we may properly attempt to change the current set of rules on utilitarian grounds, until we succeed in getting the rules changed the right action will always be to conform to them, no matter how bad they may be. This corollary seems to me sufficiently unacceptable for us to omit further consideration of this variant of utilitarianism.[19]

We are left, then, with two plausible forms of utilitarianism— the view that each act should be assessed simply in terms of its consequences, and the view that each act should be assessed, not in terms of actual rules, but in terms of the rules which it would be most useful to have accepted. Let us start by looking at justice from the point of view of act utilitarianism. It may be helpful to return here to our simple illustration of the use of principles of justice, the case of the two small boys cleaning the windows of my house. As the case was described, in attempting to act justly when payment was due, I had to balance con-

[18] Lyons, op. cit., ch. 3.

[19] For a fuller critique of actual-rule utilitarianism from an ideal-rule utilitarian position, see R. B. Brandt, 'Some Merits of One Form of Rule-Utilitarianism' in K. Pahel and M. Schiller (eds.), *Readings in Contemporary Ethical Theory* (Englewood Cliffs, N.J., 1970).

siderations of rights (each had been offered £1 beforehand) against considerations of desert (one had done a better job than the other) and considerations of need (one came from an impoverished family). Note that in coming to a decision I paid no attention to the general consequences of my action, to the over-all amount of happiness or pain which alternative courses of action might produce. Indeed, if I *had* taken general consequences into account, this would have introduced a fourth set of considerations which might well have altered my decision. I might, for instance, have reflected that the sudden acquisition of such a large sum of money would have a deleterious effect on the characters of my two employees, and have resolved to pay them a maximum of 25p each. As it was, I gave no thought to the general happiness, but considered only the *claims* which the two boys had upon me by virtue of past agreements, work performed, etc. Thus my reasoning was certainly not overtly utilitarian. However, an act utilitarian might claim that, whether or not the utilitarian criterion was consciously used, all the considerations which I took into account can be explicated in utilitarian terms. The importance I attached to keeping my original agreement with the boys can be explained in terms of the unhappiness which they would suffer if their expectations were disappointed, as well as by the need to preserve people's general trust in agreements. My wish to reward the deserving boy can be understood as a desire to encourage hard work and skill, qualities which will produce benefits for everyone in the future. My concern about the respective needs of the two boys reflects the fact that we create more happiness by giving goods to people in need than by giving to those who already have enough. Then in weighing these considerations against one another, I was actually comparing the net balance of happiness which one action would produce with the net balance produced by another. Finally, even if it is implausible to represent my thinking in this way as 'unconsciously utilitarian', at least a utilitarian will take account of the same factors as I did, and so there will be no material difference between the utilitarian's reasoning and my own—except, perhaps, that the utilitarian will be in a better position to make the final decision.

The utilitarian case looks plausible enough at first sight.

But if we examine the example carefully it will begin to seem doubtful whether my reasoning could possibly have been utilitarian (even 'unconsciously utilitarian'), or whether a utilitarian would necessarily arrive at the same conclusions as I did. First, in considering the rights which the boys had as a result of our agreement, I was thinking of the agreement itself, not of any expectations the boys might have, or of the disappointment they might suffer if I failed to keep it. For all I know, they might *not* expect adults to honour their agreements, nor can I tell what effect my breaking this agreement would have on general confidence in agreements. For the utilitarian, on the other hand, the agreement as such is irrelevant, and its only importance is as a source of expectations whose frustration would be painful. If the utilitarian could acquire *direct* knowledge of the boys' expectations (perhaps by eavesdropping?) he could ignore the agreement entirely—except in so far as he is concerned with general confidence in agreements, which anyway is doubtfully affected by this particular case. Second, in taking account of the relative deserts of the two boys, it is again implausible to suggest that my considerations were as general as the utilitarian's. I gave no thought to the incentive effects of rewarding the more skilful cleaner. I had no idea whether the boys would be cleaning windows again in the future, or whether they would pass on their experience to their friends and neighbours. Thus a utilitarian *might* reason along the same lines as I did, but only if he believed that giving a special reward *would* have incentive effects; otherwise he has no special reason to reward the more skilful cleaner more highly. Finally, considerations of need: here it seems that the utilitarian's reasoning must converge with my own, for what could be more useful than giving more to those in greater need? But even this is questionable in the particular case in hand; it might turn out that giving more to the better-off boy would create more happiness—if, for example, it allowed him to realize an important ambition for which a certain lump sum was necessary. If, in these circumstances, I still feel it right to give more to the needier boy, I must be moved by consideration of justice, not of utility.

In each case, a similar pattern of argument emerges. The utilitarian can explain why, in general, it is useful to respect rights, reward deserts, and fulfil needs; but act utilitarianism falls down because it cannot show why, in the particular case, strict attention should be paid to these considerations. At best, the act utilitarian can claim that, given certain empirical assumptions, the most happiness will be produced by recognizing the claims of rights, desert, and need. But these assumptions may well not be true, and yet there is no evidence that the strictness of the demands of justice varies according to estimates of consequences. For this reason act utilitarianism cannot be accepted as a theory of justice.

This very weakness of the act utilitarian position gives the ideal-rule utilitarian his strongest card. According to rule utilitarianism we should not try to estimate the consequences of each particular act, but rather follow the rule whose *general* consequences are best. Therefore, the rule utilitarian will argue, it may be right to adhere strictly to a rule of justice, even though, in the particular case in hand, a better result could be produced by breaking the rule; and the reason is that general adherence to common rules of justice produces more happiness than a situation in which each man tries to make a direct estimate of the consequences of his own actions. Finally, the principles of justice—rights, deserts, and needs—are precisely rules which it would be useful for people to accept, for the kind of reasons which the act utilitarian gave in attempting to incorporate justice into *his* theory.

The pure form of rule utilitarianism defined above assesses rules wholly in terms of their utility. Thus for a rule to be justified it has to be shown, not merely that acceptance of the rule would produce happiness, but that it would produce more happiness than the acceptance of any alternative rule. Granted that the rule utilitarian can show why rules are useful, can he show that the rules of justice, as we normally understand them, are more useful than other rules which might be proposed?

Consider the principle that deserving actions (such as skilful window-cleaning) should be rewarded. We may grant that it is useful for people to adhere to this rule; more happiness will be produced if desert is generally or universally rewarded than if it is not, because the expectation of reward will encourage people to acquire useful skills, perform deserving actions, etc. But is this rule *more* useful than any alternative? Surely not: a more useful rule would be to reward desert only in those cases where we believe that giving a reward will act as an incentive to acquire useful skills, etc.; rewards given in other cases are, from the utilitarian point of view, wasted—the benefits given could almost certainly be used in better ways.[20] Thus it seems that the rule utilitarian must endorse, not the principle of desert as we normally understand it, but a modified principle which takes account of the *consequences* of rewarding desert.

The rule utilitarian may say in reply that the point of having rules—the reason why it is useful to have them—is to simplify the process of reaching a moral decision, and to make it easier for men to predict one another's behaviour. To achieve these desirable ends, it is necessary that the rules adopted should be relatively simple. In the abstract, the modified desert principle might seem more useful than the one we have now, but in practice it would be too difficult to apply, given limited human capacities for prediction. Such an argument is hard to assess, since we lack empirical evidence about how well people perform as moral agents when using principles of different types. On the other side, it may be pointed out that we already act on 'incentive' principles in many cases—we quite often give people benefits, not as deserved rewards, but as direct inducements to perform some act in the future—and these actions are not noticeably unsuccessful. In the absence of firm evidence on either side, one must, I think, remain sceptical of the rule utilitarian's claim to have shown that the principles of justice can be incorporated into the rule utilitarian framework, although the negative considerations here are less decisive than in the act utilitarian case.

Rule utilitarianism, however, suffers from an additional failing which act utilitarianism avoids as it has so far provided us with no guidance in cases where two rules come into conflict. Suppose the rule utilitarian could convince us that the ordinary principles of rights, deserts, and needs would form part of a rule utilitarian framework. What ought we to do in cases where these principles conflict, as they did in our imaginary example? The rule utilitarian appears to have three options here: either he can leave us to weigh one rule against the others as best we can; or he can recommend that in such cases a straightforward

---

[20] For an example see below, ch. 3, pp. 93–4.

calculation of the consequences of the alternative actions available should be made; or he can put forward a secondary rule
for dealing explicitly with cases in which primary rules conflict.
But if the first option is chosen, rule utilitarianism loses its
systematic aspect, which after all constituted the initial appeal
of utilitarian theories; if the second option is chosen, rule
utilitarianism becomes indistinguishable from act utilitarianism in a large number of cases; and if the third option is chosen,
it is difficult to see what rule could be proposed (for instance,
any straightforward ranking of the three principles of justice
will certainly be unacceptable). So it is doubtful whether
adopting an ideal-rule version of utilitarianism would help us
much in precisely those cases of moral dilemma which it was
designed to resolve.[21]

Can we reach a general conclusion about utilitarian theories
of justice? Utilitarians can show, it seems, that justice is
generally beneficial to society, but they cannot explain why, in
particular cases, the distinctive claims of justice should be
weighed separately from considerations of utility. Hume saw
the problem with great clarity:

That Justice is useful to society, and consequently that *part* of its
merit, at least, must arise from that consideration, it would be a
superfluous undertaking to prove. That public utility is the *sole*
origin of justice, and that reflections on the beneficial consequences
of this virtue are the *sole* foundation of its merit; this proposition,
being more curious and important, will better deserve our examination and enquiry.[22]

It seems, however, that the distributive character of justice—
its concern that each individual should receive his due—cannot
be accommodated to theories such as utilitarianism which,
whatever sophistications they may introduce, ultimately make
the rightness of actions depend upon the sum total of happiness
produced. We are dealing here with two irreducibly different
types of moral demand, both important in their own right, and
attempts to make them coalesce are futile; it would be equally

[21] There are further objections to ideal-rule utilitarianism which cannot be
considered here for reasons of space. The reader should consult Lyons, op. cit.,
pp. 136–60.
[22] D. Hume, *An Enquiry Concerning the Principles of Morals*, Section III, Part I in
Enquiries Concerning the Human Understanding and Concerning the Principles of Morals,
ed. L. A. Selby-Bigge (Oxford, 1902), p. 183.

fruitless to attempt to reduce utility to justice. John Rawls
takes this insight as his starting-point in developing a contractual theory of justice which is intended to remedy the deficiencies of utilitarianism. He sums up his dissatisfaction with utilitarianism in the following words:

If, then, we believe that as a matter of principle each member of
society has an inviolability founded on justice which even the
welfare of everyone else cannot over-ride, and that a loss of freedom
for some is not made right by a greater sum of satisfactions enjoyed
by many, we shall have to look for another account of the principles
of justice. [23]

Utilitarianism has one valuable contribution to make to the
theory of justice. If, as Hume suggests, our respect for justice
derives at least partly from its utility, we may legitimately
expect that in circumstances where it is no longer socially
useful its salience will be sharply reduced. Even if the basic
moral demand of justice is not founded on utility, it may still
be a necessary condition of the emergence of justice that it
should be socially useful, and conversely where a strict observance of rules of justice would be socially harmful, we may
expect that much less emphasis will be placed on the virtue.
The sociological evidence presented in Part III will be seen to
support this proposition. Thus even if utilitarianism cannot
explain the value of justice, it may none the less provide a helpful theory of the conditions under which justice will flourish in
human societies. [24]

4 *The Contractual Theory of Justice*

We have seen that the impetus behind John Rawls's contractual
theory of justice is a recognition that utilitarianism cannot
accommodate our firmly held conviction that 'each person
possesses an inviolability founded on justice that even the welfare of society as a whole cannot override'. To replace the utili-

[23] J. Rawls, 'Distributive Justice' in P. Laslett and W. G. Runciman (eds.),
Philosophy, Politics and Society, 3rd Ser. (Oxford, 1967), p. 59.

[24] A valuable contribution towards such a theory is made by Hume in *A Treatise
of Human Nature*, ed. A. D. Lindsay (London, 1911), Book iii, Part II, section 2,
and in *An Enquiry Concerning the Principles of Morals*, Section III. It is of some interest
to observe that Rawls, although strongly critical of utilitarian theories of justice,
is prepared to endorse Hume's account of the 'circumstances of justice'. See Rawls,
A Theory of Justice, section 22.

tarian account, Rawls proposes the following general conception of justice:

All social primary goods—liberty and opportunity, income and wealth, and the bases of self-respect—are to be distributed equally unless an unequal distribution of any or all of these goods is to the advantage of the least favored.[25]

His discussion, however, is usually conducted in terms of the more specific conception of justice expressed in the following two principles:

(1) Each person is to have an equal right to the most extensive basic liberty compatible with a similar liberty for others.
(2) Social and economic inequalities are to be arranged so that they are both
(a) to the greatest benefit of the least advantaged; and
(b) attached to offices and positions open to all under conditions of fair equality of opportunity.[26]

These principles are to be applied in the following 'lexical order'; principle (1) is to be fully satisfied before principle (2) is allowed to operate; and principle 2 (b) is to take similar precedence over 2 (a). I shall call principle (1) the principle of equal liberty, principle 2 (a) the difference principle, and principle 2 (b) the principle of fair equality of opportunity. The point of the lexical ordering is to establish a strict priority among the different demands of justice in Rawls's theory. An equal liberty has first priority, followed by the demand for fair equality of opportunity. Only when these are fully satisfied can we turn to arranging social and economic inequalities so that they work to the greatest benefit of the least advantaged member of society.

Rawls attempts to justify this theory in two contrasting ways. First, as we have already noted,[27] he believes that an acceptable moral theory must accord with our intuitive moral judgements, or at least with those intuitive judgements which we are not prepared to abandon in the light of the theory which is being offered. He therefore tries to show that the theory of justice

[25] Rawls, *A Theory of Justice*, p. 303.
[26] This is a slightly simplified version of the principles as set out in Rawls, op. cit., pp. 302–3.
[27] See p. 31.

takes account of the common sense precepts; his hope is that
'the two principles of justice may not so much oppose our
intuitive convictions as provide a relatively concrete principle
for questions that common sense finds unfamiliar and leaves
undecided'.[28] Second, Rawls attempts to provide an independent justification for the two principles by showing that they
would be adopted by rational individuals placed in a situation
in which they were ignorant of their personal qualities and their
place in society. One might say that, just as utilitarians often
wish to provide a deductive 'proof' of the principle of utility,
so Rawls wants to obtain a deductive grounding for his theory
by proving that it is the necessary choice of men placed hypothetically in 'typical circumstances of justice'.

I have elsewhere subjected this second chain of argument to
critical examination, and it must now be regarded as very
doubtful whether the theory of the hypothetical situation lends
much support to Rawls's two principles of justice.[29] I propose,
for present purposes, to disregard this aspect of the theory
entirely, and to concentrate simply on the relationship between the two principles and our ordinary notions of justice,
as previously analysed. Our question is whether Rawls's
principles adequately synthesize ordinary judgements of justice
without contradicting any that are firmly held. We may also,
I suggest, focus our attention on principles 2 (a) and 2 (b),
since the principle of equal liberty is relevant to legal and
political justice rather than to social justice. As interpreted by
Rawls, it covers such issues as freedom of conscience and the
rights of citizens to participate in government, whereas the
distribution of wealth and related matters fall within the
ambit of the difference principle and the principle of fair
equality of opportunity.[30]

The first point to notice about Rawls's principles 2 (a) and
2 (b) is that they are not distributive principles in the same
strong sense as the ordinary principles of justice. They do not
specify some property of the individual which will determine
what his share of society's goods shall be. The difference prin-

---

[28] Op. cit., p. 319.
[29] See R. Keat and D. Miller, 'Understanding Justice', *Political Theory*, ii (1974).
[30] See Rawls, op. cit., ch. 4. It is doubtful whether the principle of equal liberty,
as Rawls defines it, can properly be regarded as a principle of justice. See Keat
and Miller, op. cit., section 3.

ciple states that goods should be distributed in whatever way creates most benefit for the least advantaged member of society. The principle of fair equality of opportunity is distributive in form, since it demands that positions and offices should be allotted on the basis of ability and skill (rather than on the basis of birth or influence), but it should be made clear that the principle states nothing about the levels of reward which may be attached to different positions and offices. Thus there is nothing in the two principles which directly prescribes how wealth and other goods should be distributed to persons; in this respect the contractual theory of justice resembles utilitarianism. We might think, therefore, that we have already uncovered a rather sharp divergence between this theory and ordinary notions of justice. But Rawls has a line of defence against this criticism which must be removed before we can make any further progress.

Rawls distinguishes between three types of justice, which he designates perfect procedural justice, imperfect procedural justice, and pure procedural justice. Perfect procedural justice exists where, in a division of goods, we have both an independent criterion of a fair distribution and a procedure which is certain to produce that fair outcome. An example is the division of a cake between a number of men, where, assuming that the fair division is taken to be an equal division, we have a method (the man who cuts is to take the last piece) which is guaranteed to produce the desired result.[31] Imperfect procedural justice exists where, although we have an independent criterion of a fair outcome, no method exists which is certain to produce that outcome; at best we can claim that a certain method is *likely* to produce the result sought. Rawls instances the institution of a criminal trial, whose methods are aimed at producing fair results (that those and only those guilty of crimes are convicted) but do not succeed in their aim on every occasion. Finally, in cases of pure procedural justice, we have no independent criterion of a fair outcome, but only criteria for fair methods and procedures. Thus in a game of roulette, the betting procedure is fair, provided that the wheel is unbiased and so forth, and, Rawls claims, we call the result-

[31] Strictly speaking, a number of additional assumptions must be made. See Rawls, op. cit., p. 85.

ing distribution of money fair, whatever it is, on the grounds that it is the outcome of a fair procedure. Now the point of making these distinctions is that Rawls wishes to maintain that social justice is pure procedural in character. There are no independent criteria for judging, for instance, whether a given allocation of money resources to persons is just or unjust. Rather, such an allocation is just if it has arisen through the operation of fair procedures and unjust otherwise. Rawls sketches an institutional framework which he believes will realize 'background justice'. There is to be a competitive market economy, a 'transfer branch' of government to guarantee a basic social minimum, another branch to prevent the formation of monopolies, and so on. Once these institutions are working, Rawls claims, there is no need to examine the precise distribution of goods to persons that results, since its fairness will be guaranteed by the procedures which have produced it.

Plainly, if such an account of social justice could be sustained, it would undercut my critical objection to Rawls's theory—that it does not prescribe how wealth and other goods should be distributed to persons—and make the rest of my discussion redundant. But the account can be attacked on at least three grounds. First, it is arguable as a general point whether there is such a notion of pure procedural justice as Rawls describes. Do we actually call the results of betting games fair or, even more pertinently, just?[32] It is of some interest that Rawls subtly weakens his claim when he states:

If a number of persons engage in a series of fair bets, the distribution of cash after the last bet is fair, or at least not unfair, whatever this distribution is.[33]

Note the qualifying clause 'or at least not unfair'. This suggests that we are much readier to describe the outcome of a crooked game as unfair than we are to describe the outcome of a fair game as positively fair.

Second, Rawls's two principles do not themselves represent a pure procedural conception of justice, although he appears to believe that they do. Consider the difference principle and

[32] For similar doubts, see B. Barry, 'On Social Justice', *Oxford Review*, v (Trinity, 1967).
[33] Rawls, op. cit., p. 86.

the principle of fair equality of opportunity. Each of these prescribes a certain outcome, in the first case an arrangement of inequalities which maximizes the benefit of the least advantaged, and in the second case a distribution of offices according to ability and skill. Had Rawls wished to make his account of justice pure procedural, he should have omitted the two principles altogether and prescribed only the institutional framework; for instance, if one maintained that whatever distribution resulted from the workings of a free market economy was fair, this would be a pure procedural interpretation of justice. But in Rawls's case the institutions are set up to *satisfy* the two principles.

Third, it is implausible to suggest that the ordinary notion of justice has a pure procedural form. When people discuss the justice of distributions of wealth, for example, they are concerned about the claims which each man has to the amount of wealth he possesses. It is not that institutions such as the free market are seen as fair in themselves, and therefore that whatever distribution arises from them is also fair; rather, institutions are assessed in terms of independent criteria of distributive justice, such as desert and need. The situation is one of imperfect procedural justice, since the outcome can be judged independently, but no sure way of reaching the fair outcome can be discovered.

We may therefore pass over Rawls's idea of pure procedural justice and consider the relationship between the two principles of justice and the common sense criteria—rights, deserts, and needs—as substantive theories of justice. To what extent do the two principles succeed in accommodating these ordinary criteria of justice? Rawls claims that his theory has a place for individual rights. Once just institutions are established, individuals participating in these institutions will form certain expectations about how they are to be treated, and these in turn will give rise to entitlements.[34] But how far does this match up to the ordinary principle of rights? Rawls appears to give no weight to rights which are established in *unjust* societies, i.e. in societies which do not satisfy the two principles; yet it is surely part of the ordinary principle that *all* rights have some claim to recognition even though their claim may be outweighed by other considera-

[34] Op. cit., p. 313.

tions of justice. Furthermore, there seems no reason why rights should be particularly stable in Rawls's just society. Suppose, for instance, it turns out that, due to changing economic circumstances, the position of the worst-off could be materially improved by expropriating wealthy landowners without compensation. It seems that Rawls must endorse this policy, since there is nothing in the two principles which requires him to pay attention to the rights of those such as the landowners whose advantaged position does not contribute to the well-being of the worst-off. Rawls, in fact, seems less able to incorporate rights into his theory than the utilitarian, for while the utilitarian could give some weight to the frustrated expectations of the landowners in such a case, Rawls cannot do this unless the landowners were so badly affected that they actually became the worst-off members of society themselves.

Let us turn next to the concept of desert. Rawls here makes a division between 'the common sense precepts of justice', such as the precept 'to each according to his contribution' or the precept 'to each according to his effort', and the claim of moral desert, i.e. the claim of virtue to a reward. I wish, for reasons that will be stated later, to consider all these claims as claims of desert. Rawls argues that the 'common sense precepts' are taken into account by his theory because they 'simply identify features of jobs that are significant on either the demand or the supply side of the market, or both'.[35] Someone who makes a larger than average contribution is creating more value for his firm, and it is therefore worth paying him a higher wage if market conditions demand it. Thus Rawls, like the utilitarian, interprets rewards as incentives which are needed to encourage people to acquire skills, work harder, take on unpleasant work, etc. As we have seen, such a distributive practice does not correspond to one which rewards desert. Two jobs may require precisely the same amount of skill, effort, etc., but it may happen that there is a surplus of men to undertake one and a shortage of men to undertake the other. In this situation the incentive principle will justify paying one job at a higher rate than the other, but from the point of view of desert (and justice) they must be rewarded equally. Again, Rawls's difference principle may permit the payment of exceptionally high re-

[35] Op. cit., p. 305.

wards to people with scarce but useful talents if those people will only exercise their talents when they are highly paid for doing so. Provided that the worst-off gain on balance, such inequalities of reward are vindicated by Rawls's theory, but they cannot be regarded as deserved.[36]

Before leaving the concept of desert, something must be said about Rawls's principle of fair equality of opportunity. It would be possible to regard equality of opportunity as a principle of efficiency, since we may assume that filling offices on the basis of ability and skill leads on the whole to more competent performance of the tasks attached to the offices. But Rawls does not view the principle in this light.[37] Reversing the lexical ordering for a moment, let us ask why it should matter, in a society that satisfies the difference principle, whether the advantaged positions are obtained on a basis of equal opportunity or not. Rawls states:

. . . if some places were not open on a basis fair to all, those kept out would be right in feeling unjustly treated even though they benefited from the greater efforts of those who were allowed to hold them. They would be justified in their complaint not only because they were excluded from certain external rewards of office such as wealth and privilege, but because they were debarred from experiencing the realization of self which comes from a skillful and devoted exercise of social duties.[38]

Now since, in any case, only a certain number of favoured positions will be available, so that not everyone will be able to enjoy the rewards of responsibility, what does the complaint of

---

[36] Rawls tries to evade the conclusion that his theory falls down over the principle of desert in two ways. First, he interprets desert to mean 'moral desert' and then has no difficulty in showing that the common sense precepts do not aim to reward desert in this sense. But if, as seems likely, the sense or senses of 'desert' which are relevant to social justice do not include the moral sense, this demonstration becomes irrelevant. Second, Rawls is sceptical about the whole notion of desert, since he believes that a man's character, and even his willingness to make an effort, is socially determined; and since 'it seems to be one of the fixed points of our considered judgments that no one deserves his place in the distribution of native endowments', the assertion that 'a man deserves the superior character that enables him to make the effort to cultivate his abilities' must be regarded as equally problematic (Op. cit., p. 104). Here, however, we must suspend judgement until the general relationship between the thesis of determinism and the concept of desert has been explored. (See below, chapter 3, section 3.)

[37] See Rawls, op. cit., p. 84.

[38] Op. cit., p. 84.

those excluded come to? Surely that not all of those currently receiving high rewards actually *deserve* them, since some of them are less able than some of those excluded. Despite his rejection of the notion of desert, Rawls actually requires it to establish the justice of his principle 2 (b). Of course, equality of opportunity does not amount to a complete principle of desert unless it is supplemented by some other principles regulating the size of the rewards attached to each of the various offices; but conversely, a notion of desert is required to establish equality of opportunity as a principle of justice.

Finally, we must look at the concept of need in the light of Rawls's two principles. It seems to me that here Rawls's principles fare rather better, and certainly better than does utilitarianism. The difference principle, which demands that inequalities be arranged so that the worst-off enjoy the maximum benefit possible, will normally also ensure that basic needs are fully catered for; or, reversing the point, any departure from the difference principle, by depriving the worst-off to some extent, runs the risk of satisfying needs less efficiently than a Rawlsian arrangement.

It must nevertheless be stressed that Rawls's theory does not incorporate the distributive principle of need which we found to be one part of the ordinary idea of justice. The difference principle does not prescribe a distribution of resources according to need, but instead requires whatever distribution of resources will most effectively satisfy the needs of the worst-off. Indeed Rawls's over-all argument depends on the assumption that if, instead of distributing goods according to need, economic inequalities are allowed to develop, and to act as incentives, production will increase to such an extent that everyone's needs will be more fully satisfied. But although this result may be justified on grounds of humanity, it may be considered less just than a situation in which resources are allocated strictly according to need. Fewer needs may be satisfied in the latter situation, but they are satisfied more fairly.

In summary, the two principles of justice are not particularly successful in accommodating the ordinary precepts of justice, and my opening claim—that principles which were not strictly distributive could not be expected to converge with the distributive principles of rights, deserts, and needs—appears to have been borne out. Before moving to a general verdict on Rawls's theory, however, I want to consider whether principles 2 (a) and 2 (b) may not stand up as principles of justice in their own right. Fair equality of opportunity has already been categorized as one part of a desert principle. But is it not possible that the difference principle, which is really the most original part of Rawls's theory of justice, could be taken as a self-supporting criterion of justice, independently of the more orthodox criteria previously discussed? The idea that inequalities should only be permitted when they benefit the least advantaged members of society has a strong intuitive appeal.[39] Does the difference principle express a sense of justice which is more basic than the ordinary precepts of rights, desert, and need?

The difference principle can be viewed in a number of ways. Brian Barry, for instance, sees it as 'one possible compromise point between two ultimate principles, namely the utilitarian principle and the principle of equality.'[40] In the same general vein, someone predisposed towards equality might regard it as a criterion of justified inequality—departures from equality being rational if everyone stands to benefit by them. Again, we might adopt Rawls's suggestion that the difference principle 'provides an interpretation of the principle of fraternity', on the grounds that when it is satisfied everyone will be in a position to justify his advantages to everyone else. The question we must ask, however, is whether the difference principle can be interpreted as a principle of *justice*; and it seems to me that it can only be so interpreted by relying once again on the notion of desert. For consider the position of someone who is gaining a larger than average reward in a society which conforms to the difference principle: what inclines us to say that this reward is just? It is surely a sense that he is *earning* the reward by contributing to the well-being of those worse off than himself. This is further confirmed when we recall that the difference principle may license the payment of exceptionally high rewards to some people simply because they refuse to exercise their valuable

[39] This is not the only way in which the difference principle may be interpreted, but it is the rendering which may most plausibly be regarded as a principle of justice. See further, Keat and Miller, op. cit., Section II.

[40] Barry, op. cit., p. 42.

skills without such payment. Under these circumstances, would
we still regard the rewards as just (even if we thought them
justified)? Surely not: and the reason is that the rewards
are no longer deserved. Thus the difference principle's appeal
as a principle of justice appears to derive from our feeling that
those who contribute to the well-being of the worst-off deserve
some reward. Rawls has not added a fundamentally new principle to our ideas of justice, but has rather presented a variation
on a well-established theme.

Let us conclude by comparing Rawls's theory of justice with
the utilitarian theory from the point of view of the ordinary
principles of justice. Utilitarianism diverges from ordinary
ideas in two important ways. First, it is a wholly 'forward-
looking' theory—it judges actions to be right or wrong solely
on the basis of their future effects. The common idea of justice,
however, includes 'backward-looking' elements; for example,
when somebody is said to have a just claim to a reward on
grounds of desert, a present act (giving the reward) is seen as
right because of its relationship to a past act (the act which
earned the reward). Second, utilitarianism is an aggregative
theory—it judges actions to be right or wrong according to the
net quantity of happiness they produce—whereas the common
idea of justice is concerned with the distribution of benefits
among persons. Now Rawls's theory is also forward-looking,
with the possible exception of the principle of fair equality of
opportunity (which has been shown to involve the notion of
desert). The size of incomes and other rewards is not to be
fixed in such a way that they fit the past, but in such a way
that the greatest benefit is produced in the future for the
least advantaged members of society. And although Rawls's
theory is not strictly aggregative, because it does not allow the
few to be deprived to obtain a greater balance of happiness for
the many, it is not distributive either since it contains no principles directly prescribing an allocation of benefits and burdens
to persons. In short, the contractual theory of justice appears
to be less a radical alternative to utilitarianism than a modification of the utilitarian theory, differing from that theory
chiefly in demanding the maximum benefit for one particular
group in society—the worst-off—instead of the maximum benefit for society at large. While this may come a little closer to our

ordinary sense of justice than the unmodified utilitarian position it still appears to diverge too far from well-established judgements to satisfy the requirements which both Rawls and the modern utilitarian propose for an acceptable moral theory.

Since neither of the systematic theories of justice we have examined has been found satisfactory, we must return to the principles of justice which we uncovered in our investigation of the concept's ordinary use. These principles have yet to be subjected to thorough examination. We must try to clarify the concepts which are used to express them, discover the moral significance of each principle, and make certain that, as previously claimed, they represent irreducibly different demands of justice. The following three chapters are devoted to such an examination. After it has been completed, we shall be better placed to understand the nature of the conflict between the principles, and to indicate how a choice might be made between them.

II

RIGHTS

---

1 *Legal and Moral Rights*

A familiar starting-point for those who wish to analyse the concept of a right is the distinction between legal and moral rights—between the rights of an individual which arise from his position within a system of positive law (as property-owner, say, or as party to a contract) and those which arise in other ways, for example from a promise or agreement which has no legal status. But a moment's reflection shows that this dichotomy is too simple. For most people possess a great number of rights of different kinds, as a consequence of their roles as employees, club members, participants in group activities, etc., and these rights cannot properly be assimilated either to the legal or to the moral category. My right as a university teacher to mark examination scripts is directly neither a legal nor a moral right (though it may *become* a moral right under certain conditions). One could of course resolve this by stipulating that all non-legal rights should be counted as 'moral', but it would not be a helpful resolution; for should not moral rights be seen as arising from moral rules in much the same way as legal rights arise from legal rules?

Nevertheless, the practice of focusing one's attention on legal and moral rights is not wholly misguided. The other kinds of right (which we might group together under the heading 'institutional rights') can be seen to fall in between the two pure types, legal and moral. The rules of a university, with their fixed procedures, tribunals, rights of appeal, and so on, are like a legal system in miniature. Having a right as a member of a university is much like having a legal right. By contrast, if I draw up an agreement with a group of friends setting out how we are to use a house which we share, this is quite like a rather formal and detailed promise; and the rights which I

52

have that others should perform what is laid down in the rules
are like rights to have promises fulfilled. Roughly, I think,
the closeness with which an institutional right approaches the
legal 'ideal type' depends on three factors:

(1)　The extent to which the rules conferring the right are
clearly laid down.

(2)　The extent to which definite penalties are established
for those who violate the right.

(3)　The extent to which specific individuals are designated
to impose such penalties.

If other rights have this intermediate status, we can see why
political theorists should have paid most attention to legal and
moral rights proper. These are the cases which present the
greatest difficulties of analysis, and of the two groups moral
rights are the harder to deal with from a philosophical point
of view. The political philosopher is well advised to avoid the
technical analysis of types of legal right, which should be left
to those with a thorough knowledge of the practice of law.
I shall take for granted the results of one such analysis
(Hohfeld's) and ask whether the same analytical schema can
correctly be applied to moral rights. But one general remark
must be made about law before we turn away from it.

In what I have said so far, I have taken for granted a positivist account of law. A clear distinction between legal and
moral rights has been assumed, and legal rights have been
presented as arising in a straightforward way from the rules
of positive law. Law, in other words, has been seen as a set of
rules whose content is relatively clear and fixed, and in some
cases these rules create rights in the individuals who are
subject to them. But this account of law can be called in question by an objection on the following lines.

The positivist account of law makes it seem more cut and
dried than it either could or should be. Legal rules are never
as precise as the account suggests, they have to be freshly
interpreted for each specific case, and such interpretation
modifies the rule for the future. Therefore, establishing that
you have a legal right is not simply a matter of citing the
relevant rule; you have also to justify the interpretation you
propose to place on the rule, and to do this it is necessary to

bring forward moral considerations. These, however, should not be seen as extra-legal grounds, imported from outside to repair the inadequacies of the law, for they may be included within the law as *legal principles*.[1]

Although this objection may tell against a naive legal positivism, it does not seem to me decisive against more sophisticated versions. The positivist may allow that rules of law do not interpret themselves, that there are hard cases in which the law as it stands gives no clear indication as to what the legal rights of the various parties are. The question is how this situation should be viewed. For the positivist it indicates a failing in the law, and it becomes appropriate to go outside the law itself to consider the moral aspects of the case, in order that good law should be made for this and other similar cases in the future. But such instances must be seen as exceptional, not characteristic of the way in which legal rights are established. For critics such as Dworkin, on the other hand, it is the difficult cases which reveal to us the essential nature of law.

Fortunately, we do not have to decide on the general issues involved for our special purposes. We are interested only in what it is to have a legal right, and here we may say that for the great majority of cases the positivist theory will do. To decide what someone's legal rights are, it is enough to consult the relevant rules of law, without bringing in moral considerations. It would be most odd to say that whenever someone takes an object belonging to me, I have to produce moral grounds for asserting my legal right to the thing concerned. Not only would this be a clear misdescription of what actually happens, but a legal system which had this quality would have obvious practical disadvantages. Thus whatever the merits of an anti-positivist view as a general account of law, it does not help us to understand the central, characteristic cases of having a legal right.

Let us pass on to moral rights. There are several fundamental issues to be settled before we can begin a detailed analysis of the concept of a moral right and its relation to the concept of justice. The first is whether it is meaningful to speak of moral rights at all; for it has occasionally been argued that only *legal*

---

[1] See R. Dworkin, 'Is Law a System of Rules?' in R. S. Summers (ed.), *Essays in Legal Philosophy* (Oxford, 1968).

rights can properly be described as rights. This point of view was classically expressed by Bentham, and more recently in a paper by W. D. Lamont.[2] In Bentham's eyes,

Rights are, then, the fruits of the law, and of the law alone. There are no rights without law—no rights contrary to the law—no rights anterior to the law. Before the existence of laws there may be reasons for wishing that there were laws—and doubtless such reasons cannot be wanting, and those of the strongest kind—but a reason for wishing that we possessed a right, does not constitute a right.[3]

Bentham's argument was that a claim to a moral or natural right was a misleading way of claiming that a certain legal right *ought* to exist. It was misleading because to state that a right existed was to state a *fact*, namely that sanctions would be imposed on any individual who interfered with the relevant goods enjoyed by the right-holder. But the asserted 'moral rights' did not have this factual existence; they were fictions. Bentham's account is wrong in two ways, however. Firstly, it is simply not true that the purpose of making 'moral right' claims is to demand that the corresponding legal right should be created. In many cases this would be a most implausible intention to ascribe to the person making the claim—for example, in the case of moral rights arising from promises. Secondly, Bentham's account is inconsistent, in so far as he is prepared to admit that moral duties may be backed by sanctions in the form of social disapproval, ostracism, etc. His views that to have a right is to be the beneficiary of a duty, and that to have a duty is to be faced by a threat of sanctions, if something is not done, may be inadequate in themselves,[4] but if he holds these views he is bound to admit the existence of those moral rights corresponding to acknowledged and sanctioned moral duties.

As for Lamont's claim that 'rights follow from law. If no law, no rights', this turns out on inquiry to depend upon a broadening of the concept of law beyond our ordinary understanding of that idea, until moral rules are seen as a type of law. This

---

[2] W. D. Lamont, 'Rights', *Proceedings of the Aristotelian Society*, Supp. vol. xxiv (1950).
[3] Cited in C. K. Ogden, *Bentham's Theory of Fictions* (London, 1932), p. cxxviii.
[4] On the former view, see also below pp. 63–5.

should generally be regarded as a sterile and confusing proposal to make, but the inclination to make it at all may be illuminating. It indicates that when we are thinking and talking about rights, we are working in a legalistic area of morality. The kind of reasoning involved in reaching the conclusion that someone has a moral right is like the reasoning of a judge or lawyer trying to establish that someone has a legal right. This is the kernel of truth in the view that all rights are legal rights. Otherwise there is nothing in what Bentham and Lamont say to make us change our usual practice of ascribing moral rights to people, without thinking either that such rights should be legally recognized, or that some esoteric form of law is involved anyway.

A more serious objection to the idea of moral rights is that 'moral right' is such a vague expression that to say 'A has a moral right to X' is to say no more than 'It is morally right that A be given X' or 'A ought to be given X'. If this were true, it would prohibit rights from being regarded as distinctive grounds for justice-claims. However, I believe that the criticism can be met. Consider a typical situation in which moral rights are created: the making of a promise. A promises B that he will give B a certain object; this creates in B a moral right to be given the object, and the right persists until B receives it *unless* he voluntarily releases A from his obligation. But suppose it turns out that the object concerned will be extremely harmful to B, or that B will use the object to harm others. It is then no longer right to give B the object—but his moral right to it persists (the moral right is overridden by the requirement that we avoid causing serious harm whenever we can).

The argument can be put in another way. If we say 'A ought to be given X, because he has a moral right to it', the second clause does not simply reiterate the first. There are other types of reason which might be advanced instead—for instance, that giving X to A will maximize the general welfare. If there are six men in a boat at sea, and only one of them can row, it may be right to give the whole of the last loaf of bread to that one, in the hope that he can row them ashore. But has he a right to it? Could he complain if a general decision was taken to divide the bread equally and to forgo the added chance of reaching land? I think not.

There is some temptation to expand the concept of a right to include these cases, and casual everyday use could no doubt be cited in support. But I shall try to show that such expansion should be resisted, since the central use of this concept is to make a particular kind of moral claim, rather than to express rightness in general. We shall see later that there are a limited number of grounds upon which moral rights can properly be based, and the general welfare is certainly not one of these.

A weaker (and more plausible) version of the previous position is the view that 'A has a moral right to X' means 'It would be just to give X to A'; or as Raphael puts it 'justice is co-extensive with rights'. This would avoid the objections stated above, provided of course that one does not identify justice with the whole of morality; but it would be equally damaging to my thesis that rights are *one* type of ground for justice-claims. The view was argued for by Mill:

Justice implies something which it is not only right to do, and wrong not to do, but which some individual person can claim from us as his moral right.[5]

The reasons Mill gives for asserting this are instructive, for they show why it is tempting to enlarge the concept of a right until all 'justice claims' can be expressed as 'right claims'. Whenever an injustice occurs, there is some person who is wronged—whether he is robbed, not kept faith with, or treated worse than he deserves. Thus, Mill says, injustice implies two things—a wrong done, and some assignable person who is wronged. He then makes the tacit assumption that when an individual is wronged, some moral right of his is violated. Hence the original assertion. But the tacit assumption is false. Consider a case in which someone is treated worse than he deserves. A devoted nurse who has sacrificed a number of years of her life to look after a sick person gets no part of the inheritance when the person dies. The nurse has been wronged (and an injustice has been committed), but it is incorrect to say that she had a moral right to any part of the inheritance. The wrong and the injustice arise directly from her deserts, and it is mistaken to interpose an imaginary right between the desert and the wrong.

[5] J. S. Mill, *Utilitarianism* in *Utilitarianism; On Liberty; Representative Government*, ed. A. D. Lindsay (London, 1964), p. 46.

If the invalid had promised, or had even indicated, that he would be leaving something to the nurse, the case would be different; but even then her rights would arise from the promise and not from her deserts. Mill's mistake is an easy one to make, but it leads to considerable confusion through failure to discriminate between different grounds for asserting that an act is just or unjust. I shall have more to say later about why the concepts of desert and entitlement must be kept distinct.

2   *The Concept of a Right*

Thus far I have attempted to defend the view that moral rights can serve as a distinctive type of basis for making justice-claims against the contentions (1) that there are no such things as moral rights, (2) that to have a moral right to something is simply for it to be *right* for you to have that thing, (3) that to have a moral right to something is simply for it to be *just* for you to have that thing. It is worth noticing that these attempts at conceptual dissolution have much less plausibility in the case cf legal rights, and it is not necessary to repeat the argument as it applies to them. Having cleared away some initial difficulties, we can go on to ask; what *are* moral rights? What do we mean when we say that people have them, and what grounds do we give for our claim? How are rights related to duties and obligations? And when do rights become relevant to social justice? Some misleadingly simple answers to these questions may be avoided by starting from Hohfeld's classic analysis of legal rights, and asking whether the classification he proposed can profitably be extended to moral rights as well.[6]

Hohfeld's general point was that the concept of a right is ambiguously used to cover four different sorts of legal relation, and that much confusion has occurred in consequence. He proposed instead that four separate terms should be used for the different relations. The four terms which are normally now used (modifying Hohfeld's original suggestions) are 'claim-right', 'liberty', 'power', and 'immunity'. A person has a claim-right to do or have something when another person has a duty to let him do or have that thing. An example of a claim-right is A's right to a piece of land which he owns,

⁶ W. N. Hohfeld, *Fundamental Legal Conceptions as Applied in Judicial Reasoning* (New Haven and London, 1964).

corresponding to the duty of B and others to stay off the land. A person has a liberty to do something when he is under no duty *not* to do that thing. For example, A's right to speak freely in public places is a liberty, since it corresponds to his lack of any duty to refrain from speaking. A power is the legal ability to change people's claim-rights and duties in certain respects. For example, A's right to make a will is a power, because it enables him to grant new rights to B and others, and to impose duties on his executors. An immunity, finally, is a legal gua-rantee against the imposition of certain duties by another person (or for that matter the granting of certain rights)—it corresponds, in other words, to someone else's lack of (legal) power in a certain respect. Thus in a state with a constitution guaranteeing freedom of speech, each citizen has an immunity against the legislature's imposing duties which restrict free speech.

To what extent is this division of rights replicated in the moral sphere? It appears that all four categories of moral rights exist. Moral claim-rights, like legal claim-rights, are the kind we most often have in mind when speaking of 'rights' without qualification. If A promises B that he will lend B a book, then B has a claim-right to be lent that book, correspond-ing to A's duty to lend it to him.[7] As for moral liberties, we may again use the example of A's right to speak freely, which is a moral as well as a legal liberty. To say that A has a right to speak freely means that he has no moral duty not to speak

---

[7] A point which might be raised here concerns the relationship between the concepts of duty and obligation. It is more natural to speak of promises as giving rise to *obligations* than as giving rise to *duties*. In the case in question, we would normally speak of A's obligation to lend the book. The matter is excellently discussed in R. B. Brandt, 'The Concepts of Obligation and Duty', *Mind*, lxxiii (1964). His conclusions, in brief, are as follows: In the case of both concepts, we must distinguish between *paradigm* uses and *extended* uses. Paradigm uses are a subclass of uses which (a) are felt to be especially natural uses of the term; (b) occur in special contexts having features in common. The paradigm use of 'obligation' is in a context where two people are involved, and a prior transaction has occurred: either a promise or agreement has been made between them, or one has bestowed a benefaction on the other. The paradigm use of 'duty' is in the context of a person's occupying a position within an organization ('official duties', for instance). But both concepts can properly be applied in a much wider range of situations, and in their extended uses Brandt concludes that there is little difference between the two terms. Accepting this conclusion, I have for simplicity's sake spoken throughout of the relation between rights and duties, even in contexts where 'obligation' would be the more natural term to use.

freely. An example of a moral power would be A's right to make a gift of one of his possessions. In exercising this right, he alters the (moral) rights and duties of other people, as he does in the analogous legal case.

The existence of moral immunities is more problematic. I think it can be said that *if* there are inalienable moral rights, these rights would be made up of both immunities and claim-rights or liberties. Consider again the right to speak freely, understood as a moral right. If this is held to be inalienable (as it was in traditional natural rights theory), then not only does A have the liberty to speak freely (absence of duty not to), but he is not liable to be put under a contrary duty. It can never become his duty not to speak freely. He has an immunity against all moral agents in this respect, whatever he does. This at least shows that the idea of a moral immunity makes sense, whether or not any such rights actually exist.

Of the four types of moral and legal right we have distinguished, claim-rights are obviously of central importance to social justice. When we speak of a person's rights to material goods, to wealth, to education, or to the fulfilment of agreements, we are in each case thinking of claim-rights which imply corresponding duties on the part of other people. Liberties, as their name suggests, are mainly relevant to the ideal of personal freedom. Powers and immunities are rarely considered outside of strictly legal contexts. In the following discussion, therefore, I shall focus my attention on claim-rights and their relationship to social justice with no more than a passing mention of the other categories of rights. Although we have given a general definition of a claim-right, we have yet to establish when it is that individuals are granted them, and how precisely they stand in relation to duties.

One position that has been taken up here is the thesis of the 'strict correlativity' of rights and duties: A's right against B implies, and is implied by, B's duty to A. This position supplements the view contained in Hohfeld—that a claim-right implies a corresponding duty—by adding the reverse implication—a duty implies a corresponding claim-right. Ross advocated the correlativity thesis, at least in the case of duties to human agents.[8] He was prepared to draw the implication

---

[8] See W. D. Ross, *The Right and the Good* (Oxford, 1930), esp. ch. 2, appendix 1.

that since we speak of duties of beneficence, we must also speak of rights to beneficence. Ross appears not to have found this objectionable (though he admitted that current usage resisted such a broadening of the concept of a right). However, were we to accept Ross's claim, it would destroy the distinctive character of statements about rights. 'A has a right to X' would become equivalent in meaning to 'A ought to be given X', and we have already given reasons for rejecting this equivalence. Ross thought that our reluctance to talk about rights to beneficence arose from a feeling 'that there is something indecent in making a *claim* to beneficence', but this is hardly pertinent since we can readily think of cases of undeniable rights which it would be thought wrong, on many occasions, to stand upon or press. The trouble lies elsewhere. There are well-defined criteria for ascribing rights to people; something quite specific has to be done by them or by others in order for us to say that they have a right. 'Being in a position to benefit from someone else's action' is too broad and imprecise a basis upon which to found a right. Ross's view overlooks this feature of the assertion of rights, and therefore prevents a proper appreciation of the role which such assertions play in moral and political argument.

Another way in which the correlativity thesis might be maintained, to avoid the difficulties of the previous position, is by limiting the concept of 'duty' more narrowly than does Ross. One would maintain that of all the actions one ought to do, only some are properly called duties, and that the distinguishing characteristic of the latter class is that they are actions undertaken to respect the rights of others. But this certainly runs counter to ordinary use. Some examples: the invalid who is cared for by his devoted nurse has a duty to deal fairly with her, i.e. to reward her services after his death, even though she does not have a right to any benefit from him. An eminent painter, contemplating destroying his works, has a duty to preserve them for the benefit of humanity as a whole, though no individual has a right that he should. If you perform some supererogatory action which brings me immense benefit, I have a duty to find some proper way of expressing my gratitude, though you have no right that I should do this. These cases show that we do not normally restrict 'duty' in the way suggested;

at the same time neither do we expand it to include everything that we ought to do. This is shown by such classic
examples as the soldier who throws himself on a grenade to
save the lives of the rest of his platoon—'beyond the call of
duty'[9]—as well as much slighter instances; one ought from
time to time to give unexpected presents to one's close friends,
but we would hardly speak of a duty here. This suggests that
for a morally right action to be a duty, it must at least (a) have
sufficiently important consequences, (b) be within the capacities of a normal person. There is no need for our purposes to
make this any more specific. The essential point is that as we
ordinarily understand the concept of duty, it has a scope (1)
narrower than that of morally right actions, (2) *wider* than that
of actions demanded by the rights of others.

Is there any general way of characterizing those cases in
which duties do give rise to corresponding claim-rights? Two
recent suggestions have been offered by Hart[10] and Lyons.[11]
In Hart's view, a person who has a right is in a position either
to demand that the corresponding duty be performed, or to
waive the duty. He has, so to speak, control over the incidence
of the duty. Hart distinguishes such a person from someone,
who merely stands to benefit from the performance of a duty.
In his example, a man extracts a promise from a friend to
look after his mother. Here it is the son who has the right to
have the looking-after done, and the mother, although benefiting, has no right arising from the promise. Yet Hart himself
admits that this account will not do for all cases. The rules
of the criminal law are generally said to confer rights on
individuals not to be killed, assaulted, etc., but the individuals
concerned have no option whether or not to enforce the corresponding duties. Or, to take a non-legal case, if an agreement
is made between a number of people which establishes rules
to govern their respective activities, each man has a right

[9] See J. O. Urmson, 'Saints and Heroes' in A. I. Melden (ed.), *Essays in Moral Philosophy* (Seattle, Washington, 1958).

[10] H. L. A. Hart, *Definition and Theory in Jurisprudence* (Oxford, 1953); 'Are there any Natural Rights?', in A. Quinton (ed.), *Political Philosophy* (Oxford, 1967); 'Bentham: Lecture on a Master Mind', in R. Summers (ed.), *More Essays in Legal Philosophy* (Oxford, 1971).

[11] D. Lyons, 'Rights, Claimants and Beneficiaries', *Amercian Philosophical Quarterly*, vi (1969).

against all the others that they should comply, yet he cannot himself choose to release them from the performance of their duties. Hart tries to deflect the full force of this criticism in his later article ('Bentham') by contrasting the strict use of the concept of a right (in cases where the individual can control the incidence of the duty) with a wider use in such instances as those I have mentioned. But are we correct to suppose that these latter instances are somehow peripheral? May it not be that one reason for depriving a person of the choice whether or not to exercise his right is the overriding importance of that right to him? This hypothesis would fit the circumstances of the criminal law, where the most serious kinds of harm that could be done to a man are prohibited by legal duties over which he has no control. In the sphere of civil law, by comparison, where a person generally has a choice whether or not to press his rights, much less serious forms of injury are involved. Hart wants to establish a basic connection between the having of a right and the exercise of free choice, and no doubt the connection holds in many cases, but it seems equally vital to link rights with basic security of the person. If I have a right to something which is respected by others, I have a certain expectation that I will be able to enjoy it in the future whatever the over-all balance of advantage may turn out to be, and this expectation exists whether or not it is within my power to press or waive the corresponding duty. Of course, having definite expectations for the future does of itself increase my freedom, for I can now choose between alternative courses of action knowing that I will actually be able to *take* them, and not be stopped by unforeseen intervention; so perhaps Hart's connection between rights and free choice can be re-established in a different way. But his original suggestion must be rejected.

Lyons defends a modified version of Bentham's theory that to have a right is to be the beneficiary of someone else's duty. To take care of Hart's objections to the general view (as stated above), Lyons distinguishes between those who merely benefit from the performance of a duty in some way or other, and those who are the *direct, intended* beneficiaries of the duty. Some duties are not aimed at any specific person in this sense, and so do not confer corresponding rights (e.g. my moral duty to pay taxes, which does not correspond to anyone else's right).

Other duties will be directly intended to benefit some people, and may incidentally benefit others; only those in the first category are said to have rights. Lyons, therefore, overturns Hart's account of the son/mother case, arguing that the mother *does* have a right to be taken care of (she is the direct, intended beneficiary of the friend's duty), and further that *unless* the son also benefits in some way from the performance, it is doubtful whether he has a right at all. Lyons claims that this account comes closer to ordinary thought on the subject than does Hart's analysis.

While doubtless an improvement on Bentham's original view, it does not seem that Lyons's 'qualified beneficiary' theory is satisfactory as an account of rights. First, it is more plausible to claim that to be the direct, intended beneficiary of a duty is a sufficient condition of having a right, than to claim that it is a necessary condition. While we might be prepared to agree with Lyons that the mother in the given example has a right as well as the son, it is much less plausible to say that the son has no right unless he benefits from the friend's performance too. Lyons's argument is that unless the son really wants his mother to be looked after, the promise is frivolous and need not be attended to. But why should we accept the further proposition that if something is done which I really want done, then I benefit from that doing? This is an egoistic fallacy worthy of Bentham himself. And even if the son were to derive satisfaction from the knowledge that his wishes were being carried out, this would not make him the direct, intended beneficiary of the duty. The duty is intended to benefit the mother, and any advantages which accrue to the son are incidental. So being the direct, intended beneficiary of a duty is not a *necessary* condition of having a right, for the son certainly has one after the promise is made.

Second, there is reason to doubt whether it is a sufficient condition either. Feinberg[12] notes that in legal cases the beneficiary of a promise does not *necessarily* have a right to what is promised, but does so only in specified cases. I think this can be generalized to other types of duty, and to the moral sphere.

---

[12] J. Feinberg, 'Duties, Rights and Claims', *American Philosophical Quarterly*, iii (1966), reprinted in E. A. Kent (ed.), *Law and Philosophy* (New York, 1970). See esp. pp. 144–5 of the latter.

If my previous examples hold good, they undermine Lyons's position. The duty of gratitude to my benefactor is directly intended to benefit him, yet he has no right that I should perform it. The invalid's duty to leave part of his inheritance to his nurse is directly intended to benefit her yet she has no right to what she receives. It is, on the whole, true that if someone comes to know that he is the beneficiary of a duty (and so acts on that expectation) he is properly said to have a right to performance, but the basis of the right is the creating of expectations, not the duty itself. The case is essentially similar to that in which A acts in such a way as to give B reason to believe that some benefit will be delivered to him, even though A is under no duty to B to begin with.

Hence neither Hart nor Lyons succeeds in giving a general criterion for distinguishing the circumstances in which duties *do* confer corresponding rights from those in which they do not. Instead of looking for a general criterion, we shall have to consider the different ways in which people come to acquire claim-rights. Only when this variety of right-creating situations has been examined can we start to look for features which are common to all ascriptions of rights.

3 *Positive Rights*

In the previous section, Hohfeld's scheme for classifying rights was used to distinguish claim-rights from liberties, powers, and immunities. I want now to introduce a further distinction which cross-cuts Hohfeld's classification, and which is essential for a proper understanding of the relation between rights and justice. This is the distinction between *positive* and *ideal* rights. A positive right is constituted by its social recognition. A person has a positive right when a certain description applies to him, and, in the society in which he lives, people falling under that description are acknowledged to have rights. The simplest example is again that of promising. In our society it is acknowledged that someone to whom a promise has been made (this could be spelt out in descriptive terms) has a right that the promiser should do what he promised. The *content* of a positive right is immaterial. If someone promises me that he will stand on his head at noon tomorrow, I have a right that he should carry out his promise, although the act in itself has no moral value.

An ideal right, on the other hand, is constituted by its content. A person has an ideal right because of that to which he has the right, whether or not that right is socially recognized. Natural rights are the most familiar examples of ideal rights. A man's right to free speech, for example, is a right because of the moral value attached to being able to speak freely, not because the right is socially recognized. An ideal right may, of course, become a positive right by gaining general recognition in a given society, and indeed the intention of those who have claimed that men have certain ideal rights has been that those rights should become positive. Thus the two classes overlap. It is possible that all the ideal rights which a particular man believes exist may be recognized in his society; though it is extremely unlikely that the reverse is true, that all positive rights are ideal (would be regarded as rights even if they were not socially recognized) by anyone's standards.

It should be observed that the logical status of the two sorts of right is different. Establishing the existence of a positive right is a matter of empirical investigation. This is not of course to say that these rights can be observed in the way that tables and chairs can; they are not physical objects. It is a question of what people do, and how they describe what they are doing. For such rights to exist, individuals must assert and recognize them, and these assertions must be taken as reasons for performing, or not performing, the appropriate actions. To establish that people in our own society have positive rights derived from promises, we should point out that promisees are disposed to assert their rights, and promisers to admit that they have obligations to do what was promised; furthermore, that these obligations are generally fulfilled, unless good countervailing reasons can be given. It will not always be so simple to discover whether rights exist in a positive form: for instance, a society may pay lip-service to certain ideal rights, such as the right to free speech, yet in practice fail to recognize them in some cases. Do individuals have positive rights here, which are just rather readily overridden? Or is the society's commitment only to the rights in their ideal form? Besides this type of problem, there is also the circumstance in which social consensus fails. One section of society acknowledges a certain kind of right, another section does not. For instance, there may be disagreement about whether a promise made under a certain form of duress is binding. In such a case it will be impossible to give a simple answer to the question 'Does Smith have a right that Brown should do X (which he promised to do)?'

The existence of these difficult cases, however, does not affect the basic point that positive rights are identified by empirical investigation. By contrast, to prove that an ideal right exists requires moral argument. What has to be shown is that some benefit or freedom is of sufficient moral value to the individual to be called his moral right; so there will be as many lists of ideal rights as there are moral standpoints (including those, such as Bentham's, which exclude the possibility of ideal rights altogether). The existence of some rights, of course, is beyond reasonable doubt, provided one is prepared to use the language of ideal rights at all; such is the case with the right to life. Among the main contenders for this agreed status are the traditional natural rights. But it should not be thought that all ideal rights can properly be called natural. At the very least, a natural right must be one which all men can possess *qua* men, and there are some ideal rights (such as the right of parents to receive special consideration from their children) which cannot possibly meet this requirement. We shall later want to examine the form of argument which is used to support the claim that an ideal right exists, whether natural or otherwise.

At the beginning of this analysis, a simplifying assumption was made, which was in effect that all legal rights are positive rights. To establish whether someone has a legal right, it is enough to consult the relevant rule of law, and the question of what the law is can itself be settled empirically (e.g. by showing that a certain rule was laid down by a competent authority). In the case of institutional rights, there is no room for doubt at all: every institutional right is positive. Whatever the temptation to suppose that an 'ideal law' stands behind the positive law and confers rights which are both ideal and legal, no one will propose a similar theory in the case of the rules of cricket, say, or the constitution of a university. Thus the division of rights into positive rights and ideal rights creates a single dichotomy between, on one side, legal rights, institutional rights, and positive moral rights, and, on the

other, ideal moral rights. What I propose to do, in this section
and the one following, is to consider positive rights, their value
and their relation to the idea of justice, before returning in
section 5 to a rather briefer discussion of ideal rights. We can
better appreciate the character of ascriptions of positive rights
if we begin by looking at the various contexts in which such
ascriptions are made. In what circumstances are people said
to have positive rights? The following contexts appear to be the
most important.

1. *Publicly established rules.* This heading covers both legal
rights and quasi-legal institutional rights. Where rules exist
and are generally agreed to be binding, they confer positive
rights in one or both of the following ways:

(a) Individuals may have rights under the rules, and these
may be claim-rights, liberties, etc. For instance, a legal rule
prohibiting assault on the person creates a (claim-) right not
to be assaulted in each person covered by the rule. The rules
of cricket (by their silence on the matter) give players the
liberty to wear caps during the game. We have already seen
that there is a difficulty in saying in general terms *when* rules
confer rights on those who benefit from their existence, but
there is no doubt that positive rights *are* acknowledged to arise
in this way.

(b) The rules may give powers which enable individuals to
confer rights on others and on themselves. The law permits
me to alienate my property, transferring the rights of ownership to somebody else. Or I can give another permission to
walk over my land, granting a liberty in place of his previous
duty to keep off.

2. *Promises and agreements.* I include here all cases in which
one individual, by a specific act, confers rights on another,
but without reference to publicly established rules. The main
sub-cases are:

(a) Promises, where A unilaterally takes an obligation upon
himself, and thereby confers a right upon B, to whom the
promise is made.

(b) Agreements, where A and B each take obligations upon
themselves and confer rights on the other (e.g. an agreement
to meet in the square at noon tomorrow).

(c) Authorizations, where A confers a right on B by explicitly removing certain obligations which would otherwise obtain. For instance, one man may authorize another to prevent him from drinking more than a certain amount in an evening (removing the normal duty not to interfere with other people's self-regarding conduct).

The point to be stressed about these cases is that the right is created by a definite act at a specific point in time, and the right so created is positive because it is generally understood that performing such an act *does* create rights.

3. *Compensation and reciprocation.* Rights to compensation arise when one person deliberately or negligently harms another, or injures his interests in some way. If I knock you over in the street, you have a right that I help you to your feet again. If I damage your house, you have a right that I make good the loss. It should be noted that in many of these cases the rights concerned depend on rights previously existing, and are therefore derivative. For instance, you have a right to enjoy the use of your house, and I have a duty to let you enjoy it. If I fail in my duty by damaging the house, this gives you a further right to compensation, and me a further duty to repair the damage as best as I can.

Rights of reciprocation arise when a person who has benefited from someone else's action is placed in a position where he can repay his benefactor in kind. Although I have argued that, in general, duties of gratitude do not imply corresponding rights in the object of gratitude, such rights may exist in particular cases, especially where B is able to perform the very same action for A as A performed for B. If yesterday you helped me to carry a heavy suitcase up the stairs, and today I meet you struggling with an equally heavy case, you would probably be justified in claiming a right to be helped. Unless such instances can be presented as loose forms of tacit agreement, rights of reciprocation must be admitted as a category of their own.

4. *Established forms of behaviour.* If people are accustomed to acting in a particular way, in time they may come to have a right to act in that way. A familiar example, in which a legal right is created, is the persistent use of a path to traverse a piece of land, which eventually establishes a right of way. Moral rights can come into existence in a similar manner. If the workers at a factory have for a long time been in the habit of taking a

tea-break during the afternoon, they have a right to continue doing this (though only a moral one), and an employer who arbitrarily orders them to stop would be guilty of violating their rights.

It is tempting to try to reduce these cases to type 2 above by use of such ideas as a 'tacit agreement' (to let people walk on one's land, etc.). This should be resisted. The person across whose land the right of way is created may have been completely ignorant of the behaviour which created the right.

5. *Legitimate expectations.* There are many ways short of explicit promising in which we can induce people to expect that they will receive goods or services. In such cases, these people may be said to have rights to what they expect. If A can show that B has led him to believe that a benefit will be forthcoming, then A has a right to that benefit, and B has a duty to give it to him. These cases depend on social conventions concerning the implications which can appropriately be derived from individual actions and utterances, and it is not necessarily enough for B to plead ignorance of the conventions for him to escape from his obligation. As social beings we have a duty to make ourselves familiar with the conclusions that others will draw from our behaviour, in cases where that behaviour has a standard significance.

On the other hand, it does not *necessarily* follow from the fact that one person's behaviour creates expectations in another, that the second has a right to have his expectations fulfilled. Someone who regularly performs a particular action may cause other people to expect that he will continue in the future, as the sun's regular rising creates an expectation that it will rise tomorrow. But if there is no convention whereby repeated performance indicates an intention to continue performing, no rights are created.

6. *Acknowledged ideal rights.* The rights which come into existence in the five preceding ways are rights regardless of their moral content. That to which a person has a right may be morally good, bad, or indifferent. But, as I noted earlier, it may happen that certain ideal rights become widely acknowledged in a society, not merely in the sense that they form part of the 'official' belief system, but that they are acted upon, and people are expected to modify their behaviour to take account of such

rights in others. These rights may of course be incorporated
into a formal system of rules, in which case they will be included
under 1. above; however, it will sometimes be inappropriate
to do this, in which case the rights will remain moral only.
Two examples in current society might be the right to be told
the truth, and the right of parents to special consideration
from their children. These rights do not originate in any of
the ways set out in 1–5. The right to be told the truth is one
which each man has regardless of conduct, and the parent's
right to consideration derives directly from his or her status as a
parent (though it can be forfeited by grossly negligent
behaviour).

4 *The Value of Positive Rights*

Examining the contexts in which rights get ascribed to people
helps us to understand the *character* of rights-claims. We want to
know how appealing to rights differs from other sorts of moral
appeal, and what is the point of a society recognizing rights
at all. If we can clarify these matters, we will be able to make
better sense of the relationship between rights and justice.

Plainly, the paradigm case of a right being used is where the
individual who has the right knows that he has it and acts
upon it, while other people recognize his right and adjust their
behaviour accordingly (by performing their obligations, not
imposing obligations on the right-holder, etc., according to
the nature of the right). What advantages accrue to the individual in such a case, and why should we think of rights as
morally valuable? The main advantages, I would argue, are
security and *freedom*. The relative weight attached to these two
values will vary between different cases. Claim-rights in
particular are linked to the value of security, for the right-
holder knows either that he will be protected in the future from
certain kinds of interference or harm, or that he will actually
receive certain benefits. Of course we can form reasonable
expectations about the future which have nothing to do with
our possession of rights, but a point which emerges clearly
from the foregoing analysis is that expectations very often
take on the character of rights, when they fall into the category
of 'Established forms of behaviour' or of 'Legitimate expectations'. Conversely, a right which falls into disuse, so that people

cease to have expectations about behaviour on account of it, loses its character as a right. A law becomes a 'dead letter'. A right of way which nobody uses ceases to be a right of way.

If the existence of rights confers security on the individuals who possess them, it might be thought that the value of having and claiming rights can be understood in utilitarian terms (as Mill, for instance, maintained). However, this would be wrong for various reasons. The most straightforward reason is that a particular right may have no positive utility at all; in fact its exercise may be harmful both to the person who possesses it and to others. Furthermore, even if the possessor of a right benefits from the security which it brings him, this does not mean that the right is generally beneficial to society. Like other principles of justice, the principle of rights is distributive in form—it specifies what treatment is due to particular individuals—and the value implicit in such a principle cannot be assimilated to aggregative ideals such as the general happiness. Thirdly, the benefit which a right confers is a benefit of a particular kind: it consists in security of expectation about the future. A utilitarian theory of rights is likely to blur this point by suggesting that if anything is essential to our happiness, it becomes one of our rights:

If [a man] has what we consider a sufficient claim, on whatever account, to have something guaranteed to him by society, we say that he has a right to it.[13]

By contrast, our analysis has suggested that rights are rarely ascribed to an individual on a basis of this sort (the exceptions are acknowledged ideal rights), but rest instead upon such facts as his legal status and his past history (as party to an agreement, for instance). What it is that we have rights to may be quite trivial; the value of having a right is often the value of expectation-fulfilment alone. Your standing on your head at noon tomorrow is morally worthless in itself; my right that you should do so is important because I can arrange my activities around that moment in the knowledge that you will perform the required action. Yet simultaneously I may have no positive right to sufficient food to keep me alive. A utilitarian

[13] J. S. Mill, op. cit., p. 49.

approach will tend to disguise such paradoxes as this, which arise unavoidably in our thinking about rights.

Besides giving security of expectation, the possession of a right often increases a man's freedom. In the case of liberties and immunities this feature is predominant, but a claim-right may also confer freedom of choice, especially where (as Hart stresses) the right-holder has the option to waive or press his right. This again gives us an important clue to the character of ascriptions of rights, and helps us to differentiate them from other kinds of moral judgements, particularly those which simply recommend that individuals shall be awarded certain tangible benefits for the satisfaction they will bring. We confer rights and impose obligations because we believe that people ought to be free to act in different ways, and to have control over their future circumstances irrespective of the good or bad use we think they will make of such freedom.

It is important to consider fully why we want to say that people have rights to do things which they ought not to do. Surely, if some action ought not to be done, then that is its cardinal feature; and why must we be perverse and insist that nevertheless the person involved has a right to do the action? There are at least two reasons for such perversity. First, the existence of a right may set moral limits to what we can do in practice to ensure that the wrong action is not performed. In many cases, for instance, it will be regarded as legitimate to reason with the person in an effort to persuade him not to do the action, but it will not be legitimate to take further steps to prevent him (e.g. to restrain him physically). So it will sometimes be morally correct to allow a wrong action to be performed, rather than to infringe someone's rights. Second, if the wrong envisaged is serious enough to justify any steps (e.g. if the person intends to commit a murder), insisting on a person's rights will indicate that the lesser of two evils has been chosen, and that only the gravity of the wrong in prospect was sufficient to justify interference with the person's normal liberties. In both cases we are testifying to the great importance of *this individual's* freedom and security, and setting it against the over-all good or harm which will result from his acting in a particular way.

What, then, would be objectionable in a society which did

not recognize individual rights, even if it were a society which took good care of its members? Feinberg, who has addressed himself to this possibility,[14] points out that such a society would necessarily lack the making of claims, which occurs when one stands upon one's rights and insists that other people perform their obligations. But, he argues, the making of claims is essential to human self-respect. There is a good deal in Feinberg's position here, particularly when one considers such practices as the inheritance trust. The child is the beneficiary of the estate put in trust, but it is assumed that he is incapable of exercising the rights over the estate, hence they are placed in the hands of the trustee. When he comes of age, the rights are transferred to him. Here there is a clear connection between the possession of rights and qualities such as responsibility which mark out the adult person. By giving the child rights, we recognize his status as a developed human being.

However, an objection on these lines to a society without rights seems most appropriate when the society is conceived of as run by a ruling group, who see to the welfare of the majority with a paternal eye. Here the ordinary people are aptly compared to children, receiving benefits but making no demands which they regard as legitimate either on one another or on the government; not standing on their rights. As Feinberg says, they lack self-respect. But compare the following situation: a group of friends decide to establish themselves as a community on a basis of equality. They draw up no agreements, no sets of rules, and no one is conceived to have any rights against other members. On the other hand, each person acknowledges an obligation to further the general welfare of the group, and to help other members when in need. Thus if A undertakes a project (building a house, say) which cannot properly be completed without the co-operation of other people, the community members have a duty to assist him but he has no right that they should; he cannot complain if they do not give him the help he needs.

Now it does not seem that such a community fails to cater for the self-respect of each member. Each person's needs are taken equally into account when the community members

<hr/>

[14] J. Feinberg, 'The Nature and Value of Rights', *Journal of Value Enquiry*, iv (1970).

decide what they should do,[15] and no person is under the control of any other. Yet the group's arrangements are flawed, and the flaws appear to confirm the foregoing argument about the value of having individual rights. First of all, each person is poorly placed to make plans for the future when these plans involve other people besides himself. A, building a house, may wish to carry out a series of operations at specific time-intervals. He cannot bind other people to help him at those times in the future, for this would introduce rights into the community, contrary to hypothesis. When he presents his plan to the community as a whole, the community may agree that the stages are best carried out as he suggests, and resolve to implement the plan. This certainly gives A some security of expectation, but not much. The community cannot *undertake* or *promise* to follow A's proposal. If, later, someone else is found to be in more urgent need of assistance, the members are quite justified in breaking off their help for A and going to assist the other man. A cannot demand that they continue with his plan.

Besides its failure to afford its members security of expectation, our community discourages individuality, and reduces freedom of choice. Suppose A wants to embark on some project which he regards as important but which appears ridiculous to the rest of the community (building a folly, for example). The community cannot disregard A's open expression of his wishes, yet they may well be justified in postponing this project until other more pressing tasks have been accomplished. They must in any case make comparative judgements about the urgency of different people's needs, and it is understandable that they should not regard this wish of A's as particularly important. So A will not be able to build his folly, at least in the foreseeable future. On the other hand, if we were to introduce promises and agreements into the community, then

[15] Does not this admit at least one right into our hypothetical society—the right to equal consideration of one's needs? Possibly—yet it is not a right one can stand upon or use to make claims against other people. Even if (privately) one thinks one's needs have not been equally considered, there is nothing one can do in practice to alter the decision. Hence from the point of view of Feinberg's argument, which links the having of rights to the making of claims, and finds the value of rights in the fact that they allow the individual to make claims against others, this right (if it is one) is irrelevant.

A will be in a position to agree with B, C, etc., that in return for help given to them, they will help him with his eccentric project; they may be completely repelled by his ideas, but once rights are instituted they cannot refuse to do as he wishes.

Thus we are brought back again to the way in which positive rights serve to protect the individual against the demands of his social group. In recognizing rights we are also recognizing the distinct value of each person and of his freedom, whether or not these contribute to the over-all good of the community. This is not to say that the general point of having rights cannot be understood in utilitarian terms. It is rather that a utilitarian approach cannot explain why we may want to insist upon protecting an individual's rights even at the expense of the general happiness.

The same feature of rights explains the intimate connection between the concepts of rights and justice. If justice is concerned with what is *due* to each person considered individually, it is hardly surprising that one of the facts about a person which determines what is due to him is the set of positive rights which he possesses. Putting it more formally, to say that an action respects someone's rights is to give a reason (though not a conclusive one) for regarding it as just, and to say that an action violates someone's rights is to give a reason (though not a conclusive one) for regarding it as unjust. The reason is less than conclusive in each case for (a) an action which respects A's rights may violate B's, and vice versa; (b) respecting rights may conflict with other 'just-making' considerations, i.e. deserts and needs. To illustrate, (a) you may promise a friend to meet him on a particular evening, but later discover that your parents intend to call on that same evening. The friend's right clashes with your parents' right to favoured treatment. The just thing to do will be to respect the more important of the two rights; deciding this will be a fairly complex matter, taking into account such factors as the comparative harm caused to the two parties if their rights are overridden, the firmness of the promise made to the friend, and so on. However, I do not wish to discuss in detail what is to everybody a familiar process of moral reckoning. The point is that citing the friend's right is not sufficient to establish the justice of your going out to meet him; it is a consideration which makes that action prima facie just—just in the absence of overriding considerations—but not conclusively just. (b) In a similar way you may promise to meet a friend, and it happens that on the day in question your neighbour falls ill. The neighbour has no right (against you) to be taken care of, yet he may badly *need* your assistance, and again it may be just to break your promise and violate your friend's right.

Rights and social justice likewise stand in a close relationship to one another. Although there are cases in which the violation of rights is an injustice, but not a social injustice as that idea is usually understood (an individual instance of promise-breaking would fit this description), an important part of social justice consists in respecting the positive rights which people have. The most powerful instrument for achieving this end is of course the law. Any socially just society must include a public mechanism for specifying and protecting people's rights, though it will be a matter of argument how far the existing legal system, in protecting the rights which it does, realizes justice. A balance has to be struck between (to use Raphael's terms) 'conservative' and 'prosthetic' justice— between the justice which preserves established rights and the justice which modifies these rights in terms of an ideal standard (a principle of desert or need). Each person will strike the balance differently, and the extreme positions are (1) a complete identification of social justice with the protection of rights, and (2) a thorough refusal to acknowledge any connection between *existing* rights and social justice. These clear-cut positions will be examined in the second part of the book. Even in the case of someone adopting position (2), however, the dissociation is only between existing rights and justice, and we may conjecture that the connection will be re-established in the ideal situation envisaged; social justice will consist (partly, at least)in the preservation of the positive rights which people *will* have in the society to be created.

Thus the connection between the concepts of rights and justice is repeated, in slightly weaker form, between the concepts of rights and social justice. There are some personal rights which do not really fall within the sphere of social justice, but many other rights must be taken into account when assessing the justice or injustice of social policy. This connection is quite plainly present in ordinary speech and argument, but I have tried also to explain its existence by pointing out axiological links between justice, understood as a set of principles specifying what is due to the individual as such, and rights, whose value lies in the security and freedom which they give to the person who possesses them. It is not surprising that the concept of rights should be tied more closely to justice than to aggregative concepts such as the public interest.

5 *Ideal Rights*

No account of rights and their relationship to justice would be complete without some consideration of 'ideal' moral rights—rights that are claimed for men but are not necessarily recognized in practice. It is clear that some of these rights, particularly those which are known as 'natural' or 'human' rights, represent very important moral claims, and must stand in a close relationship to justice; but it is equally clear that the value of such rights cannot be understood in the terms which were appropriate to positive rights. I shall argue that ideal rights are best analysed in terms of the concepts of desert and need; though I shall also try to show why the language of 'rights' is a natural, and at times almost unavoidable, way of expressing the claims in question.

Consider first what is surely the most important class of ideal rights: the list of natural or human rights. These rights are ideal because they are claimed for all men regardless of whether they are actually recognized in any particular society. What kinds of claim are they? Recent investigators[16] have considered it necessary to distinguish between two categories of human rights. On the one hand, there are the traditional natural rights of Locke and the French revolutionaries: life, liberty, and property, for example. On the other, there are social and economic rights which have only been claimed in recent times, such as the right to work and the right to subsistence. The main difference between the two classes is that rights in the first category are rights to be *allowed* to do things, corresponding to duties in other people not to interfere, while rights in the second category are rights to be *given* things,

[16] See particularly the contributions by M. Cranston and D. D. Raphael to D. D. Raphael (ed.), *Political Theory and the Rights of Man* (London, 1967).

corresponding to duties in other people to provide them.[17] Thus the traditional right to property meant the freedom to acquire property plus the claim that other people should not interfere with what had been acquired; it did not mean the right to be given property. On the other hand, the right to work does not just mean the freedom to seek work, but the right to have work provided. One consequence of this difference is that the traditional natural rights have more to do with the ideal of freedom, whereas the social and economic rights have more to do with social justice. A restriction of free speech, for example, would obviously be a violation of freedom, but it would not usually be considered a social injustice. The reverse holds if the right to subsistence is denied.

For this reason, the important human rights from the point of view of social justice are the social and economic claims. If we examine a document such as the *Universal Declaration of Human Rights*,[18] we shall see that these claims are mainly directed towards providing a minimum standard of decent living for each person. Thus besides the rights to work and subsistence, food, clothing, housing, medical care, and education are mentioned. Now such claims could equally well be presented as claims of need. What is actually contained in this section of the *Declaration* is a list of basic human needs, together with the principal means of satisfying them. Thus what makes this class of human rights relevant to social justice is that they are claims based upon need, and moreover of a universal and urgent kind.

If the assertion of human rights is really a way of advancing the claims of basic human need, why should the language of rights be used at all? Feinberg argues that this is perfectly comprehensible as a political device:

I accept the moral principle that to have an unfulfilled need is to have a kind of claim against the world, even if against no one in particular. . . . Such claims, based on need alone, are 'permanent possibilities of rights', the natural seed from which rights grow. When manifesto writers speak of them as if already actual rights, they are easily forgiven, for this is but a powerful way of expressing

[17] D. D. Raphael, 'Human Rights, Old and New', in Raphael, op. cit.
[18] Reprinted as an appendix to Raphael, op. cit.

the conviction that they ought to be recognized by states here and now as potential rights and consequently as determinants of *present* aspirations and guides to *present* policies. That usage, I think, is a valid exercise of rhetorical licence.[19]

We might add here that within the concept of need itself there is no distinction between the universal claims of basic human need and other claims of need which are less urgent and peculiar to specific persons. One way of making this morally important distinction is to continue speaking of human rights when the former class is in question. But from an analytical point of view, we ought to consider human rights and their relationship to social justice as one part of the principle of need. There is no reason to give them an independent status.

Besides natural and human rights, there are other ideal rights which belong only to particular categories of people. I shall discuss just one example in this class, the alleged right of parents to special consideration from their children.[20] It should be noted that this is a positive moral right in current society (i.e. parents do actually claim it, and children generally acknowledge their corresponding obligations) but I think those who would defend it would do so on ideal grounds—they would argue that even if the right were not acknowledged, it would still be a right that parents have. Thus the outcry against Godwin's views on how to decide whether to save Archbishop Fenelon or one's mother from a burning house[21] was not based simply on the fact that to accept Godwin would be to upset standing expectations, but rather on the intrinsic immorality of Godwin's position. Parenthood necessarily implies a right to favoured treatment by one's children, it is thought, and Godwin denies this.

As with the human rights discussed above, we must ask what grounds there are for saying that this right exists. It plainly cannot be justified in 'human rights' terms. It is equally plain

[19] Feinberg, op. cit., p. 255.

[20] I choose this example because it has featured in two fairly recent discussions of rights: Melden's *Rights and Right Conduct* (Oxford, 1959) and Hart's 'Are there any Natural Rights?' in *Political Philosophy*. Hart speaks of a parent's moral right to obedience from his child, but I think those who would assert such a right would prefer Melden's more liberal version used above.

[21] See W. Godwin, *Enquiry Concerning Political Justice*, ed. K. Codell Carter (Oxford, 1971), pp. 70–1.

that examining the biological relationship between parent and child cannot provide anything which is relevant to a claim of right. A third (somewhat more plausible) approach would be to attempt to argue that the right in question is always in fact positive, being derived from a promise or agreement made between parent and child. Thus the crime of a Godwin, saving Fenelon from the flames, would really consist in a breach of faith. Yet this appears unsatisfactory, for two reasons: the child is not capable of making such an agreement, and anyway the family relationship is not a voluntary one; the child cannot opt out of it, at least until he reaches a certain age.

If one asked people to say (unreflectively) why they thought parents had a right to special consideration, they would probably begin talking about the great responsibilities of parenthood, the amount parents give to their children, and so on. This suggests that what is really at issue here is a claim of *desert*—that parents deserve gratitude from their children, and deserve special consideration as an expression of gratitude. But the character of the desert claim is a little out of the ordinary, and this explains why it appears under the guise of a right. Generally speaking we think of specific individuals as having deserts, and having them in virtue of a particular action they have performed or quality they possess. In the case under consideration, however, a person deserves gratitude simply for being a parent and for carrying out the infinitely varied but commonplace activities which parents perform. He does not need to be a particularly good parent to qualify, though if he falls below a certain minimum standard he loses his claim. (As Melden points out, we may also cease to describe him as a parent: 'He wasn't a father to me', etc.) The point, then, is that almost all parents deserve special consideration from their children, not for any extraordinary feats, but just through having carried out the ordinary tasks involved in child-rearing—and this, I suggest, is why we are prone to speak of parents as having a right to consideration, as though the right inhered in the role of a parent, independently of what the person does. But strictly we should speak of parents *deserving* special consideration from their children, and from the theoretical point of view this type of 'ideal right' is best regarded as a form of desert.

I hope that this makes sufficiently clear the way in which ideal rights may, for the purpose of analysis, be reduced to the categories of desert and need. One does not want to say that ordinary use requires tightening up in this area, for there may be good practical (e.g. rhetorical) reasons for using a locution such as 'has a right to' when advancing a claim of desert or need. What has to be shown is that for the purposes of an analysis of the concept of justice, there is a sufficiently clear contrast between the 'just-making' criteria of rights, deserts, and needs for one to impose this classification on the looser use of terms in everyday life. At the beginning of the next chapter we shall want to bring out this contrast further in considering desert. In this chapter I have tried to throw some light on what it is to have a right, on how people come to have them, and on why the fact that someone has a right should be relevant to the justice or injustice or an action or policy. I have also tried to bring out what is distinctive about a 'rights' claim and its relation to justice, in such a way that the opposition between this and other 'just-making' criteria can come clearly into view in succeeding chapters. From this standpoint, the central cases of people having rights are those in which the rights have positive status. Although we continue to speak the language of rights when referring to human and other ideal rights, such language is derivative and, strictly from the analytical point of view, misleading.

III

DESERTS

---

1 *Desert, Entitlement, and Need*

In the course of the preceding chapter we had occasion to discuss the view, held by J. S. Mill and others, that the concepts of justice and rights are co-extensive; that every claim of justice can be presented as a claim of individual rights. This view we rejected, as based upon a fallacious chain of argument, but not before observing how easily the two concepts came to be identified. The ordinary use of the concept of a right is not precise, and indeed the great majority of assertions concerning justice can be re-expressed in terms of that concept without manifest verbal impropriety. The reasons for imposing a more rigorous use in this area are philosophical in character, not linguistic. They have to do with the distinctive character of rights-claims, with the values which are being appealed to when such claims are made. Desert- and need-claims, we shall see, have an entirely different moral standing. The contrast is lost if we allow casual everyday speech to blind us to the distinctions in question.

The concept of desert has a tendency to expand in the same way as the concept of a right, with similar results. In its widest, loosest sense, 'A deserves X' means 'It is fitting for A to have X' or 'X is due to A'. If we recall our abstract definition of justice as *suum cuique*, we can see how, in this widest sense, desert encompasses the whole of justice. Justice means 'to each his due'; desert refers to what it is fitting for each person to have. Hence, as Hospers put it, 'justice is getting what one deserves; what could be simpler?'[1]

Taking 'desert' in this widest sense, we can find cases in which claims of rights and need are expressed, perfectly

---

[1] J. Hospers, *Human Conduct*, p. 433.

naturally, in the language of desert. Consider the following statements.

(1a) Since £50 has been offered for climbing the rock and I have climbed it, I deserve it.[2]

(1b) The man who breasts the tape first deserves first prize.

(2a) Old-age pensioners deserve to be exempted from prescription charges.

(2b) The hungriest child deserves the last piece of cake.

On reflection it seems clear that (1a) and (1b) are really claims of rights. On the verbal level, 'deserves' can in each case be replaced by 'is entitled to'; but, more importantly, if we ask in each case for the ground upon which the person concerned should be allocated the benefit, we find typical right-creating circumstances. In (1a) we have an extended *promise* made by the person who offered the £50, hence a right in whoever fulfils the qualifying conditions.[3] In (1b) we have a set of *publicly established rules*, i.e. the rules of the race, and the man who qualifies under these rules has a right to the prize. Analogously, statements (2a) and (2b) are really claims of need. If prescription charges are to be imposed, pensioners should have special exemption because their need for medicine is especially great, both absolutely and in relation to their slender resources. The cake is due to the hungriest child because he needs it more than any of the others. As with statements (1a) and (1b), the verbal form (the use of the concept of desert) conceals the real grounds on which the claim is made.

But, it may be said, this argument rests on a false assumption. You claim that in these cases 'desert' is used in a loose sense, and the statements are really statements of a different type; but why should not people's rights and needs serve as a *basis* for their deserts? Why cannot you have genuine desert claims which are grounded on claims of rights or need? More than

[2] Taken from B. Barry, *Political Argument*, p. 112.

[3] Barry says that this example exemplifies a subsidiary sense of desert. J. Kleinig in 'The Concept of Desert', *American Philosophical Quarterly*, viii (1971), argues that entitlement, not desert, is involved. In agreeing with Kleinig, I hope that I have taken account of what is true in Barry's position.

one writer has seen nothing odd in taking need as a basis of desert.[4]

The full answer to this must wait upon the detailed analysis of the concept of desert in the following section, but by way of a preliminary this may be said: desert is a matter of fitting forms of treatment to the specific qualities and actions of individuals, and in particular good desert (i.e. deserving benefit as opposed to punishment) is a matter of fitting desired forms of treatment to qualities and actions which are generally held in high regard. If we compare the notion of rights, and consider our analysis of the types of right-creating situations, we shall see that they make no reference to the particular qualities of the individuals concerned. For instance, someone makes me a promise, and I thereby acquire a right; this happens irrespective of what I am or do. Or I qualify for a benefit under a rule; here, of course, there may or may not be a qualifying condition, but even if there is it may be one (such as 'being an adult') which segregates people without reference to their own peculiar qualities or actions.

The cases considered earlier ((1a) and (1b)) are somewhat more complicated, for in order to gain the entitlement the people concerned had to perform specific actions, probably requiring unusual personal qualities. For this reason questions both of desert and of entitlement are involved, though the questions remain separate. To become entitled to the £50, I had simply to climb to the top of the rock, nothing more nor less. To decide whether I deserved that sum, we should have to investigate several other matters, such as the difficulty of the climb (perhaps the person who made the offer had overlooked a simple route) and my own capacities as a climber. Similarly, in the case of the race, the man who is entitled to the prize—the first man to reach the tape—may not be the man who deserves to win it, as Feinberg points out. 'Perhaps the man who truly deserved to win did not in fact win because he pulled up lame, or tore his shoe, or suffered some other unforeseeable stroke of bad luck.'[5]

[4] For instance, Hospers, op. cit., ch. 9; W. Kaufmann, 'Doubts about Justice' in H. E. Kiefer and M. K. Munitz (eds.) *Contemporary Philosophic Thought, IV: Ethics and Social Justice* (New York, 1970).

[5] J. Feinberg, 'Justice and Personal Desert' in *Doing and Deserving: Essays in the Theory of Responsibility* (Princeton, 1970), p. 64.

In short, then, the reason for keeping rights and deserts distinct, and refusing to consider rights as a *basis* for desert lies in the contrast between a principle which attaches benefits to persons without essential reference to personal qualities (but *with* reference to earlier transactions, etc.) and a principle which is exclusively concerned with apportioning advantages to personal characteristics.

The principle of need is also concerning with apportioning advantages to the particular characteristics of each person. Every man should be given advantages according to the extent and nature of his needs. Yet need is inappropriate as a basis of desert; being needy cannot make us deserving. To explain this, we should look at the second point I made about desert: 'good desert is a matter of fitting desired forms of treatment to qualities and actions which are generally held in high regard'. What disqualifies needs from being taken as grounds for desert is, first, that (for most needs) everyone has them until they are satisfied, and, second, that no one wishes to have them, or admires others for having them, The point can be reinforced by considering contexts in which needs might be looked upon as valued possessions. It is, for instance, sometimes claimed that our personal needs for love and affection from others are valuable, and that those who lack these needs are deprived—'people who need people are the luckiest people in the world', in the words of a popular song. If this is so, having such personal needs is a possible basis for desert—one might at least deserve praise or congratulation for being needy in this way. If this still sounds odd, it is probably because the great majority are 'people who need people', hence there is nothing outstanding or exceptional in having the needs we have been considering.

Needs are not unique in being generally inappropriate as a basis of desert. The same is true of beliefs, or preferences, or interests; we cannot claim that people deserve benefits because of what they believe, and again the reason is that there is nothing in the actual holding of a belief (as opposed to the process of arriving at it) which we can appropriately admire.[6]

[6] I think that this can be defended against apparent counter-examples, provided by the intelligibility of such statements as 'I admire him for being a Marxist'. Such a statement implies a special background—it must refer, for example, to

I shall have more to say about 'need' later, but I hope that I have said enough at this point to justify my claim that rights, deserts, and needs must be kept separate, and that the central sense of 'desert' must be distinguished from its wider use, as featured in statements (1a)–(2b).

2 *The Concept of Desert*

I shall confine my remarks in this and the following sections to desert of benefits, or 'good desert' as it is sometimes called, and make no more than passing reference to deserved harm, whose main sub-categories are deserved blame and punishment. I think that this is not only excusable in a discussion of social justice but positively advantageous, in so far as those who have treated deserved benefit and harm together have often arrived at a distorted understanding of the former due to excessive concentration on the problems raised by the latter. When we consider what it is to deserve punishment, we quickly discover that desert here carries a moral sense—men are held to deserve punishment for moral wrongs they have committed. By analogy, good desert is given a moral sense as well, and the problem becomes one of apportioning external advantages to the moral virtues of individuals.[7] Yet few desert judgements made in practical contexts have this character. When we argue about whether a particular employee deserves a higher wage than he is now earning, we mention his skill, his responsibilities, the effort he puts into his work, but not his moral character. It is plain that the kind of desert which is relevant to social justice is rarely *moral* desert.[8]

---

the holding of Marxist beliefs under hostile pressure, so that the basis for admiration is not the content of the belief itself, but the courage shown in sticking to it.

[7] See, for instance, W. D. Ross, *The Right and the Good*, pp. 56–64.

[8] Though at the same time judgements of desert are always moral judgements. Desert is moral when based upon qualities or actions of the individual which have moral value in themselves—courage, honesty, etc. It is non-moral when based on morally neutral qualities—intelligence, ability, etc. Yet 'Jones deserves a high mark for his ability' is as much a moral judgement as 'Brown deserves a medal for his courage', in the sense that each entails a weak 'moral-ought' judgement: 'Jones ought, prima facie, to get a high mark'; 'Brown ought, prima facie, to get a medal'. Desert judgements are low-level moral judgements, only indirectly related to the universal imperatives which have been considered by some recent writers to be the central cases of moral judgements. In this respect they resemble such claims as 'His behaviour was rude', 'She is always honest', etc.

It is in fact most important to keep in mind the range and variety of judgements which we make using the concept of desert, even if the extended uses discussed in the last section are excluded.[9] Restrictive theories about the features of men's conduct which *must* serve as a basis for their deserts can often be exploded by taking examples from an area which had not been considered by the proponent of the theory. This variety shown itself in at least two ways. There is (1) the contrast between desert judgements which are broad and unspecific, and those which are more specific *either* because they state with some precision what is deserved *or* because they state from whom it is deserved. Thus compare 'Jones deserves to succeed' with 'Jones deserves at least £4,000 a year' or 'Jones deserves a salary increase from his employer'. There is also (2) the range of generic modes of treatment which may be deserved: rewards, honours, prizes, offices, income, praise, recognition, etc. The diversity here is important, because the reasons which can be given for saying that a person deserves one of these modes of treatment may be specific to that mode. The reasons for which one deserves a prize are rarely of the same kind as the reasons for which one deserves a reward.

In all these cases, however, there must be *a* reason for deserving. Whenever we make a claim of the form 'A deserves X', whatever X is, we must be prepared to indicate the feature of A, or A's conduct, in virtue of which he deserves X. If I say 'Smith deserves to win the mile', it is proper for someone else to ask 'Why does he deserve to?' and I must be able to reply (for example) 'He has trained harder than anyone else.' The reason must be a descriptive statement about the person or his conduct. I shall call such a statement the desert basis.

To understand the relationship between a desert basis and a judgement of desert, it is helpful to switch our attention away from desert proper for a moment and look at certain attitudes which one person may hold towards another: attitudes such as admiration, approval, and gratitude, for which I shall use the generic term 'appraising attitudes'. It is plain that, like judgements of desert, these appraising attitudes demand a basis, which consists of features of the person (or his conduct) towards

---

[9] For accounts which do justice to this variety, see J. Feinberg, op. cit., and J. Kleinig, op. cit. I have drawn upon these accounts in the following pages.

whom the attitude is held. If I admire someone, I must admire him *for* something (for his intelligence, or for his skill at playing the violin).

Several points are worth making about these attitudes. First, it is contingent that we have them at all. In other words, it is not hard to imagine a world in which men never took up attitudes such as admiration towards one another. Second, we do not generally have a point or purpose in holding them. If someone acts in a way which causes us to feel gratitude, we feel it because this is the response that his behaviour evokes. We may *express* our gratitude for various different reasons: to give our benefactor satisfaction, or to encourage him to benefit us in the future, for instance. But the purpose of expressing an attitude is obviously quite different from the attitude itself. Third, there is a close but complex relationship between these appraising attitudes and the concept of desert. This relationship has several aspects.

(1) If we did not adopt these attitudes towards one another, we would not and could not use the concept of desert. If the behaviour of others did not arouse our admiration and approval we could not say that they deserved honours, prizes, and the rest. The words would have no meaning for us.

(2) The range of possible desert bases coincides with the range of possible bases for appraising attitudes. I have already made use of this claim when I argued that, except in special cases, a person could not deserve on the basis of his need, because we do not admire, etc., people for their needs. The same point shows what is wrong with such a judgement as 'Jones deserves a pay increase because it would further the public interest if he had one'. We cannot admire or approve of someone on the basis of a relationship between his income and the public interest. We can only admire Jones for what Jones is or does.

(3) The existence of appraising attitudes makes intelligible the connection between a desert judgement and its basis. Consider again the connection between 'Smith deserves to win the mile' and 'Smith has trained harder than anyone else'. We would accept this fact about Smith as a reason for his desert because on the whole we admire the kind of determination and effort which goes into a course of training. Now it is

not actually necessary for me, the maker of the judgement, to have this attitude of admiration myself. I may, for instance, so thoroughly disapprove of athletics that I cannot regard the time and effort that goes into training as in any way admirable or worth while. Still, I live in a community in which most people would take up the relevant appraising attitude towards hard athletic training, and hence I can give Smith's training as a reason for his desert. (In a similar way, someone lacking any aesthetic sense can call objects beautiful and point out the features in virtue of which they are beautiful according to general opinion, even though he himself lacks the appropriate aesthetic response to those features.)

Although we have done something to limit the range of possible desert bases by exploring their connection with appraising attitudes, it does not seem that at this stage we can limit it any more narrowly. Men may take up favourable appraising attitudes towards many different features of people's character and conduct, and nothing by way of conceptual analysis can show us which of these attitudes they *ought* to take up. I shall return to this problem in the case of deserved income in section 4. But now a query must be raised about the adequacy of relating desert judgements solely to the desert basis, as this has been defined. Consider again the judgement 'Jones deserves at least £4,000 a year'. Does not this depend on the existence of a rule establishing how much people of a certain capacity are to be paid? Are we not tacitly invoking such a rule when we make the judgement, the rule therefore being as much the grounds of our judgement as the desert basis (facts about Jones)?[10]

It appears to me that if we look closely at the statement in question, we can distinguish three claims that are made by its use. There is first of all a favourable general appraisal of Jones, expressed in the claim that he deserves a reasonable income. Second, Jones's deserts (of income) are compared with those

---

[10] Cf. S. I. Benn and R. S. Peters, *Social Principles and the Democratic State* (London, 1959), p. 137:

'"Desert" is a normative word; its use presupposes a rule having two components: (i) a condition to be satisfied; (ii) a mode of treatment consequent upon it . . . We cannot estimate desert, therefore, in a vacuum; we must be able to refer to some standard or rule from which "X deserves R" follows as a conclusion.'

of other wage earners. Third, this comparison is expressed in numerical terms by the claim that £4,000 a year or more would adequately represent Jones's position on the scale of wage earners. It is plain that the third of these claims is conventional, in that the accuracy of the figure of £4,000 depends upon the wage levels enjoyed by other wage earners. Had Jones been working in 1965 instead of 1975, his deserts might have been accurately expressed by saying that he deserved at least £2,000 a year. Yet it would be odd to say that even the third claim depended on a rule; it would be better to say that it depended upon established practice—the current set of wage rates. And neither of the first two claims depends on anything of this kind. They can be derived directly from knowledge of the characteristics of Jones and other wage earners which are taken as a basis for their desert. Finally, it is the first and particularly the second claim which are really the basic desert judgements here. We could make a judgement of the second type (comparing Jones's deserts with those of other wage earners) without being able to make a judgement of the third type (stating how much income Jones deserved)—for example, if we were ignorant of current wage rates. But we could not make the third judgement without being able to make the second.

The point must be driven home, because an account of desert which construes desert judgements as derivative from rules fundamentally misconceives that concept, and makes desert into a kind of entitlement. To qualify for a benefit under a rule may well be to have a right to that benefit, but it is not to deserve it. If Brown is a Grade C official, and Grade C officials are awarded £3,000 a year, then Brown has a right to £3,000, but he does not thereby deserve it. To show that he deserves the income in question, we should have to refer to features of his job and the efforts and capacities which he puts into it; in short, to the qualities of Brown and his conduct (though with implied reference to the analogous qualities of other wage earners). Because desert is independent of rules, it forms part of prosthetic, not conservative, justice. It is a principle which can serve to modify an existing distribution of rights, for the people who have these rights may not be the people who deserve to have them, according to some criterion of desert. We may then demand that the established rules and practices be changed in order that the deserving shall come to have rights, and the undeserving to lose them. For this reason Feinberg describes desert as a 'natural' moral notion, one that is prior to institutions, rules, etc., and a standard by which such institutions and rules may be judged.[11]

The case in which these arguments may look least plausible is that of games and competitions, and the desert of prizes which results once such practices are established. For not only is it impossible to deserve first prize until a first prize has been established, but the desert basis itself (e.g. Smith's hard training in the athletic case) seems to be dependent upon the competitive institution. How could a period of training form a ground for deserving a prize unless there was to be a race *for* which the training was undertaken? If a man spends long hours running around the country, but with no race in prospect, he could not deserve anything on that basis.

Yet on closer scrutiny, it seems that although the existence of an athletic competition allows the runners' deserts to be manifested, it does not create those deserts. The basis of desert is still certain qualities which the runner possesses, such as effort and determination, and towards which we hold favourable appraising attitudes. Indeed, were we not to hold such attitudes, it is inconceivable that we should set up competitions and award prizes for athletic achievements. Here again the desert is prior to institutions and practices. Further, when such competitions are established we try to ensure that they measure accurately the qualities which we admire, and which we wish to form the basis of victory. Piaget discovered that children of about twelve would accept or reject proposed changes in the rules of the game of marbles according to whether they favoured skill in shooting, or on the other hand gave too much weight to luck.[12]

Desert, then, denotes a relationship between an individual and his conduct, and modes of treatment which are liked or disliked. When we make a judgement of desert, we are judging the appropriateness of this particular individual, with his qualities and past behaviour, receiving a given benefit or harm—an appropriateness which is made intelligible by

[11] Feinberg, op. cit., p. 56. See also pp. 85–7.
[12] J. Piaget, *The Moral Judgement of the Child* (London, 1932), ch. 1.

considering the appraising attitudes that we may take up towards the person. Having seen this, we can understand what is wrong with utilitarian attempts to reinterpret the concept as part of a consequentialist moral framework. It is not clear to me exactly how a utilitarian analysis of desert judgements might proceed, but the main possibilities seem to be as follows (corresponding to the distinction between act- and rule-utilitarianism):

(1) A deserves X = Some or all of the consequences of giving X to A would be good (i.e. would contribute to the general happiness).

(2) A deserves X = A qualifies for X under a rule whose adoption would be good (i.e. would contribute to the general happiness).

The first possibility, then, is that desert judgements should be analysed in straightforward consequentialist fashion. When we say that Jones deserves £4,000 a year, we mean that it will be useful to give him that amount, presumably because of the encouragement it will offer to himself and others to perform the valuable work he is now undertaking. Rewards and other deserved benefits are here seen as direct incentives to the production of future good. It should be apparent, in the light of the foregoing, why this fails to capture the meaning of 'desert' as that concept is properly understood. Desert judgements are justified on the basis of *past* and *present* facts about individuals, never on the basis of states of affairs to be created in the future. Desert is a 'backward-looking' concept, if we regard the present as the limit of the past; utility is a forward-looking principle. Furthermore, although the awarding of deserved benefits undoubtedly serves as an incentive to people to perform the actions or to acquire the skills which make up the basis of desert, it is unlikely that the boundaries of *this* practice will coincide with those of a practice deliberately aimed at maximizing future good. A reward can only act as an incentive if it is capable of modifying the conduct of those to whom it is given, and this generates cases in which our judgements of desert will not correspond to the proposed utilitarian principle.[13] Suppose that a certain community wants to increase

[13] The following example is adapted from Barry, op. cit., pp. 165–6.

its birth rate and so institutes a system of child benefits, giving parents special allowances or privileges for each child they have. These could be understood either as straight-forward incentives to have children, or as rewards for the performance of socially valuable actions. The difference will emerge if we imagine within the community a religious sect whose sexual practices are strictly governed by their religious beliefs, with the result that the family size of a sect member is unaffected by the introduction of the system of benefits. If the benefits are pure incentives, they will not be given to parents who also belong to the sect—the saving can be put to better use by increasing the benefits of non-members. If they are rewards, however, the sect members must be given what they deserve, for they have performed the required socially valuable actions.

The rule-utilitarian analysis ((2) above) may appear at first sight to avoid these difficulties, and to give a better account of the concept of desert. For on this theory the direct justification of a desert judgement is a description of the person who forms its subject which shows that he falls under a certain rule, and so the 'backward-looking' logic of desert is preserved. Consequences are only considered at a different point, when a justification for the rule itself is required. However, the example of the child allowances may again be pressed into service to show that the consistent rule-utilitarian will choose to adopt different rules from the person who wishes to reward desert. A rule which awards equal benefits to all parents with a given number of children is less efficient than a rule which restricts the allowances to those outside the sect but gives slightly higher sums. Provided the latter rule can be applied (i.e. provided it is possible to distinguish the members of the sect from everyone else) the utilitarian is bound to adopt it. So again we find a divergence between child allowances given as deserved rewards and child allowances given as incentives to population growth.

No doubt a utilitarian will be able to think of further arguments to show that the first rule should be adopted in preference to the second, if he wishes to show that a sophisticated utilitarianism can reproduce the outlines of the concept of desert. I want, however, to leave this debate (which has been thoroughly worked over in the opposite case of deserved punishment) to consider a more radical utilitarian position. This would abandon the attempt to make utilitarianism fit around the existing concept of desert, on the grounds that the existing concept is logically untenable. The reason is that determinism is true, and determinism is incompatible with judgements of desert as they are usually understood. The concept should either be abandoned entirely, or used in a new sense which is openly utilitarian. As Sidgwick put it:

The only tenable Determinist interpretation of Desert is, in my opinion, the Utilitarian: according to which, when a man is said to deserve reward for any services to society, the meaning is that it is expedient to reward him, in order that he and others may be induced to render similar services by the expectation of similar rewards.[14]

3 *Determinism and Desert*

The argument that determinism undermines the concept of desert is best understood when set out as two separate steps:

(1) A man can only deserve treatment (benefit or harm) on the basis of his own voluntary action, or of characteristics he has voluntarily acquired.

(2) Determinism shows that no action is voluntary in the sense required by the concept of desert.

Thus desert is first linked to voluntary, or freely chosen, action, and then determinism is shown to exclude freedom in the strong sense which desert seems to demand. Conversely, the argument can be halted at either stage. A few have denied the linking of desert to voluntary action. Many more have argued that determinism allows the requisite freedom of choice, or more strongly that only determinism allows it. I cannot hope to say anything original on the second topic, though I shall explain my position later.[15] As for the first topic, there is something to be gained by approaching it in terms of deserved benefit, and not, as usually happens, in terms of deserved punishment.

[14] H. Sidgwick, *The Methods of Ethics*, p. 284.
[15] I shall say nothing about the truth or falsity of determinism itself; I am concerned only with its implications for other principles and concepts.

One of the few who have denied that personal merit depends upon the voluntary acts of the person concerned is Hume. Hume argued that there were many qualities a man might possess which were useful or agreeable to himself or to others. Because men possessed the capacity to enter sympathetically into one another's feelings, they looked favourably upon such qualities and regarded their possession as meritorious. The list of qualities which constituted merit included natural abilities such as wit and good looks, as well as the moral virtues, benevolence, courage, and the rest. Hume discussed the view that a sharp distinction should be made between the moral virtues and other good qualities on the grounds that the moral virtues alone were voluntarily acquired, and that therefore only they should be regarded as carrying merit; but he rejected this position, pointing out that virtues such as courage 'depend little or not at all on our choice'. In fact, he argued, the distinction between virtues and other abilities has been invented by moralists who have observed that the former class alone can be implanted and encouraged by the social mechanisms of praise, blame, reward, and punishment. But ordinary men, who do not have any such social purpose in view when they judge merit and demerit, ignore the distinction, and praise natural abilities as readily as moral qualities.[16]

Hume's opinion accords well with the analysis of desert set out in the last section. If we consider the attitudes of admiration, approval, etc., it is plain that we do not adopt them only towards qualities believed to be voluntarily acquired. When we admire the superlative skill of a musician, we do not ask about the conduct which led to its acquisition before granting our admiration. The attitude is held directly towards the quality as it now exists, and the question 'voluntarily acquired or not?' is simply not considered. If the close relation between appraising attitudes and desert is admitted, it seems inconceivable that such judgements as 'Green (the musician) deserves recognition' should not be made on the same basis: on the basis of the skill alone, without reference to the manner of its acquisition. And this is indeed our practice. When we say that the prettiest girl

---

[16] D. Hume, *A Treatise of Human Nature*, Book iii, Part III, section 4; *An Enquiry Concerning the Principles of Morals*, Appendix IV in *Enquiries Concerning the Human Understanding and Concerning the Principles of Morals*, pp. 312–23.

deserves to win the beauty contest, the most skilful shot deserves to win at marbles, the ablest candidate deserves the scholarship, we look no further than the present qualities of the individuals concerned. We do not inquire into their past histories. If we were to undertake such an inquiry, we should be forced to conclude that the qualities forming the basis of desert were, to a greater or lesser extent, involuntary. Physical beauty is almost wholly inherited, skill at marbles rather less so. Intellectual capacity is partly inborn, partly formed by education, which itself is a mixture of the voluntary and the involuntary.

If we turn to cases in which an action, rather than a quality, forms the basis of desert[17] we arrive at a similar conclusion. It is true that we cannot deserve benefits for actions which are involuntary or unintentional. If I apprehend a wanted man by accident (e.g. the floor collapses and I fall on top of him) I do not deserve a reward, though I may be entitled to one. Yet if we consider actions which do constitute a basis for desert, two points stand out:

(1) even if the action is wholly voluntary, it may require personal qualities which are not—e.g. I am able to save a drowning man because of my (inherited) physical strength.

(2) Actions which are not fully voluntary may still deserve rewards and other benefits—e.g. I am blackmailed into hunting down a dangerous criminal.

It seems, then, that ordinary judgement does not support the view that a man's deserts depend upon his voluntary actions alone. But it would be wrong to think that ordinary judgement is wholly consistent on the issue. One can detect some inclination to relate desert to the quality of will which a man displays,

---

[17] Hume believed that actions only possessed merit in so far as they were taken as signs of persistent qualities belonging to the agent: 'If any *action* be either virtuous or vicious, it is only as a sign of some quality or character. It must depend upon durable principles of the mind, which extend over the whole conduct, and enter into the personal character.' *A Treatise of Human Nature*, vol. ii, p. 272. But in this belief he was surely mistaken. If a cowardly man performs a courageous deed or an unjust man acts fairly, we regard these actions as meritorious even if we are fully aware that they are exceptional and correspond to no persistent character trait. Indeed, in the former case at least, we may even regard the merit of the action as increased by its atypical character, because for a cowardly man to perform a courageous act requires both courage and unusual self-mastery.

rather than to other characteristics which affect his actions but which are outside his control. If, for instance, we go back to the case of the scholarship cited above, someone might well adopt the following attitude: it is right that the scholarship be awarded to A, the most able candidate, yet he is really less deserving than B, who has only slightly less ability but who has a much poorer academic background. B has struggled to achieve his present standard, whereas A has always been helped by superior teaching, etc. There is no doubt that this argument carries weight. Or again, consider the case of the drowning man. Suppose that two men jump in to save him, and that one manages to reach him while the other, who has tried just as hard but is physically weak, fails and has to turn back. We would say that the first man deserves more gratitude (and reward, perhaps) than the second, yet the second deserves *some* thanks for having tried to help. He could not actually do good to the drowning man because of his physical incapacity, but his intentions were as laudable as those of the man who actually brought off the rescue.

Some people would want to go further here, and say that desert *should* depend entirely upon what is within a man's control, that is on his efforts and the choices he makes. If the drowning man knew that his two would-be rescuers had tried equally hard to save him, he should recognize that they deserved equal gratitude and reward. Although ordinary judgement does not yet accept this view, it might be said that we can detect an historical trend towards its adoption. Primitive moral thinking does not distinguish between the voluntary and non-voluntary parts of conduct, and it has taken many generations to reach the developed conception of personal responsibility which we now have. We have simply failed to follow out the full implications of this conception in our use of the concept of desert. Again, it may be said, a distinction must be drawn between moral judgements and natural responses. The man who is saved from drowning naturally feels more warmly towards the swimmer who has actually rescued him. The *moral* judgement of the two men's deserts must ignore this emotional response and consider only what each intended and tried to do.

Such an argument looks most persuasive when good and ill

desert are considered together. Indeed, it has usually been advanced with reference to deserved blame and punishment, and extended by analogy to deserved praise, reward, etc. The linking of ill desert to a man's voluntary actions is well-established. We do not blame people for physical defects which they did not bring upon themselves, nor do we punish people for what they could not have helped doing. We would regard it as immoral if a law were enacted which only some people were physically able to keep (for example, a law demanding that every citizen should run five miles each day). In other words, to deserve blame or punishment a man must have committed a wrong act which he could have avoided committing. Why, then, should we not restrict deserved praise, etc., to those actions which a man has voluntarily performed, or those qualities which he has voluntarily acquired?

We have seen that ordinary judgement does not support this conclusion (though neither does it clearly repudiate it). We praise the highly intelligent and the skilful, despite the fact that we do not blame the stupid and the clumsy. But the view we are now considering would wish to impose a greater consistency on our thinking, by bringing our judgements of deserved benefit into line with our judgements of deserved harm. Against this, it may be said that there is a real moral difference between the two kinds of desert. Inflicting harm upon a person is an evil in itself, hence it can only be justified by a stringent type of desert. (Many, of course, would say that even this is not sufficient justification; we shall not consider such a view here). A man only deserves harm when he 'brings it upon himself' by a voluntary action. But since conferring benefit is generally speaking a good, we can afford to be less stringent in our judgements of desert. Certainly, it would be extremely difficult to separate the voluntary from the nonvoluntary aspects of character formation, and so to tell which of a man's qualities were proper grounds for desert. Perhaps the revised principle for ascribing good desert would be impossible to use in practice.

Returning, then, to the principle that a man can only deserve treatment (benefit or harm) on the basis of his own voluntary actions, or of characteristics he has voluntarily acquired, our assessment must be as follows. So far as deserved benefit goes, ordinary thinking gives us no clear guide as to whether the principle is to be accepted. In some of our judgements we base desert entirely upon voluntary action, in others we do not. Further, the philosophical arguments in favour of the principle are not decisive. The verdict must be: not proven.

Now for someone who rejects this principle, determinism creates no difficulties for the concept of desert, or at least for good desert. This was Hume's position, believing as he did both in determinism and in a concept of personal merit which made no reference to voluntariness. It is perhaps the most comfortable position to take on the issue. Yet because I feel that the arguments for the principle have *some* weight, I want to look very briefly at the further question whether someone who accepts the principle is forced to choose between determinism and desert; whether a concept of desert based on voluntary action is incompatible with the thesis of determinism.

Let us take determinism to be the thesis that every event has a causally sufficient set of antecedents. Why should this be thought to raise difficulties for our concept of voluntary action? A direct problem occurs only if a voluntary action has to be in some way uncaused; that is to say, if the series of happenings within the agent which lead up to it must include at least one for which there is no causally sufficient set of antecedents. Holders of this position have spoken of a 'contra-causal type of freedom' being required.[18] Their opponents argue that a voluntary action is simply one whose causal antecedents are of a particular kind. According to this view, when we describe an action as voluntary, we are not ruling out causal explanation in general, we are simply excluding certain *kinds* of causal antecedents—such circumstances as physical coercion, threats, fits of madness, etc.[19] Obviously, if this latter view is correct, there is no incompatibility between determinism and our concept of voluntary action.

At first sight it seems that the 'compatibility' view must be correct. Take a simple example: A makes a suggestion to B,

---

[18] See C. A. Campbell, 'Is "Freewill" a Pseudo-problem?' *Mind*, lx (1951).
[19] See especially A. G. N. Flew, 'Divine Omnipotence and Human Freedom' in A. Flew and A. MacIntyre (eds.), *New Essays in Philosophical Theology* (London, 1955); A. J. Ayer, 'Freedom and Necessity' in *Philosophical Essays* (London, 1954); P. Nowell-Smith, *Ethics* (Harmondsworth, 1954), ch. 20.

who considers it, and then acts upon it. B's action is voluntary, but can be causally explained by reference to A's suggestion and B's mental make-up; there is no incompatibility here. However, to be certain that B's action really was voluntary, we should have to be sure that his present character and mental dispositions were not produced by factors of an inadmissible type—for example, that he had not been rendered susceptible to suggestions of a certain type through brain-washing. Our concept of voluntary action excludes cases where the disposition to act has been induced by constraining factors. To take a practical example, lawyers have been able to secure acquittals (from 'ordinary men' in the jury box) by exhibiting their clients' behaviour as the inevitable outcome of circumstances beyond their control—home backgrounds, early experiences, etc.

This throws the relationship between determinism and voluntary action into a new light. For determinism may be taken to have the consequence that every action can ultimately be shown to result from causes which are commonly held to exclude freedom. This would not follow directly from the determinist thesis, but from the observation that as we gain in knowledge of the immediate and more distant causes of human action, we find that more of these actions have to be shifted from the voluntary to the non-voluntary category, since they turn out to be consequences of one or other of the varieties of constraint. Determinism, however, entails that there are no breaks in the chain of causation which leads up to any action, and therefore that there is no inherent reason why our knowledge of the causal antecedents of action should not be increased indefinitely, It is therefore possible, given sufficient knowledge, that the number of actions believed to be voluntary will eventually shrink to zero, every action being interpreted as the outcome of constraining causes such as coercion or indoctrination.

Even if we accept this, however, it is still a moot point whether our concept of voluntary action should be abandoned as a result of a belief in determinism. For we cannot yet explain most human actions in the way that the determinist promises us we shall—i.e. in such a way that their non-voluntary character is apparent. Until we can, there seems no alternative but to go on using the traditional concepts. We may also follow Strawson[20] in pointing out how our ordinary dealings with people are infused with attitudes which depend upon contrasting voluntary and non-voluntary actions—attitudes such as resentment, gratitude, and forgiveness. To treat people at all times as the objects of circumstances rather than as free agents would, if it were possible at all, mean a transformation of human relationships. Since we normally only regard people in this way when we believe that they are incapable of sustaining ordinary interpersonal relations—say as a result of mental derangement—Strawson implies that the transformation would necessarily be a loss. He asks how it could possibly be *rational* to make this change as a result of an abstract belief in the consequences of determinism.

To summarize, the argument that determinism undermines the concept of desert is open to attack at both its stages. The claim that a man can only deserve benefits (in particular) on the basis of voluntary actions or qualities cannot be convincingly vindicated; and neither can the claim that determinism destroys the distinction between the voluntary and the non-voluntary. People are willing to believe both that a man deserves rewards and other benefits for the actions he performs, and that these actions can be explained in causal terms. If, therefore, we find that the concept of desert has become less popular in recent years, we cannot, in the case of good desert especially, explain this change by reference to a growing belief in determinism. An explanation of a different kind must be sought.

4 *Principles of Economic Desert*

One of the most important, and yet most difficult, problems which arises in an inquiry into desert and its relation to social justice is that of the basis upon which judgements of economic desert should be made. By economic desert I mean desert of monetary and other rewards for socially useful work—for doing one's job, in a society which has such a division of labour. Which features of a man's work activity should be taken into

---

[20] P. F. Strawson, 'Freedom and Resentment', *Proceedings of the British Academy*, xlviii (1962).

account when we judge that he deserves such-and-such a reward? J. S. Mill used this problem to illustrate the ambiguities of an intuitive notion of justice, one which was not controlled by the overriding principle of utility. Conflicting principles, he argued, could be defended with equal force in terms of fairness and justice; only considerations of utility could definitely settle which principle should be chosen.[21]

The principles which have seriously been put forward as determinants of economic desert can be reduced to three:

(1) Contribution: A man's reward should depend on the value of the contribution which he makes to social welfare in his work activity.

(2) Effort: A man's reward should depend on the effort which he expends in his work activity.

(3) Compensation: A man's reward should depend on the costs which he incurs in his work activity.

I shall argue later that (3) is not a genuine alternative to the first two principles. It is a refinement which may be used in conjunction with either (1) or (2). The problem, as I see it, is to adjudicate between (1) and (2) (which are in genuine competition), and then to consider in what circumstances (3) can properly be used as a modifying principle.

In what follows I shall examine the arguments which have been used in defence of these principles, in order to see whether any of them count decisively in favour of one principle at the expense of the others. Only arguments which are internal to the concepts of desert and justice will be considered. It is probably true that the most convincing reasons which can be given for taking contribution, rather than effort, as a basis for reward are utilitarian in character. By rewarding people according to the value of their different contributions, we encourage them to develop the skills and abilities which produce a superior contribution, and this result is socially useful. But to use such utilitarian arguments to establish a principle of desert seems to me inconsistent. If one starts from utilitarian premisses, and regards rewards as incentives to acquire useful skills, etc.,

---

[21] J. S. Mill, *Utilitarianism* in *Utilitarianism; On Liberty; Representative Government*, pp. 54–5.

the correct principle is to reward only those contributions which would not be made in the absence of such reward, the contributions, in other words, which have to be called forth by material incentives. The case is exactly analogous to the case of the child benefits discussed on pp. 93–4 above. In both instances the utilitarian argument gives us a different principle from the genuine principle of desert. For this reason, it may be left out of consideration, despite the fact that it is often employed by defenders of the contribution principle.

Among those arguments for principle (1) which remain on the ground of justice, the best-known, historically speaking, begins from the claim that every man has a right to the whole product of his labour.[22] If we consider a state of nature, such as that constructed by Locke, we shall see how plausible is the view that when men produce in isolation from one another, and with land and raw materials in plentiful supply, they each deserve to retain whatever they can make by their own labour. The argument is that the essential justice of this distribution is not affected by the transition from a state of nature to an actual society. Although people no longer produce objects independently of one another, the principle may be preserved by awarding to each the value which he contributes to a joint product. Thus 'the whole product of his labour' now means 'that part of the product of combined labour which he has contributed.'

However, even if we accept this principle when applied to a hypothetical state of nature, it is not clear that the shift to real society can be made without invalidating the argument. There are differences between the two situations which must be taken into account when we assess the justice of possible modes of distribution.

First of all, it is no longer true that land and raw materials are freely available to everyone. It may happen instead that some men, in producing the greatest product of which they are capable, engross such a proportion of the existing natural resources that the remainder cannot even satisfy their basic needs. In this situation the right to the whole product of labour loses its justification; it rested upon the supposition of complete

---

[22] For the history of this claim in socialist thought, see A. Menger, *The Right to the Whole Product of Labour* (London, 1899).

independence—no man's acts having a significant effect upon any other man.

Second, in a civilized society, the value of the goods which a man can produce depends upon technique and skills which he has not discovered for himself. It is implausible to see his productive output as wholly being due to his own qualities and efforts. So again the justice of rewarding him with the whole product of his labour is put in question.

Third, there is the problem of estimating the value of individual contributions to a jointly made product. Since this is a general difficulty for the contribution principle, I shall hold it over for discussion at a later point.

It appears for these reasons that to argue for each man's right to the whole product of his labour by analogy with a Lockean state of nature is mistaken. Historically, the doctrine proved most telling when used by socialists against idle landlords, rentier capitalists, etc.—men who, it was argued, reaped rewards without making any contribution to production at all. But the negative principle—no product, no reward—is much easier to justify than the positive claim that each man's reward should be proportional to the product of his labour. We must look elsewhere for possible justifications of the contribution principle.

One such attempt at justification makes the implementation of the principle a matter of commutative justice. It looks for a fair exchange between individual and society. Consider the following situation: two men are employed to make radio sets, each man making complete sets by himself. One of the two, by virtue of greater skill and dexterity, is able to produce twice as many sets as the other. He is therefore, so to speak, adding twice as many goods to the total stock of his society, and, assuming that the radios are needed, contributing twice as much to the level of social welfare. Is it not then fair that his society should give him in return a remuneration which is double that of the unskilled man? An exchange is taking place in which the individual is supplying one kind of goods and services, and receiving in return the means to other goods and services. Does commutative justice not demand that the man who supplies a double quantity of goods receives back twice as much in exchange?

This argument seems hard to answer at first sight, yet its force is lost when we see that a question-begging assumption has been made at the outset. In comparing the remuneration of work to an exchange between individual and society, we take it for granted that each person has a complete right to the object which enters into the 'exchange'. We assume that the two men own the radios they produce as a farmer owns the cattle which he drives to market. In other words, the argument rests on a prior premiss that each man has a right to the whole product of his labour. If this premiss is granted, there is a good case on grounds of commutative justice for saying that the product of labour should be converted fully into economic rewards. But the premiss itself is faulty, as my previous arguments have suggested.

Two defences of the contribution principle have been found unconvincing. I come now to two difficulties with the principle. The first is that a man's actual contribution may only properly be regarded as a measure of his desert when we can be sure that extraneous factors have played no part in bringing about that contribution. In practice the opposite is true. How much each man actually contributes depends upon environmental factors such as the fertility of the land he is cultivating, the accuracy of the tools he uses, the conditions he works under, and so on. The point is really an elementary one. If the principle of contribution is to be a genuine principle of desert, then rewards must be proportional *not* to actual contributions but to that part of each man's contribution which can be attributed to his own abilities and efforts. This does not invalidate the principle, but it means that it must be stated more carefully than it often is, and that its application is less simple than at first appears. To illustrate, a piece-work system of payment might look to be a perfect application of the contribution criterion, but this is actually only so if it is certain that the environmental factors are identical for each man involved in the system. There are countless ways in which this can fail to be so—consider, for example, work involving the use of machines which are more easily operated by right- than by left-handed people.

The correct principle, then, is not that each man should be rewarded according to the value of his contribution, but that he should be rewarded according to the *average* contribution which someone with his skills and abilities, employed in a particular way for a particular time, would make. By taking the average we eliminate the effect of extraneous factors. This has the further practical implication that the usual method of remunerating wage earners—namely fixing an hourly rate for the job on the basis of the skills involved, and multiplying this by the number of hours worked—may not be less fair than the piece-work system. For, although the former method fails to discriminate between the highly skilled worker and the merely competent one, it at least ensures that extraneous circumstances do not benefit some at the expense of others.

The argument up to this point has been based on the assumption that contributions can be independently measured. The second difficulty for the contribution principle emerges when we consider situations in which two or more men are working co-operatively to bring about a common result. The problem here is more than merely the practical one of measuring contributions in such a situation; it is the question of whether any meaning at all can be given to the idea of an individual contribution. Perhaps this is best brought out by considering first a case in which the difficulty *is* simply a practical one. Consider the problem of estimating how much each member of a tug-of-war team is contributing to the common pull. The pulls of the different members are straightforwardly cumulative, and one can imagine ingenious devices for measuring individual performances. The difficulties here are merely technical ones. Compare the following situation: two men are employed in shifting sacks, and when they are left to work alone one can shift 6 sacks an hour and the other can shift 8, so that if extraneous factors are ignored, the contribution theory will require that they are paid, say, 60p and 80p an hour respectively. They are then set to work together and manage (by some division of labour) to shift 21 sacks an hour between them. How should the 210p an hour which is due to them be divided up? The contribution theory gives no method of choosing between the following three solutions:

(1) They should share the sum equally—105p each.

(2) They should retain their original wages and then divide up equally the extra earned through co-operation—95p (60p +35p): 115p (80p +35p).

(3) They should divide the whole so that the ratio between their earnings is preserved—90p:120p (since 90/120 = 60/80).

To say 'each should get an amount equivalent to what he himself contributes' is no solution, precisely because 'contribution' has not yet been defined in this situation, and to define it is already to have chosen (1), (2), or (3). This example also represents a *reductio ad absurdum* of one proposal for avoiding the problems involved in measuring contributions to a joint product—the proposal that contribution is to be measured by the marginal product of each man's work, i.e. the difference between the size of the product when X is working and the size of the product without him. The absurdity in our case is that if the first man is working alone and the second comes to join him, they will be paid, on the marginal product criterion, 60p and 150p respectively, while if the first man joins the second the rates will be 130p and 80p respectively; but there is no reason to suppose that their relative contributions (however we define these) are different in the two cases.

Faced with these formidable difficulties, one may be tempted to retreat still further from the idea of contribution as a basis of desert and to substitute a composite of effort, ability, and skill, hoping thus to preserve the general character of the contribution principle in contrast to the much more egalitarian principle of effort alone. Yet it would be most odd to take ability in itself as a basis of economic desert, regardless of how such ability was used. At least one would have to limit it to 'useful ability usefully employed'. Suppose, though, that we have two men of equal ability working equally hard, one of whom has chosen to employ his abilities in a much more valuable way than the other, does it not seem that the former deserves a greater reward than the latter? If this correctly reports common thought on the matter, it shows that the idea of contribution retains a powerful hold in cases where contributions can be clearly established and where the other difficulties we have mentioned can be circumvented.

We have now seen that the main justifying arguments for

adopting contribution as the basis of economic desert are unsatisfactory, and that although the principle seems intuitively acceptable (i.e. self-justifying in terms of ordinary thought) it presents much greater difficulties of application than is commonly realised—both because the relative size of contributions may be dictated by extraneous factors, and because in co-operative situations the idea of an individual contribution may have no meaning. One of the great merits of the principle of effort is that it avoids such difficulties, and can be applied in a fairly straightforward manner. However, I doubt whether ease of application is sufficient in itself to recommend the principle, and we must ask whether it can be justified in terms of desert and justice.

The argument in its favour is usually expressed as follows: a man can only deserve reward for what it is within his power to do. If two men try equally hard, and work for an equally long time, they deserve equal remuneration even if one of them, by virtue of superior ability, manages to produce more goods, or goods of a better quality. According to this view it may be expedient to remunerate superior skill, etc., but it is not just, and the skilled man does not *deserve* more than the unskilled, assuming that each does the best he can.

This argument depends upon the more basic claim that a man's deserts depend wholly upon his voluntary actions. We have examined this latter claim in the previous section, and returned a sceptical verdict upon it: there are no conclusive reasons for restricting the basis of desert in the way suggested, and the counsels of common sense are divided on the question. I do not propose to reopen this issue here, but I want to point out that even if we accept the principle that men only deserve benefits for what they have voluntarily brought about, this does not of itself justify the principle that rewards should be proportional to efforts. For certain of the skills and abilities which a man uses in his work are the products of *previous* voluntary actions—for example, the decision to attend training courses—and there is no reason to tie desert to present voluntary actions at the expense of earlier ones.[23] Surely the voluntary decision to acquire a useful skill should be rewarded in the future when the skill is exercised?

[23] Cf. Barry, op. cit., p. 108.

Thus the logical consequence of adopting the principle that desert depends on voluntary action is not that effort alone should be taken as a desert basis at the expense of all differences in ability and skill, but rather that effort and *voluntarily* acquired abilities should be separated from innate abilities and abilities which are implanted by other people, desert to be based upon the former group alone. The resulting principle may be almost impossible to apply, since any useful piece of work will require a combination of effort, innate ability, and acquired ability, and one cannot usually say how much of the result should be put down to the voluntary acts of the person concerned. Certain features, for example a man's physical size, can be ruled out completely, but this will not get us anywhere near the heart of the problem.

The principle of effort alone seems, therefore, to lack any real justification. That it should continue to receive serious consideration as a principle of economic desert may be explained by (a) its undoubted simplicity; (b) a failure to grasp the points made in the last two paragraphs—the principle being considered a corollary of the view that desert depends upon voluntary action; (c) the fact that the principle may represent a *practical* solution for someone who is sceptical about the whole notion of desert but is unwilling to propose that social wealth should be distributed entirely on the grounds of need. A socialist, for instance, may doubt that one man deserves more than another on the basis of differences in ability, but regard a distribution according to need (without any reference to work performed) as utopian. Marx argued that the principle of effort would be the appropriate mode of distribution in a socialist society which had recently emerged from capitalism, before the expansion of the productive forces enabled the principle of need to be implemented. This does not, of course, prove anything about the intrinsic fairness of the principle.

We come finally to the principle of compensation: a man's reward should depend upon the costs he incurs in his work activity. Work is costly when it is, for example, unpleasant (a dustman's job), arduous (a miner's job and a surgeon's, in different ways), or dangerous (a steeplejack's job). In each case the cost should be repaid through increased remuneration, and what we call 'reward' is really compensation for the loss incurred while the person is at work (in the case of dangerous work, it may be seen as an insurance against the possibility of future loss). This seems undeniably fair; yet I believe that the principle needs clarification before it can be properly assessed. Its apparent simplicity conceals the fact that it can be interpreted in two different ways. First, we might regard costs as facts about an individual's activity which serve as a basis for his desert in the same way as, say, the skill he displays. But second, we might understand costs not as a basis for desert, but rather as a reduction in the benefit which a person is receiving, so that he should be given extra economic benefits to make good the loss. Here we are computing an over-all level of benefit which a man is enjoying, taking into account the rewards he gets and the costs he incurs, and then proportioning this over-all level (rewards minus costs) to his deserts. On the first reading, costs are seen as increasing a man's deserts; on the second, as reducing his rewards.

Why does it matter which interpretation of the principle we choose? Suppose that we use it as the sole determinant of a person's remuneration, in other words not in conjunction with either of the other two principles. If we take the first reading we have a genuine distribution according to desert: men's deserts are different because of the different costs they incur in their work, and rewards should be proportional to desert. But if we take the second reading we have an equal distribution: men should receive equal rewards, but in so far as one man's work is more costly than another's, the loss should be made good by increased monetary income. Feinberg, who interprets the principle in this sense, puts the point admirably:

The principle that unpleasant, onerous, and hazardous jobs deserve economic compensation, unlike the claim that superior ability deserves economic reward, is an equalitarian one, for it says only that deprivations for which there is no good reason should be compensated to the point where the deprived one is again brought back to a position of equality with his fellows. It is not that compensation gives him more than others (considering everything), but only that it allows him to catch up.[24]

[24] J. Feinberg, 'Justice and Personal Desert', Appendix, in Feinberg, op. cit., p. 93.

However, the principle that each man should enjoy an equal level of reward, in spite of differences in ability, effort, etc., is not a principle of desert for it implies that any possible basis of desert, any quality which might be thought relevant to the determination of income, is actually irrelevant to the question of how much reward a man should receive. Interpreted in this way, the claim that costly work deserves compensation employs the concept of desert only in the extended sense identified at the beginning of the chapter; it means simply that it is fitting for costly work to be adequately compensated.

Which interpretation of the principle of compensation is correct? The following considerations seem relevant. If we consider work which is costly, such as the dangerous and extremely arduous work which a miner performs, we may distinguish, first, the pain, deprivation, and unpleasantness suffered by the person concerned, and, second, the various qualities such as courage and endurance which he may display in the course of his work. Generally, when we think of work as involving human costs, we have the first group of features in mind—we are thinking of what the person is suffering, not of the good qualities he is displaying. I do not think that these features can serve as a basis for desert, for reasons which have already been outlined in my discussion of need as a possible desert basis. In summary, a desert basis consists of personal attributes which are generally held in high regard. Pain cannot therefore be a ground for desert, though the courage shown in withstanding pain might be. In so far as we consider the costs themselves which are involved in work (and not the qualities displayed in bearing those costs), our judgements of deserved compensation must be intepreted in the second way—not as desert judgements in the true sense, but as judgements about the making good of unwarranted deprivation. I suggest that the bulk of cases fall into this category.[25]

The upshot of this rather intricate discussion is that the

[25] This is certainly true for work that is unpleasant or onerous, such as refuse-disposal or road-making. Some dangerous work requires positive qualities of courage and endurance—e.g. a deep-sea fisherman's work—but in other cases the hazards are unpredictable—e.g. work on a construction site where heavy objects occasionally fall and strike people—and here extra pay as compensation could not be based on individuals' deserts.

principle of compensation is not really a desert principle at all, but rather an indication of additional factors to be taken into account when rewards are calculated. It can be used in conjunction with the principles of contribution or effort, or on its own as an egalitarian principle. We must look finally at the problems involved in assessing 'costs'. It is sometimes claimed (for example by Feinberg) that the main outlines of the current distribution of income can be proved fair by appeal to the principle of compensation. This rests on the assumption that highly paid jobs (top managers, administrators, professional men, etc.) carry with them responsibilities which are onerous to the people concerned. Being answerable for decisions, knowing that other people's futures depend upon your judgement, such factors create strain and anxiety which, it is said, are much more costly than simple physical exertion. Can such claims be justified?

It seems that once we move away from the unquestionable cases of costs involved in work—physical debilitation, health risks, and the like—we enter an area of great uncertainty. First, there may be no consensus on what is a cost: one man may find decision-taking stimulating, another may find it exhausting. Second, the costs associated with responsibility, if they are costs, go hand-in-hand with the benefits of exercising power, of being one's own master, and so on. If we count up the psychological costs of a job, we must surely reckon the psychological gains as well. Perhaps the only certain way of estimating costs would be to examine people's preferences for types of work in the absence of income differentials and other extraneous factors. (This assumes that people are fairly well-informed about the work involved in different occupations.) Any job which was systematically shunned could be judged to have special disadvantages deserving compensation. Unfortunately, the results of such a procedure must remain hypothetical. While this is so, compensation arguments can only carry conviction when they appeal to the restricted set of unquestionable costs mentioned above. This means that few of those in jobs which are currently highly paid can be shown to deserve their remuneration by way of compensation. If they do deserve the rewards they are getting, it must be on the grounds of contribution, ability, etc.

In our discussion of the various principles of economic desert we have uncovered a confused tangle of beliefs. Neither of the first two principles (contribution and effort) can be given an independent justification, and the third principle, which is undoubtedly valid, is seen not to be a principle of desert at all. Ordinary judgements of economic desert may appeal to the value actually contributed by a given person, the skills and abilities he employs in his work, or the effort he puts into it. There appears to be no orderly method of combining these features—it is a matter of personal judgement which is given most weight.

Such a conclusion may seem unnecessarily pessimistic. Is there no theoretical standpoint from which judgements of economic desert can be brought into some sort of consistency? One possible line of enquiry is to ask how the concepts of desert and justice are related. When we judge that someone deserves a reward or some other benefit, do we imply that it is a matter of justice that he gets it? If we do not always imply this, what distinguishes the one set of cases from the other? These questions are taken up in the following section. They are important questions in themselves, but we may also hope that they lead us towards a solution of the problems of economic desert.

5 *Desert and Justice*

If we examine the relationship which exists in our ordinary thinking between the ideas of desert and justice, we find that it is weaker than the corresponding relationship between rights and justice. When considering rights we found that if A has a right to X, this is always a prima facie reason for regarding it as just that A be given X; but in the case of deserts, the fact that A deserves X is not always taken even as a prima facie reason for regarding it as just that he be given it. To see this we need to look at a number of different situations in which people's deserts are estimated:

(1) Competitive situations: If Smith deserves to win the first prize in a race (he has trained hardest, is the fastest runner, etc.), this is *no* reason to give him the prize, or to regard it as just that he gets it, except in some cosmic sense of

'justice' which carries no implications for human actions.[26] If Brown is first through the tape, then he becomes entitled to the prize and it is just that he and he alone receives it. It is not the case that in reaching this conclusion we weigh Smith's deserts against Brown's entitlement, and then decide that Brown has the stronger claim of justice to the first prize; questions of desert do not enter into our judgement in such a case. Of course, we have already noted that the rules of races and other competitive events are usually arranged with the intention that the deserving shall win the prizes, so that if a set of rules repeatedly allows the undeserving to win, this may be a sign that the rules are unfair (to *show* that they are unfair, we should have to discover why the deserving keep losing). However, this general point about the criterion for rules being fair does not entail that in a particular case the prize should be given to the most deserving competitor; on the contrary, once rules are established, it is the person who qualifies under them who should justly receive the prize—and this is the only consideration relevant to the justice of that act.

(2) A practice of rewarding desert: Governments usually take it upon themselves to confer honorific titles on those of their subjects who are judged to have made substantial contributions to the nation's welfare. If someone is deserving in this respect, i.e. has made a sufficient contribution, is it a matter of justice that he gets an honour? It seems to me that the answer depends upon whether the practice of conferring honours operates in his society or not. If the government has not instituted such a practice, it cannot be accused of injustice towards any particular deserving subject, nor can the subject complain of unfair treatment. There is no general obligation to confer honours on worthy individuals. On the other hand, if the practice exists, then any deserving person who is overlooked is unjustly treated when less deserving men receive their titles.

[26] We do sometimes speak of the result of a race as fair, meaning that the positions of the competitors correspond to our judgements of their merits. However, this fairness is not something which anyone has a duty to promote—it would be absurd if we asked the runners to adjust their running speed to get a 'fair' result, or demanded that the officials interfered with the rules to the same end. It would no longer be a race if either of these things happened. By the same token, an 'unfair' result may occur even though everyone has acted exactly as he should. This is why I describe this sense of justice as 'cosmic'.

Once the government has decided to confer honours, it must make sure that they are given to the deserving in proportion to their deserts.

It may be thought that this case should really be seen as a case of rights, not of deserts. Does the government not arouse legitimate expectations of future honours among certain of its subjects, and so give them a right to those honours in due course? Is this not why we think it unjust if someone is overlooked? There is no doubt that the practice of conferring honours may take on this character; for example when Civil Servants automatically receive an honour on reaching a particular level in the Service. But I think this should be seen as a corruption of the practice, not as its essence. The reason that the regular awarding of honours does not confer rights to those honours is that no qualifying conditions are (or should be) laid down. The basis for an honour is 'contribution to the nation's welfare' —an extremely general criterion which cannot be translated into any precise set of qualifying rules. Nevertheless, the case seems to occupy an intermediate position between pure desert on the one hand and entitlement on the other. For, as I have argued, to have a just claim on an honour two conditions must be fulfilled:

(a) You must be deserving in the relevant respects.
(b) A practice of conferring honours must exist in your society.

(3) Rewards proper: If someone freely confers a benefit on me—for instance, saves my life or restores a valuable possession to me—he deserves to be rewarded, and it is a matter of justice that he is. I treat him unjustly if I fail to offer him an appropriate token of my gratitude (the offer may be refused; justice is satisfied if it is sincerely made). By contrast to case (2), this relationship between desert and justice holds whether or not I make a practice of giving rewards. My benefactor may be the first person who has helped me in an important enough way to deserve reward, but it is none the less just if he gets his reward, and unjust if he does not. Moreover, the relationship holds even if no social practice of rewarding exists. If we discovered a society in which no one ever rewarded anyone else, it would be inappropriate to blame any particular indi-

vidual for not giving rewards, but we should still describe the society as an unjust one. Doubt has occasionally been cast on this view, for instance by Godwin, who challenged the justice of personal rewards along with other benefits usually thought to be deserved.[27] But this clearly runs counter to the deliverances of the 'common moral consciousness', which recognizes our duty to reward acts of beneficence whether or not there exists a practice of conferring rewards.

These three different cases illustrate the complexity of the relationship between desert and justice. In the first, A's deserving X (Smith's deserving to win first prize) is no reason for regarding it as just that he be given it. In the second, A's deserving X (a man's deserving an honour) is a reason for regarding it as just that he be given it only when others like A are usually given X. In the third, A's deserving X (your deserving a reward) is always a reason for regarding it as just that he be given it (though one should add the reminder: not a conclusive reason, since, for example, if my resources are limited, there may be more powerful claims of justice upon them than your desert of reward). It is plain that merely to be deserving, without specification of what is deserved or from whom it is deserved, does not give rise to claims of justice. It is only in special circumstances that you can put forward your deserts as grounds for saying that you have been fairly or unfairly treated.

If one looks at the problem from the point of view of a person concerned to act justly in choosing between alternative ways of distributing goods, a similar conclusion emerges. If I have to allocate a coveted office, or fix a scale of wage payments, I am not obliged to consider everyone's deserts in every respect before coming to a decision. The good I am distributing will determine the type of desert which is relevant—in the case of the office it is ability to occupy that position, and other kinds of desert, whether moral virtue or athletic prowess, can safely be neglected. This way of putting it is perhaps too simple: there may be controversy both about the nature of the good

[27] 'Gratitude therefore, if by gratitude we understand a sentiment of preference which I entertain towards another, upon the ground of my having been the subject of his benefits, is no part either of justice or virtue.' W. Godwin, *Enquiry concerning Political Justice*, p. 71.

being distributed, and about the precise basis on which it is deserved. Thus a professorship may be regarded as a reward for a long-standing contribution to the welfare of a university department, or as an office awarded on grounds of ability. This disagreement over what is being allocated will be reflected in differences about what should be taken as a basis for deserving the post. And even if it is agreed that the post is an office to be filled on the basis of ability, there may still be disagreement about the respective weights to be given to, for instance, scholarship and administrative skill. But these complications do not invalidate the essential point, that in deciding upon the just allocation of a good, it is not necessary to take account of desert in general, but only of those deserts which are relevant to the good being distributed.

How do things stand when we consider social justice? In speaking of social justice we have in mind the distribution of goods such as wealth, housing, and education among the people who make up a society. One of the criteria we use in assessing the justice of such a distribution is that it should correspond to desert. But which kind of desert? This will clearly vary from one good to the next. In the case of education—for example, if a restricted number of university places have to be allocated—then in so far as desert is taken as the ground of allocation, it must be based on academic achievement in the period prior to university entrance. On the other hand, no one has suggested that income should be proportional to academic success. Indeed, it is income which poses the most difficult problems, for it is by no means clear what the basis of desert should be in this case. It is useful here to take up Sidgwick's idea that the desire to reward socially valuable services arises through universalizing the impulse of gratitude.[28] That is to say, just as an individual wishes to repay his benefactor in proportion to the benefits he has received, so he will wish society as a collective body to reward its members to the extent to which it benefits from their activities. If this analogy can be sustained, it provides the most defensible interpretation of economic desert. The basis of desert will be the value which each individual has contributed to the com-

[28] Sidgwick, op. cit., pp. 278–83.

mon stock of society, or more strictly that portion of the value which is due to his own efforts, skills, and abilities. We therefore return to the principle of contribution, but now justified rather differently, as a reward conferred by society on its individual members, understood by analogy to private rewards.

This conclusion is not without its difficulties. One objection to construing income as a reward is that when people take on a job, their motive is often the purely selfish one of getting income, and any social benefits which may result are, from their point of view, accidental. Yet although the paradigm case of deserving a reward may be that in which the action that forms the basis of desert is undertaken disinterestedly, it does not seem that having the right motive is a necessary condition of desert. For instance, I may dive into the sea to save a drowning man, making the shrewd calculation that I shall be rewarded for so doing, yet if I am successful I still deserve a reward, even if, as some might argue, I am less deserving than if I had performed the same action for altruistic reasons. Having the wrong motive may lessen a person's desert, but it does not extinguish it.

Other difficulties concern the evaluation of a person's contribution to society. We have already examined the problem of disentangling one man's contribution from another's, and of estimating how much of the value each man creates is due to his personal qualities rather than to extraneous environmental factors. It is also difficult to find a way of measuring the value of goods and services. Demand is obviously a poor guide, at least in the short run, since people can be induced to demand goods which bring them little benefit. In the case of individual rewards, we think that the extent of gratitude should depend upon the actual benefit which one person has conferred upon another, benefit being assessed in terms of the recipient's needs and interests. A similar criterion would seem appropriate in the social case, but there are additional problems to be faced because society is composed of individuals with different needs and interests. Thus the goods which an artist contributes to society may be of great value to some people, but of little or no value to many others. The most hopeful suggestion is that public opinion will, in the long run, come to a reasonably correct estimate of the relative value of different goods and services; but at best this could only be expected to happen for those goods and services from which most people benefited fairly regularly (medical services, for instance). Although the contribution criterion seems abstractly just, the problems of applying it are formidable.

How strong is the relationship between desert of social reward and justice? We cannot overlook the possibility of someone basing his conception of social justice entirely on one or both of the other two criteria (rights and needs). More commonly, however, justice is felt to consist at least partly in rewarding people according to their relative contributions to society. The connection between desert and justice here is certainly stronger than in the case of honours; the common opinion is that, whether or not there is a practice of rewarding people according to their contributions, there ought to be greater rewards for greater services to society. My intuition, however, is that most people would be readier to abandon social rewards than private rewards. Perhaps the reason for this is that private gratitude is an essential member of the set of personal attitudes which we identified at the close of section 3. To abandon private gratitude and its tangible expressions, it would be necessary to give up a whole range of emotions and beliefs which make up interpersonal relationships as we now enjoy them. If this intuition is correct, the connection between desert of income and justice is stronger than that between desert of honours and justice, but weaker than that between desert of private rewards and justice.

There is in any case no doubt that most people in present-day Britain, say, hold a view of social justice which gives a large place to making incomes correspond to personal deserts.[29] The difficulty with the idea that income should be given as a reward for services to society is not to find abstract arguments in its favour, but to indicate how it might conceivably be put into practice. We shall see later that committed supporters of a desert-based idea of justice have usually combined that notion with a theory of society which resolves the problems of measuring desert—for instance, they have argued that a free market economy effectively allocates goods according to desert without deliberate human intervention. Against this, adherents of a

[29] Some useful empirical evidence is given in B. Barry, 'On Social Justice', p. 41.

need-based notion have used the difficulty of establishing and measuring desert as a good reason for abandoning the concept entirely. It remains to be seen whether 'needs' are easier to identify than 'deserts' have proved to be.

IV

NEEDS

---

1 *The Relevance of Needs to Justice*

To claim that the concepts of rights and deserts form conceptually legitimate criteria for applying the idea of justice is hardly controversial. Although some thinkers have adopted, as a substantive moral view, the position that needs and needs alone should form the basis for a just distribution of resources, these thinkers have not (to my knowledge) ever claimed that other views were conceptually improper. In the case of the concept of need, however, matters are different. An influential minority view in political philosophy is that, conceptually speaking, needs have nothing to do with the concept of justice. To use needs as a basis for just distribution is not so much morally reprehensible as conceptually confused. I shall be looking at substantive arguments against the 'needs' interpretation of justice in the second part of the book; here I want to clear away, much more briefly, the conceptual claim.

Since it can hardly be denied that people often *do* use the criterion of need as a basis for their judgements of justice, it might seem that the conceptual argument has nothing from which to start. But the strategy adopted in two recent versions of the minority view is to argue that on such occasions people are *really* appealing to one of the other criteria of justice, even though the concept of need is explicitly used. In other words, what are apparently 'deviant' uses of the concept of justice can be brought back into line by reinterpreting the need claim which is offered in support as a claim of right or desert. Since I have myself engaged in this kind of conceptual tidying-up in earlier chapters, no objection can be made in principle to the project; but I shall try to show that the attempted assimilations fail to capture the sense of the original needs claims.

Consider first the view put forward by J. R. Lucas.[1] Justice is centrally a matter of apportioning benefits to individual deserts. But this is not the only principle:

Indeed, it may be specifically over-ridden, as in a Mutual Insurance Society: we may make it an explicit principle of our community that need shall be a ground of apportionment, and then of course justice will require that each man shall receive what he needs, in the same way as under a legal system justice requires that each man shall have his legal due.[2]

Lucas claims that 'the same principle governs the National Health Service and various other aspects of the Welfare State'.[3]

What is being maintained here is that needs can form a basis for justice if and only if they are also rights, deriving from a prior agreement or an established set of rules. For instance, I contract to join a mutual insurance society, the terms of the contract stating that whenever a member is in need, he shall receive assistance. If I am later in need, what makes it a matter of justice that I am helped is not my need *simpliciter*, but my need as giving me a title to assistance according to the terms of the contract. Does this adequately reflect 'ordinary thinking' about justice, for instance in the case of the welfare state? I do not think so. One consequence of Lucas's view is this: although we can say that an individual living in a country with a welfare state who does not receive the expected benefits has been unjustly treated, we cannot say that a country *with* a welfare state is more just than a country *without* one. Since, in the latter case, there are no agreements or established rules which would lead people to expect that they would receive benefits, they are not being unjustly treated even if, say, they are given no unemployment benefits. From Lucas's point of view, the original decision to found a welfare state must be based on some value other than justice, such as social utility (*once* the institution is operating, claims of justice can arise, but not before). But this contradicts 'welfare state philosophy',

---

[1] J. R. Lucas, 'Justice', *Philosophy*, xlvii (1972).
[2] Ibid., p. 237.
[3] Ibid., p. 242.

which surely regards the establishment of the welfare state itself as a matter of justice. In other words, it is his needs as such which form the basis of an individual's just claims on society, not needs in the guise of rights.

To press the argument further: since not all morally relevant cases of need are cases in which the individual has some prior expectation that his need will be satisfied, under what general principle do these cases fall, if not the principle of justice? Lucas appears to imply that the satisfaction of needs is here a matter of humanity, or generosity, or benevolence—virtues which are, of course, quite distinct from justice. But although considerations of need are certainly relevant to the practice of these virtues, there is also a distributive principle of need which forms part of social justice. Suppose, for instance, that I am authorized to distribute a limited amount of food during a famine. If we take humanity in its simplest sense, any distribution of the food which helps to relieve the suffering of one or more persons will satisfy its requirements. If we take a more rigorous definition of humanity, as the duty to minimize the total amount of suffering in any situation (i.e. as a 'negative utilitarian' principle), then distribution according to need may or may not be required by humanity, depending on empirical factors. For example, I may decide that I can do most good by concentrating my limited supplies of food on a few families and allowing the others to starve. If I succeed in minimizing suffering in this way, I have satisfied the criterion of humanity, but I have treated the families I have left to starve unfairly. They have not received their due share of food, in accordance with their needs. Thus the distributive principle of need, which is part of justice, cannot be reduced to the general duty to satisfy needs, which is part of humanity or benevolence.

My reply to Lucas, then, is twofold: (a) one cannot plausibly maintain that all need claims which are popularly held to be matters of justice are disguised right claims; (b) one cannot assimilate distributive need claims to principles such as humanity or benevolence. Let me now consider an attempt to reinterpret familiar claims of need as claims of desert. The attempt is made in the following passage by N. M. L. Nathan which requires quoting in full:

As I have already mentioned, desert-dependent senses of 'just' are frequently juxtaposed with senses on which a situation can be just only if each person is affected in a way equal in value to his neediness. But there is not much evidence that such need-dependent senses are at all popular. Social critics do admittedly often enough point to relations between the effects of a situation and the needs of those affected by it when they claim that the situation is unjust. It is often said, for instance, that because unintelligent children from deprived areas have a relatively greater need, it is unjust to devote the largest share of the country's educational resources to the intelligent children of well-off parents. But perhaps, in examples like this, the inequality between the neediness of those affected by a situation and the value of the effects of the situation on them is being simply treated as a symptom of injustice in a desert-dependent sense. Suppose you think that a distribution of educational resources would be desert-dependently just if the value of the resources each child had devoted to him was equal to his scholastic performance. Unintelligent and deprived children find it more difficult to perform well scholastically. You could therefore not hold that a distribution of resources which gives them no more than the intelligent children of well-off parents is desert-dependently just. And in fact I can think of no case in which people would actually say that an action was unjust because of its relation to the needs of those affected and in which the action was not also unjust in some desert-dependent sense.[4]

Nathan centres his claim that judgements of justice apparently based on need are really based instead on desert on his example of the deprived children, so that if we can show that his interpretation of this case is erroneous, we shall have done enough to discredit the general thesis. Nathan's argument is that if two children reach equal academic standards and one, because he comes from a deprived background, finds it harder to do so than his privileged classmate, the deprived child deserves more resources than the other. However, this hardly corresponds to what the 'social critics' of the passage have in mind. Their view (if I may speak for them) is that children from deprived areas reach a lower standard than those from privileged backgrounds, and so they should be given more resources to help them do better in the future. The deprived children are not more deserving than the others in any sense

[4] N. M. L. Nathan, *The Concept of Justice* (London, 1971), pp. 35–6.

(they may even be less deserving, since they may try less hard than the privileged children, besides getting worse results). The claim is that the privileged children, having already reached a high academic level, *need* less resources devoted to them than the deprived ones who have fallen behind.

If further argument is required, consider again the position of someone with food to distribute during a famine, who decides, as a matter of justice, to allocate it according to need. In what sense does he suppose that the neediest person is also the most deserving? On the contrary, I should claim, he entirely ignores questions of desert in so far as he considers only the features of each man which are relevant to his needs (e.g. his bodily condition).

The lesson to be drawn here is that, if one wishes to discount the criterion of need as a basis for justice, one cannot do so on conceptual grounds alone. People who use need claims to ground their judgements of justice mean what they say. To show that they are misguided, one must engage in substantive moral argument, not rely on conceptual analysis alone. This is not to say that the concept of a need is perfectly clear as it stands. There are in fact a number of problems with the concept, some of which I shall try to resolve in the following section.

2 *The Concept of Need*

In this section I shall examine the meaning of need statements, and I want to begin by looking at an analysis of the concept which, if it were correct, would have even more radical implications than the positions considered in the previous section. This analysis is given by Brian Barry in his book *Political Argument*. Barry argues that statements of the form 'A needs X' are incomplete, and must be filled out in the form 'A needs X in order to do Y'. It follows that needs do not provide an independent justification for any policy, since their whole justificatory force derives from whatever end (Y) is being invoked when the concept is used. To say, for instance, that men should be given food because they need it is not to provide a justification, since it can always be asked 'What is the food needed for?', and the answer to this ('To keep them alive') provides the real justification for the giving of food. Barry concludes that the political philosopher has to take no special account of needs since 'the only interesting questions arise in connection with the ends'.[5]

If this analysis were correct, it would *a fortiori* be the case that needs cannot stand as an independent principle of justice, and I must therefore begin by showing what is wrong with Barry's position. In order to do this, a distinction must be drawn between three different types of need statements:

(1) 'Instrumental' needs (e.g. 'He needs a key', 'She needs a driving licence').

(2) 'Functional' needs (e.g. 'Surgeons need manual dexterity', 'University lecturers need books').

(3) 'Intrinsic' needs (e.g. 'Men need food', 'He needs someone to understand him').

Now statements in the first category clearly presuppose that the agents referred to have certain further ends which generate their needs, and so these statements can rightly be said to require filling out in the way that Barry suggests. Thus 'he needs a key' becomes fully comprehensible only when filled out in such a form as 'he needs a key in order to enter his house'; and 'she needs a driving licence' must be expanded into 'she needs a driving licence to drive a car', or something similar. The first example is a straightforward case in which what is needed (the key) is a physical means to the end postulated (entering the house); whereas the second case is slightly more complex in that the need statement depends for its truth upon a set of conventional rules—having a driving licence does not enable her physically to drive a car (she can do that anyway) but it *permits* her to drive a car within the law. Despite this difference, the examples are essentially similar in that what is needed is instrumental to some further (distinct) end, and the need cannot be understood unless this further end is supplied. However, this is not true of need statements in the second and third categories. To say that surgeons need manual dexterity is comprehensible as it stands, and the statement cannot be regarded as in any way incomplete. Were we to try to fill it out in Barry's way, we would find that the expansion was more or

---

[5] Chapter III, section 5A.

less vacuous. Thus one might try 'surgeons need manual dexterity in order to be surgeons' or 'surgeons need manual dexterity in order to do their job', but one has hardly added any new information in either case. Of course it is possible for someone to ask 'Why do surgeons need manual dexterity?', but in giving an answer one would be involved in explaining what it was to be a surgeon to someone who knew little about the role, not in supplying distinct ends *for* which the surgeon's dexterity was needed. In the case of 'functional' need statements, then, to adopt Barry's analysis would be to misrepresent the meaning of the original statements.

The same holds of the third category, 'intrinsic' need statements, which are the ones that really concern us here. Barry suggests that with statements such as 'men need food', the end is fairly obvious, and so it can be omitted without linguistic impropriety. But, logically speaking, the form of such statements is still 'A needs X in order to do Y'. However, I want to suggest that to construe 'intrinsic' need statements in this way is to misconstrue them, since what is needed in these cases is not a *means* to an end but a part of the end itself. In other words, *if* one undertakes to supply an end here, one is simply filling out a whole of which the thing needed is one part. Compare the two statements 'he needs a key (in order to enter his house)' and 'he needs someone to understand him (in order to achieve mental well-being)'. In the first case, what is needed (the key) is a mere means to the end, and once the end is reached (the house is entered) the key is needed no longer and may be dispensed with. In the second case, what appears as a 'means' (having someone to understand him) is really part of the 'end' indicated (a state of mental well-being). The understanding person is not employed and then dispensed with, rather the proximity of such a person is (partly at least) what constitutes a state of well-being for the subject of the statement. The means –end form distorts the sense of the original claim; and similarly, I should argue, for other statements in the third category.

What, then, do 'intrinsic' need statements really mean? It is tempting to try to give an account of these statements in terms of the simpler concept of a want. In fact, no such account is adequate, but the attempt to provide one helps us to a better understanding of what a need is.

Consider first the simple equivalence: 'A needs X' = 'A wants X'. This equivalence fails to hold in either direction. For (a) we often say of people that they want things which they do not need; for instance, a child who demands a lollipop, makes efforts to get one, etc., certainly wants a lollipop, but we are most unlikely to acknowledge that he needs one. (b) We (rather less often) say of people that they need things which they do not want. We might say of the same child that he needs to eat more healthy food, though he gives us every evidence that he wants to do no such thing. The point is that wanting is a psychological state, which is ascribed on the basis of a person's avowals and his behaviour (we use behaviour as a criterion when we cannot ask the person directly to tell us what he wants, or when we think that he is being disingenuous). Needing, on the other hand, is *not* a psychological state, but rather a condition which is ascribed 'objectively' to the person who is its subject.

If a direct link between the concepts of 'need' and 'want' cannot be established, an indirect link may be proposed instead. An analysis of the following form might be suggested:

'A needs X' = 'A would want X, under certain favourable conditions'.

An example of this type of analysis can be extracted from the following passage by Marcuse, although the terminology used is somewhat different.

We may distinguish both true and false needs. 'False' are those which are superimposed upon the individual by particular social interests in his repression. . . . In the last analysis, the question of what are true and false needs must be answered by the individuals themselves, but only in the last analysis; that is, if and when they are free to give their own answer. As long as they are kept incapable of being autonomous, as long as they are indoctrinated and manipulated (down to their very instincts), their answer to this question cannot be taken as their own.[6]

If we put 'false needs' = 'actual wants which are not needs, in the true sense' and 'true needs' = 'needs', then Marcuse is claiming that under conditions of freedom individuals' preferences are to be taken as defining their needs, but not other-

[6] H. Marcuse, *One-Dimensional Man* (London, 1968), pp. 21–3.

wise. Although such an analysis avoids the straightforward objections to the earlier suggestion ('A needs X' = 'A wants X'), it runs into two other difficulties:

(a) The danger of circularity. Is it possible to identify the favourable conditions under which wants are to be taken as an authentic guide to needs without including among those conditions some specification of what people's wants will actually be? In Marcuse's case, can he identify a condition of freedom independently of specifying what choices people will actually make in such a condition? Suppose, for instance, that in a situation in which people were apparently free from indoctrination and manipulation, they continued to want large quantities of consumer goods (taken by Marcuse to be a 'false' need). Would Marcuse admit that this want actually constituted a 'true' need, or would he not rather insist that indoctrination was still present, albeit in a disguised form?

(b) It may be questioned whether the proposed analysis really explicates the meaning of needs claims. For instance, it seems quite in order to say of a person 'He needs X, but he will never be in a condition such that he wants it'. One might say this because one believed, for example, that the person concerned was too unreflective ever to realize that he needed X. Thus 'he needs a more equal relationship with his wife, but he will never see that'. In such cases, there are *no* conditions under which the person will want what he needs, but we nevertheless continue to speak of the person as having the needs in question.

If we consider what we have in mind when we ascribe needs to a person, we shall, I believe, recognize that we are thinking not of the person's wants, whether actual or hypothetical, but rather of the consequences for the person of *not* having what is needed. We are thinking of the harm which the person will suffer through not being given what we say he needs. Thus a better definition of the concept of need than either of those proposed is the following:

'A needs X' = 'A will suffer harm if he lacks X'.

This makes good sense of the 'intrinsic' need statements with which we began: 'men need food' ('Men will suffer harm if they lack food'), 'he needs someone to understand him'

('He will be harmed if he does not have someone to understand him'). Yet although the analysis is a useful starting-point, it is obviously incomplete until some account is given of the concept of harm. Evidently harm can occur in various forms—physical, emotional, intellectual, etc.—and each of these will be required to explicate the corresponding type of need. Although it seems at first sight fairly simple to define physical harm (and thus, by extension, physical needs) it is much less easy to see what constitutes emotional or intellectual harm; and this problem must be resolved, for an adequate account of 'needs' cannot stop short at physical needs.

A satisfactory understanding of 'harm' must avoid two incorrect but inviting extreme positions:

(1) The view that the concept of harm can be applied to a person on the basis of general empirical criteria, without reference to the aspirations and ideals of the person concerned. This would be to suppose that the concept of human harm is an exact analogue of, say, the concept we apply to a plant when we say that certain environmental conditions are harmful to it. In the latter case there are agreed physical criteria for applying the concept—stunted growth, a failure to reproduce, etc. It might appear that in the human case physical harm is understood in the same way; but even here what counts as an injury to one man may not count as an injury to another, because their aspirations are wholly different. This is vividly illustrated in a story told about the philosopher Brentano:

Brentano was blind at the end of his life. When friends commiserated with him over the harm that had befallen him, he denied that his loss of sight was a bad thing. He explained that one of his weaknesses had been a tendency to cultivate and concentrate on too many diverse interests. Now, in his blindness, he was able to concentrate on his philosophy in a way which had been impossible for him before.[7]

If we are prepared to accept Brentano's own opinion about what harmed him and what did not, we have here a case in which a loss which would be harmful to almost any other man was actually beneficial to a particular person.

[7] Cited in D. Z. Phillips and H. O. Mounce, 'On Morality's having a Point', *Philosophy*, xl (1965), p. 316.

(2) It is equally wrong to suppose that the concept of harm can be applied only from the point of view of a strong theory of human nature—a definite account of how human beings ought to live and the kind of satisfaction they ought to enjoy. From such a standpoint harm will be assessed in terms of departures from the ideal which is postulated—any condition will be judged harmful which deflects people from living in accordance with the standards in question. Such an account of harm is certainly possible, but it is neither necessary to adopt such a strong view, nor is it desirable. An example may illustrate this. Consider Marx's theory of human nature, as advanced especially in the *Economic and Philosophical Manuscripts.*[8] This theory includes a specification of human needs, and thus of the conditions whose absence is harmful to men (Marx's theory of alienation may be considered as an account of how men are harmed by capitalist society). Among these needs are the following: the need to perform productive work, the need to enjoy a reasonably high level of consumption, the need to form solidary relationships with other men. Consider now a religious ascetic who wants nothing more than simple food, shelter, and a chance of communion with God. Marx is committed to the view that *nevertheless* his real needs are those laid down in the theory of human nature. Of course Marx can offer us an explanation of why it is that the ascetic fails to perceive his true human needs (this explanation also forms part of the theory of alienation). But what is disturbing here is the size of the gap between the ascetic's felt needs and the needs which Marx attributes to him. Although Marx may (rightly or wrongly) be stating what needs the ascetic ought to have, it seems difficult to deny that, as a matter of fact, the ascetic's needs are for solitude, the simple life, etc.

These doubts are further supported by the observation that the ascetic appears to have a definite and stable idea of the kind of life that he wants to lead. If his aims were incoherent, or constantly changing, we should be readier to apply to him a doctrine such as Marx's, which identifies a man's needs independently of his aims. And this suggests the following conclusion about the concept of harm: to determine what counts as harm for any given person, it is necessary first to identify the

---

[8] See T. B. Bottomore (ed.), *Karl Marx: Early Writings* (London, 1963).

aims and activities which are central to that person's way of life. Let me refer to these aims and activities collectively as the person's 'plan of life'. I take it that a person has to have such a plan, for a person's *identity* is established by the aims and activities which constitute his plan of life, and without such an identity he could hardly be regarded as a person in the full sense, rather as an organism of a certain type which was potentially a person. (The connection between a person's plan of life and his identity can be brought out by considering the responses which may be made to the question 'Who are you?'; in reply one mentions aspects of one's plan of life—e.g. what work one does, what social relationships one stands in, etc.)

Plans of life can take different forms. They may consist, for instance, in (a) carrying out a certain social role, such as a work role or a family role—or some combination of these; (b) the pursuit of a social ideal, such as the liberation of one's country or the creation of a classless society; (c) a project such as cataloguing all the plants in South-East Asia; (d) the attempt to develop personal relationships of a particular type. This list is by no means exhaustive. I believe that the notion of a plan of life can be applied quite generally to human beings, although the idea that a person should choose his plan of life from among a number of available alternatives is specific to technologically advanced liberal societies. In traditional societies, a person's plan of life is generally laid down for him in advance, and he adopts it without reflective consideration; such a person may not be able to articulate his plan of life in the way that the modern liberal can, but this does not mean that he has not got one.

Once it has been established what a man's plan of life is, his activities can be divided roughly into two groups—those which are essential to his plan and those which are non-essential. 'Essential' activities include: (1) Those activities which actually make up the plan of life (e.g. in the case of the man whose plan of life is to catalogue the plants of South-East Asia, collecting plants for cataloguing, etc.). (2) Those activities which are necessary to support the activities listed under (1) (e.g. for all men, eating food; for most men, maintaining satisfactory personal relationships with others). Most people also engage in non-essential activities such as consuming superfluous food and drink, going to entertainments, and playing games. The point about these activities is that, although they generally bring pleasure to those who participate in them, their cessation would not significantly interfere with people's plans of life. They are not integrally connected with a person's central aims, and so his identity as a person is not at stake if he is prevented from engaging in them, even though he may resent the loss of pleasure which results.

We are now in a position to put forward our account of 'harm' and thereby our account of 'need'. Harm, for any given individual, is whatever interferes directly or indirectly with the activities essential to his plan of life; and correspondingly, his needs must be understood to comprise whatever is necessary to allow these activities to be carried out. In order, then, to decide what a person's needs are, we must first identify his plan of life, then establish what activities are essential to that plan, and finally investigate the conditions which enable those activities to be carried out This account may be recommended on two grounds. First, it explains how we may say (what we certainly say in practice) that the needs of different people are very diverse. Thus compare a European intellectual with a Russian peasant of the Tsarist period. Each has, let us assume, a reasonably coherent plan of life, but those plans of life are quite different, and so the two men have different needs. The European intellectual needs books, because without books he cannot engage in the activity of thought which is central to his plan of life, whereas the Russian peasant does not. On the other hand, the Russian peasant may be said to need a certain type of religion, because religion enables him to fit his own life into the order of the world, while the European intellectual has no such need. Second, this account of 'need' makes sense of the wants/needs distinction. When we say that a person wants something which he does not need, we imply that that which is desired, although possibly a source of pleasure, is not a necessary part of that person's plan of life. If he did not get it, his plan of life would not be significantly disrupted. Moreover, we can intelligibly say that people do not know what their needs are, for although a person must in some sense know what his plan of life is (even if he cannot articulate that knowledge) he may not know what conditions are necessary to support that plan; in fact he is most unlikely to know what *all* the conditions are, given that among them will be highly complex bodily states, such as vitamin-levels.

Up to this point I have apparently been offering a wholly empirical account of 'need'—i.e. an account which makes the question of what someone's needs are a wholly empirical question; and this contrasts sharply with some other recent analyses, notably those given by Benn and Peters[9] and Peters.[10] However, although I want to maintain that questions about needs are predominantly empirical in character, I believe that evaluative elements enter to a small extent into the determination of needs, in the following way. We have seen that a person's needs must be understood to comprise whatever is necessary for him to carry out his plan of life. In making such a judgement, we are implicitly acknowledging that the plan of life which we have uncovered is intelligible to us—intelligible not only in the sense that it can be coherently described in meaningful language, but in the sense that we can understand how, for the person who has it, that plan of life has significance and value.[11] It is not that we ourselves must find the plan valuable, but that we must be able to see how someone else may value it. Thus if confronted with a pyromaniac we are likely to say, not that he needs a plentiful supply of matches, access to barns, etc., but that he needs psychiatric help. Our reason for saying this is that we do not regard a series of attempts to start destructive fires as making up an intelligible plan of life. We therefore judge the pyromaniac's needs to comprise, not the conditions necessary for his present 'plan of life', but the conditions which are necessary for him to engage in other plans of life that *are* intelligible. Such judgements are clearly evaluative in character: what we are prepared to describe as intelligible depends upon our sympathies and our moral standards. Some people will be prepared to find a wider range of plans of life intelligible than others, and this will be reflected in their judgements about needs. It may still be said, however, that need judgements are

[9] S. Benn and R. S. Peters, *Social Principles and the Democratic State*, ch. 6, section III.

[10] R. S. Peters, *The Concept of Motivation* (London, 1958), pp. 17–18.

[11] The distinction between these two senses of 'intelligibility' is drawn by A. J. Watt in 'The Intelligibility of Wants', *Mind*, lxxxi (1972).

weakly evaluative only, because although they depend on judgements of intelligibility, they do not depend on our preferences for one plan of life over another. Consider again the Russian peasant and the European intellectual. It would be hard to deny that both have plans of life that are intelligible; neither can be dismissed in the same way as the pyromaniac's 'plan of life'. The question of which plan of life—the peasant's or the intellectual's—is to be preferred is a matter of acute controversy, not only among peasants and intellectuals. But this controversy should not affect our assessment of the needs of the two men. Having accepted both plans of life as intelligible, the question of what the respective needs of Russian peasants and European intellectuals are becomes an empirical one.

We see, then, that disputes about a person's needs can take a number of forms:

(1) Disputes about what conditions are actually necessary for someone to carry out his plan of life.

(2) Disputes about the precise nature of someone's plan of life.

(3) Disputes about whether someone's plan of life is intelligible or not.

My claim is that only in the third case do evaluative elements enter into the question of what a person's needs are. In the first two cases the dispute is in principle capable of being resolved by empirical methods. This does not mean that such a dispute can be resolved easily, for the empirical questions may be highly complex (even such a question as 'how much food does a healthy person need to eat?' is hard to answer). The point is that such difficulty should not be taken as evidence for the view that need judgements always depend upon values. In most cases, disagreements about the nature and extent of a person's needs can be settled by reference to matters of fact, albeit of a somewhat intricate nature.

3 *The Expansion of Needs*

It is a matter of common observation that people's needs change as time passes, both in nature and in extent. In the kind of society we inhabit, they are generally thought to be undergoing a process of expansion; and it is important to decide whether this process tends towards any finite limit, or whether needs are potentially infinite in extent, for this will influence our understanding and application of the principle 'to each according to his needs'. According to one view, it is possible with enough resources (some might argue, even with current resources properly distributed) to satisfy everyone's needs; and we would then have to decide how, from the point of view of justice, any surplus should be distributed. According to the other view, needs may be expected to expand as fast as resources, and consequently there will never be sufficient goods available to satisfy everyone's needs completely; in this case justice will be taken to mean the *proportionate* satisfaction of needs (an equal proportion of each person's needs should be satisfied).

In technologically advanced societies, it has been accepted as a matter of course that levels of production will steadily rise, and as a result that people's wants will change and increase. Men are expected to want larger amounts of things previously produced, such as food, and to develop tastes for new commodities which could not be produced before. It is sometimes argued that needs must expand in the same way. This seems to be implicit in the view put forward by Benn and Peters that 'needs' must be understood in relation to a standard of living which is conventional and which changes over time.[12] A similar thesis had earlier been stated in sociological form by Halbwachs.[13] With particular reference to the working class, Halbwachs argued that when wage increases gave the workers more money than they needed to buy the basic necessities such as food, they began to purchase new types of goods hitherto unavailable to them. Thus American workers in the 1920s were found to be in possession of cars, radios, washing machines, etc. These new goods quickly become part of the conventional standard of living expected by the class as a whole, and they were therefore considered as needs by the individual workers. Halbwachs backed up this claim by showing that when wages slumped, the workers did not give up buying the new goods, but saved on the basic items—food and clothing—by, for example, eating less meat but more vegetables. He also pointed out that workers and salaried employees (e.g. bank

---

[12] See Benn and Peters, op. cit., ch. 6, section III.
[13] M. Halbwachs, *L'Évolution des besoins dans les classes ouvrières* (Paris, 1933).

clerks) divided up their budgets in different ways even when
their incomes were equal, and he took this as evidence that
the needs of the two classes were different. In short, a person's
needs depend upon the conventional standard of living which
his social group expects, and (under modern conditions)
regularly expand to include new items.

We are in no position here to quarrel with Halbwachs's
sociology, but we can, I think, find fault with the terms he
chooses to express his findings, terms which are also used by
Benn and Peters. It is worth pointing out that by relating
needs to a conventional standard of living, one not only implies
that personal needs must expand as the standard of living rises,
but also that if the customary standard is low enough, needs
are likewise diminished. Benn and Peters seem prepared to
accept this consequence:

Where poor sight is common and spectacles rare, there would be no
basic need for spectacles.[14]

I hope that this conclusion is sufficiently disturbing to make the
reader question the premises from which it is derived. Surely,
to decide whether a man needs spectacles, one does not have to
find out how many of those around him already possess a pair.
The alternative account of 'need' which was put forward in the
previous section makes better sense of the case. According to
that account, a man needs spectacles if he will be harmed by the
lack of them, and to determine whether or not he will be harmed
we must refer to his plan of life. Thus if a man lives by hunting
and his sight is so poor that he can hardly see the game, then
he needs spectacles—whether or not his fellow hunters have
them already.

What, then, of the expansion of needs? It is of course true
that plans of life change as society develops under the impact of
technology, and to that extent needs must alter. To continue
with the example of the working class, the course of this century has seen definite changes in working-class patterns of life,
resulting particularly from the shortening of work hours and the
consequent growth of leisure activities. At the same time it
must be said that for most people the 'core' of their plan of life
has remained the same: to hold a stable job, bringing in

[14] Benn and Peters, op. cit., p. 146.

sufficient income to support a home and family. To that extent we may say that needs have not changed very much, certainly not as much as the wants and expectations which people actually entertain. There is ample evidence (including, of course, that of Halbwachs) to show that people now expect to possess a great number of commodities which they could not have expected to possess had they been living, say, a hundred years ago. We have no reason to deny the psychological reality of these desires, but equally we have no reason to describe them as needs. Radios, sewing machines, electric toasters, washing machines (to use some of Halbwachs's examples) are *not* needed because they are not essential to people's plans of life, even though they are convenient, useful, and widely demanded. I am not suggesting, as some critics of modern society have suggested, that people's wants for such objects are not really wants at all, but simply insisting, for the sake of clarity, and in order that necessary moral distinctions can be made, that 'wants' and 'needs' be kept apart.

A problem which must be taken up here is whether a person's plan of life might not include his having a certain status. For example, people customarily compare their material position to that of other members of their 'reference group' (which has been chosen in one way or another),[15] and it will be said that part of a person's plan of life may be to keep up materially with the rest of his reference group, and that he therefore needs as many consumer goods as the current norm in that group prescribes. In defence of this claim, we might point out that people who fall behind in the race for material possessions may experience status anxieties which are plausibly enough construed as harmful.

However, we must observe that it is not the goods themselves that are needed in order for the person to carry out his plan of life. For it is not the absence of, say, a washing machine as such that makes it impossible for a particular individual to fulfil his plan, but rather the absence of a washing machine in circumstances in which other people have one, and he knows that this is the case. The situation could be remedied with equal success

[15] For a discussion of the factors which influence the choice of reference groups, see W. G. Runciman, *Relative Deprivation and Social Justice* (London, 1966), esp. ch. 2.

either by giving him a machine or by removing everyone else's (or indeed by persuading people to stop regarding washing machines as marks of social status). So to say that he needs a washing machine is misleading: what he actually needs is parity of goods with other members of his reference group. It follows that in this context the need for any particular good can only be an instrumental need—a necessary means of maintaining status, given a particular level of consumption already enjoyed by the reference group as a whole.

Furthermore, the notion of a person needing status must be scrutinized carefully. It may be broken down into two quite different elements. There is first of all the need for recognition—i.e. the need to be acknowledged as an equal by one's peers, to avoid being placed in a position of inferiority. This need is real enough, since a person's self-respect may depend upon his gaining recognition in this sense. It should be noted, though, that its fulfilment does not require that society should contain a series of unequal statuses. On the contrary, it can be plausibly argued that the need for recognition is met most completely in a society of equals, since each man's peer group then becomes the whole of society. However, the notion of a need for status may also be understood in a second way, to mean the need to occupy a superior position in society—a position commanding greater wealth or prestige than at least some of the other positions available. Interpreted in this way, the need for status appears to create a problem for our attempt to limit the expansion of needs, since it may be claimed of some people that they need extremely large quantities of material goods to satisfy their need for status.

I have two doubts about such a claim. The first is whether the need for status, in this second sense, is really a need at all—whether, that is, it can reasonably be shown to be an essential part of an intelligible plan of life. It is quite comprehensible that people should seek wealth and prestige as a means to carry out some further undertaking, but is the quest for superior status for its own sake really something that we can regard as a coherent plan of life? We saw in the previous section that such questions about the intelligibility of plans of life cannot be settled in a purely empirical way, and it may be that my doubts here are a result of democratic sympathies and an incapacity to understand, for instance, the value of an aristocratic mode of life in which the possession of status is a necessary condition of the other activities which make up that mode of life. Perhaps this is true. I think, though, that we are entitled to ask whether people who speak of a need for status in such cases are not confusing the status itself with those material advantages usually associated with a particular status in the past.

Even if we are prepared to regard the need for a superior status as a genuine need, a second doubt arises. The doubt is whether such a need can be relevant to questions of justice. For a feature which differentiates this particular need from almost every other need is that, necessarily and not merely contingently, not everyone can have it satisfied. As a matter of logic, only some people can hold superior positions. We therefore meet a problem which is also met, for instance, in discussions of freedom. There it is pointed out that to give each man unlimited freedom allows everyone to encroach upon his neighbour's freedom. The problem is usually solved by discounting at the outset freedom which can only be exercised at the expense of other people's freedom, so that if one wishes, for instance, to employ a principle of maximum freedom, one will maximize only with respect to freedom which can be exercised without infringing the freedom of others. Similarly, I suggest, when we interpret justice as the equal satisfaction of needs, we should discount those needs which (necessarily, not merely contingently) cannot be satisfied consistently with their equal satisfaction on the part of others.[16]

I believe, therefore, that the existence of needs for status does not upset the view that people's needs are fairly well defined and limited in extent. Generally, a need for status means a need to be respected as an equal by one's social group; and if it is taken to mean a need for *superior* status, then firstly it is doubtful whether such needs exist, and secondly, even if they

---

[16] I hope that the distinction between needs which *contingently* cannot be satisfied universally and needs which *necessarily* cannot be satisfied universally is clear enough. If a man needs to engage in space travel, this need *contingently* cannot be satisfied universally, since there are not at present enough resources to permit everyone to travel in space. If a man needs to be the only man travelling in space, then of course this need *necessarily* cannot be satisfied universally. My proposal is that in implementing the principle of needs as a principle of justice, we should take into account needs of the first type but not needs of the second type.

do exist, it is doubtful whether they are relevant to questions
of justice. However, the need for status in the first sense is unquestionably important, and it may help to explain why other
needs appear to expand faster than they actually do.[17] Someone
who lacks the goods which would give him a comfortable status
in his reference group will certainly feel a need for those goods,
and cannot be expected to see that his actual need is for status,
not for the goods themselves. It has of course already been
established that what a person feels he needs may not be an
adequate guide to what he actually needs, but in this case we
have especially good reason to expect that felt needs will expand beyond real needs.

A similar tendency results from the confusion of instrumental
needs with intrinsic needs. Someone may feel that he needs a
washing machine, without asking himself whether this is an
intrinsic need or merely a need with respect to some end which
does not form part of his plan of life. If one asked him to specify
what the washing machine was needed *for*, the instrumental
character of the need would surely emerge. Thus a plausible
answer might be 'I need the washing machine in order to wash
my clothes at home with little effort'. It is most unlikely that the
end cited here could form an essential part of anyone's plan of
life, and so the need is seen to be instrumental. Such distinctions are rarely made in practice, however, and the resulting
confusion between instrumental and intrinsic needs lends
currency to the thesis that needs are expanding at a rapid rate—
whereas in fact they are changing only as fast as plans of life
change, that is to say quite slowly.

A final point which must be made here concerns needs
which are rather ill defined, such as the need for self-respect
or the need for close personal relationships. Benn and Peters
say of needs such as these that 'they are too indeterminate to
provide criteria for income distribution', and this is surely
correct. One cannot use the need for self-respect as a direct
basis for distributing income, although one may be able to say
in general terms what kinds of economic distribution are most
likely to foster self-respect all round. Yet although we cannot

[17] In this paragraph and the one following I draw upon D. Braybrooke, 'Let
Needs Diminish that Preferences may Prosper', *American Philosophical Quarterly
Monograph Series*, No. 1 (Oxford, 1968).

lay down precise conditions for satisfying the need for self-respect, there is no reason to believe that among these conditions will be a large quantity of material possessions. It is therefore wrong to use the vagueness of these needs as a way of reintroducing the expansion thesis; they do not generate subsidiary needs for ever-increasing amounts of material goods.

4 *Needs, Justice, and Equality*

The analysis which has been offered in the previous section implies that a situation is possible in which all the needs of the members of a society have been satisfied, and yet there is material wealth left over. This generates the following conceptual problem: given that justice as distribution according to need gives us no direct indication as to how the surplus is to be allocated, can this conception of justice be extended in a logical way to deal with such a situation? I shall attempt to resolve this problem in the present section.

It might first of all be said that if the situation described were to arise, the correct policy would be to cut back production until just enough goods were produced to satisfy everyone's needs. But, although this answer might be the proper expression of some ascetic principle, it could hardly be offered as a matter of justice, at least if we accept the view that justice concerns the distribution of wealth and not the aggregate amount produced. So this response does not seem to offer a solution.

It might, secondly, be suggested that an alternative principle such as desert should be used to govern the distribution of the surplus once needs have been satisfied. Such a solution carries a certain intuitive appeal—which may be expressed in catchphrases such as 'Bread for all before jam for some'—although the two parts of the combined formula may tend in practice to generate moral conflicts within the thinking of its adherents. The proposed conception, however, in no way represents an extension of the 'needs' conception of justice. Rather, two quite different principles are being used in combination, with the principle of need being given the priority.

A third suggestion, which I want to endorse, is that the surplus should be distributed so as to achieve an equal level of well-being for everyone, through the proportionate satisfaction of wants. In other words, the logical extension of the principle of need is the principle of equality, interpreted as the claim that every man should enjoy an equal level of well-being.[18] Equality is achieved by giving first priority to the satisfaction of needs, and then by satisfying as large a proportion of each person's further desires as resources will allow—it being assumed that resources are not sufficiently abundant to gratify every wish.

It may be asked whether any sense can be given to the idea of satisfying an equal proportion of each person's desires. What does it mean to say that we have satisfied one-third of A's wishes, one-third of B's, and so on? I propose to answer this by introducing the notion of an individual 'scale of well-being', in the following way. We are to suppose that each person is asked to consider all the possible ways in which resources might be allocated to him, over and above the allocation which satisfies his needs. He is also asked to indicate which allocation he would regard as giving him the greatest well-being, and which he would regard as giving him the least; and then to place other allocations on a scale between these two extreme points. Once we have such a scale for each person, we can interpret the principle of equal well-being as the claim that each man should enjoy as high a position on his scale as every other.

This principle, it should be said, falls short of being a complete conception of equality. For one thing, it ignores factors which might influence the construction of scales of well-being and which the egalitarian would certainly wish to consider. If, for instance, people were here and now asked to set up their scales of well-being, the results would no doubt reflect established inequalities of wealth. The poor would be satisfied with a smaller allocation of resources than the rich, because their wishes were confined by their limited experience of sources of enjoyment. Nevertheless the principle does give an answer to an important question which every egalitarian must face: given that people exhibit a wide variety of tastes and wishes (over and above those inherent in their different plans of life), in what does an equal distribution of resources consist? The principle of equal well-being satisfactorily answers this

[18] 'Well-being' is here a blank term to be used indiscriminately for 'pleasure', 'happiness', 'self-realization', etc., as one chooses. Egalitarians may accept my general formulation of the principle of equality while differing over the precise nature of the state which is to be enjoyed equally by each individual.

question, though it needs to be complemented by other principles regulating the *development* of tastes and wishes (for example, principles of educational equality).

It may be objected that the principle of equal well-being, interpreted in the way suggested, could never be successfully implemented, because it gives an incentive to each person to overestimate the amount of resources he would require to be fully satisfied. It would pay each person to indicate that an infinite allocation of resources would satisfy him, and that any lesser amount would bring him no satisfaction at all. Egalitarians may respond that equality in any case can only be achieved if men do not behave in a wholly self-interested way; however, the objection has sufficient force to explain why egalitarians have sometimes opted for an equal distribution of income as an expression of the principle of equality. This is not because they are moved by a desire to create a uniform, undifferentiated society (as critics of equality sometimes suggest),[19] but because an equal distribution of the surplus once basic needs have been met is a rough and ready way of achieving an equal level of well-being, if scales of well-being cannot be constructed or cannot be relied upon. It *is* rough and ready because some people's desires may cost more to satisfy than others', and not necessarily because they are desires for luxury in itself. One man wants to play the piano, another to play the flute. If income is distributed equally, the first man will have to forego satisfaction for longer than the second, until he has saved enough from his income to buy a piano. This shows why the equal distribution of income is an imperfect expression of equality, and why in contexts in which mutual confidence is possible men will return to the principle of equal well-being—for instance, by holding all goods in common, and allowing each person to take what he wants. This in effect is to allow

---

[19] See I. Berlin, 'Equality', *Proceedings of the Aristotelian Society*, lvi (1955–6); H. J. McCloskey, 'Egalitarianism, Equality and Justice', *Australasian Journal of Philosophy*, xliv (1966). Berlin writes: 'The fanatical egalitarian . . . will tend to wish so to condition human beings that the highest degree of equality of natural properties is achieved, the greatest degree of mental and physical, that is to say, total uniformity—which alone will effectively preserve society, as far as possible, from the growth of inequalities of whatever kind.' (Loc. cit., p. 314.) For an egalitarian response to charges of this kind, see R. H. Tawney, *Equality* (London, 1964), pp. 49–50.

each person to decide how far up his scale of well-being he should be, taking into account the resources available to the community. The pure principle can be implemented (if at all) only in small communities, in large societies the cruder criterion of equal incomes will have to be used. But, I should argue, in both cases the intention is the same; to achieve a state in which as far as possible each man enjoys the same level of well-being as every other.

What in fact is the relationship between this principle of equality and the principle of need? At first sight the connection between the two principles appears to run in one direction only; it is fairly clear why the principle of equality should imply the principle of need, but less clear why the converse implication should hold. For, if one is aiming to bring about a state in which equal levels of well-being are enjoyed, one's first priority will be to satisfy everyone's intrinsic needs. This becomes particularly plain if we recall the connection between an individual's needs and his plan of life, and we may further observe that the satisfaction of (non-essential) desires is often only worth while for individuals who have an established plan of life. However, why should not one satisfy needs and then distribute the surplus in some fashion other than an egalitarian one? There is no strict inconsistency here, but there is an incongruity which can be brought out by considering the premisses which underlie the principle of need.

The satisfaction of needs can be regarded in two ways: either as a matter of justice or as a matter of humanity. I have already noted the views of those such as Lucas who regard the satisfaction of needs as a matter of humanity, and have indicated that a rather different principle of need emerges from this perspective. In this case the underlying premiss is simply that human suffering should be avoided. But if the satisfaction of needs is seen as a matter of justice, a different underlying premiss is required. The premiss is difficult to state with any clarity, but it may be expressed by saying that every man is as worthy of respect as every other. That is to say, although men plainly differ in moral virtue, in merit, in personal success, in usefulness to society, there is an underlying equality which consists in the fact that each man is a unique individual with his own aims, ideals, and outlook on the world, and that consequently he must be treated as such. This, it seems to me, is what Mill had in mind when he said, 'If a person possesses any tolerable amount of common sense and experience, his own mode of laying out his existence is the best, not because it is the best in itself, but because it is his own mode'[20]—and the same intuition has been expressed in different terms by a great number of other writers.[21] Further, this premiss is required to show why each man has an equal claim to carry out his plan of life, and hence to have satisfied the needs which are related to that plan of life. Unless the premiss is granted, we cannot show why it is *unjust* (and not merely inhumane) to satisfy one man's needs and not the needs of another. But the same premiss can be used to take us beyond the satisfaction of intrinsic needs, for it also shows why each person has an equal claim to benefits which are not needed in the true sense. Although the satisfaction of non-essential wants is not as vital to a person's individuality as the satisfaction of his needs, nevertheless individuality *is* expressed in, for instance, pleasurable or creative activities which do not form part of a plan of life. Therefore, to allow some people to enjoy these benefits to a greater extent than others is to violate the principle of equal respect, because one is permitting an obstacle to individuality to remain in one case but not in the other; and this is inconsistent with an equal respect for the individuality of each man. The loss of respect is not, of course, to be compared with that involved in humiliating a person, or allowing him to starve to death, but there is a small loss nevertheless.

It is therefore in order to regard the principle of equality as a natural extension of the principle of need, and indeed the two principles are frequently run together in the writings of egalitarians. It is a further question whether the principle of equality should be regarded as a principle of justice—whether in fact, the idea of justice as distribution according to need is more fully expressed in the principle of equality. To make the

[20] J. S. Mill, *On Liberty* in *Utilitarianism; On Liberty; Representative Government*, p. 125. It should be observed that this is certainly not a utilitarian argument.
[21] Among contemporary writers, see especially B. Williams, 'The Idea of Equality' in P. Laslett and W. G. Runciman (eds.), *Philosophy, Politics and Society*, 2nd Ser. (Oxford, 1962); W. K. Frankena, 'The Concept of Social Justice', section VII, and G. Vlastos, 'Justice and Equality', section II, both in R. B. Brandt (ed.), *Social Justice* (Englewood Cliffs, N.J., 1962).

extension, it would be necessary to find a new distributive principle to supplement the principle of need—'to each according to his wants' is the formula suggested by the foregoing analysis. Is this a principle of justice? Some recent analyses of the concept have included similar criteria.[22] Against this, it may be held that 'wants' (remembering that these are 'non-essential wants') do not constitute a strong enough claim on resources to ground a demand of justice. Although it may be desirable that men's wants should be equally satisfied, it might be said, this is not a matter of justice provided that all needs are fully catered for. The kind of example which might be used to support such an argument is the following: consider a society in which resources are distributed according to need, but in which the surplus, once needs have been satisfied, is put into a national lottery and handed out to a small number of lucky individuals. Is this an unjust society? It is a moot point. If one held that the arrangements were fair, this would presumably be on the grounds that each man stood an equal chance of winning a prize, such a virtue being held sufficient to offset the unequal satisfaction of wants. Contrast the situation where *everything* goes into the lottery, so that many people are left with their needs unsatisfied. This is unquestionably unjust. The example shows, I think, that if the proportionate satisfaction of wants is a principle of justice, it is much less compelling than the principle of need.

A further consideration which throws light on the relationship between justice and equality is the following. Even if the same state of affairs (one in which every man enjoys the same level of well-being) satisfies both the principle of equality and the idea of justice we are now considering, the two concepts may nevertheless be distinct: they may point to different aspects of the one situation. I suggest that the notion of equality refers primarily to the end result—the equal levels of well-being enjoyed—whereas justice refers to the way in which each man has been treated—namely, according to his peculiar needs and wants. This corresponds to the general conception of justice as '*suum cuique*'. Because 'just treatment' means 'treatment fitted to the individual', it also means in practice treatment which

[22] See W. Frankena, op. cit., p. 11; A. Honoré, 'Social Justice' in *Essays in Legal Philosophy*, p. 81.

is different for each person; whereas 'equality' points directly to the identical levels of well-being which are the outcome of such different treatment.

The safest conclusion to draw here is that the 'needs' conception of justice and the principle of equality stand in a peculiarly intimate relationship to one another which is still less than an identity. The intimacy consists, first, in the fact that the equal satisfaction of needs is the most important element in bringing about full equality; and, second, in the fact that the premiss which underlies distribution according to need also underlies equality in the broader sense. One could say that the principle of need represents the most urgent part of the principle of equality. This urgency finds its expression in our undoubted willingness to regard the satisfaction of needs as a matter of justice, compared with our uncertainty about the satisfaction of other wants. This conclusion, at any rate, is sufficient for my purposes. We have seen that any attempt to drive a wedge between the principle of need and equality is misguided. This attempt is sometimes made on the grounds that the principle of need is a principle of *inequality*—it demands that people should be treated differently, because their needs vary. But this is a mistake. It is certainly true that to satisfy everyone's needs it is necessary to mete out different physical resources to different people. This, however, is not inegalitarian, because the principle of equality does not demand that each person should receive the same physical treatment, rather that each person should be treated in such a way that he achieves the same level of well-being as every other. Because people have varied needs and wants, physical resources such as food, medicine, and education should not be assigned in equal quantities to each man, but in different proportions to different people, according to their peculiar characteristics. No serious egalitarian has thought otherwise.

I shall therefore make the working assumption that egalitarians are committed to the view that justice consists (minimally) in a distribution of resources according to need, and that this forms a primary part of their conception of equality. This assumption will be required in the remainder of the book, since the material to be studied refers as often to 'equality' as to 'need'. It is of course important to distinguish equality in the sense used here (the principle that every individual should enjoy an equal level of well-being) from other, weaker senses of the term—such as political equality, equality before the law, or equality of opportunity. But provided this elementary caution is observed, the assumption seems to me to be a perfectly reasonable one.

CONCLUSION

In this first part of the book, I have attempted to separate the common notion of social justice into three elements. Each of the three criteria which have been distinguished—rights, deserts, and needs—forms a part of that notion, and each is irreducible to the others. Although the key terms are sometimes used loosely in ordinary speech, so that the boundaries between the criteria may become blurred, if we focus our attention on the most characteristic uses of each term, we shall see that 'rights', 'deserts', and 'needs' are used to make quite different kinds of moral claim. Even though we must begin from ordinary language, we should not hesitate to impose a more precise use of terms if important distinctions are in danger of being lost.

Besides the distinctiveness of the three criteria of justice, the other main theme of this part of the argument has been the failure of theories which claim to synthesize the conflicting claims of justice into a single principle or consistent set of principles. We have returned several times to utilitarianism, while dealing rather more briefly with the contractual theory of John Rawls. In the case of utilitarianism, I have tried to bring out as clearly as possible the contrast between aggregative and distributive principles, and the reasons why an aggregative principle such as utility cannot accommodate the distributive principles of social justice. The principle of utility is concerned with the over-all amount of happiness enjoyed by the members of a society, and in many circumstances this is an important, or even overriding, political consideration. But we are also concerned to deal justly with each member taken separately, sometimes even at the cost of a net loss in total happiness. The three criteria of justice testify to this concern for the individual, the principle of rights by guaranteeing security of expectation and freedom of choice, the principle of desert by recognizing the distinctive value of each person's actions and qualities, the principle of need by providing the prerequisites for individual

plans of life. Of course, these different ways of showing concern for the individual are likely to conflict with one another;
but over and above this, they stand in common opposition to the
demands of social utility.

In our attempt to clarify the criteria of justice, we found it
impossible to dispel a good deal of the vagueness which surrounds the ordinary concepts of rights, deserts, and needs. The
concept of a right was perhaps the most precise: it proved feasible to define a set of right-creating conditions such that if a
person satisfied any one of them, he would be said to have a
right. The concept of need came next in order of precision:
within certain limits, the question whether a person had a certain need could be settled empirically, although not without
difficulty. Desert was the least precise concept: it proved hard
to decide which of the possible bases of desert should be chosen
for the allocation of any particular good, although in the case of
deserved income an attempt was made to defend a version of
the contribution principle. None of the three criteria, however,
was sufficiently precise for its practical application to be a
straightforward matter. Thus over and above the problem of
choosing between, or balancing off, the criteria, there remains
the problem of showing how any of them could be used as a
practical guide to social policy, a quality obviously to be desired
in a principle of social justice.

Our investigation of the three principles of justice has therefore produced the following conclusions. First, each is a distinct
principle, embodying a particular type of moral claim. Second,
each is (to a different degree) hard to define theoretically, and
therefore hard to implement as a practical notion of social justice. This furnishes the starting-point for the second part of
my inquiry. How would single-minded defenders of each
principle try to justify that principle, and how would they
evade or resolve the difficulties of implementing it? My claim
is that these problems are answered by adopting a view of
society which supports the principle in question at the expense
of its rivals. I shall therefore examine the writings of three
representative thinkers—Hume as an advocate of the principle
of rights, Spencer as an advocate of the principle of desert,
Kropotkin as an advocate of the principle of need. In the case
of each thinker, I shall begin by examining his interpretation of

justice and his attacks on rival interpretations; next I shall outline his general views about how men behave and how societies function; finally I shall attempt to relate interpretation of justice to view of society in such a way that the vindicating role of the social model becomes apparent. We begin our inquiry with Hume.

PART II

V

HUME'S THEORY OF JUSTICE

1 *Hume's Conception of Justice*

Hume's thinking about justice is chiefly to be found in two places, Book iii of the *Treatise of Human Nature* and the *Enquiry Concerning the Principles of Morals*.[1] Between these two works, separated in time by eleven years, there are a number of differences; some slight, others more substantial. I shall assume that, as far as Hume's conception of justice is concerned, these differences are not fundamental, and I shall draw on both sources to describe that conception, except when differences between the works are explicitly pointed out. This follows most interpretations of Hume, including Kemp-Smith's *The Philosophy of David Hume* (London, 1941).

Justice is discussed in the *Treatise* in the context of an inquiry into the nature of virtue. Hume begins *Treatise*, Book iii, by asking 'In what does the distinction between moral good and moral evil consist?', but quickly propounds the view that the objects of moral evaluation are not *actions* but *persons* and their qualities. The distinction between virtue and vice is logically prior to that between right and wrong, and actions are regarded only as signs of the possession of relevant qualities. Justice is taken as a virtue which a man may possess. However, the impact of this initial move is modified when Hume arrives at the detailed discussion of justice, for justice is defined, not as a disposition or an attitude of mind, but as a set of principles governing men's actions. The virtue of justice must consist in acting in conformity to these principles.

Hume asks two questions about justice:

---

[1] References to David Hume's *A Treatise of Human Nature* (hereinafter *Treatise*) are to the edition of A. D. Lindsay (London, 1911), and to Hume's *An Enquiry Concerning the Principles of Morals* (hereinafter *Enquiry*) to that of L. A. Selby-Bigge (Oxford, 1902).

How do men come to adopt the principles of justice which they do?

Why do they consider that justice so established is a virtue?

We should observe that in posing these questions Hume is not *explicitly* or *directly* concerned to provide a justification for the principles of justice he spells out. Perhaps this is a consequence of his general view, that moral distinctions cannot be arrived at by the use of reason, but derive from the feelings of men as they contemplate the words and actions of others. The philosopher, because he appeals only to reason, cannot establish any moral principles as such. Nevertheless, if we accept Hume's account of why it is that men have adopted the principles of justice he describes, we are bound to admit that these principles should be adhered to, if we have any regard for the welfare of our fellows. In that sense, Hume's account is both explanatory and persuasive.

In Hume's eyes, the concept of justice is intimately bound up with that of property. Yet, for reasons we shall examine below, he is unwilling to define justice in terms of property. Hume's definition can be set out as follows: the *rules* of justice are conventions whereby material goods (wealth, land, possessions, etc.) are ascribed to particular individuals; and the *virtue* of justice consists in respecting this ascription, by refraining from appropriating the goods of others, and ensuring that wrongly appropriated goods are returned to their owners.

Now, since when a set of rules of this kind is generally acknowledged, it is correct to say that individuals have rights to their goods, we could define justice as respect for the rights of individuals to their goods; or again (these rights constituting property) as respect for the property of others. These definitions follow from Hume's, and can be considered as equivalent to his. He himself occasionally uses them.[2] But from Hume's point of view they would be misleading. They suggest to the unwary that individuals naturally have rights to material objects, or that property is a natural relationship between a

---

[2] 'It is thus *justice*, or a regard to the property of others, *fidelity*, or the observance of promises, become obligatory, and acquire an authority over mankind.' (D. Hume, 'Of the Original Contract' in *Essays Literary, Moral and Political* (London, n.d.), p. 279.)

man and an object; and that therefore justice can be understood as a moral obligation to respect the *pre-existing* rights of individuals. According to Hume's account, on the other hand, the two ideas, justice and property, are entirely interdependent. Where there are no rules of justice, there is no property, only possession, and individuals have no rights to objects, they only have them in their power. This is a straightforward repudiation of a theory such as Locke's, in which individuals have rights by nature to the things which they appropriate. Hume insists that human convention is the sole origin of justice, rights, and property.

This is also why Hume describes justice as an artificial virtue. He means by this that there is no natural motive to perform acts of justice, as there is for acts of benevolence, such as helping a man who is in pain. For, in the absence of conventional rules of justice, in what would this motive consist? Obviously not in respect for the rights of others, for *ex hypothesi* there are none such. Nor does Hume think that we should be moved by the natural feeling of sympathy to leave people in possession of the goods they held. No doubt this would sometimes be the case, but equally, in other circumstances, sympathy would dictate that goods be given to those who could best make use of them, or to those who had established themselves in our favour.

But although justice is an artificial virtue, and the rules of justice are human conventions, Hume makes it clear that these are not 'mere' conventions. Justice is vital to human society, and no society could afford to lack the conventions in question. For this reason, Hume says,

Though the rules of justice be *artificial*, they are not *arbitrary*. Nor is the expression improper to call them *Laws of Nature*; if by natural we understand what is common to any species, or even if we confine it to mean what is inseparable from the species.[3]

I conclude that we may legitimately speak of justice, in Hume's account, as respect for the rights of others; provided we always remember that an individual's right is an ascription of a good to a person in accordance with a rule of justice.

[3] *Treatise*, vol. ii, p. 190.

2 *The Rules of Justice*

Let me now consider the rules of justice Hume lays down, before going on to look at the relation he establishes between justice and the public interest. A rule of justice, we remember, must link a descriptive statement about an individual to an ascription of a property right. It must, in other words, lay down what an individual must do in order to gain a right over something. In the *Treatise* Hume lists five such rules, followed by a sixth of a rather different kind. His designations for these rules—present possession, occupation, prescription, accession, succession—are confusing, and need clarification. It would really be better to call them *principles* instead of rules,[4] for they are general considerations which may on occasion conflict with one another, and which are given precise embodiment in the rules of civil law.

Hume claims that his first rule of justice—present possession —operates only at the foundation of society. If men were to come together to institute a system of property, their guiding principle would be that each man should be given a property right over those goods which he already possessed. Construed in this way, the application of the principle is severely limited, particularly in view of Hume's critical attitude towards 'contractual' theories of society. He prefers an evolutionary hypothesis in which men come to respect the rules of justice as they increasingly see the advantage of so doing. But, extending Hume in his defence, present possession can also be seen as a residual principle which applies when no one can be sure of other titles to property. If two landowners have lost all record of the original boundary between their properties, they will probably agree to abide by the present division.

It would be absurd, though, to make present possession the sole rule governing property, for this would obliterate the distinction between justice and injustice. The thief, as present possessor of stolen goods, would have a perfect right to them. Hume's second rule, occupation, corrects this. A better name would be 'original possession'. The right to an object resides with the man who possessed it first, provided of course that he has not voluntarily alienated his title.

[4] For the distinction between rules and principles in a legal context, see R. Dworkin, 'Is Law a System of Rules?' in *Essays in Legal Philosophy*.

But original possession may come into conflict with another of Hume's rules—prescription or *long* possession. Hume sees this principle as taking effect when the original title to an object has become obscure. In that case, the person who has possessed it over a long period of time is considered its owner. In legal practice, though, the two rules may clash, as when a man who fences off a piece of his neighbour's ground, and remains sufficiently long in possession, becomes in English law the owner of that land, despite his neighbour's original title. Nor is this without moral justification.

The last two rules of justice are relatively straightforward.

We acquire the property of objects by *accession*, when they are connected in an intimate manner with objects that are already our property, and at the same time are inferior to them. Thus, the fruits of our garden, the offspring of our cattle, and the work of our slaves, are all of them esteemed our property, even before possession.[5]

Hume points out, against Locke and his school, that labour is not the important factor here (my fruit tree may continue to fruit even though I do nothing to it) but simply the relationship of physical proximity between the two objects concerned. By succession, Hume intends the transfer of possessions from parent to child on the grounds of their personal relationship alone—i.e. independently of the expressed will of the parent.

These rules, Hume says, guarantee the stability of property which is absolutely essential to human society. But men also need to adjust their possessions to their individual needs, and so there is instituted 'transference of property by consent'. This presupposes, of course, that people already have established titles to their goods, and hence is dependent upon the first five rules. Various forms of words are evolved to allow people to transfer their property to other hands.

3 *Justice and the Public Interest*

We must now consider the relation of these rules, and of justice in general, to the public interest.[6]

---

[5] *Treatise*, vol. ii, p. 212.
[6] Hume uses 'the public interest' in the *Treatise* and 'utility' in the *Enquiry* with, so far as one can tell, an identical meaning. No doubt this reflects changing intellectual fashions.

Justice, Hume says, is artificial. The rules of property are established because men see that it is to their advantage to have them. Each man, that is to say, sees that it is in his own interest. In general, Hume thinks, men are moved by both self-love and benevolence, neither completely selfish nor completely altruistic. If they were entirely benevolent, there would be no need for justice, for each man would willingly give to his neighbour the things he needed. So Hume rests justice on the sure foundation of self-love.[7] Society with rules of property is better for everybody (even the poorest) than society without.

And even every individual person must find himself a gainer on balancing the account; since, without justice, society must immediately dissolve, and every one must fall into that savage and solitary condition, which is infinitely worse than the worst situation that can possibly be supposed in society.[8]

What is most important is that there should be some rules ensuring the stability of possessions; exactly what form these rules take is less important. Hume puts this point clearly in the *Enquiry*:

We must ever distinguish between the necessity of a separation and constancy in men's possession, and the rules, which assign particular objects to particular persons. The first necessity is obvious, strong, and invincible: the latter may depend on a public utility more light and frivolous, on the sentiment of private humanity and aversion to private hardship, on positive laws, on precedents, analogies, and very fine connexions and turns of the imagination.[9]

He examines in some detail how far the rules he has laid down can be given a utilitarian justification. Most of them, he finds, can be explained both in terms of the public interest and in

---

[7] According to Hume, men adopt rules of justice out of an awareness of their own interests. It is a further question why they come to regard justice as a moral virtue. To answer this, Hume refers to the feeling of sympathy: for instance, my sympathy with the victim of an injustice leads me to regard the perpetrator as morally vicious. But sympathy could not be the original motive for establishing rules of justice; it is too fluctuating and partial a feeling. Cf. D. D. Raphael, 'Hume and Adam Smith on Justice and Utility', *Proceedings of the Aristotelian Society*, lxiii (1972–3).

[8] *Treatise*, vol. ii, p. 202.   [9] p. 310.

terms of the imagination—he means by this the tendency of the human mind to connect together objects which are placed in physical proximity to one another. (This in turn derives from the mind's dissatisfaction with a physical arrangement which is merely contingent. Hume notes that we like to arrange the books in our library in some determinate order. In this case we are creating a real order from objects whose significance is already established—by their titles, subject-matters, etc. In the former case, the order is an invention of the mind, which 'spreads itself on external objects', as Hume says in another context, and superimposes the intelligible relation of property upon mere physical juxtaposition.) For example, the present possession rule can be accounted for on utilitarian grounds: it harms a man more to be deprived of an object which he already possesses than it benefits someone else to be given it. Equally, it can be explained by reference to the imagination: the physical relationship between man and object possessed suggests a more permanent and orderly relationship, namely ownership. Hume sees no need to discover a principal cause here. Over all (especially in the *Enquiry*) he thinks that the general rules of property (the five principles) have a utilitarian foundation, as well as an origin in the imagination, whereas their detailed application in civil law—how long is 'long possession'?—need have none. As before, what is important is that there should be some precise, known rule, so that the order of society is maintained. A direct contrast with Bentham might be drawn here.

Hume's case that justice as a whole is founded on the public interest (rather than having an independent moral status) is made by considering the empirical conditions under which justice is thought to be valuable. In different circumstances—in a hypothetical state of material abundance, for example, or in a famine—the rules of property are abandoned because they no longer contribute to human welfare. Strictly speaking Hume's argument does not prove his case. If justice and the public interest are actually independent values, there may be circumstances in which the public interest is allowed to override justice. When, in a famine, the public open the granaries, without the consent of their owners (Hume's example), they do not wholly cease to respect the claims of ownership, but rather allow these claims to be overridden by considerations of humanity and the public interest. As to the other argument, that in a society of material abundance Humean justice would have no place, since no man would have any reason to keep goods to himself, this is interesting and plausible; but again it does not show that in society as it is, justice has a utilitarian foundation. It proves only that the belief in justice arises from a society of moderate scarcity, not that men have this belief because they see it is in the public interest to have rules of property.

As a matter of fact, Hume doubts whether the majority of people grasp the connection between justice and the public interest. They act justly through habit and education, and this is all that is required of them. In fact, Hume says, 'A single act of justice is frequently contrary to *public interest*'.[10] What does he mean by this?

The kind of case he has in mind is that of an object disputed between two men, one of whom is likely to make good use of it, and the other to squander it to no one's benefit; but the second man has the better title under the rules of property. Justice demands that the object be given to him, and, Hume says, the public interest suffers.

This statement of Hume's needs careful reading. Does he mean that the public interest really demands that the first man be given the good, but that men habitually follow fixed rules which are useful in most cases but not in this? Or does he mean that the public interest in the first man's having the good is only an immediate, short-term interest, while the real interest of the people is to have fixed and stable rules? We could discover the answer to this if we knew what Hume would advise a benevolent man to do in this situation, having to decide which of the two was to be given the object; a difficult point to decide, since Hume, as I mentioned earlier, does not make explicit moral recommendations. But a big clue is given to us in the *Enquiry*, when Hume in passing mentions the case of Cyrus. Cyrus, in Xenophon's account, was called on during his schooling to adjudicate the case of a tall boy with a short coat who had forcibly exchanged coats with a small boy in a coat too long for him. Cyrus decided to leave things as they now

---

[10] *Treatise*, vol. ii, p. 201.

were, since each boy had a coat that fitted him. But his teacher punished him for taking this decision. Here is Hume's comment on the affair:

Cyrus, young and unexperienced, considered only the individual case before him, and reflected on a limited fitness and convenience, when he assigned the long coat to the tall boy, and the short coat to the other of smaller size. His governor instructed him better, while he pointed out more enlarged views and consequences, and informed his pupil of the general, inflexible rules, necessary to support general peace and order in society.[11]

Hume obviously considers the teacher's position right and Cyrus' wrong. If this is his view, his arguments need filling out, perhaps in the following way. The benefits of a system of justice accrue only when the rules of property are absolutely inflexible. Even if, on a particular occasion, they are broken on grounds of benevolence, this weakens their hold over the opinions of others, and encourages further breaches. We cannot be sure that such future breaches will also be made with benevolent intentions, for this would be to postulate general benevolence on the part of humanity, and if *this* held true, justice would not be needed at all. The point of having rules of justice is to restrain immediate love of gain for a benefit which is long term, and to achieve this the rules must be uniformly enforced.[12]

Hence Hume's assertion 'a single act of justice is frequently contrary to public interest' must not be read literally. The point of this remark, and others like it, is to emphasize the contrast between obligations of justice and feelings of sympathy, and so to bear out Hume's central thesis, that justice is an artificial virtue. Given the context of his writing, this was an important thesis to establish, but one cost was the confusion he has created for subsequent readers about justice and the public interest.

4 *Hume's Conception of Justice and the Alternatives*

Hume's conception of justice surprises modern readers by its narrowness. He equates justice with respect for the rights of

[11] *Enquiry*, pp. 304–5.
[12] A similar reading of Hume is found in Broad's *Five Types of Ethical Theory* (London, 1930), p. 94.

others as established by conventional rules, and refuses to discuss the question whether these rules themselves, and the resulting distribution of rights, are just. For him the question makes no sense. Since Hume has admitted that the main rules of justice are adopted in part for their utility, he ought, for consistency's sake, to allow that utilitarian reasons may be offered for changing them; (though as Plamenatz remarks, Hume in fact took it for granted that the rules would never change). But there is no hint of a broader concept of justice in Hume.

Hume's contemporaries would have found this less surprising than we do.[13] The modern use of ideal standards of social justice to recommend the wholesale transformation of society dates largely from a more recent period. However, traditional discussions of justice as an individual virtue, such as Aristotle's, had included reference to the ideas of merit and equality. It is therefore still a problem why Hume omits these broader principles of justice from his analysis of justice as a virtue. In fact, he does in various places reveal his attitude towards desert and equality as possible criteria of distribution, and we can learn a good deal about the justification of his own position from his opinions on this subject.

Curiously, Hume takes distribution according to desert as an example of how sympathy and justice can come into conflict. Suppose I have to decide whether a set of possessions belongs to a beneficent man or a selfish miser. My 'natural feelings' for the merit of the former prompt me to award the goods to him; but if I am to abide by the principles of justice, I must ignore all questions of character and personal circumstance, and consider only their respective titles to the goods under the established rules. Hume, however, elsewhere acknowledges the moral claim of the desert criterion:

---

[13] Although one of them, Thomas Reid, attacked Hume for the narrowness of his concept of justice. Reid's own view was that justice consisted in respect for certain natural rights—life, liberty, etc.—and Hume was faulted for his exclusive concentration on property. The implication of Reid's position is that some weight must be given to considerations of need, as well as to established rights, in making judgements of justice; but Reid does not pay any attention to desert in this context, nor does he consider equality as a principle of justice except in situations (such as famine) where equality is necessary to protect everyone's right to live. See T. Reid, *Essays on the Active Powers of the Human Mind*, ed. B. A. Brody (Cambridge and London, 1969), Essay v, ch. 5. (I am grateful to Professor Raphael for drawing my attention to Reid.)

We shall suppose that a creature, possessed of reason, but un-
acquainted with human nature, deliberates with himself what rules
of justice or property would best promote public interest, and
establish peace and security among mankind: His most obvious
thought would be, to assign the largest possessions to the most
extensive virtue, and give every one the power of doing good,
proportioned to his inclination. In a perfect theocracy, where a
being, infinitely intelligent, governs by particular volitions, this rule
would certainly have place, and might serve to the wisest purposes:
But were mankind to execute such a law; so great is the uncertainty
of merit, both from its natural obscurity, and from the self-conceit
of each individual, that no determinate rule of conduct would ever
result from it; and the total dissolution of society must be the
immediate consequence.[14]

In short, then, Hume's attitude towards distribution according
to desert is this: both natural sympathy and abstract reason
suggest that material goods should be apportioned to deserts,
as an ideal. But practical experience confirms that this would
be wholly unworkable, and would destroy the stability of
property which Hume thinks is so important. There could
never be agreement among men on a standard of merit, or on a
method of applying such a standard in a particular case, and
so a rule based on merit could not be implemented impartially.

It is of course true to say that Hume does not give the desert
principle a fair hearing. By interpreting merit as 'virtue' in
this passage, he overlooks the possibility of a more down-to-
earth criterion of merit, such as the quantity of goods a man
produces. What is chiefly of interest, though, is the kind of
reason Hume gives for rejecting the principle—one that
stresses certainty and stability of possessions. I shall return to
this later.

Hume also recognizes the moral justification for an egalitarian distribution, albeit as an instrument of utility:

It must also be confessed, that, wherever we depart from this
equality [of goods], we rob the poor of more satisfaction than we
add to the rich, and that the slight gratification of a frivolous vanity,
in one individual, frequently costs more than bread to many
families, and even provinces.[15]

---

[14] *Enquiry*, pp. 192–3.　　[15] *Enquiry*, p. 194.

Despite this, Hume is resolutely opposed to equality in practice, which he regards as a false hope. He considers two forms of egalitarian society:

(1) A society without property. Hume discusses this in order to prove that justice entirely derives from the public interest. He maintains that such a society would be the natural consequence if either of two conditions were fulfilled.

(a) An abundance of goods relative to human wants ('For what purpose make a partition of goods, where every one has already more than enough?')

(b) Unlimited generosity on the part of men, so that goods are freely given to those who need them ('Why raise landmarks between my neighbour's field and mine, when my heart has made no division between our interests?')

Hume cannot envisage either of these conditions being satisfied. As production of material goods expands and diversifies, new tastes are acquired—tastes for luxuries take their place alongside basic needs for food and clothing—and so there are always more wants than there are goods to satisfy them. And as to unlimited generosity, Hume thinks that this may be approached in certain small groups, particularly in the family and among intimate friends, but whenever it has been tested (by 'imprudent fanatics') in communal experiments, human selfishness has always ensured the failure of the schemes. So here we find two fairly straightforward 'human nature' claims being used against equality. The known characteristics of human beings (expanding desires, limited generosity) prevent the working of what would otherwise be the best arrangement, namely goods held in common and distributed according to need.

(2) Hume also considers briefly an alternative egalitarian system, one which retains private property, but distributes it equally. In this case, he argues, it will be impossible to prevent inequalities re-emerging, because men's unequal capacities and talents will allow some to acquire wealth at the expense of others. If this is prevented by a continued enforcement of equality, the incentive to work will be lost, and society reduced to extreme indigence.

These arguments against equality are not to be found in the *Treatise* (although some of the same points are there made in Hume's discussion of the origin of justice). We may suppose that in the years between the composition of the *Treatise* (1732–6) and the production of the *Enquiry* (1751) Hume became further acquainted with the views of egalitarians and felt it necessary to combat them, by confronting the moral claim of equality with what he took to be the evident facts of human life. This supposition is given partial confirmation by the fact that Hume, while he was working on the *Enquiry*, was also collecting material for his *History of England*.[16] The first two volumes of the *History* to appear (in 1754) covered the Stuart period, and included brief mention of the Levellers, who, Hume asserts, 'insisted on an equal distribution of power and property, and disclaimed all dependence and subordination'.[17] Hume plainly abhorred the propagation of such ideas, and comments:

Every man had framed the model of a republic; and, however new it was, or fantastical, he was eager in recommending it to his fellow citizens, or even imposing it by force upon them.[18]

He refers to the Levellers again in the *Enquiry*, calling them 'a kind of *political* fanatics, which arose from the religious species', but he obviously considered their ideas to be sufficiently dangerous to warrant an open rebuttal in the paragraphs which followed.

5 Hume's Model of Society

We have now established Hume's theory of justice and his arguments against rival theories. But to bring out the full significance of this theory and these arguments, we need to set them in the context of his assumptions about human nature, and his model of the social order. Too often, I think, Hume has been interpreted in relation to later utilitarians—to Bentham especially. From the point of view of these writers, Hume's

[16] See E. C. Mossner, *The Life of David Hume* (London, 1954), pp. 232–3.
[17] D. Hume, *The History of England* (Oxford, 1826), vol. vii, pp. 136–7.
[18] Ibid., p. 136.

influence is clear and important,[19] and the relationship justifiably stressed by historians of political philosophy. On the other hand, this has often meant reading back into Hume assumptions which do not really belong there.

In an obvious sense, Hume's moral philosophy was utilitarian. He justified the existence of rules of justice in terms of their utility, and refused to see justice as an independent moral value; though even here we must go carefully, for he plainly did not think that the *sense* of justice could be explained in utilitarian terms, or that the utilitarian ground of the rules was necessarily apparent to those who followed them. Hume also shared certain assumptions historically connected with utilitarianism, such as the analysis of motivation in terms of pain and pleasure (though Hume was not a psychological egoist), and the belief in an economic policy of free trade. These similarities have led some commentators to attribute to Hume the full utilitarian 'picture' of society, of separate individuals pursuing their calculated ends in competition with one another, held together only by bonds of mutual interest. They have then seen his distinctiveness in his political conservatism—in his unwillingness to countenance political disobedience, his opposition to legal reform, etc.—in contrast to the radicalism of Bentham and Mill. Stewart's usually sound reading of Hume lays much stress on the role of competition in his social thought. The rules of justice, Stewart thinks, are intended to convert destructive competition into advantageous competition.[20] In a similar vein, Plamenatz writes:

[Hume] saw society, not as a refuge from terror, but as a kind of market for the more efficient satisfaction of wants . . . His was already the Godless and sinless and calculating world of the Utilitarians and economists, where the great business of life is to get as much comfort as possible at the cost of the least inconvenience.[21]

---

[19] We remember Bentham's comment on the *Treatise*: 'For my own part, I well remember, no sooner had I read that part of the work which touches on this subject [the origin of government], than I felt as if scales had fallen from my eyes. I then, for the first time, learnt to call the cause of the people the cause of Virtue.' *Fragment on Government*, in *Fragment on Government and an Introduction to the Principles of Morals and Legislation*, p. 50.

[20] J. B. Stewart, *The Moral and Political Philosophy of David Hume* (New York and London, 1963).

[21] *Man and Society* (London, 1963), vol. i, pp. 324–5.

This seems to miss the real tenor of Hume's thought. What needs to be done is to assemble the countervailing evidence, which suggests quite a different conception of society and man from the utilitarian stereotype.

It is worth remarking at the outset that Hume was not a political economist. He produced a social theory purporting to explain the basis of social organization, and more particularly of the rules which men felt obliged to follow. He wrote about politics, about the justification of political obedience, and, in a different vein, about the workings of party politics. He also composed a number of essays on economics, where he was concerned to point out certain misapprehensions concerning, for example, the role of money in the economy, and to make recommendations for economic policy. But these three activities were kept separate from one another. If one considers the various essays which Hume wrote during the course of his life, it is easy enough to arrange them into the different categories. There is no systematic attempt to analyse society in terms of its economic constituents, and little attention is paid to the fundamental concepts of political economy: value, division of labour, capital, rent, etc. It is worth remembering that the writings of the political economists (Adam Smith's *The Wealth of Nations* was published in the year of Hume's death) were intended as much more than an explanation of how the economy worked; indeed the abstraction implied in this phrase, that 'the economy' can be studied as an entity in itself, was foreign to their thought. Political economy showed why men associated into societies, why they adopted the rules they did, why they established governments and legal systems. The omission of a political economy from Hume's work is not accidental; it indicates that his own thoughts on these questions moved in different paths from those of the utilitarian economists.

Let us pose the question: is man, in Hume's view, naturally fitted for society? This question, to begin with, suffers from the ambiguity of the term 'nature' which Hume dissects with much precision.[22] Taking the term in Hume's third sense (where it is contrasted with what is 'artificial') his answer appears to be this: if a man could be conceived as existing

[22] See *Treatise*, vol. ii, pp. 181–3.

outside of society, his every instinct would be to establish or enter a social order; in that sense he is naturally a 'social animal'. But at the same time his passions disqualify him for society. There is no question of men's natural urges combining harmoniously to yield social order, as there is, say, in Smith. With reference to one of these passions, Bonar comments:

Unlike Adam Smith, Hume by no means regarded the desire of wealth as a force which shaped society in any good sense. It is rather a disintegrating influence which needs to be counteracted.[23]

In Hume's view society can only be maintained by an artificial constraining of natural passions. In this respect he stands with Hobbes, and not with the optimistic utilitarians. The similarities and differences between the two are worth pursuing.

Hume repeatedly states his opinion that men are not the rapacious egoists depicted by Hobbes. They are moved to consider the interests of others as well as their own—indeed, 'It is rare to meet with one in whom all the kind affections, taken together, do not overbalance all the selfish.' But this is of little help in establishing social order, since men's natural affections are afflicted by *partiality*—i.e. a tendency to prefer the good of one's family, friends, immediate neighbours to that of more distant persons. This tendency makes society quite as impossible for Hume as rampant egoism does for Hobbes.

For both Hobbes and Hume, the escape from a hypothetical asocial condition is made possible by *reason*, which discovers a set of rules whose observance creates a social order. Reason does not oppose the natural passions, in the sense of recommending goals which run counter to those naturally desired, but only suggests ways in which the passions can be more fruitfully satisfied. Instead of immediate gain, followed by equally swift loss, stability of property is indicated, and so forth. But reason is weak; men are more likely to pursue their strong natural desires than to listen to its dictates; and so a more immediate motive to perform the reasonable action is required.

In Hobbes, we know, this motive is fear—fear of the sovereign. Hume is less pessimistic than Hobbes. He concedes that a simple social order may exist without government, provided

[23] J. Bonar, *Philosophy and Political Economy* (London, 1968), p. 116.

the social group remains small, so that the consequences of each individual's action can be seen by him. But in a larger society, where an unjust, partial action on my part brings about no visible disadvantages, the problem recurs; what can supplement the feeble voice of reason and hold men to their obligations, without which society will dissolve?

Hume's answer is that three separate causes work together to this end: government and law, custom and habit, and the love of reputation. He is emphatic that government by itself cannot maintain the system of moral rules. It may coerce a few individuals, but must itself rest on the opinion of the majority. Thus habit and custom must bear a good deal of the weight in Hume's theory. Most just and virtuous acts are performed unreflectively, with no perception of their contribution to the public interest, but simply because the individual has become used to doing acts of this kind. Even if his interest lies elsewhere, he will feel, strongly, that he 'somehow ought' to do such-and-such an action. This habit is inculcated in him by his parents, and strengthened by the effects of education. Hume also admits that the 'artifices of politicians' may contribute to the same end, though for obvious reasons he is unwilling to go as far as Mandeville and say that politicians produce the moral distinctions themselves. We could sum up Hume's view in the ugly modern word 'socialization'. Without socialization from childhood, moral rules would not be followed.

Hume's men are also sensitive to the judgements of others. His society is one in which honour plays an important part (more of this later). Thus fear for our reputation and love of respect supply an additional motive to perform virtuous acts in opposition to our immediate interests.

I have excluded here any mention of the very force which gives actions their moral character—sympathy in the *Treatise*, 'sentiment of humanity' in the *Enquiry*. These are essential components of Hume's system of thought. If we did not possess these feelings, we would be unable to make moral judgements at all. But, on the other hand, if they were powerful, determining influences on conduct, the whole system of 'artificial virtues' would be unnecessary. Hume's scheme is sufficiently complex to accommodate virtuous action done for its own sake—out of sympathy for the suffering of others, or out of an understanding of the connection between justice and the public interest, coupled with a disinterested regard for the public interest. Hume admires the men who are capable of such actions; but he has too little confidence in the majority of men to believe that these motives are sufficient in themselves; hence the crucial role given to the factors listed above.

It follows that in Hume's eyes the social fabric has a rather delicate character. The habit of acting according to moral rules must be built up gradually, and so stability is a cardinal virtue of societies. Although he maintains that the state of nature is a 'philosophical fiction', he is not reluctant to use it as a dreadful warning of what may happen if the rules of property are not strictly respected:

> . . . it is impossible for men to consult their interest in so effectual a manner, as by an universal and inflexible observance of the rules of justice, by which alone they can preserve society, and keep themselves from falling into that wretched and savage condition which is commonly represented as the *state of nature*.[24]

If men's desire to follow these rules were based on reason-directed self-interest, or on regard for the public interest, a single breach would not disturb their attitudes. But because they are mainly governed by custom, it is essential that the custom be preserved and enforced. 'We are afraid to put men to live and trade each on his own private stock of reason'—the statement is Burke's, but the sentiment might equally well be Hume's.[25]

Plamenatz justly remarks on the oddness of Hume's assertion:

> That there be a separation or distinction of possessions, and that this separation be steady and constant; this is absolutely required by the interests of society, and hence the origin of justice and property. What possessions are assigned to particular persons; this is, generally speaking, pretty indifferent; and is often determined by very frivolous views and considerations.[26]

---

[24] *Treatise*, vol. ii, p. 235.

[25] Acton has brought out the resemblance between Hume's and Burke's attacks on abstract reason in the name of 'custom' (Hume) and 'prejudice' (Burke). Hume criticizes those who seek to create 'perfection' in man when this involves the destruction of useful 'byasses and instincts' which govern human conduct. See H. B. Acton, 'Prejudice', *Revue internationale de philosophie*, vi (1952).

[26] *Enquiry*, p. 309.

We can perhaps now come closer to understanding Hume's reasons for asserting such a paradox. Hume is convinced that any attempt to assign possessions to individuals on the grounds of merit or suitability will quickly call in question the whole system of property, and hence threaten the stability of society. The same would apply to general principles of distribution which seek to alter existing titles to property, such as the principle of desert. These principles would undermine the hold of custom over men's behaviour. Once the notion that the present distribution of property is not sacrosanct is abroad, it will be impossible to restrain the natural impulses of greed. We must always remember that:

This avidity alone, of acquiring goods and possessions for ourselves and our nearest friends, is insatiable, perpetual, universal, and directly destructive of society. [27]

I wish to argue that Hume's underlying pessimism, expressed with uncharacteristic vehemence in this sentence, coupled with the central role assigned to custom and habit in rendering men fit for civilization, provides the main support for his theory of justice. The arguments against the alternative conceptions (meritorian and egalitarian) fall into place against this general background. Justice as respect for established rights, without regard to how those rights are distributed among persons, is intelligible when it is seen as the principle which restrains men from destructive greed. If men are governed more by custom than by reason, then the less the customary distribution of rights is disturbed, the better. This is the central connection. There is, however, more to be said about Hume's conception of society which reinforces my case.

Hume's image of society is not a competitive one. I can find no evidence that he discusses competition at all. It is true that he favours industry and commerce, claiming that a commercial society offers its members a higher standard of living than an agricultural one, but commerce and competition are hardly the same, even if historically they have come to be associated. Contrary to all this, the society which Hume portrays is a hierarchical one, divided into ranks, and he displays no

[27] *Treatise*, vol. ii, p. 197.

enthusiasm for the idea that a man should seek to better hin.self in the eyes of the world, and surpass his rivals:

It is necessary, therefore, to know our rank and station in the world, whether it be fixed by our birth, fortune, employments, talents, or reputation.[28]

As this quotation shows, the hierarchy is not a rigid one—the man of personal ability may try to gain a high place in society— but neither does Hume dispute the claims of birth to such position. He has no sympathy for the meritocratic notion that a man's position in society should depend solely upon his individual merits—the idea of the career open to talents. It is better to cultivate the qualities which are appropriate to your present social position, than to seek for a better one on the basis of natural ability:

He will always be more esteemed, who possesses those talents and accomplishments, which suit his station and profession, than he whom fortune has misplaced in the part which she has assigned him.[29]

In short, Hume was satisfied with the graded society of his day, and counselled his readers to adapt themselves to their rank, showing due (though not excessive) deference to those above them and due (though not excessive) superiority to those below. Willey, who notes Hume's love of order and his content- ment with existing society, attributes it largely to the fact that England (unlike France, for example) had already had its religious reformation and its bourgeois revolution.[30] It is not entirely clear what he intends by the second half of this claim, but presumably he has in mind such things as the thorough demolition of feudalism, the establishment of parliamentary government, and the guaranteeing of many individual rights. Socially and politically, however, the aristocracy was still predominant. Hume's ideal is in no sense a bourgeois one, if by that is meant a society dominated by self-made entrepre- neurs, where wealth and power come as a result of a competi- tive struggle between men initially in a position of equality.

---

[28] *Treatise*, vol. ii, p. 293.
[29] *Enquiry*, pp. 241–2.
[30] B. Willey, *The Eighteenth Century Background* (London, 1940), ch. 8.

A further strand can be added to this argument if we examine the ideals of individual behaviour which Hume advocated. In both *Treatise* and *Enquiry* he discusses at length the personal virtues. Leaving aside the major ones, justice and benevolence, which we have already considered, Hume endorses such virtues as: good manners, constancy in friendship, dignity of character, self-esteem, courage, politeness, wit, eloquence, decorum, 'a certain je ne sais quoi'. These, of course, are the qualities ordinarily admired in polite society in the eighteenth century. Hume also mentions industry and frugality, but the balance of his discussion leaves him much closer to the aristocratic Shaftesbury's idea of the 'virtuoso'—cultivated, disinterestedly virtuous, attractive to society—than to the 'bourgeois man' of Benjamin Franklin. To develop this a little: although Hume speaks of virtues as being admired for their utility, he does not mean by this their usefulness in a material sense but, very often, the pleasure they give to the possessor or to others around him; a position which Shaftesbury also held. On the other side, if we compare Hume's catalogue of virtues to the thirteen listed in Franklin's *Autobiography*, two salient facts emerge. First, Franklin lays great stress on the two virtues of industry and thrift—less perhaps in the *Autobiography* than in *The Way to Wealth*, a collection of sayings from *Poor Richard's Almanack*, published as a Preface in 1758.[31] There industry and thrift are represented as the basis upon which all other virtues depend. In Hume they are simply two among many. Second, there are two items which appear as virtues in Franklin's list, but as vices in Hume's. These are silence and humility. Hume comments:

Celibacy, fasting, penance, mortification, self-denial, humility, silence, solitude, and the whole train of monkish virtues; for what reason are they everywhere rejected by men of sense, but because they serve to no manner of purpose; neither advance a man's fortune in the world, nor render him a more valuable member of society; neither qualify him for the entertainment of company, nor increase his power of self-enjoyment? . . . We justly, therefore, transfer them to the opposite column, and place them in the catalogue of vices.[32]

[31] B. Franklin, *Autobiography*, ed. W. MacDonald (London, 1948); *The Way to Wealth* (London, n.d.).   [32] *Enquiry*, p. 270.

I think that this disagreement on silence and humility epito-
mizes the difference between Hume and his contemporary
Franklin, who has been taken by others as one of the prime
exemplars of the 'bourgeois ethic' or the 'spirit of capitalism'.[33]
Hume's educated men in the higher reaches of society are
expected to entertain with their wit and eloquence, and should
possess a proper measure of self-esteem. Franklin's are working
men—artisans or small traders. Their speech is utilitarian.
'Speak not but what may benefit others or yourself: avoid
trifling conversation,' Franklin tells them. They are to comport
themselves without pride.

We can now attempt a summary of the argument. We began
by seeing that Hume clearly espouses a conservative conception
of justice—of justice as respect for the established rights of
others—and attacks the two alternative conceptions. This, I
argued, could be understood only in the wider context of
Hume's thinking about society, and to achieve this understanding it was necessary to rid ourselves of the 'utilitarian'
interpretation of Hume. Hume held a utilitarian moral
philosophy, but did not see society as the utilitarian economists
did, as the interplay of competitive, egoistic individuals, held
together by bonds of mutual interest. To bring out the contrast in its strongest form compare the following two statements, one by Hume, the other by the utilitarian economist
McCulloch:

This avidity alone, of acquiring goods and possessions for ourselves
and our nearest friends, is insatiable, perpetual, universal, and
directly destructive of society.[34]

Since society is nothing more than an *aggregate collection of individuals*
it is plain that each in steadily pursuing his own aggrandizement
is following that precise line of conduct which is most for the public
advantage.[35]

---

[33] Most notoriously in Max Weber's *The Protestant Ethic and The Spirit of Capitalism*
(London, 1930). See also Maria Ossowska, *The Social Determinants of Moral Ideas*
(London, 1971).
[34] *Treatise*, vol. ii, p. 197.
[35] J. R. McCulloch, *Principles of Political Economy*, cited in E. Halévy, *The
Growth of Philosophic Radicalism* (London, 1972), pp. 500–1.

Hume (a) was very conscious of the need for habit and custom to supply a restraint on the destructive passions; (b) saw and approved a society in which traditional status was more important than individual merit; (c) took as his ideal the eighteenth-century aristocratic virtues, and not the 'bourgeois' ones. Given these views, is it not entirely comprehensible that he should have rejected the criteria of merit and equality as principles of justice, and restricted his notion to that of rights? Or, inverting the question, to defend such a position is it not necessary to view man and society somewhat in the manner that Hume did? Can one resist the moral claims of merit and need unless one takes Hume's pessimistic view about the need for established order, for unchanging rules of property?

VI

SPENCER'S THEORY OF JUSTICE

1 *Spencer's Moral Philosophy*

To gain a proper understanding of Spencer's theory of social justice, we must begin by looking briefly at three general aspects of his moral philosophy: the distinction which he draws between Absolute and Relative ethics, his attitude towards utilitarianism, and the ethical implications of his theory of evolution. We saw in Hume how a moral philosophy which was formally utilitarian could rest on assumptions which were quite different from those generally held by the utilitarian school. In Spencer, too, a formal commitment to the principle of utility might conceal from us the real nature of his moral and social thought. I shall attempt in this section to remove any misapprehensions by examining the relationship between Spencer and the classical utilitarians.

Spencer understood the distinction between Absolute and Relative ethics thus: Absolute ethics is the study of those moral principles which should be adopted and followed in ideal circumstances; that is to say, in a society which is constituted as it should be. Relative ethics is the study of those principles which should be followed in existing society, taking account of its imperfections. The need for a system of Relative ethics is fairly clear, since the consequences of acting on ideal principles in an imperfect society might be disastrous. Spencer, however, argues that Absolute ethics is the proper subject-matter for scientific (or philosophical) study. His books on ethics contain a system of Absolute ethics, a set of principles for a perfect society. His attitude towards Relative ethics is not entirely clear. In his first work, *Social Statics*, he appears to dismiss it out of hand:

. . . it will very likely be urged that, whereas the perfect moral code is confessedly beyond the fulfilment of imperfect men, some other code is needful for our present guidance. . . . To say that the imperfect man requires a moral code which recognises his imperfection and allows for it, seems at first sight reasonable. But it is not really so . . . a system of morals which shall recognise man's present imperfections and allow for them, cannot be devised; and would be useless if it could be devised.[1]

In the work which forms his major discussion of ethical questions, *The Principles of Ethics*, Spencer is prepared to recognize the importance of Relative ethics, but continues to insist on the priority of Absolute ethics. The analogies which he employs suggest that in his eyes only Absolute ethics can be studied as a pure science, while Relative ethics is related, as it were, to the position of moral technology—an approximate application of the principles of Absolute ethics. For instance, he compares Absolute ethics to a science of ballistics which studies the motion of projectiles through a vacuum, while Relative ethics is analogous to practical gunnery, which must take account of the effects of air resistance and other disturbing factors.[2]

Spencer's views about Absolute ethics help to explain his attitude towards utilitarianism. He dissociated himself from the main utilitarian school, as represented by Bentham, the Mills, and Sidgwick, yet claimed still to hold the greatest happiness of the greatest number as the supreme moral end. The difference, as he saw it, lay in three main points.

First, Spencer labelled his system 'rational utilitarianism' as opposed to the 'empirical utilitarianism' which had hitherto been espoused. Clearly, to make utilitarianism into a practical philosophy, it is necessary to find out in what ways and by what methods the general happiness may be advanced. Spencer claimed that his predecessors had done this in a thoroughly pragmatic way, establishing generalizations on the basis of observed correlations between events, and using such generalizations to guide future actions. In other words, their utilitarianism had been filled out by an inductive social

[1] *Social Statics* (London, 1851), pp. 463–5.
[2] The contrast between Absolute and Relative ethics became the subject of several exchanges between Spencer and Sidgwick. Sidgwick believed that the basic task of the moralist was to establish what the individual ought to do here and now, without reference to hypothetical perfect societies. See H. Sidgwick, *The Methods of Ethics*, Book i, ch. 2, and Book iv, ch. 4 section 2.

science. Spencer's utilitarianism, on the other hand, was filled out by a deductive system of science, which began with the fundamental laws of the universe, holding true of all objects, natural and social (the most important were the laws of evolution). The practical rules through which the general happiness would be achieved were asserted as corollaries of these fundamental laws:

. . . Morality properly so-called—the science of right conduct—has for its object to determine *how* and *why* certain modes of conduct are detrimental, and certain other modes beneficial. These good and bad results cannot be accidental, but must be necessary consequences of the constitution of things; and I conceive it to be the business of Moral Science to deduce, from the laws of life and the conditions of existence, what kinds of action necessarily tend to produce happiness, and what kinds to produce unhappiness. Having done this, its deductions are to be recognized as laws of conduct; and are to be conformed to irrespective of a direct estimation of happiness or misery.[3]

Spencer's distinction between 'rational' and 'empirical' utilitarianism follows directly from the prior distinction between Absolute and Relative ethics. His utilitarianism consists of a set of principles for use in a perfect society. These principles are derived, not from empirically observed human behaviour, but from human behaviour as the laws of nature tell us it should be.

Second, Spencer accused other utilitarians of making the general happiness the direct object of pursuit, of demanding that people should act with perfect altruism on all occasions. In his eyes, the general happiness could only be attained indirectly, mainly through egoistic action regulated by his principles of justice. It should be stressed that Spencer's attack is highly misleading, since the utilitarians both recognized the beneficial consequences of egoism, particularly in economic life, and acknowledged the need for secondary principles to serve as practical guides to action. J. S. Mill and Sidgwick, in particular, carefully examined the relation between the ultimate moral end—the general happiness—and secondary moral principles, especially principles of justice. It is never-

---

[3] From a letter to J. S. Mill, cited in *The Principles of Ethics* (London, 1893), vol. i, p. 57.

theless true that the position which Spencer maintained here is different from that envisaged by Mill and Sidgwick. For Spencer thought it was *never* appropriate to appeal to the principle of utility in a situation of dilemma; he thought that the secondary principles were entirely adequate by themselves. Mill and Sidgwick thought that often there was no need to look beyond the secondary principles, but that sometimes these principles were ambiguous, or gave no guidance at all, and here it was appropriate to consult utility directly. This difference forces us to ask whether Spencer was a utilitarian in any real sense at all. I think it is better to see him as a thinker whose attachment to intuited moral principles was backed up by a quasi-scientific appeal to 'the laws of life', and the whole system capped by the assumption that the general happiness must necessarily be promoted thereby. The principle of utility could be left out of the argument, and replaced by some other ultimate end—by the will of God, for example, as it was in *Social Statics*—without altering the details of the system at all.

The third failing which Spencer found in traditional utilitarianism was its apparent egalitarianism. He argued that Bentham and J. S. Mill, to make their general happiness principle workable, needed to add the assumption that 'everyone was to count for one, and no one for more than one' or that 'everyone had an equal right to happiness'. This assumption is in fact contained in the utility principle itself, but Spencer regarded it as an additional intuited principle with dangerously egalitarian implications. I believe he saw the matter somewhat as follows. Suppose you are authorized to distribute certain resources which serve as means to happiness. There are a number of possible recipients, each having an equal claim to be considered. It is an empirical matter which distribution will create the greatest sum total of happiness. This will depend on the needs, capacities, etc., of the various individuals. It will *not* depend on their past conduct as such.

Spencer abhorred this moral outlook. He saw it as the outlook of utilitarian legislators and officials, who attempted to alter the 'natural' distribution of benefits by appealing to the considerations I have outlined—in practice, generally speaking, redistributing in favour of the most needy. For in Spencer's eyes there is no question of a quantity of happiness, or means

to happiness, to be distributed on the basis of empirical calculation. Each benefit is already earmarked for a particular individual, on the basis of his past actions, in accordance with the
fundamental laws of nature. In a concrete situation, therefore,
individuals do not have 'equal rights to happiness'—they have
different rights to different amounts of benefit. In short, the
talk about 'equal rights to happiness', combined with direct
appeals to the principle of utility, encouraged a certain way
of construing utilitarianism, which supported intervention in
the economic workings of society to increase over-all happiness
—a kind of 'managerial utilitarianism', one might say. Spencer
insisted, we remember, that the 'laws of conduct' were to be
'conformed to irrespective of a direct estimation of happiness
or misery'.

We can now see that all of Spencer's differences with
utilitarianism were as much political as philosophical in origin.
He feared that the traditional version of that doctrine could
be shifted in a collectivist or interventionist direction through a
change in empirical beliefs about society. He wished to set out
a form of 'utilitarianism' which was necessarily tied to a rigid
set of rules of conduct, especially to the economic principles of
laissez-faire. Now this conclusion may seem surprising in the
light of Spencer's commitment to the evolutionary hypothesis.
Spencer and the other evolutionary thinkers, through their
awareness of historical change and social variety, were widely
believed to have escaped from the utilitarian straitjacket, with
its abstract individuals and its universal laws of social life.
Spencer believed this too. He attacked the utilitarians for
failing to see that what constitutes happiness varies from one
society to the next, and therefore that the rules which serve to
promote happiness must be specified in relation to each society.
The same is true of social institutions: we should not judge the
institutions of the past in terms of their value for present society:

When there has been adequately seized the truth that societies are
products of evolution, assuming, in their various times and places,
their various modifications of structure, and function; there follows
the conviction that what, relatively to our thoughts and sentiments,
were arrangements of extreme badness, had fitnesses to conditions
which made better arrangements impracticable.[4]

[4] *The Study of Sociology*, intro. T. Parsons (Ann Arbor, 1961), p. 364.

And thus, as Burrow puts it, Spencer 'was supposed to have superseded the old, narrow utilitarianism by calling in the aid of comparative documentation and the theory of evolution'.[5]

How can these views be squared with those previously discussed? The answer lies in Spencer's concept of evolution.[6] Evolution is not merely change, not merely a succession of societies embodying different institutions and standards of value, it is progress towards a definite end, which can be shown to have the highest value. The end is static, and its character can be ascertained scientifically. Thus there is a bifurcation in Spencer's moral thinking. On the one hand, the moral principles appropriate to fully evolved society (i.e. Absolute ethics) can be determined by rigorous deduction, are fixed and unchanging. On the other hand, the many less developed social forms exhibit a great variety of moral systems, and must be understood in their diversity, not reduced to a single utilitarian standard. As we shall see, fully evolved society meant for Spencer a purified form of the market society which had developed in nineteenth-century England, with various remnants of earlier ('militant') society removed.

So curiously enough, Spencer's attempt to 'historicize' utilitarianism by taking full account of the facts of social change ends by reinstating the free market economy as the natural social order, seen now as the end-product of a long process of evolution. His ethical theory is entirely directed towards this ideal form of society, and its central concept is justice.

2 *Spencer's Conception of Justice*

Spencer divided up his treatment of the ethics of social life into three components: 'Justice', 'Negative Beneficence', and 'Positive Beneficence'. I think it is fair to say that he sees justice as the essential framework which makes life in modern societies possible at all, while the two kinds of beneficence are adornments, which make it somewhat more pleasant and gracious. Justice is plainly the most important moral principle, in practical terms, for Spencer.

[5] J. W. Burrow, *Evolution and Society* (Cambridge, 1970), p. 180.
[6] There is no space here for a full discussion of Spencer's doctrine of evolution, which has recently been treated admirably by J. W. Burrow (op. cit.) and by J. D. Y. Peel in *Herbert Spencer: the evolution of a sociologist* (London, 1971).

The fundamental principle of justice Spencer expresses simply as: 'each individual ought to receive the benefits and the evils of his own nature and consequent conduct'.[7] When we act, and especially when we produce, we naturally create certain benefits, depending on our efforts, skills, and capacities, and these benefits ought to be secured to us. Conversely, though I shall not pursue this side of Spencer's argument, if we act foolishly, we create harm for ourselves, and this we must also bear. Plainly, then, Spencer identifies justice with a distribution according to desert, desert here being interpreted as 'achievement' and not as 'effort' (though Spencer appears not to have noticed the distinction being made, and was often careless in his use of language—see the passage below); the same distribution, in fact, that another school of thought called 'the right to the whole product of one's labour'. Here is a fuller statement of Spencer's position:

Justice then, as here to be understood, means preservation of the normal connexions between acts and results—the obtainment by each of as much benefit as his efforts are equivalent to—no more and no less. Living and working within the restraints imposed by one another's presence, justice requires that individuals shall severally take the consequences of their conduct, neither increased or decreased. The superior shall have the good of his superiority; and the inferior the evil of his inferiority. A veto is therefore put on all public action which abstracts from some men part of the advantages they have earned, and awards to other men advantages they have not earned.[8]

It may, however, be questioned whether Spencer, in recommending this distribution, is recommending it *because* it is a distribution according to desert. I shall argue that this is so, at least in part. There are three ways in which his principle of justice might be justified:

(1) On the grounds that its implementation serves the general happiness.
(2) On the grounds that it conforms to the 'laws of life'.
(3) On the grounds that it gives each individual what he deserves.

[7] *The Principle of Ethics*, vol. ii, p. 17.
[8] *The Principles of Sociology*, vol. ii (London, 1882), p. 700.

From the foregoing discussion of utilitarianism, it will be seen
that Spencer cannot make a direct use of (1). There is, for
example, no question of reinterpreting each deserved reward
as an incentive to future activity on the part of the individual
and others, as there is in Sidgwick. For Spencer, the connection
between justice and the general happiness can only be established by an argument of type (2). Thus there is no problem
for him of possible conflicts between desert and utility. A strict
adherence to distribution according to desert is guaranteed
to produce the greatest happiness.

This leaves (2) and (3). Spencer characteristically surrounds
his discussions of the principle of justice with natural-scientific
arguments. He claims, for example, that the principle that
benefits should be proportioned to conduct is an expression of
the law 'that among adults the individuals best adapted to the
conditions of their existence shall prosper most, and that
individuals least adapted to the conditions of their existence
shall prosper least—a law which, if uninterfered with, entails
survival of the fittest . . .'[9]

At another point, he argues that the same law is involved in
organic life, where 'every muscle, every viscus, every gland,
receives blood in proportion to function. If it does little it is
ill-fed and dwindles; if it does much it is well-fed and grows.'[10]
However, it would be quite wrong to think that Spencer
arrived at his principle simply as a corollary of certain biological laws which he had discovered. This is partly a matter of
the analogies being bad ones. As Sidgwick pointed out, the
analogy with the organism would suggest that 'each labourer
will receive the means of carrying on his labour in the most
efficient manner', which is not at all the same as receiving
wealth in proportion to the value of his labour, as Spencer
wants.[11] The 'survival of the fittest' argument is likewise odd,
since Spencer himself rejected natural selection as the most
important mechanism of evolution at the level of human
society, preferring instead the inheritance of functionally produced modifications (i.e. 'Lamarckian' rather than 'Darwinian'

[9] *The Principles of Ethics*, vol. ii, p. 17.
[10] Ibid., p. 9.
[11] See H. Sidgwick, *Lectures on the Ethics of T. H. Green, Mr. Herbert Spencer and
J. Martineau* (London, 1902), p. 204.

evolution).[12] More generally, though, we may question whether moral principles can *ever* be derived from this kind of scientific analogy.[13] A much more plausible supposition is that Spencer began with strong moral intuitions about the propriety of rewarding desert, and clothed these intuitions in a scientific dress. His direct attachment to the concept of desert shows through in passages such as these:

(Speaking of the advantages of co-operative production)

One more aspect of the arrangement must be named. It conforms to the general law of species-life, and the law implied in our conception of justice—the law that reward shall be proportionate to merit . . . Excluding all arbitrariness it would enable reward and merit to adjust themselves.[14]

(Discussing 'animal ethics')

. . . during immaturity, benefits received must vary inversely as the power or ability of the receiver. . . . Throughout the rest of its life, each adult gets benefit in proportion to merit—reward in proportion to desert: merit and desert in each case being understood as ability to fulfil all the requirements of life. . . . Does any one think that the like does not hold of the human species? . . . Can he assert that outside the family, among adults, there should not be, as throughout the animal world, a proportioning of benefits to merits?[15]

In Spencer's account, then, justice necessarily implies inequality of reward, according to the capacities and efforts of different individuals. As we shall see, he is strongly critical of socialists who would give equal returns to labourers of different capacity. Yet his attachment to the notion of desert is some-

[12] See Spencer "The Factors of Organic Evolution" in *Essays Scientific, Political and Speculative* (London, 1891), vol. 1, esp. pp. 460–2.
[13] This doubt can be supported on both philosophical and historical grounds. The philosophical arguments against deriving moral principles from scientifically discovered laws of evolution have been set out by (among others) A. Flew in *Evolutionary Ethics* (London, 1967). From a historical point of view, Himmelfarb has shown that the scientific authority of Darwin was cited in support of a wide range of religious, moral, and political doctrines. See G. Himmelfarb, 'Darwinism, Religion and Morality: Politics and Society' in L. M. Marsak (ed.) *The Rise of Science in Relation to Society* (New York, 1964).
[14] *The Principles of Sociology*, vol. iii (London, 1896), pp. 563–4.
[15] *The Man versus the State*, ed. D. Macrae (Harmondsworth, 1969), pp. 136–7.

times subject to qualification. This has two sources: his fear that the principle of desert could be applied in a way exactly opposite to that which he preferred; and his determinism.

First, Spencer insisted that deserts could not be humanly measured. Thus it was no use aiming for a system in which a man's deserts were judged, and then an appropriate reward was given to him. This, he thought, was what would happen under socialism (of the non-egalitarian variety). He drew a distinction between 'the artificial apportionment of greater rewards to greater merits' and 'the natural achievement of greater rewards by greater merits'. Spencer thought that an individualistic, competitive society ensured that the 'natural rewards' of a man's labour were given to him; under socialism the apportioning would have to be done by human estimation.

Thus when we find Spencer critical of the notion of merit— for instance when he attacks the view that men should have *rights* in proportion to their merit—he is very often attacking a type of society in which merit is estimated in an objectionable way.

Second, Spencer believed that the character and capacities of each individual were formed for him by the combined influences of heredity and social environment. Nevertheless he thinks it proper that the superior shall benefit from their superiority, while the inferior take the consequences of their deficiencies. (This at least is demanded by justice, and beneficence should not modify the principle to any great extent.) This position, clearly, is not without paradox; and Spencer sometimes acknowledges it:

But such deficiencies in the shares of happiness some men get by co-operation, as arise from the inferior natures they inherit, or from the inferior circumstances into which their inferior ancestors have fallen, are deficiencies with which justice, as I understand it, has nothing to do . . . We have to accept, as we may, the established constitution of things, though under it an inferiority for which the individual is not blamable, brings its evils, and a superiority for which he can claim no merit, brings its benefits; and we have to accept, as we may, all those resulting inequalities of advantages which citizens gain by their respective activities.[16]

---

[16] *The Principles of Ethics*, vol. ii, p. 472.

Despite such admissions (and we should observe that even here nature rather than men receives the blame) Spencer continues to use the principle of desert without hesitation in the bulk of his writings. Clearly, on this point, the implications which he drew from his scientific studies were not sufficient to upset a deeply held moral conviction.

3 The Secondary Principle of Justice

Spencer's practical conclusions were not normally derived directly from his fundamental principle of justice, but from a secondary principle which he stated as follows: 'Every man is free to do that which he wills, provided he infringes not the equal freedom of any other man.' This is used interchangeably with the desert principle as a statement of the law of justice—Spencer taking it for granted that the two were equivalent. Since this is obviously a major assumption, we need to look further at why Spencer should have introduced the secondary principle, and why he assumed an equivalence between fundamental and secondary principles.

On my reading, Spencer regards the 'equal liberty' principle partly as a statement of the conditions under which rewards can be naturally proportioned to merits, and partly as an independent moral standard, whose evolution in human thought he traces in some detail. From a statement of the conditions under which justice could be realized, he made it into a definition of justice itself, and gave it priority in practical argument. Why? Principally, I think, because the desert principle itself *could* not be applied directly, and attempts to do so could only have harmful consequences. We return here to his attacks on socialism as a system in which rewards are adjusted to merits by deliberate human action. To prevent the fundamental principle from being interpreted in this way, the individualist conditions for justice are incorporated into the definition of justice itself—a familiar enough intellectual tactic.

Spencer, then, takes it that a society in which men have equal liberty—possess equally a number of rights, which he lists in successive chapters of *The Principles of Ethics*—will achieve a distribution of benefits according to deserts, and so conform to the basic laws of life. We might have expected some detailed argument to support this; if we did, we should be disappointed. Perhaps Spencer thought his assumption too obvious to need arguing. A sympathetic critic could write:

The close connection between this formula [equal liberty] and the principle of benefits in proportion to merits is so clear as to require no prolonged explanation.[17]

Let us try to sketch in the argument which is lacking here. It was, as we have seen, integral to Spencer's position that deserts could not be measured directly. He speaks of justice as maintenance of the natural relation between actions and benefits. If we consider an isolated producer no problem arises, for the very object he makes, or the food he grows, forms the natural result of his actions. But Spencer wants to extend the notion of 'natural consequence' to situations where products are exchanged, and this can only be done by introducing some standard of value, so that when equivalents are exchanged each still receives the 'natural consequences' of his actions, in an extended though perfectly intelligible sense.

So let us consider a society made up of independent producers, exchanging their goods with one another on the basis of free bargaining. Assume that the value of an object is determined by the quantity and quality of labour which goes into producing it, and that this value is therefore also a fair measure of the deserts of its producer. Assume also that a free market, through the law of supply and demand, ensures that objects exchange in proportion to their values. Then it follows that each producer will receive a quantity of goods proportionate to his deserts in the market. This, of course, is the traditional theory of market fairness which can be found in the writings of the classical economists from Smith onwards. Spencer, who produced no economic theory of his own, seems simply to have taken over the economists' principles. He is always proud to point out that his deductions from the laws of life accord with the existing findings of political economy.[18] Here he is willing to accept that market demand gives an adequate measure of the value of someone's product:

[17] H. S. Shelton, "The Spencerian Formula of Justice", *International Journal of Ethics*, xxi (1910–11), p. 300.
[18] See *The Principles of Ethics*, vol. ii, pp. 154–5; *Social Statics*, pp. 459–60.

Under this universal relation of contract when equitably administered, there arises that adjustment of benefit to effort which the
arrangements of the industrial society have to achieve. If each as
producer, distributor, manager, adviser, teacher, or aider of other
kind, obtains from his fellows such payment for his service as its
value, determined by the demand, warrants; then there results
that correct apportioning of reward to merit which ensures the
prosperity of the superior.[19]

Not only was value adequately measured by demand, but if
supply and demand were not allowed to operate, there was no
way in which value could be estimated.

I impute this argument to Spencer partly because it seems
the only way in which his two principles (desert and equal
liberty) can reasonably be linked, and partly because it was
included in the common stock of individualist thinking at the
time. As Sidgwick wrote in 1883:

It certainly seems to me that the prevalent acquiescence in the
results of competitive distribution—at least among persons whose
principles of conduct are not consciously utilitarian—is largely due
to the more or less definite conviction that free competition affords
the best realisation possible, in a community of human beings, of
the principle that 'every man should have the opportunity of
obtaining a fair return for his labour'.[20]

It hardly needs saying that the argument used here is open to
severe criticism, which can be arranged under two heads:
(a) errors in the argument even assuming the stated conditions
to hold—i.e. that we are describing a society of independent
individual producers; (b) errors involved in transferring conclusions derived from such a society direct to a capitalist society,
composed of owners of capital, managers, workers, etc. I shall
remark later on Spencer's ability to ignore these salient features
of contemporary society, which really transform the significance
of such notions as 'free competition'. For the moment it is
worth reminding ourselves briefly of the criticisms under head
(a) which Sidgwick sets out with his customary lucidity.[21]

[19] *The Principles of Sociology*, vol. ii, p. 701.
[20] *The Principles of Political Economy* (London, 1883), p. 503.
[21] *The Methods of Ethics*, Book iii, ch. 5. section 6.

The claim that free competition and free bargaining ensure that each gets what he deserves fails for a number of reasons. Fundamentally, it assumes perfect knowledge and perfect competition. In fact, men may be poor judges of the value of each other's products. Their tastes may change rapidly, forcing down the rewards of those who make the old products, and inflating the rewards of those who make the new. The parties to a bargain may be far from equal; monopolies may develop among the sellers, or the buyers may need the products sold so badly that they are prepared to pay whatever the sellers ask. All these factors may affect the market prices of commodities, but it is hard to see how they can affect the deserts of their producers. For example, 'it does not seem that any individual's social Desert can properly be lessened merely by the increased number or willingness of others rendering the same services'.[22]

In short, there is no reason to think that a competitive market gives us more than the crudest approximation to a distribution according to desert. Spencer's silence on this problem is illuminating. It suggests that he is so firmly wedded to *both* ideals that he is not prepared to contemplate the possibility of their diverging. That free competition produces rewards in line with deserts is really a premiss of his system of thought, and as such beyond the need for argument. We have seen that such views were the stock beliefs of one school of thought at the time, and were held more confidently than they could be today. I shall later examine Spencer's lifelong attachment to free competition and free contract as a mode of social organization.

4 *Alternative Conceptions of Justice*

What attitude did Spencer have towards the two alternative notions of social justice—distribution according to established rights, and distribution according to needs? In discussing the former alternative we run into a difficulty, which can be briefly explained. It arises from the distinction between Absolute and Relative ethics outlined earlier. Spencer's principles were intended to apply to a perfect society, and not

---

[22] Ibid., p. 288.

directly to the existing one. In a perfect society the conflict between 'rights' and 'deserts' cannot arise. Men make contracts, and so acquire the rights to goods and services; but according to the argument in the last section, the quantity of these goods and services will match the recipients' deserts. Each person will have a right to the benefits he deserves, and to no more than he deserves. Respecting rights and ensuring that desert gets its reward come to the same thing. Sidgwick noted this feature of Spencer's argument when he observed that the distinction between conservative and ideal justice does not occur in Spencer. This is necessarily the case so long as we confine ourselves to talking about an ideal society, for the problem of whether to protect rights established in *our* society does not then arise.

Nevertheless, we should expect to find Spencer adopting a hostile attitude towards rights acquired, not by contract (and so satisfying the principle of desert) but by force, occupation, etc. This is confirmed by his treatment of property in land. Opposition to private ownership of the land was one of the striking features of the early work *Social Statics*. There Spencer distinguished sharply between landownership and other forms of private property, and while he strongly supported the latter, he argued that the land should be publicly owned and leased to individuals on the basis of competitive bidding. This was because the supply of land was necessarily limited, and had already been exhausted by appropriation in the past.

In his later writings such as *The Principles of Ethics*, Spencer tried to play down the opinions of his radical youth. The trouble was that readers of *Social Statics* had not realized that its principles were meant to apply only in the distant future, and Spencer had been involuntarily recruited as a champion of the land nationalization school led by Henry George. This was not at all to his taste. He therefore partially retracted his commitment to public ownership of the land. While admitting that pure deduction from the principles of justice pointed in this direction, he produced empirical arguments to show that such a scheme would not work. It would not be possible to form satisfactory estimates of the present value of the land to compensate its owners for the labour they and their ancestors had expended on it, and a state-managed scheme would suffer from all the 'vices of officialism' (see Appendix B to *The Principles of Ethics*). This is a notorious occasion on which Spencer entirely contradicts his stated method—abandoning 'rational utilitarianism' for the worst kind of 'empirical utilitarianism' (there was, after all, no direct evidence about how the scheme Spencer had put forward in *Social Statics* might work).

The point to note, however, is that Spencer does not attempt to show that the landowner has a just claim to his land, based on customary right. He still believes that 'ownership established by force does not stand on the same footing as ownership established by contract'. His willingness to let the landowners retain possession of their land is prompted, not by a respect for custom and the rights it creates, but by fear of the state and the consequences of further extension of its powers. He is prepared to see, at some future stage, the principles of *Social Statics* adopted:

As that primitive freedom of the individual which existed before war established coercive institutions and personal slavery, comes to be re-established as militancy declines; so it seems possible that the primitive ownership of land by the community, which, with the development of coercive institutions, lapsed in large measure or wholly into private ownership, will be revived as industrialism further develops.[23]

Spencer, then, divided rights into those acquired by force (which had no foundation in pure equity) and those acquired by contract (which could be justified by the principle of desert). His lack of respect for rights as such must be seen in relation to his image of a perfect industrial society which maintains itself entirely through a network of individual contracts, without need of those forces which Hume stressed as necessary to fit men for society—custom, prejudice, the artifices of politicians. This contrast will be developed further below.

Spencer's attitude to the principle of distribution according to need is easier to establish. He attacks the principle persistently and directly. Or rather, he attacks the principle as a principle of public policy. There is, he says, an absolute distinction to be drawn between the ethics of the family and

---

[23] *The Principles of Sociology*, vol. ii, pp. 643–4.

the ethics of the state. Within the family, benefits are inversely proportioned to merits—most is given where least is deserved; in society at large, benefits are directly proportioned to merits. Socialists and communists, advocating the principle 'from each according to his capacity, to each according to his needs', are accused of extending the régime of the family to the whole community. Spencer here makes the curious assumption that a person's needs can be identified with his lack of merit, but this need not detain us. The point, properly stated, is that within the family benefits tend to be allocated according to need, and this is the principle which communists are attempting to extend. Spencer attacks this both in its strongest form— when it is maintained that all goods should be distributed according to need—and in weaker forms, for example when collectivists advocate a partial shift in the direction of need, say through the provision of free public libraries. His funda- mental objection is that such proposals are unjust, by his standards. They necessarily involve depriving some of the deserving of a part of their rewards, in order to supply the undeserving with benefits. Furthermore, once the natural connection between merit and reward has been interfered with, it cannot be re-established. Socialist attempts to retain an element of desert alongside distribution by needs must fail because, as we have seen, there is no way in which desert can be measured except via the operation of a free market.

But Spencer, besides setting one standard of justice against another, brings up two supporting arguments. The first is psychological. If the need principle is to be implemented, everyone must be prepared to give his labour and talents freely to the community without reward. The more able will actually be in a worse position than the less able, for the jobs they perform will be more taxing and exhausting. They must be perfect altruists. On the other hand, the less able, being also perfect altruists, must feel perpetually guilty that others are sacrificing themselves on their behalf. 'The implied mental constitution is an impossible one.' The only alternative to these arrangements is a return to a system of compulsory co- operation. The state would physically compel each individual to work at the task for which he had the capacities, at the cost of eroding individual liberty. Spencer sees this second type of socialism as a return to the 'militant' type of society which had existed in the past.

To these familiar objections to the principle of needs, Spencer adds one of his own (though it has been used by others since). This is the biological argument from the 'survival of the fittest'. The superior, Spencer argues, must be allowed to gain the benefits of their superiority. This will induce them to reproduce and create further superior individuals. Conversely, the inferior must take the evils of their conduct, to prevent them from perpetuating inferiority. This plan guarantees the gradual improvement of the human race in accordance with natural laws. Clearly, a distribution according to need would frustrate it, by setting superior and inferior on an equal footing so far as capacity to produce offspring is concerned. Spencer pulls no punches in describing the consequences:

Fostering the good-for-nothing at the expense of the good, is an extreme cruelty. It is a deliberate storing-up of miseries for future generations. There is no greater curse to posterity than that of bequeathing them an increasing population of imbeciles and idlers and criminals. To aid the bad in multiplying is, in effect, the same as maliciously providing for our descendants a multitude of enemies.[24]

There is no need here to spend time in exposing the weaknesses of Spencer's argument. He has to show both that the qualities which make up 'superiority' are directly transmitted by heredity, and that policies which aid the 'inferior' will encourage them to produce more children. Neither proposition stands up well to empirical investigation.

To sum up, Spencer's argument against distribution according to need, besides directly repudiating it in the name of *his* conception of justice, appeals to the inescapable fact of individual egoism and to the beneficial consequences of a competitive struggle for rewards. As we shall see in the next section, Spencer regards egoism not simply as a datum of human nature but as morally valuable, since a society in which each person pursues his own interests will actually enjoy more happiness than one in which each person directly attempts to promote the general interest.

[24] *The Study of Sociology*, p. 314.

5 *Industrial Society*

Spencer's sociology was presented within the framework of a contrast between 'militant' and 'industrial' societies. These should be seen as genuine ideal types in Weber's sense: abstract constructs which serve as poles between which actual societies can range. So far there have been no 'unmixed' militant or industrial societies, but only societies which are predominantly of one type (Spencer's ideal is a pure industrial society, but this is placed far into a hypothetical future). Industrial societies are distinguished, not by the degree to which their members are engaged in work rather than warfare, nor by the incidence of industry as opposed to agriculture, but by the form of co-operation they embody, which Spencer terms 'voluntary co-operation'. 'Co-operation' is here used, not in its usual comparatively narrow sense to identify a particular mode of organizing work, but in an extended sense, to refer to any set of rule-governed relationships into which men enter for their mutual advantage. It is important to remember this when reading Spencer, for it implies among other things that the usual contrast between competition and co-operation disappears, competition (at least where it takes place according to some agreed rules) becoming simply one of the possible forms of co-operation.

A system of voluntary co-operation is distinguished by the following four characteristics:

(1) Each man can choose the kind of occupation he will adopt, instead of being assigned to it by birth or authoritative command.

(2) He works for the rewards which he can gain, not under compulsion or for fear of sanctions.

(3) He competes freely with other individuals for these rewards.

(4) He is free to make contracts with others as he wishes.

In Marx's vocabulary, 'voluntary co-operation' refers to a set of relations of production, and so industrial society is identified by its relations of production. Capitalist production is seen by Spencer as one form of voluntary co-operation—though not the only type possible. In fact, as Spencer acknow-

ledges in some places, capitalism only fits the ideal type
imperfectly. The capitalist satisfies the four criteria listed, but
not so the worker. Although he is free to choose between types
of industry and between employers, once he is taken on he is
compelled to work at a certain task, and his hours and rewards
are fixed for him:

The wage-earning factory-hand does, indeed, exemplify entirely
free labour, in so far that, making contracts at will and able to break
them after short notice, he is free to engage with whomsoever he
pleases and where he pleases. But this liberty amounts in practice
to little more than the ability to exchange one slavery for another;
since, fit only for his particular occupation, he has rarely an opportunity of doing anything more than decide in what mill he will pass
the greater part of his dreary days.[25]

For this reason Spencer ideally prefers 'co-operation strictly so
called', that is to say co-operative companies run by associations of workers sharing the profits between them according
to the principle of justice. Yet he doubts whether the character
of workmen is sufficiently advanced to permit this, and shows
an amazing capacity for double vision towards capitalism itself,
at times writing in the vein of the previous passage, at other
times suggesting that capitalism already satisfies the criteria
for voluntary co-operation.

Spencer agrees with Marx in seeing the relations of production (the type of co-operation) as determining the other aspects
of society. The social structure of industrial society is created
by the network of contracts entered into by individuals in their
economic capacity. There is no inherited social status: a man's
place is determined by his actions, by the agreements he makes,
and the rewards they bring him. There are no rigid institutions
which constrain people to act in ways they would not otherwise
do, whether by compulsion or by the sanctity of custom; every
institution is a voluntary association, created and sustained
by the free agreement of the individuals who wish to use it to
gain certain specific ends. Thus the society is remarkably fluid:

. . . with the cessation of those needs that initiate and preserve the
militant type of structure, and with the establishment of contract as

[25] *The Principles of Sociology*, vol. iii, p. 516.

the universal relation under which efforts are combined for mutual advantage, social organisation loses its rigidity. No longer determined by the principle of inheritance, places and occupations are now determined by the principle of efficiency; and changes of structure follow when men, not bound to prescribed functions, acquire the functions for which they have proved themselves most fit. Easily modified in its arrangements, the industrial type of society is therefore one which adapts itself with facility to new requirements.[26]

Spencer wished industrial companies to convert themselves into true voluntary associations. In an essay on 'Railway Morals and Railway Policy' he argued that firms should be established by a contract which set out in precise terms the aim which the organization was designed to achieve. Each person investing in the company would know exactly how his money would be used. It would then be illegal for the company officials to add new undertakings to the company's business—nor could this be done by majority vote. It would require the unanimous consent of the shareholders; in effect a redrafting of the contract of incorporation.[27]

The same logic was applied to the state. Spencer argued that it should be seen as a joint stock company, set up by men for certain limited purposes, even if no 'deed of incorporation' could be found in history. From this position, essentially contractual in its character (although Spencer repudiated traditional contractual views because he thought they assumed a historical contract), he was able to deduce the essential functions of the state by asking: what would men in industrial society agree to by way of state action from a position where no state existed? His answer, briefly, was 'negative regulation': preventing individuals from encroaching upon one another's area of freedom, by the impartial administration of justice, and especially by the rigid enforcement of contracts. To this was added external defence.[28]

In this way both the social structure and the social institutions of industrial society were erected on the basis of free contract. Spencer's model provoked a famous attack from

[26] *The Principles of Sociology*, vol. ii, p. 704.
[27] 'Railway Morals and Railway Policy' in *Essays Scientific, Political and Speculative*, vol. iii, esp. pp. 88–96.
[28] See *The Man versus the State*, pp. 157–61.

Durkheim,[29] who maintained that a society founded entirely on unregulated contract could not possibly be stable. If men were subject to no moral regulation, their egoism would dissolve society into a state of war between each man and the next. In Durkheim's eyes, contracts were not simply expressions of mutual self-interest. They were subject to the moral control of society, which determined the forms of contract which were permissible, and imposed obligations on the individuals concerned which they did not necessarily desire.

Spencer could have admitted that this was the character of existing contract. He looked forward to a time when the existing authoritative regulation of contract would be completely abolished and adult individuals would be free to make whatever agreements they chose. His disagreement with Durkheim was less about the character of current contractual relations than about the stability of a society such as he envisaged. Here Durkheim correctly understood Spencer to be advocating a society composed of egoistic individuals, needing no moral rules to coerce them into social behaviour.

This may seem odd, because a first glance at Spencer suggests that he saw the course of evolution as running from egoism to altruism; 'underlying the gradual development of industrialism was a shift in men's characters from the egoism of the savage to the altruism of the forward spirits of the modern age'.[30] But Spencer's use of the term 'altruism' is misleading. He applies it to any actions other than those which serve our immediate self-interest. Thus to keep a disadvantageous contract when there is a chance to break it is to behave altruistically. Spencer devotes a good deal of space[31] to showing that altruism in this sense is in everyone's long-term interests. He therefore maintains that the contrast frequently drawn between egoism and altruism is obscuring. By acting 'egoistically' we add to the general happiness; by acting 'altruistically' we promote our own interests as well. On the other hand, he seeks to show that 'pure' altruism—actions which aim directly to promote the general happiness—is self-defeating. He looks

---

[29] See E. Durkheim, *The Division of Labour in Society* (New York, 1964), Book i, ch. 7.
[30] J. D. Y. Peel, op. cit., p. 200.
[31] See *The Principles of Ethics*, vol. i, chs. 11–14.

forward to a future state in which the scope for altruism will steadily decrease, as everyone gets better at taking care of himself. Finally, there are three spheres left for altruism. The first is the rearing of children. The second is 'pursuit of the social welfare at large'—but this must steadily dwindle. The third is the occurrence of natural disasters, 'flood, fire and wreck'. Spencer anticipates the complete evanescence of the notion of duty, and the emergence of a social condition in which 'pleasure will accompany every mode of action demanded by social conditions'.

The process of social evolution, in other words, is also the process whereby human nature is moulded into a shape such that men's selfish activities fit harmoniously together and the general good results. The society envisaged is a competitive one. Spencer vacillates in his attitude towards competition, some- times glorying in it, sometimes accepting it with a show of reluctance. Again, we must distinguish between primitive competition, which knows no rules and is directed towards immediate advantage on both sides, and civilized competition, conducted within the rules required by justice—i.e. princi- pally, that people shall keep their agreements. Yet, strikingly, Spencer is prepared to use military metaphors in describing the latter, for instance when condemning 'law-making based on the assumption, that it is the duty of the State, not simply to insure each citizen fair play in the battle of life, but to help him in fighting the battle of life'.[32] Nor should we forget the frequent references to 'the struggle for existence' and 'the survival of the fittest'.

I have already suggested that Spencer's attitude towards capitalism is complex, and that it would be wrong to see him merely as an apologist for private enterprise. He is capable of describing the degradation of the labourer under advancing industrialism in a manner that would not come amiss from Marx; but then to conclude

It seems that in the course of social progress, parts, more or less large, of each society, are sacrificed for the benefit of the society as a whole. In the earlier stages the sacrifice takes the form of

[32] 'Parliamentary Reform' in *Essays Scientific, Political and Speculative*, vol. iii, p. 369.

mortality in the wars perpetually carried on during the struggle for existence between tribes and nations; and in later stages the sacrifice takes the form of mortality entailed by the commercial struggle, and the keen competition entailed by it. In either case men are used up for the benefit of posterity; and so long as they go on multiplying in excess of the means of subsistence, there appears no remedy.[33]

A similar ambiguity can be found in Spencer's treatment of the relation between capitalism and his notion of justice. In his discussion of co-operation in the proper sense, he is ready to admit that co-operative production is able to yield a much closer correspondence between merit and reward than is possible under capitalism. He sees that employers, in endeavouring to keep wages low, will give the worker less than 'the natural consequences of his actions'. But now compare what he has to say about capitalism and (collectivist) socialism. Warning his readers, in *The Man versus the State*, of 'the coming slavery', he argues that slavery is a matter of degree, and that 'a man is enslaved to the extent to which he has to labour for someone else's benefit':

The essential question is—How much is he compelled to labour for other benefit than his own, and how much can he labour for his own benefit? The degree of his slavery varies according to the ratio between that which he is forced to yield up and that which he is allowed to retain; and it matters not whether his master is a single person or a society.[34]

Spencer reviews several forms of slavery, and concludes that socialism will simply be another form, with society as master taking an individual's products from him, and giving him back as much as it sees fit. What is remarkable is that the possibility of 'slavery' in capitalist society is not even considered. Spencer seems to have overlooked the fact that the worker under capitalism does 'labour for other benefit than his own'—that he receives less than the full value of his products. If we accept Spencer's rather odd idea that a man's slavery is determined by 'the ratio between that which he is forced to yield up and

[33] *The Principles of Sociology*, vol. iii, p. 516.
[34] *The Man versus the State*, p. 101.

that which he is allowed to retain', then it is surely an open and empirical question whether this ratio is greater or less under socialism than under capitalism. One cannot help but think that Spencer is here accepting the mystique of capitalism, which disguises the transfer of benefits from worker to employer under the form of an equal exchange of values, through the device of the free contract of employment.

The paradoxes we have discovered can be illuminated by viewing capitalism in relation to Spencer's social ideal.[35] Spencer wished for a society composed of independent producers who grouped themselves into associations for mutual advantage. It was assumed that these men started on a substantially equal footing, so that the contracts they made were freely entered into, none bargaining from a position of inferiority or weakness. Within the association, independence was preserved, no individual was to be indebted to any other, and so competition of a non-destructive kind was continued, and rewards were proportional to merit. There were to be no status barriers between men, nor was there to be any dictation from above; decisions were to be made by mutual agreement (unanimous agreement on the articles of association, majority decision thereafter within the limits laid down at the outset).

The claim I now wish to make is that Spencer looked at capitalism through the glass of this ideal. He took it that capitalism largely conformed to his vision of industrial society, though he sometimes recognized where it fell short of his requirements. What he could *not* see was that capitalism might differ in quite a fundamental way from the image which he held. Thus at one moment he was able to understand that the worker did not match up to his ideal of the independent individual freely entering into agreements; but he could not follow through the implications of this point, and had to nullify it by bringing in biological arguments about the necessity of sacrificing the weaker individuals. Similarly, he could see that employers were capable of depriving their employees unfairly, but not that the workers might be treated more fairly in general under socialism (he remains in the grip of the illusion that free bargaining must produce fair results in the round, even if not in particular cases). Even more notably,

[35] I am indebted here to J. D. Y. Peel, op. cit.

there is no discussion throughout his work of class conflict; Spencer simply did not see the structure of capitalism in terms of a vertical division between middle and working classes. As Peel observes, in so far as Spencer uses the concept of class at all, he does so in a much more old-fashioned way to denote functional groups—iron producers, cloth producers, etc.

It was this manner of construing capitalist society in terms of an ideal which was really pre-capitalist, and whose social basis was steadily eroded by capitalist development, that doubtless made Spencer so popular as an 'ideologist', particularly with American businessmen. They were able to overlook his criticisms[36] for the sake of seeing capitalism presented as a competition between free and equal individuals in search of rewards, a competition sanctioned by natural and biological laws. Having described this model of industrial society at some length, we must go on to relate it more specifically to the concept of social justice.

6 *Industrial Society and Social Justice*

Hume's theory saw justice as consisting in the maintenance of rules of property which established a social order. As part of this social order, each individual had rights and obligations, acquired by birth or by his social activities. In Spencer's industrial society there is no social order of this kind at all. The idea that the individual has rights and obligations independent of his choosing, that he has to take his place in an authoritatively established hierarchy, belongs to the disappearing regime of status. In its place there is to be a social network which is the resultant of individual free contracts. This network is mutable, non-coercive, voluntaristic. Justice can no longer be a *constraint* on individuals seeking their private ends. It becomes instead an expression of their independence and individuality.

[36] And also the belated insertion of a third type of society beside the militant and industrial forms, deemed superior to both, in which work is subordinated to 'higher activities'—intellectual and artistic. See *The Principles of Sociology*, vol. i, p. 563. This appears to be a pure afterthought on Spencer's part, which is mentioned only in a single paragraph of the above-mentioned work. It has no connection with the rest of Spencer's system; nor does the transition from 'industrial' to 'aesthetic' society fit Spencer's principle of evolution in any way I can see. The third type of society is truly 'a wheel upon which nothing turns'.

Spencer's individuals are atomistic and competitive. They inherit no obligations to the social whole which has produced them, and hence any expenditure of talent and energy which is socially useful must be recompensed at the appropriate rate, which is agreed on in advance. Individual activities are shown to be useful by the social demand for them, and demand, as we have seen, is an adequate measure of the value of each activity. Egoism therefore becomes a virtue rather than a vice. Rewards gained in the open market are socially just, however great they are, because to gain them a man must have contributed sufficiently to the welfare of society. The same argument can be applied to each component of society, such as an industrial undertaking. The only condition on which a free, self-contained individual will enter a co-operative undertaking is that he should receive a fair recompense for his labour, and this is given quantitative expression in the principle that he shall be rewarded according to his deserts. He will not take on any additional obligations, or recognize any responsibility to help the other members of the undertaking if they are in need. If he does help them, it will be out of pure beneficence, for justice is satisfied when each gets out of the undertaking an equivalent of what he has put in. If a man felt obliged to render assistance to the needy, both his own independence and the independence of the recipient would be compromised.

Justice as distribution according to desert can thus be seen as the natural outcome of the type of society which Spencer advocates. As Barry puts it:

'Desert' flourishes in a liberal society where people are regarded as rational independent atoms held together in a society by a 'social contract' from which all must benefit.[37]

Likewise the alternative conceptions of justice are discounted. Established rights are seen as constituting formal status differences, which serve as barriers to the ambitions of the free individual. The most striking examples, we have seen, are rights of property in land, which are the prerogative of the few, and thus limit the range of options open to the majority of men, however talented. The same would hold of special privileges, transmitted by birth. They would constitute an

[37] *Political Argument*, p. 112.

artificial hierarchy, directly incompatible with the type of social structure Spencer wants, in which esteem is gained on a competitive basis.

Furthermore, Spencer has no need of the restraining influence of custom and tradition. Unlike Hume, he does not fear the consequences of universal egoism, because he believes that human nature can be so moulded that egoism assumes socially beneficent, not socially harmful, forms. Thus established rights not only run counter to the basic logic of industrial society, they also have no positive function to perform.

The only personal rights that Spencer wants respected are those which arise from contract as a corollary of the principle of desert. For the principle of rights as such (which takes no account of how rights are acquired, but only of the fact that they are recognized and that individuals form expectations on the basis of them), Spencer has no time.

The principle of need is seen by Spencer as the proper principle of distribution within the family, and this is because the social organization of the family is the direct opposite of the social organization of society at large. In the family context, individuals are generous, altruistic, and recognize open-ended obligations to one another. None of this is possible in society. Here men are necessarily independent and competitive, tied together not by the bonds of mutual need but by the possibility of mutual profit. Such individuals cannot recognize that others have a just claim on them when in need, even to a limited extent. The others are their competitors, and have shown by their present condition that they are of small worth in the 'struggle for existence' (even altruism, we remember, should ideally be limited to helping those discomfited by *natural* disasters, not by their own inadequacies). Besides this, recognition that those in need have a just claim upon the better-off individual violates the requirements of independence, and the notion that all obligations are contractually acquired, as I argued above.

My claim, then, is that Spencer's image of society compels one to adopt a notion of justice which centres on the concept of desert, rather than the concepts of rights or needs. I should also wish to press the converse claim, that when a person stresses the interpretation of justice as desert to the exclusion of the other ideas, he is most likely to do so because he views society roughly as Spencer did—emphasizing individualism, independence, competition. There is no point in asking which element—the view of society or the conception of justice— Spencer arrived at first, for both were common property in the provincial, dissenting background from which he came. What we have found is that Spencer's model of society provides most of the arguments which bear out his interpretation of justice; so debate about that interpretation must be broadened to take in the model as a whole.

VII

KROPOTKIN'S THEORY OF JUSTICE

1 *Introduction*

While Hume was a consummate philosopher, and Spencer a mediocre one, it is very doubtful whether Kropotkin should be thought of as a philosopher at all. Certainly, it cannot be disputed that his leading role was that of a pamphleteer and a propagandist. Most of his books were compiled from leaflets, articles, and speeches written primarily for political purposes,[1] with the result that their theoretical level is closer to the political tract than to political philosophy. It might therefore be considered obligatory to approach Kropotkin as a political agitator, and to apply to his works criteria appropriate to tracts and manifestos, rather than criteria appropriate to political philosophies. Previous commentators have adopted this view, outlining Kropotkin's plans and ideals, and contenting themselves with a few critical remarks on their realism or utopianism. It has not been felt useful to subject Kropotkin to the kind of critical scrutiny one might apply to Rousseau or Marx.

Two reasons can be given for departing from this pattern and for treating Kropotkin in the same manner as Hume and Spencer. Kropotkin himself thought that he was doing something more than producing revolutionary calls to action. He believed that he was creating a political philosophy of anarchism, which would place anarchist principles on a scientific basis; hence, in large measure, his analysis of the role of

---

[1] Of Kropotkin's four most important books (for our purposes) only *Ethics: Origin and Development* was prepared as a book, and this had to be compiled from notes after Kropotkin's death. *Mutual Aid* originated as a series of articles in the periodical *Nineteenth Century*. *The Conquest of Bread* was a compendium of speeches and articles published in various places, including *Le Révolté* and *Freedom*. *Modern Science and Anarchism* began as a short pamphlet, and was later expanded.

'mutual aid' in human evolution, and his history of ethics. Second, there *are* things of philosophical interest in Kropotkin, particularly in this context his analysis of the concept of justice. Kropotkin wholly lacks the lucidity of, say, Hume: he is muddled and inconsistent. However, if one is prepared to be tolerant at first (even if critical later), to discover what Kropotkin might have been saying if he had been able to express himself more clearly, there are rewards to be gained from a study of his work. This cannot be proved in advance, but I hope that it will be shown in the course of the discussion.

To follow this preliminary claim, something should be said about Kropotkin's general philosophical standpoint. Firstly, he was thoroughly imbued with nineteenth-century positivism. He believed that the methods of the natural sciences could and should be applied to all phenomena, including men and societies. He was characteristically hostile to theology and metaphysics, which he regarded as socially harmful superstitions, relics of a pre-scientific era. (He included here the dialectic, which he thought was another piece of metaphysical lumber.) The scientific method he identified with the inductive–deductive method: to begin from facts established by observation and to infer from them empirical generalizations which can then be tested by deriving predictions and checking them against further observations. It is worth mentioning that Kropotkin, unlike some other members of the positivist school, was a practising natural scientist, and his work as a geographer was held in high regard.

Connected with Kropotkin's positivism, though not entailed by it, was his naturalistic approach to human phenomena. He saw men as biological creatures, to be studied as part of the natural order. He had no hesitation in transferring directly to men generalizations derived from the observation of animals, and his books on mutual aid and ethics have substantial sections on 'mutual aid among animals', and 'animal ethics' respectively, which are by no means picturesque adornments but solid parts of the argument. As he put it:

Since man is part of nature, and since the life of his 'spirit', personal as well as social, is just as much a phenomenon of nature as is the growth of a flower or the evolution of social life amongst the ants and the bees, there is no cause for suddenly changing our method of investigation when we pass from the flower to man, or from a settlement of beavers to a human town.[2]

Kropotkin's attitude towards evolution is more problematic. He worked in an intellectual milieu which was powerfully influenced by evolutionary thinking, and he acknowledged substantial debts to Darwin, Spencer, *et al.* He commended the evolutionary method. Yet his own practice runs counter to it. In place of Spencer's theory of a grand transition from militant to industrial societies, Kropotkin put forward a conception of man and society which was essentially ahistorical. For instance, the argument of *Mutual Aid* is that at all times men have developed institutions which enable them to render necessary services to each other. Modern society, and especially the modern state, has attempted to destroy these institutions for mutual aid, but they persist in springing up in the face of opposition—for they correspond to an immutable trait of human nature. In fact Kropotkin sometimes claims that the whole of history can be understood as a struggle between two human characteristics, the feelings of solidarity which lead to mutual aid, and the desire to subject other men to one's will. Now this is clearly a most anti-evolutionary way of seeing things, and we may want to ask why Kropotkin should have thought (as he did) that an anarchist-communist society would shortly be evolved from the breakdown of capitalism, given that human nature is essentially unchanging. Kropotkin hints at two types of answer:

(1) A theory of moral progress: Although moral ideas are produced by natural human characteristics (such as feelings of sympathy) and are to that extent unchanging, they become progressively more refined over the course of history. We shall shortly be able to illustrate this in the case of justice. Since anarchist principles are the fullest development of these moral ideas, anarchy is the final outcome of history.

(2) A theory of technological progress: The tendency of technological change in modern societies is to make individuals more dependent on each other, and to render even less plausible the view that each man can succeed on his own in the face of

[2] *Modern Science and Anarchism*, in *Kropotkin's Revolutionary Pamphlets*, ed. R. N. Baldwin (New York, 1970), p. 152.

competition from other men. Anarchist communism is the explicit recognition of a state of affairs which is created by contemporary modes of production, but concealed in contemporary thinking.

Kropotkin never makes any attempt to reconcile these two lines of thought about why society will evolve towards anarchist communism, and in general his thinking about evolution curiously combines insistence upon unchanging features of human life with confidence in a revolutionary change, creating a society which is in many ways the direct opposite of what has gone before.

Two further points must be made about Kropotkin's broad position. First, his positivist commitment carried the corollary that moral principles could be founded on scientific evidence. He saw moral philosophy from the seventeenth century onwards as a continuing attempt to create a 'naturalistic' ethics, once the religious basis of earlier ethical systems had been destroyed. How precisely Kropotkin understood the relationship between science and morality is less easy to decide, but he appears to have had it in mind that science could (a) identify persistent moral values, in animals and different human societies; (b) explain psychologically why these values should have been adopted; (c) justify the values, by showing that adhering to them has desirable social results.

It is plain that this programme leaves unanswered the question of what are 'desirable results' and by implication the question of the ultimate moral end. Kropotkin sensed the gap here, but what he says in *Ethics* is tantalizingly vague:

The end of morals cannot be 'transcendental', as the idealists desire it to be: it must be real. We must find moral satisfaction *in life* and not in some form of extra-vital condition.[3]

In practice, Kropotkin wavers between a utilitarian view and an evolutionary commitment, according to which moral values are justified by their contribution to the preservation of the species.

Second, Kropotkin's conception of science is that of a steady accumulation of knowledge. Each scientist builds on the

---

[3] *Ethics: Origin and Development* (London, 1924), p. 12.

shoulders of the last—there is in no sense a series of 'revolutions' in which existing science is overthrown and a new scheme of knowledge created. This cumulative model is taken over into philosophy. Unlike most philosophers, who see their views as standing in direct contradiction to those of the people with whom they disagree, Kropotkin sees philosophy as a cooperative enterprise, with each thinker adding a new refinement to the system constructed by his predecessors. In his history of ethics, hardly anyone is entirely written off, each moralist is credited with having seen something valuable even if he is wrong in other respects.[4] This makes Kropotkin's *Ethics* a uniquely charitable contribution to the genre, but it has the bad consequence that thinkers whose opinions are really quite contrary to Kropotkin's are presented as being fairly close to him. In particular, he generally underestimates the distance between Spencer and himself, and since this relationship is important for our general argument, I will discuss it in detail in the following section.

2 *Kropotkin and Spencer*

In the course of this chapter, Kropotkin's conception of justice and his social ideal will be presented as sharply opposed to those of Spencer. If this interpretation is correct, we might expect to find that the former's lengthy comments on Spencer are highly critical of his views.[5] In general, this is not so, and an explanation must be provided. Three factors seem important.

(1) There is first of all Kropotkin's general inclination to present knowledge as a cumulative growth, noted above. It may be added that anarchists in general tend to stress the affinities of their views with more 'respectable' positions,

---

[4] The only major thinkers of whom Kropotkin has little good to say are Hobbes and T. H. Huxley (on Huxley see below). The chapter on Nietzsche was not written, but from other evidence Kropotkin would probably have been highly critical of him as well. Among those who receive (qualified) bouquets are Plato, Aristotle, Locke, Hume, Smith, Kant, Hegel, Bentham, Mill, Darwin, Spencer, Proudhon. Marx, it should be noted, is not discussed.

[5] Kropotkin's views on Spencer are to be found in the following places: *Modern Science and Anarchism*, 2nd ed. (London, 1923); *Herbert Spencer: Sa Philosophie*, in *La Science moderne et l'anarchie* (Paris, 1913), (expanded French version of previous work); *Ethics: Origin and Development*, esp. chs. 3 and 12; 'Co-operation: a reply to Herbert Spencer', *Freedom* (Dec. 1896–Jan. 1897).

perhaps to deflect the charges of extremism and absurdity which naturally come from more conventional thinkers. The result, in the case of Kropotkin and Spencer, is that Kropotkin sees himself as modifying and correcting Spencer, rather than as repudiating him.

(2) On many points, particularly points of method, the two were in wholehearted agreement. Spencer's positivism, and his conception of a synthetic philosophy which applied the same methods and principles to all phenomena, were fully acceptable to Kropotkin. So was his general understanding of evolution, although Kropotkin thought that he was badly wrong in points of detail. Kropotkin applauded Spencer's agnosticism, and his sociological treatment of religion as a natural phenomenon, susceptible of explanation by natural causes. We can say in general that Kropotkin's ambitions closely resembled those of Spencer.

There was an area of political agreement, too. Spencer's repeated attacks on the state, his defence of individual liberty, his thorough anti-militarism (to say nothing of his refusal to accept public honours), were bound to earn the approval of an anarchist looking for allies. *Social Statics*, which Kropotkin thought was Spencer's best work, contained the famous attack on the private ownership of land, and Kropotkin could not see why Spencer had failed to extend the analysis to other forms of private property, particularly industrial capital. He thought that 'a breath of communism' infused the work.

(3) Third, there are a good many points at which Kropotkin fails to understand Spencer's real intentions, sometimes excusably, sometimes not. This is particularly the case with Spencer's ideal of a society based on voluntary co-operation. To begin with, Kropotkin seems not to have understood the significance of the fact that capitalism was considered by Spencer as an example of 'voluntary co-operation', and even when he considers Spencer's advocacy of co-operation in the narrow sense (see above p. 199) he fails to recognize the distance between the latter's ideal and his own 'free agreement'. Spencer, I have argued, was thinking of contractual relationships between independent individuals, preserving private property and remunerating according to merit. Kropotkin, I shall argue later, was thinking of solidaristic relationships

between individuals, producing in common and distributing according to need. It has already been pointed out that Spencer confused the issue by appropriating the term 'co-operation', with its misleading implications, for his system. On the other hand, Kropotkin cannot be fully excused, for he was only too aware that the existing institutions calling themselves 'co-operatives' often turned out (particularly in Britain) to be examples of what he called 'co-operative egotism', retaining all the individualistic and acquisitive features of capitalist society. They were 'imbued with a narrow egoistic spirit which stands in direct contradiction to the spirit which Co-operation is intended to develop'.[6]

Kropotkin's failings here reflect on the crucial difficulties of his own anarchist-communist system, to which I will return later. However, he could hardly ignore certain specific differences between his proposals and Spencer's, and where he faced these differences he put them down to failures on Spencer's part to emancipate himself from the bourgeois thinking of his early days. His attachment to private property was to be explained partly by timorousness, an unwillingness to espouse violently heterodox beliefs, partly by his love of liberty, and his conception of private property as a bulwark against the power of the State (as was the case with Proudhon, Kropotkin believed). As to Spencer's advocacy of remuneration according to merit, this was a survival of his commitment to the 'bourgeois and religious' idea of 'just retribution'. In discussing the behaviour of men and animals in terms of merits and rewards, Spencer had abandoned his naturalistic standpoint. Scientific inquiry would show that his proposals for remuneration in a co-operative enterprise were unsupported by evidence:

Spencer seems not to know that what he advocates as the highest development of co-partnership is already practised, for hundreds of years since, by millions and millions of most ordinary men. More than that. Just because these men know the institution of 'co-operative piece-work' from a very long experience, they continually abandon in it the principle of 'reward proportionate to merit' within their own co-operations—probably because they have been convinced by experience of the impossibility of carrying this principle through,

[6] 'Co-operation: a reply to Herbert Spencer'.

and find that far from being *justice*, as Spencer believes, it is a crying *injustice*.[7]

The other main area of overt disagreement between Kropotkin and Spencer was over Spencer's view that the course of evolution was a perpetual struggle for existence between individuals of the same species to acquire scarce natural resources. The whole of *Mutual Aid* (whose main argument is that co-operation between individuals to master their environment, not competition, is the principal motor of evolution) could have been written to refute Spencer. In fact, it is overtly directed against Huxley's position in the essay 'The Struggle for Existence', where he argues that life among animals and primitive men is a condition of continual warfare:

. . . the weakest and stupidest went to the wall, while the toughest and shrewdest, those who were best fitted to cope with their circumstances, but not the best in any other sense, survived. Life was a continual free fight, and beyond the limited and temporary relations of the family, the Hobbesian war of each against all was the normal state of existence.[8]

In attacking Huxley, Kropotkin fails to mention the implications which his adversary drew from this state of affairs—namely that moral standards are developed in direct opposition to natural processes. As Huxley put it, 'the ethical progress of society depends, not on imitating the cosmic process, still less in running away from it, but in combating it'.

In place of ruthless self-assertion, it demands self-restraint; in place of thrusting aside, or treading down, all competitors, it requires that the individual shall not merely respect, but shall help his fellows; its influence is directed, not so much to the survival of the fittest, as to the fitting of as many as possible to survive.[9]

In fact, then, Huxley's moral conclusions are close to those of Kropotkin, though this is not acknowledged in *Mutual Aid*.[10]

[7] Ibid.
[8] T. H. Huxley, 'The Struggle for Existence in Human Society', *Collected Essays*, vol. ix (London, 1894), p. 204.
[9] T. H. Huxley, 'Evolution and Ethics', op. cit., p. 82.
[10] Regrettably, most secondary works on Kropotkin have accepted his account of Huxley uncritically, so that a most misleading impression of the latter is produced. The worst offenders are Woodcock and Avakumovíc, *The Anarchist Prince* (London, 1950), pp. 333–4, where Huxley appears as an apostle of ruthless capitalism.

In *Ethics*, where Huxley's contrast between nature and morality is recognized, he is written off as intellectually bankrupt—Kropotkin believing that the only alternative to deriving moral conclusions from observation of the natural world was to derive them from a supernatural basis (religious or metaphysical).

It is Spencer, who *did* derive moral conclusions from the 'struggle for existence' in nature, who should be the real target of *Mutual Aid*. Yet perhaps Kropotkin was more willing to forgive Spencer's errors about the condition of primitive men and animals (which, after all, could be corrected by producing fresh evidence) than he was to condone Huxley's separation of moral questions from scientific questions, a separation which threatened the whole of Kropotkin's philosophical position. Elsewhere Spencer is in fact criticized, though never as strongly as Huxley. Spencer incorrectly follows Hobbes in seeing primitive societies as made up of isolated and warring individuals. He overestimates the importance of struggle *within* each species for food, etc. His defence of egoism ignores the fact that the benefits which each individual appropriates are social benefits—the products of a long history of civilization.

To conclude, Kropotkin recognizes that there are divergences between Spencer and himself on the concept of justice, on the form which a future society should take, and on the natural relationships which exist between men (and animals). I have suggested that he is inclined to underestimate the extent of these divergences, because of the favour with which he regards other features of Spencer's position. The conclusion of *Herbert Spencer: Sa Philosophie* is optimistic. Forgive Spencer his 'bourgeois' pronouncements, which can be explained by his love of liberty; correct his misunderstandings of the capitalist system; overlook his defence of private property, which springs from his fear of the state: and you will make a good anarchist-communist out of him. One can agree with this in a sense, but it must be added that those elements which Kropotkin regards as 'lapses' on Spencer's part are in fact the central tenets of his political philosophy.

3 *Kropotkin's Analysis of Justice*

Kropotkin never wrote his projected work on the basis of ethics, and so we must rely for his opinions on the mainly historical discussion in *Ethics*, and on a few other sources, such as the pamphlet on *Anarchist Morality*. His moral theory is centred on a division between three levels of moral activity, which he labels Mutual Aid, Justice, and Self Sacrifice (or Morality proper). These elements must be explained briefly, before we look more fully at Kropotkin's analysis of justice.

By mutual aid Kropotkin means helpful activities performed by one individual for another out of an instinctive feeling of human solidarity. It involves a natural, sympathetic response to someone else's need. The activity is performed without thought of reward, and it is not undertaken upon any principle of distribution—i.e. there is no requirement that individuals receive fair or equal treatment. Thus, developing Kropotkin here, we might regard mutual aid as a sub-moral phenomenon, out of which morality proper grows.

The notion of justice arises when a community recognizes that each of its members has an equal claim to recognition and respect. This notion is expressed in various principles, interchanged rather haphazardly by Kropotkin, of which the most important are the golden rule—treat others as you would like them to treat you under similar circumstances—and the principle of equal rights. When one is acting from justice, then (as opposed to mutual aid) one is (a) acting from a principle; (b) recognizing that some specific benefit or service is demanded of one—is due to the recipient. This behaviour is therefore properly described as moral. It is, however, also recognized that others will owe you similar services on appropriate occasions in the future, and hence the morality involved is a 'contractual' morality.

This is why Kropotkin sometimes attempts to reserve the title of morality proper for the third level—self-sacrifice. Activity at this level is supererogatory, given in excess of what is due to others without thought or hope of reciprocal gain. It springs, on the one hand, from the original feelings of solidarity, which move men to help each other beyond the demands of justice, and on the other from a human urge to create and express oneself. Kropotkin sees the self-sacrifice principle as the source of progress and invention in human society, and produces some of his most expansive prose in its vindication.[11]

[11] See *Anarchist Morality* in *Kropotkin's Revolutionary Pamphlets*, pp. 105–13.

Let us now consider Kropotkin's conception of justice in more detail. His remarks on justice are scattered throughout his discussion of the history of ethics, and it must be said that these remarks are extremely confused. He consistently identifies justice *both* with equity and with equality, which, in the ordinary meaning of these terms, is self-contradictory. However, through this confusion a certain position can be seen to emerge, which is worth stating clearly for it is of some interest.

Kropotkin identifies the concept of justice with a certain formal principle, whose content changes over time, these changes representing in some sense an ever more adequate working-out of the implications of the original principle. The formal principle has already been stated; treat others as you would like them to treat you under similar circumstances. This is the generic concept of justice. Clearly it yields of itself no definite prescriptions, for its interpretation depends on how a particular individual would like to be treated by others in given circumstances. For instance, in a society based on honour, each man might wish to be put to death if he betrays his comrades in battle, hence when another does this, it is fair that he should be killed. It may at least be said, however, that the principle contains implicit recognition of the equal rights of each individual, for it contains the minimal demand that no one should be ill-treated *except* when he has violated one of the relevant rules.

Kropotkin sees the earliest specific conception of justice in the Mosaic principle 'An eye for an eye, and a tooth for a tooth'. He gives an example of two men involved in a quarrel, in the course of which one of them inflicts an injury on the other. Justice demands that an equivalent injury be inflicted on the first man; this, Kropotkin says, ensures the re-establishment of the disturbed equality—not, of course, an absolute equality, but simply an equality of injuries.

The second conception of justice mentioned in *Ethics* is justice according to the law. Kropotkin is thoroughly critical of this interpretation, arguing that while the law pretends to protect the equal rights of all men, it actually sanctifies inequality. While discussing Aristotle, he points out that when 'justice according to the law' is applied in a slave society it divides men into different classes and justifies slavery.

It was not until the French revolution that the egalitarianism implicit in the formal principle of justice was drawn out in the demand, first of all, for political and civil rights, and then, following from this, for genuine economic equality. It is not at all clear how Kropotkin understands the relationship between the golden rule and the principle of material equality, but it is plain from constant reiteration that he does see some relationship, and that the rule, once properly understood, gives rise to the demand for equality.[12] For instance, in discussing Kant, he remarks 'The application of any rule to *all men without exception* leads unavoidably to the conception of the *equality of all men*', yet the necessity is not explained. Elsewhere the two things are identified:

Besides this principle of treating others as one wishes to be treated oneself, what is it but the very same principle as equality, the fundamental principle of anarchism?[13]

There is considerable unclarity here, and further evidence of Kropotkin's philosophical deficiencies. The important point for our purposes is that Kropotkin regards men's understanding of the idea of justice as developing through history and culminating in the idea of equality. To discover the more precise interpretation which he gave to the principle of equality, we must leave the *Ethics* and examine *The Conquest of Bread*, which sets out a model for an anarchist-communist society and deals with the problem of distributive justice in such a society.

The question of the principles according to which benefits

[12] An attempt to connect the two principles is made in the following passage from *Modern Science and Anarchism*:

'. . . only those who consider *others* as their *equals* can obey the rule: "Do not do to *others* what you do not wish them to do to you". A serf-owner and a slave merchant can evidently not recognize the "universal law" or the "categorical imperative" as regards serfs and negroes, because they do not look upon them as equals. And if our remark be correct, let us see whether it is possible to inculcate morality while inculcating ideas of inequality.' *Modern Science and Anarchism*, 2nd ed., p. 74.

Kropotkin's claim is that we can only adopt the golden rule towards those whom we consider as our equals. But the equality which is required here is only formal; we must give equal consideration to each man's claims, and discriminate only where there are relevant grounds for doing so. Substantial economic equality is neither a logical nor an empirical prerequisite.

[13] *Anarchist Morality* in *Kropotkin's Revolutionary Pamphlets*, p. 98.

should be distributed under socialism was one which agitated and divided socialists at the time when Kropotkin was writing. One group, whom we shall follow Kropotkin in calling the collectivist socialists, advocated a distribution according to social contribution—hours of work being multiplied by some factor to represent skill, responsibility, etc.; this principle, which is plainly a type of desert principle, is to be found in the writings of Saint-Simon and his disciples. A second position was that of the mutualists (following Proudhon) who claimed that each person should be given a labour cheque for the number of hours he had worked, with no distinction made between types or qualities of labour. While less inegalitarian than the collectivist proposal, this obviously falls short of absolute equality, both because individuals may work for different lengths of time (though ideally Proudhon hoped that they would receive equal wages) and because their needs will be different (one having a family, the other not, etc.). Proudhon accepted this degree of inequality because he believed that pure communism would mean the destruction of individual independence and would encourage idleness among the workers (see *What is Property?* (New York, 1970)). In an early essay[14] Kropotkin had adopted Proudhon's mutualist position, but he quickly changed his opinions, and became one of the leading spokesmen for the communist view, which demanded distribution according to need. In *The Conquest of Bread*, he clearly regards the principle of need as the authentic expression of the demand for human equality, while the collectivist and mutualist solutions are half-hearted compromises with the existing inequalities of capitalism. He begins by linking justice to equality:

There is only one way in which Communism can be established equitably, only one way which satisfies our instincts of justice and is at the same time practical; namely, the system already adopted by the agrarian communes of Europe. . . .
   In a word, the system is this: no stint or limit to what the community possesses in abundance, but equal sharing and dividing of those commodities which are scarce or apt to run short.[15]

---

[14] 'Must we occupy ourselves with an examination of the Ideal of a Future System?' in *Selected Writings on Anarchism and Revolution*, ed. M. A. Miller (Cambridge, Mass., 1970).   [15] *The Conquest of Bread* (New York, 1926), pp. 58–9.

Kropotkin further refines this position when he makes it clear that 'equal sharing and dividing' does not mean arithmetical equality, but a sharing according to need. He thinks this is already recognized by the common people who are not 'tainted with middle-class prejudices':

If you were to give utterance, in any gathering of people, to the opinion that delicacies—game and such-like—should be reserved for the fastidious palates of aristocratic idlers, and black bread given to the sick in the hospitals, you would be hissed. But say at the same gathering, preach at the street corners and in the market places, that the most tempting delicacies ought to be kept for the sick and feeble—especially for the sick. Say that if there are only five braces of partridge in the entire city, and only one case of sherry, they should go to sick people and convalescents. Say that after the sick come the children. For them the milk of the cows and goats should be reserved if there is not enough for all. To the children and the aged the last piece of meat, and to the strong man dry bread, if the community be reduced to that extremity.

Say, in a word, that if this or that article of consumption runs short, and has to be doled out, to those who have most need most should be given. Say that and see if you do not meet with universal agreement.[16]

We have seen so far that Kropotkin interprets justice as distribution according to needs, and we also know something about the way in which he intends the principle to be understood. First, in the case of goods which are available in abundance (such, in some circumstances, as water and grazing land) each person is to have free and unlimited access to their enjoyment. Second, in the case of basic needs (such as the needs for food and shelter) there is sufficient consensus on what people's needs are, and how they may be satisfied, for the principle to be applied voluntarily, without the necessity for any authority to interpret and enforce it. Kropotkin is firmly opposed to 'authoritarian' versions of communism, such as that of Cabet, in which the individual's activities are to be wholly directed by a public authority, and his goods assigned to him in the same way.

What, however, of needs other than the basic ones? Communist theories may roughly be divided into 'ascetic' models,

[16] Ibid., pp. 59–60.

which advocate the suppression of as many desires as possible and a return to simple modes of living, and 'expansive' models, which argue that human productive powers, liberated in a communist society, will allow more needs to be created and satisfied than ever before. (This distinction does not necessarily coincide with the authoritarian/libertarian distinction.) Among ascetic communists were Mably and Cabet, and it was this type of communism which was attempted in practice, for instance in the American settlements. Kropotkin saw this as an important reason for their failure, and aligned himself with the expansive school:

Man is not a being whose exclusive purpose in life is eating, drinking, and providing a shelter for himself. As soon as his material wants are satisfied, other needs, which, generally speaking, may be described as of an artistic character, will thrust themselves forward. These needs are of the greatest variety; they vary with each and every individual; and the more society is civilized, the more will individuality be developed, and the more will desires be varied.[17]

Since these new needs will differ from one person to the next, we cannot expect that they will attract the same universal recognition as basic needs. So Kropotkin leaves it up to each individual to satisfy them. He calculates that everyone is obliged to work for no more than five hours a day to produce the basic necessities, leaving a good deal of time in which other interests can be pursued, mainly through voluntary associations which spring up in every field of human activity.

At the same time Kropotkin argues that as productivity increases, further items are transferred from the class of 'luxuries' to the class of 'necessities'. Thus he assumes that the consensus on what are to count as human needs, which could plausibly be held to exist in the case of the absolute necessities of life, can be preserved while the content of 'human needs' is expanded. Indeed, he even believes that needs can be studied scientifically, and advocates a new science of Political Economy: 'The study of the needs of mankind, and the means of satisfying them with the least possible waste of human energy'.

Kropotkin's case would be strengthened here if he employed the distinction between needs and wants to mark off those

---

[17] Ibid., p. 95.

demands which the community is obliged to satisfy from those which the individual may satisfy in his leisure time. But even if this were done, there would still be the problem of deciding what each person's needs were, over and above the basic necessities common to all men. The 'science' of political economy may give theoretical answers; but the community needs some mechanism for deciding in practice what is to be produced after the essentials of life have been secured. Kropotkin's failure to specify any such mechanism is a weakness to which we shall return later.

Kropotkin's main defence of the 'needs' interpretation of justice is that it represents a strict corollary of the communist mode of production. In fact he believes that the experience of anarchist communism will automatically incline people towards this principle of distribution (see his remarks on Spencer, pp. 215–16 above). At the very beginning of *The Conquest of Bread* there is a chapter entitled 'Our Riches' in which he presents the sum total of resources available to his contemporaries as the product of centuries of human co-operation, making it absurd for any one individual to claim that he had created an object entirely by himself, and hence that he has a right to appropriate it:

Under pain of death, human societies are forced to return to first principles: the means of production being the collective work of humanity, the product should be the collective property of the race. Individual appropriation is neither just nor serviceable. All belongs to all. All things are for all men, since all men have need of them, since all men have worked in the measure of their strength to produce them, and since it is not possible to evaluate every one's part in the production of the world's wealth.[18]

In communist society, this interdependence will become apparent, since work will largely be performed in common, whereas capitalist society tends to disguise it. However, Kropotkin sees tendencies even within capitalism towards adoption of the principle of need:

. . . new organisations, based on the same principle—*to every man according to his needs*—spring up under a thousand different forms; for without a certain leaven of Communism the present societies

[18] Ibid., p. 10.

could not exist. In spite of the narrowly egoistic turn given to men's minds by the commercial system, the tendency towards Communism is constantly appearing, and it influences our activities in a variety of ways.[19]

He instances 'museums, free libraries, free schools, free meals for children; parks and gardens open to all; . . . water supplied to every house without measure or stint'. Along with this embryonic recognition that what matters is an individual's needs goes recognition that deserts do *not* matter:

When you go into a public library . . . the librarian does not ask what services you have rendered to society before giving you the book, or the fifty books, which you require.[20]

In short, justice as distribution according to need is explicitly linked by Kropotkin to a type of social order which is constantly reappearing in the midst of a hostile capitalist environment, and which will emerge fully when communism is realised. The connection between conceptions of justice and images of society, which had to be drawn out in the case of Hume and Spencer, is explicitly present in Kropotkin.

4 *Alternative Conceptions of Justice*

Kropotkin says little about justice conceived of as the protection of rights in the broadest sense, but he has a good deal to say about an important sub-category, justice according to the law. We have already seen that he regards this as one historically important conception of justice, and that he is critical of it. It is now time to explore his attitude more fully.

Kropotkin drew a sharp distinction between law and custom. By 'custom' he meant those socially useful rules which social groups evolve to preserve peace and harmony—their positive morality, in fact. He saw custom as originating in the sociable instincts of men, and its rules as being enforced by arbitrators—third parties appointed to settle disputes between warring individuals. This, by and large, was how primitive peoples conducted their affairs. Rules of custom, of course, confer rights, but the rights in question are *equal* rights; the rules were not rules of property, but concerned such matters as the

[19] Ibid., p. 26.   [20] Ibid., p. 27.

protection of human life and the fulfilment of mutual obligations. I shall argue later that Kropotkin was insufficiently critical of custom and its effects, but for the moment it is the contrast between custom and the law which must be emphasized.

Law, according to Kropotkin, does not grow from within society, but is imposed from above by groups seeking domination. Its content is an artful combination of the rules which are useful to society as a whole, taken over from custom, and rules which are useful only to the dominant class. In this way the natural respect felt for custom becomes transferred to the law as a whole; the institution is further preserved by the natural conservatism of the human race, which prefers what is ancient and established to what is untried. The law becomes a powerful instrument of exploitation, a cover for the injustices created by private property. Kropotkin sees no justification for the rights which law confers:

When, for example, the law establishes Mr. So-and-So's right to a house, it is not establishing his right to a cottage he has built for himself, or to a house he has erected with the help of some of his friends. In that case no one would have disputed his right. On the contrary, the law is establishing his right to a house which is *not* the product of his labor; first of all because he has had it built for him by others to whom he has not paid the full value of their work, and next because that house represents a social value which he could not have produced for himself. The law is establishing his right to what belongs to everybody in general and to nobody in particular.[21]

Thus, Kropotkin repudiates Hume's arguments for the necessity of strictly enforced legal rights by maintaining that the self-restraint and the security of expectation which law is supposed to provide can be achieved without law, by custom and mutual agreement. Furthermore, the fact that the distribution of rights among persons is itself unjust, something which Hume was prepared to overlook in the name of security, becomes of paramount importance to Kropotkin. The latter is indeed unwilling to sanction any individual appropriation at all, on the grounds that no individual can justly claim an exclusive right to an object which is inevitably the result of the

[21] *Law and Authority*, in *Kropotkin's Revolutionary Pamphlets*, p. 212.

co-operative labours of many men. In Kropotkin's eyes, Hume's understanding of justice takes the concept outside the sphere of morality, and makes it merely an attribute of positive law:

Most interesting is Hume's attitude to the conception of justice. He certainly could not overlook its influence and he recognized the significance of justice in the development of moral conceptions. But either because he did not venture to ascribe a preponderance to reason in its struggle with feeling, or because he understood that in the final analysis justice is the recognition of the equality of all the members of society,—the very principle that was not recognized by the laws,—Hume forbore to break as sharply with the existing laws as he had already broken with religion. Accordingly, he removed justice from the realm of ethics and pictured it as something that develops independently in society, as the result of regulations imposed by the State.[22]

Kropotkin was no less critical of the concept of desert than of the concept of legal rights. Generally, he linked the principle of rewarding merit with the principle of retribution for wrongdoers, and regarded both as survivals from primitive thought, having ultimately a religious origin. His more specific attacks on the idea of differential rewards for work were made as part of his criticisms of 'collectivist' socialism, understood in the sense explained earlier. The main argument is the obverse of his vindication of the principle of needs. The collectivists are proposing an entirely new type of social organization, but retaining a form of distribution which is at best appropriate to the existing system:

Collectivists begin by proclaiming a revolutionary principle—the abolition of private property—and then they deny it, no sooner than proclaimed, by upholding an organisation of production and consumption which originated in private property. . . . Well, for us it is evident that a society cannot be based on two absolutely opposed principles, two principles that contradict one another continually. And a nation or a commune which would have such an organisation would be compelled to revert to private property in the instruments of production, or to transform itself into a communist society.[23]

[22] *Ethics: Origin and Development*, p. 203.
[23] *The Conquest of Bread*, pp. 156-7.

Why is there a contradiction between collective ownership and a system of differential wages for work? Kropotkin argues that by proclaiming common ownership of all available resources, one is saying that no individual shares can properly be distinguished. The resources are the collective work of many individuals—past and present—and we can say that each has contributed something, but we cannot say how much any specific individual has contributed. But differential rewards imply the reverse assumption—that it *is* possible to estimate individual contributions. There is a contradiction between the attitude taken up towards resources created in the past, which are regarded as indissolubly social, and the attitude adopted towards newly created resources, which are jealously divided up between individuals.

This attack has two aspects. There is first the technical difficulty in establishing individual contributions. In the past, in a simple peasant society for example, it may have been possible to allocate resources fairly to individuals, for they produced in relative isolation. But interdependence is the rule in modern societies. Kropotkin takes the example of a coal-mine, and examines its social organization. There is the man who operates the cage, the boy who signals to him, the miners themselves, the engineers. How can we maintain that any one of them is more essential to the mine than any other?

All those who are engaged in the mine contribute to the extraction of coal in proportion to their strength, their energy, their knowledge, their intelligence, and their skill. And we may say that all have the right to *live*, to satisfy their needs, and even their whims, when the necessaries of life have been secured for all. But how can we appraise the work of each one of them?[24]

Beyond the technical impossibility of measuring contributions, however, there is a more fundamental objection. Common ownership is animated by a certain spirit, a generosity, which is in direct contrast to the egoism which capitalist society breeds. But differential rewards represent a reassertion of personal selfishness—each man working for what he can get out of the process of production. Kropotkin's criticisms in this vein of Spencer's scheme for 'individualistic' co-operation have

[24] Ibid., p. 163.

already been noted (pp. 215–16). He argued that Spencer was trying 'to conciliate two opposite currents of ideas and habits which exclude each other'. On the one hand, co-operation implies mutual aid, and each man recognizing his obligations to the others, while on the other, a distribution by desert is a return to the bourgeois notion of 'chacun pour soi et Dieu pour tous'. Furthermore, distribution by desert, instead of bringing men into closer contact with one another, tends to separate them by a re-establishment of the class system, an aristocracy of experts being divided from the majority made up of ordinary workers.

Kropotkin was no more sympathetic than Spencer to the striking of a balance between the principles of desert and need, though for quite different reasons. He considers the view of one De Paepe, a collectivist socialist, who wished to temper distribution by merit with social intervention on behalf of children, the aged, the sick, etc. Kropotkin notes that capitalist society—'this stepmother of a society against whom we are in revolt'—has also been obliged to modify its individualism to help the needy. In both cases the help amounts to the same thing: charity. The attitude which Kropotkin is describing is easily understood. For someone who believes that each individual has a just claim to appropriate a share of the social product for himself (on the grounds of his contribution), any measure of redistribution in favour of the needy becomes a matter of benevolence or charity, whether this is organized by the state or by private associations. This is very clear in Spencer. Justice demands that each is rewarded according to his deserts, and poor relief etc. is a matter of benevolence. (Spencer drew the implication that it should remain voluntary, and be carried out entirely by private bodies.) In Kropotkin's eyes, even if charity is organized by the state, it is still charity— implying condescension and *largesse* on the part of the rich. Only by recognizing that the needy have a *just* claim to the resources they require can mutual respect, which is the essence of true community, be obtained.

It might be said in criticism here that Kropotkin has neglected the possibility of a conception of justice which includes *both* criteria, needs and deserts. For instance, it may be held that everyone's basic needs are first to be satisfied, and then any surplus is to be distributed in proportion to desert. Such a conception is generally thought to underlie the institutions of welfare-state capitalism. However, in Kropotkin's defence, it should be pointed out that this understanding of social justice is psychologically difficult to preserve, since it is made up of two dissonant elements. It is easy to return to regarding the needy as objects of charity, rather than as individuals having just claims on the grounds of their need. This is particularly true of the unemployed, whose deserts in the sense of contribution to production are nil, and it is a familiar observation that many people, including the unemployed themselves, do regard unemployment benefit as a type of charity, with a consequent loss of self- and mutual respect.

5 *Mutual Aid*

Kropotkin's claim to have placed anarchism on a scientific foundation arose largely from his theory of mutual aid, and especially from his book of that name written to refute the 'struggle for existence' view of evolution held (with the qualifications I have noted) by Spencer, Huxley, and followers of Darwin in general. I shall therefore examine the meaning and importance of mutual aid before, in the next section, approaching the anarchist-communist ideal.

An initial distinction must be drawn between narrower and wider senses of 'mutual aid'. In our discussion of Kropotkin's theory of ethics, we saw that Kropotkin contrasted Mutual Aid, Justice, and Self Sacrifice as forms of moral activity, and here mutual aid was understood as an instinctive tendency to help other human beings in need, without the intrusion of such ideas as rights, obligations, and duties which characterize the more reflective forms of moral activity. When, however, in *Mutual Aid*, Kropotkin speaks of mutual aid institutions and practices developing among men, he is making a wider use of the term, for these institutions certainly contain elements both of justice and of self-sacrifice. What makes them forms of mutual aid are the motives from which they are established, the fact that they are directed towards satisfying the needs of each of the participants, and the fact that they are organized on a voluntary basis, not imposed by someone in a position of authority.

Kropotkin constantly claims that mutual aid is a 'natural' phenomenon; and the main evidence for this is the continual re-creation of mutual aid institutions in the face of hostile forces, most notably the centralized state. It is 'natural' in two senses: first, it can be explained as a product of evolution, since, according to Kropotkin, those species which have developed the practice of mutual aid have fared better in their struggle with the environment than species in which competition between individuals is the rule. Secondly, it corresponds to an innate tendency in human nature, a natural instinct of sociability. Surprisingly, at first sight, Kropotkin credits Darwin with being the first to recognize the importance of this instinct. Darwin's significance lay primarily in two points. First, he saw that the social instinct could be used to give an explanation of the genesis of moral ideas and sentiments; second, he realized that the same forces were at work in animals as in man.

The character of this instinct deserves closer study. Kropotkin sometimes used the term 'sympathy' to describe it, though at other times he showed that the term was misleading. He also used 'solidarity', which is probably more accurate. The substantial point is that the feeling which underlies the instinct is experienced towards *all* human beings *qua* human beings when they are in need. Kropotkin was clear that it is not *love* that is involved, since love is necessarily restricted to a few people whom one knows intimately, and sympathy has the same restrictedness—i.e. one is sympathetic towards those whose tastes or qualities are thought to be admirable. The feeling of solidarity involves the capacity to put oneself in the place of another and to experience the feelings and sensations which he is experiencing, irrespective of whether one knows the person, admires him, or has any social links with him. Only this, Kropotkin claims, can create genuine morality:

The more powerful your imagination, the better you can picture to yourself what any being feels when it is made to suffer, and the more intense and delicate will your moral sense be. The more you are drawn to put yourself in the place of the other person, the more you feel the pain inflicted upon him, the insult offered him, the injustice of which he is a victim, the more will you be urged to act so that you may prevent the pain, insult, or injustice.[25]

[25] *Anarchist Morality* in *Kropotkin's Revolutionary Pamphlets*, p. 95.

Two points must be made in criticism of Kropotkin here. First, it is almost certainly false that everyone possesses the instinct of solidarity as explained here—i.e. the capacity to enter imaginatively into other people's feelings, especially their suffering.[26] Second, among those who do possess the instinct, it does not seem that it is 'natural' in the sense of being innate, but rather that it is cultivated, partly through moral education itself. In other words, although Kropotkin was right to stress the importance of mutual aid and solidarity in human societies, it is doubtful whether he added anything valuable when he tried to explain the existence of one in terms of the other.

Analysis of the contents of _Mutual Aid_ (London, 1907) reveals that it runs over a number of themes, only some of which are directly related to mutual aid as understood here, though all of them are broadly relevant to Kropotkin's advocacy of anarchism. There is (1) the claim that human beings are naturally sociable, and more particularly that primitive men did not live singly or in small family groups but in tribal societies; that it is therefore wrong to see human society as a product of the state, which is actually a much later development superimposed upon existing societies; (2) the claim that common ownership of the instruments of production is a viable arrangement, and occurs at least as frequently as private ownership; (3) the claim that where human societies are beyond the reach of the state, they spontaneously evolve methods for restraining aggression and settling disputes, generally involving the use of an arbitrator whose rulings are voluntarily accepted by the people concerned (the only sanction available, other than moral condemnation, being expulsion from the social group); (4) cases of simple generosity or altruism, whether spontaneous (miners volunteering to go down a mine after an explosion to rescue their trapped colleagues (pp. 276–7)) or ritualized (the Hottentots invariably dividing up a gift which they have received among everyone present (p. 90)); (5) cases of institutions developed to help people in need, but to a strictly limited extent, specified in

---

[26] Kropotkin partly realized this when he recognized that among primitive peoples solidarity, and its tangible results, extend only as far as the individual's own tribe.

advance (the Kabyles' practice in which someone threatened
by poverty can convoke an 'aid'—he gives a meal to the
community, and in return they cultivate his fields for him
(p. 143)); (6) cases of institutions which involve open-ended
commitments to assist others (the agreement made between
members of medieval guilds in which each undertook to help
his 'brothers' in many ways (pp. 171–3)—see also below.)

These distinctions must be drawn to make a proper assessment of the value of Kropotkin's book. The argument makes
a strong impact on the reader, but it does so largely because of
the unspecifie nature of the position which is being attacked.
Probably *Mutual Aid* should be read as a series of counter-
examples to the Hobbesian view that men are naturally
selfish, rapacious, and untrustworthy; however, it is some
distance from this to a vindication of the anarchist-communism
which Kropotkin intended to support. The particular aspect
of his view which interests us, namely the claim that distribution according to need will naturally be adopted as a principle
of social justice, is given no support by (1)–(3), nor, on consideration, by (4) and (5); for there is plainly a great difference
between acts of generosity occurring within a system of private
appropriation, and a wholesale adoption of the principle of
need; and similarly, the 'restricted' mutual aid institutions
included under (5) exist on the boundaries of non-communist
systems, and can well be regarded as 'insurance policies'
adopted for selfish reasons by individuals who cannot predict
with certainty that they will not find themselves in need at
some future date. (This aspect is fairly clear in another of
Kropotkin's examples which belongs in category (5), the rule
among Caucasian peasants that 'when the cuckoo cries and
announces that spring is coming, and that the meadows will
soon be clothed again with grass, every one in need has the
right of taking from a neighbour's stack the hay he wants for
his cattle'—though until then the hay is privately owned
(pp. 128–9).)

It is thus only the examples belonging under (6) which bear
directly on the possibility of a communist society; i.e. institutions animated by the spirit of solidarity in which each individual is bound to render assistance to his fellows in so far as
they need it. The primary example in Kropotkin's argument

is the medieval guild, which comes closer to his ideal of anarchist-communism than anything else in *Mutual Aid*. Kropotkin
was of course not alone in seeing the guild as a forerunner of
socialism. It is necessary, however, to look critically at the
validity of the comparison to see whether the type of mutual aid
practised in the guild can really be used as a basis for a 'scientific' theory of communism.

The features of the guild which Kropotkin noted, and which
seem particularly relevant are the following: first, the general
commitment to an ideal of brotherhood, given expression,
for instance, in the demand that guild members should abandon
all outstanding feuds with one another. Second, the agreement
to help each other when in need, particularly in illness and on
the occasion of a quarrel with an outsider; in both these cases
the guild members were prepared to go to great lengths to
fulfil their obligations. Third, the method of settling disputes
within the guild by arbitration. Fourth, the view of work
as a social function—performed for the guild according to
craft standards, the price of the object being fixed by the guild
as a whole. Finally, the common purchase of food and raw
materials for the use of the guild.

One cannot inquire here into the extent to which these aims
were realized in practice, but it does seem important to mention
some other well-established features of the guild system whose
implications run counter to those which Kropotkin wished
to draw. The guilds existed in a hostile environment, and a
good deal of their *raison d'etre* seems to have been a mutual
interest in combating other groups—especially in keeping
prices fixed at a high level and in resisting the military power
of the barons. Nor were they fully egalitarian. It is true, as
Kropotkin argues, that they recognized an obligation to help
those members in need,[27] and they aimed for a type of equality
which may be called Rousseauian—namely that no man
should be one-sidedly dependent on any other. Beyond that,
however, it was up to each member to earn what he could
within the rules of the guild, and substantial inequality seems

---

[27] However, a recent writer observes, 'In their character as fraternities, both
occupational and parish gilds had sharpened sanctions by grudging any grant
from their loan or relief funds to members who failed in business through laziness,
intemperance, or "folly".' S. L. Thrupp, 'Gilds', *International Encyclopaedia of the
Social Sciences* (New York, 1968), vol. vi.

to have resulted.[28] Finally, we should not overlook the fact
that the guilds were also *religious* brotherhoods, and that this
may be as much the reason for their commitment to 'fraternity'
and 'mutual aid' as any natural instinct of solidarity—something which Kropotkin, with his thoroughly critical attitude
towards religion, could not have acknowledged.

The implications which I wish to draw from this (regrettably
brief) discussion are as follows. Kropotkin was surely right to
hold up the guilds as a refutation of certain perennial mis-
conceptions about human activity, most notably the 'egoistic
individualism' of, among others, Hobbes and Spencer. He
was also right to see certain communistic elements in the
guilds, both in their general spirit and in their practice of
mutual aid. However, the mutual aid element still remains a
minor aspect of an institution which was predominantly
directed towards self-advancement (as is the case with Kropotkin's other examples), and so no straightforward implication
can be drawn for future communist societies. There is always
the gulf between a partial recognition of the principle of need,
which occurs in many social contexts, and its full adoption
under communism.

Besides these fairly predictable conclusions, something else
emerges. Kropotkin was not acute enough in seeing the ambiguities in notions such as 'mutual aid' and even in 'solidarity'.
For mutual aid can be practised either for selfish reasons or
for unselfish ones. We have already observed two circumstances in which mutual aid can be seen to correspond to the
self-interests of the parties concerned. First, it may take the
form of an 'insurance' against possible future disasters, as is
the case with the Kabyles' institution of aids. It is not necessary
for my argument to claim that the conscious motives of the
people who take part in the aids are selfish—i.e. that they are
acting from a deliberate calculation of their interests. In the
concrete case under consideration this is probably untrue,
since custom and convention are clearly of great importance
in such societies. However, I do wish to suggest that the
institution is sustained by a general sense that each person
may be a beneficiary in the future. Second, mutual aid may

[28] See S. L. Thrupp, 'The Gilds', *Cambridge Economic History of Europe* (Cambridge, 1963), vol. iii.

mean mutual support against outsiders; this is, in greater or lesser measure, the case with mutual aid in the guilds, a point which is vividly illustrated by Kropotkin's own observation that the obligation to support a guild member in a quarrel with an outsider was maintained whether the brother was unjustly accused of aggression or really was the aggressor. (This could include going to court to support by oath the truthfulness of his statements—presumably, in some instances, in the conscious knowledge that what he said was untrue.) The same ambiguity infects 'solidarity': this may mean a sense of the common humanity of all men as such (involving the capacity to enter sympathetically into their feelings), or it may mean a sense of unity with your own sectional group, into which the existence of other, potentially hostile, groups enters as a necessary ingredient. Clearly, it will not do to present instances of the latter as partial realizations of the former, since it is essential to group-solidarity that it is non-universal, but unfortunately this is just what Kropotkin tries to do.

Two of the key features of Kropotkin's ideal society are that it is universal and that it is fully communistic. This means, first, that there are no external enemies to be resisted, and, second, that some individuals (those with the greatest needs) will persistently receive more of the benefits produced socially than will others. It therefore requires the practice of quite specific forms of mutual aid and solidarity. The chief conclusions we have reached through our analysis of Kropotkin's theory of mutual aid are (a) a sceptical assessment of his claim to have provided a scientific basis for anarchist communism; (b) a clearer understanding of the sense which 'mutual aid' must carry if it is to be the practice which sustains a communist society.

6 *Anarchist Communism*

Kropotkin was not afraid to be specific about the kind of society he would like to see after a revolution—indeed he was a good deal less specific about the process of revolution itself. Some features of this ideal have already been touched upon, but a fuller examination is now required.

It hardly needs saying that Kropotkin envisaged a society from which the state, law, and all coercive forms of authority had disappeared. Its basic unit was the self-regulating commune. The commune was intended to be a largely self-sufficient productive unit, combining in a given territorial area both agricultural and industrial functions. (The arguments for the abolition of the separation between rural and industrial areas were set out in the mainly descriptive work *Fields, Factories and Workshops* (London, 1899).) It would allocate the individual to a productive task and supply him with the goods he needed. It would also be responsible for such measures of control and discipline as Kropotkin was willing to admit. The different communes were to be linked together in loose federations by agreements among themselves—plainly with no superior enforcing authority.

Kropotkin says very little about how productive work itself would be arranged. There is the question of (a) what is to be produced, and (b) who is going to produce it. In his earliest essay he speaks of a majority decision on the types of production to be counted as essential, but this is not mentioned later, and one must take it that he is relying on a universal consensus. The difficulties with this have been alluded to above (pp. 223–4). He also assumes that each individual will freely choose the kind of work he is to perform. This is made slightly less implausible by the additional assumptions of (1) a short working day; (2) elimination of intrinsically unpleasant jobs by scientific advances; (3) improvement in the conditions of many more (he gives examples in *The Conquest of Bread* of a modernized steel factory and a modernized mine.) However, although we should expect a natural spread of aptitudes, it seems unlikely that everyone's first preference for type of work would exactly meet the requirements of production—hence there would have to be some mechanism of allocation. Kropotkin took up and answered the objection that if no sanctions are applied it will be impossible to get people to work at all, but to me this seems the lesser difficulty. Kropotkin is surely right when he says that most people want to do socially useful work, particularly if the work is pleasant and they are allowed to be self-directing; but it is unrealistic to believe that a division of labour and a proper co-ordinating of work activities can be achieved without authoritative regulation of some kind.

Kropotkin did not in fact believe in complete individual

licence, as is made clear in his comments on 'individualist' anarchism, the main anarchist alternative to his own view. The individualists believed that everyone should keep to himself and refrain from interfering with others, but this was wholly unrealistic:

> It is impossible to conceive a society in which the affairs of any one of its members would not concern many other members; still less a society in which a continual contact between its members would not have established an interest of every one towards all others, which would render it *impossible* to act without thinking of the effects which our actions may have on others.[29]

Such individualism, he believed, was liable to degenerate into 'Nietzschean' individualism, in which the emphasis on individual self-assertion justifies the superior person in doing whatever he will, even if this consists in oppressing others. Kropotkin contrasted with this the goal of individuality, a goal which does not contradict but rather presupposes the acknowledgment of social responsibilities—'the individuality which attains the greatest individual development possible through practicing the highest communist sociability in what concerns both its primordial needs and its relationships with others in general'.[30]

Yet if on one side Kropotkin was concerned to differentiate his position from that of the individualists, on the other he was strongly opposed to the authoritarian communism of such thinkers as Cabet. It was perhaps unfortunate that these writers had not paid sufficient attention to the question of individual freedom, but Kropotkin's attacks seem unduly harsh (he had probably derived his opinions from Proudhon), and this may have prevented him from making a realistic approach to the question of how 'communist sociability' can be put into practice. Natural feelings of solidarity and their sublimation as principles of morality may be sufficient to make people wish to perform useful work, but work has to be organized and co-ordinated, and so a method of making decisions is needed. If men are genuinely prepared to practise mutual aid, then no compulsion will be necessary to enforce the decisions reached, and it is difficult to see why the loss of individual

---

[29] *Modern Science and Anarchism*, 2nd ed., p. 71.
[30] 'Letter to Nettlau', in *Selected Writings on Anarchism and Revolution*, p. 297.

liberty is greater than that which Kropotkin was willing to allow on other occasions—for instance, he admits that our moral obligation to keep promises is a restriction on our absolute freedom, but a necessary one.

Kropotkin himself said that the problem facing mankind was how to solidarize everyone's efforts and maximize well-being, while at the same time keeping and enlarging individual freedom. He thus recognized an implicit tension between the two aims, and what has been suggested is that in the case of the organization of production, the commitment to individual freedom, coupled with a pessimistic view of all political arrangements, prevented a realistic solution to the problem of solidarizing efforts. The same tension runs through his account of the more general social relationships which will prevail. He was clearly opposed to the Spencerian model of independent individuals linked by free contracts, for the very ideas of mutual aid and solidarity imply that people are and should be joined by close emotional ties, so that they may spontaneously sympathize with each others' needs. This suggests tightly knit social groups which generate solidarity by the sheer amount of contact between their individual members. But Kropotkin recognized that such closeness could easily become oppressive, and could create a stifling conformism. In specific terms, for instance, he opposed the practice of taking all meals in common and of living in 'fraternities'; he thought that the family would persist largely unchanged in communist society, and that families would live in separate houses. Furthermore, the individual must feel free to leave the commune and establish himself elsewhere. One of the reasons why isolated communes (for example, experimental communities in America) had failed was that each person had only the choice between staying in the commune and returning to a capitalist society which he had already rejected. In a federation of communes he could move to a more congenial group.

As to the regulation of anti-social activities, Kropotkin rejected any infliction of punishment in the ordinary sense on the offender. The only sanctions to be used were, first, moral pressure, and, second, the threat of expulsion from the group. He relied heavily on the influence of morality, which would have to be emancipated from its religious background so that it might grow naturally from the instinct of solidarity. We may in fact distinguish three factors which unite to restrain an individual from acting in a way which might harm others:

(1) The natural feeling of solidarity towards the other, making any infliction of pain repugnant.

(2) The collective weight of custom—rules of behaviour which are unreflectively followed because they have become traditional.

(3) A more reflective grasp of the principle of justice: 'treat others as you would like them to treat you under similar circumstances'.

It is very important to bear in mind Kropotkin's account of how people came to think and act morally. He did not believe that the principles of morality could be reached by abstract reason alone; despite the formal similarity between his own generic principle of justice and Kant's categorical imperative, their derivation was quite different. Kropotkin's principle arose from human instincts of solidarity and the practice of helping one another; from feeling as opposed to reason. It follows that the extent to which men act on moral principles depends upon the kinds of relationship they have with one another, and that morality is supported by a society in which fellow-feeling is encouraged. April Carter has argued that the anarchist belief in a natural harmony between men, which will replace an imposed order, takes one of three forms: 'the reign of economics, in which a hidden hand will promote a natural coincidence of interests; the reign of reason in accordance with natural law or historical evolution; and the traditional community exemplified by peasant villages or tribal organization'.[31] It is plain from what has been said so far that Kropotkin does not use the first model, which is above all characteristic of the individualist school; nor, as we now see, does he use the second, whose most famous exponent is probably Godwin. He belongs in the third group (where Carter places him), relying on the forces which are most obviously present in traditional communities to induce men to act morally and so to produce a harmonious social order. But such communities are notorious for setting limits to individual freedom, and for confining

---

[31] A. Carter, *The Political Theory of Anarchism* (London, 1971), p. 78.

individuals to a small number of traditional patterns of life. Custom is thus double-edged. It may reduce the need for *external* restraints on people and so increase their sense of freedom, but at the same time diminish the number of options open to them. As Carter puts it, Kropotkin, 'appeals to the rule of custom without examining its possibly restrictive effects on individuality or the development of intellectual culture'.[32]

Here we have returned again to Kropotkin's basic difficulty in reconciling the 'communist' and 'anarchist' parts of his programme; or putting it another way, in reconciling the demand for solidarity (which is the necessary condition for social justice) with the demand for personal freedom (which is the necessary condition for the growth of individuality). This difficulty is not a consequence of any inadequacy on Kropotkin's part, but a genuine problem of the compatibility of two important values—important both to socialists and to others. Marx, for instance, believed both that men should live in much closer community with others than they were able to do under capitalism, and that each man should develop his powers to their fullest extent, without considering that the two aims might conflict. Because he said so little about communist society, it is less easy to see the problem with him than it is with Kropotkin. Phrases such as 'the free development of each becomes the condition for the free development of all' are merely obscurantist.

In order to relate Kropotkin's vision of communism to his understanding of social justice in the next section, it is necessary to stress the themes of solidarity and community in his writing, at the expense of the theme of individual freedom. To the extent that Kropotkin pursues the latter theme, and sees resemblances between his 'free communism' and Spencer's 'free co-operation', he is led towards a different conception of justice, one based on individual deserts rather than needs. It is perfectly natural that individualists such as Tucker should have advocated securing to each man 'the whole product of his labour'—an interpretation of justice as desert. Kropotkin was puzzled that his fellow anarchists should adopt such positions, and was critical of them, but he never fully grasped that much profounder questions lay underneath these apparently technical issues of distribution.

[32] Ibid., p. 86.

7 *Communist Society and Social Justice*

It is an interesting coincidence that both Hume and Spencer,
in their critical remarks on the principle of equality, regard it
as the appropriate mode of distributing goods within the family
group. Because of the kind of personal relationships which
exist in the family, they argue, it is natural that benefits should
be given according to need—and conversely, the *difference*
between family relationships and broader social relationships
shows why the principle is inapplicable elsewhere. The main
qualities of family life are affection, friendship, generosity,
altruism, all preponderating over their opposites, while outside
the family it is the other way round.

It is equally interesting that Kropotkin broadly accepts this
position—accepts, that is, that the principle of need can be
adopted only by a group having the qualities which Hume and
Spencer mention—but tries to avoid the implication they draw
by arguing that society can be remade in such a way that the
qualities of the family are extended throughout. Naturally
there has to be some modification. In place of love and friendship, relationships which a man can only have with a small
number of others, Kropotkin sees solidarity as the emotional
tie which underlies communism. Generosity and altruism,
however, are taken over directly from family to society, and to
a certain extent this is true also of personal closeness, the degree
of intimate contact between people. Behind this transference,
there is the sense, which Kropotkin shares with Hume and
Spencer, that as a principle of justice distribution according
to needs can only be self-imposed by individuals whose broader
relationships with one another are of the right kind.

The cardinal features of these relationships are *altruism*,
putting others' interests before one's own, and the sense of
interdependence, or as Kropotkin puts it, the feeling that 'a
service rendered to any individual is a service rendered to the
whole of society'. These features do not of themselves entail
the adoption of the principle of need, for a society of altruists
might have no principles of justice at all, but simply allow
benefits to be distributed through acts of personal generosity.
However, it can plausibly be maintained that, practically
speaking, they are necessary conditions for the adoption of the
principle. One consequence of giving to each according to his

needs is that some people will be perenially allocated a greater share of social resources than others, even if they have done nothing to produce those resources (this is, for instance, true of the chronically sick). Such an arrangement could only be found tolerable by altruists. Furthermore, it is through their sense of interdependence that men can feel justified in satisfying the needs of one particular person. For they will understand that their action forms part of an extended series of acts which jointly benefit all of the individuals who make up society. Thus one's moral duty to others can be performed in aiding a single person.

The two features I have mentioned are in turn linked to other aspects of Kropotkin's communist society. If we recall Kropotkin's insistence that feeling, rather than reason, is responsible for generating moral principles, it becomes apparent that the altruistic attitude is produced by feelings of solidarity. In order to consider it right to put others' interests before one's own, it is necessary to have a sympathetic understanding of others' suffering when in need, and others' happiness when needs are satisfied. (This, again, is a practical rather than a logical necessity.) The sense of interdependence is likewise socially determined. Capitalist society, through its characteristic institutions, fosters the impression that each person is an independent self-subsistent unit, while communism has the reverse effect, proving to its participants that the individual stripped of his inherited social resources could do nothing, and that he depends for his well-being on the activities of everyone else. In short, then, it is impossible to consider Kropotkin's defence of the principle of need in isolation from his broader advocacy of a communist society. On the one hand, the inhabitants of such a society would naturally be inclined to see justice as consisting in the satisfaction of needs, and would have profound objections to the other interpretations of that concept; on the other hand, if consideration of Kropotkin's social ideal is omitted, his principle of justice looks pitifully ill defended. For instance, he presupposes altruism— yet he also tries to show the conditions under which altruism is no longer beyond human capacities. The ideal as a whole may be thought utopian, of course, but at least it must be attacked at that level—as a whole.

It may be said: cannot justice as distribution according to need simply be regarded as a moral principle known to be correct through rational consideration, which requires no support from more general views about society? For instance, did not Godwin believe something of this kind—that reason alone is sufficient to persuade us that our neighbour's needs should take precedence over our own superfluities? However, this overlooks the character of the objection made to the principle of need. Consider Hume again. He is fully aware of the moral claims of equality, in the absence of other considerations. His condemnation is based on the impracticability of the principle, on the impossibility of any society implementing it. Thus a defence of the principle of distribution according to need cannot rest at showing the abstract rationality of the principle; it must further show that it could be applied in an actual society. We may, of course, wish to follow Godwin in maintaining that the principle's rationality is sufficient to guarantee its acceptance, but we must at least explain how the sources of 'prejudice' and 'distortion' which have hitherto prevented men from acting on (or even acknowledging) the principle of need will be removed in future society.

So it does appear correct to stress the links between Kropotkin's understanding of justice and his idea of communist society, and indeed to regard his view of society as the indispensable background to that understanding. Further, I should argue that Kropotkin provides the most plausible justification that can be given for a conception of social justice linked entirely to the concept of need. If, as I have suggested, there are serious difficulties with Kropotkin's ideal, then defenders of this interpretation of justice will have to find ways of meeting them.

CONCLUSION

The theme which underlies the foregoing studies is that in adopting one or other of the rival conceptions of social justice, one is neither deciding on the correct use of a shared concept, nor making an isolated moral choice, but rather committing oneself to a much wider view of what societies are and ought to be. If, for instance, we were to object to Hume that there are perfectly legitimate uses of the concept of justice for which he does not allow, this would be to miss the real point: namely that Hume is trying to persuade us to restrict the concept's use in the way he recommends, because of the role which justice plays in society as he sees it. It may now be useful to develop this general theme more explicitly, by emphasizing the contrasts between the three writers we have considered. One way of drawing out the point is to look at the defence which each writer offers of his own interpretation of justice and the criticisms he makes of the other interpretations. What strikes one immediately is that defence and criticism make perfectly good sense within the context of the social theory each writer expounds, but look pretty weak when confronted with a different social theory. Let us consider each writer in turn.

Hume's grounds for construing justice as the defence of established rights conferred by rules of property are, we remember, the social necessity of having such rules, of their being stable, and of their being strictly enforced. This in turn is justified by his underlying pessimism about human nature, and especially about the destructive possibilities of egoism when not restrained by principles of justice. He attacks desert principles on the grounds that they leave too much room for dispute and destroy the certainty which rules of justice must have. He attacks need principles on the grounds that they presuppose wholly unrealistic alternatives—the main alternatives being material abundance or unlimited human generosity. In Hume's terms, all this is wholly acceptable. But how would these arguments appear to Spencer and Kropotkin? Spencer would agree with Hume that rules of property were necessary, but would completely disagree that the *content* of the rules was irrelevant so long as the rules were stable and strictly enforced. On the contrary, Spencer would argue, the value of rules of property resides in the distribution of benefits they produce. If the existing rules fail to achieve a distribution according to desert (for example, by depriving some men of the opportunity to acquire property) they must be changed; and Hume's conservative arguments against change have little weight in Spencer's eyes. While Hume fears egoism, Spencer sees properly directed egoism as the main source of human well-being; while Hume acknowledges the value of custom and prejudice, Spencer sees them as obstacles to progress. Because they disagree at this level, they cannot agree on the merits of Hume's arguments about justice.

Similarly, Hume's attack on a distribution by merit is circumvented by Spencer. In Spencer's view, the problem of estimating merit is irrelevant, because a free market economy achieves this result without deliberate human intervention. Hume might question this, but he has then to discuss Spencer's general model of 'industrial society', and again the dispute has moved beyond a restricted discussion of justice to wider problems.

If we turn to Kropotkin, we find that like Spencer he can see no value in rules of property as such, and indeed sees the existing rules not as social necessities but as the impositions of a privileged class. However, his difference with Hume does not take the same form as Spencer's. Rather than regarding egoism as an endemic quality of human beings, he sees it as a perversion engendered by a competitive society, and one which will be replaced by an altruism which is 'natural' to men. Thus Hume's supporting arguments for the conservative interpretation of justice are shown from Kropotkin's point of view to be invalid. By the same token, Hume's attacks on equality are turned on their head. Equality *does* require men to be different from men as we know them—but men can be changed, and generosity will predominate over selfishness. The contrast between the family as a social group and society at large is held by Kropotkin to be unsound. Society, made up of associated communes, can come to embody the main (positive) features of the present family.

We may conclude, then, that if Hume is to persuade us that his interpretation of justice as the protection of rights is correct, he has first to get us to accept his social theory in general, including his view about the limited possibilities of human behaviour. His theory of justice is sanctioned by the ordinary use of language (we do quite often mention someone's rights as a reason for its being fair, or just, to provide him with a benefit) but so equally are the other theories. Appeals to linguistic use are necessarily indecisive.

We can deal more briefly with Spencer and Kropotkin, since many of the arguments repeat themselves. Spencer's criticisms of Hume's approach to justice have been mentioned. His attacks on distribution according to need are broadly similar to those which Hume marshals, although Spencer focuses more specifically on the problem of providing incentives to work. From Kropotkin's position this is easily dealt with: the incentive to produce is always the existence of unsatisfied human needs, and there is no necessity for individual incentives because men naturally produce as members of communities for the community. In overt defence of the principle of desert, Spencer tries mainly to show that it corresponds to natural laws and that therefore its implementation must necessarily produce the greatest benefit possible. Hume, we have seen, recognizes desert as an ideal criterion of distribution, but denies that it can be advantageously implemented—'the total dissolution of society must be the immediate consequence'. Kropotkin is at one with Hume in denying that individual deserts can be satisfactorily compared, but goes further in seeing no value in the principle even as an ideal. He disputes, of course, Spencer's contention that distribution by desert is 'natural'—hence the assembled examples of animals, etc. taking care of each others' needs irrespective of 'deserts'. This particular dispute seems especially tangential, for whether Spencer or Kropotkin is right about animal behaviour, they are both equally wrong in thinking that such behaviour is in any way relevant to the set of rules of justice which men ought to follow.

If we set aside Spencer's biological arguments, we can see that the real basis for justice as desert lies in the model of industrial society as a conglomeration of co-operative units into which individuals enter by free contract. For different reasons both Hume and Kropotkin would find this inadequate. Hume would object to a social order based on human rationality alone, without custom or hierarchy. Kropotkin would point to the lack of true community. Both would deny that such a society could function as Spencer believes that it will. In attacking Spencer's model, they would also be attacking his theory of social justice.

Let us turn finally to Kropotkin. We have already examined his criticisms of justice as the protection of rights, and justice as desert. What defence does he offer for identifying justice with a distribution according to need? The main argument, we have seen, is an appeal to the fact that all available resources are the *collective* work of humanity, and therefore should rightly belong to society as a whole. Individual appropriation is unjust, and from the social point of view it is only individuals' needs that give them a just claim to a share of resources. Hume's response to this would be as follows: it may be true that the rules of property give individuals exclusive rights to things which are really collective products, but this is no objection because of the great benefits which the system of property confers. These benefits do not depend on the precise manner in which resources are assigned to individuals. In this way Hume can deflect the force of Kropotkin's argument. Can Spencer do the same? He, it is true, relies on being able to differentiate individual contributions to a collective product, but he can circumvent Kropotkin's attack by pointing out that the market itself identifies such contributions by granting unequal rewards. If Kropotkin is unable to tell whether an engineer or a miner contributes more to the working of a mine, Spencer's reply is that the engineer, by being able to command a higher reward in the open market, proves his superior contribution.

Again we reach the conclusion that so long as each theorist is granted the assumptions of his own general position, his arguments about justice are hard to combat. From another position, they are easy to demolish. It might be thought that this leads to a sceptical conclusion, but the contrary is true. If adoption of a theory of justice were simply a matter of picking one principle at the expense of others without justifying reasons, then scepticism about justice-propositions would be appropriate. What I have attempted to show is that much wider issues of social theory are involved. It may then be said that the choice between views of society is equally arbitrary, but this hardly bears serious examination. Although one's schedule of values may to some extent influence the view of society one decides to adopt, much of the debate between different ways of looking at society takes place on the ground of empirical sociology. However, this is not the place to consider such general issues. What I hope to have shown is that arguments about social justice cannot fruitfully remain *merely* arguments about justice, but must be conducted in a broader context in which competing ideas about the nature of society are given a central place.

PART III

VIII

SOCIAL JUSTICE IN SOCIOLOGICAL PERSPECTIVE

1 *Introduction*

In my inquiry up to this point I have tried to explicate the familiar idea of social justice, first by separating its three distinct, conflicting elements, and then by showing how each element corresponds to a different way of viewing society, represented in my analysis by the political theories of Hume, Spencer, and Kropotkin. Each of these images of society (the stable order, the competitive market, the solidaristic community) plays a part in the thinking of our contemporaries. Any given person will adhere most closely to one image in particular, and to the corresponding conception of justice. Rather than explore the reasons for these individual differences, however, I want to ask whether ideas of justice do not vary systematically from one social context to the next. Some writers have suggested that men everywhere share a common sense of justice, which can be expressed as a general principle that incorporates more specific conceptions of justice.[1] Although this may hold of the most basic notions of justice (such as the golden rule: treat others as you would like them to treat you under similar circumstances), I shall try to show that substantive ideas of social justice—the principles used to assess the distribution of benefits and burdens among the members of society—take radically different forms in different types of society. To do this, I shall start by comparing the social ideas characteristic of three such types. The types will be referred to as primi-

[1] Among recent social scientists, see G. C. Homans, *Social Behaviour: Its Elementary Forms* (London, 1961), ch. 12; L. Kohlberg, 'From Is to Ought: How to Commit the Naturalistic Fallacy and Get Away with It in the Study of Moral Development', in T. Mischel (ed.), *Cognitive Development and Epistemology* (New York and London, 1971).

tive societies, hierarchical societies, and market societies. Our own society will later be presented as a modified form of market society.

This classification is not meant to be an exhaustive social typology: many societies do not belong to any of the three categories. The purpose of the classification is rather to enable us to form a better understanding of the social ideas of market societies by looking at the corresponding ideas of societies with very different structures. In describing each type of society, I shall pick out its most distinctive features, without suggesting that these features will be wholly absent in the other types. Thus primitive societies will display, to a small degree, traits which are characteristic of market societies, and so on. The types are distinguished by the relative prominence or insignificance of features which will be found in societies of every kind.

Let me now outline the three social types to be used in the analysis, before discussing briefly the kind of explanation of social ideas which is to be attempted. Primitive societies, first of all, are small-scale societies in which the basic nexus between man and man is kinship. Men in these societies gain subsistence by hunting and gathering, tending flocks, or simple agriculture. The division of labour is not extensive, and there is no strong, well-defined system of political authority; if such authority exists at all, it will be vested in the village headman or council of elders. Contract, although it may occur occasionally, is not an important feature of these societies.

In hierarchical societies, men are arranged vertically in social strata, each stratum having a definite rank in the hierarchy. There is a strong, though not universal, tendency for economic dominance, social prestige, and political power to combine in the hands of the group at the top of the hierarchy. Each person is assigned to a stratum largely on the basis of his birth, since social mobility is low or non-existent. Stratum membership confers traditionally established rights and obligations, and largely determines the type of work which the individual will perform. Contract is again not an important feature of these societies.

I shall confine my discussion to a particular sub-type of hierarchical society, namely feudal society. In this sub-type the social mobility of individuals is slight rather than non-existent; a man is not tightly bound within the stratum of his birth (whereas in caste society, for example, there is no individual social mobility and each stratum forms a self-contained social unit with its own rules and authority structure).

Market societies, finally, are typically large, economically developed societies, in which the basic nexus between man and man is contract. The division of labour is extensive, and each man is formally free to decide upon his occupation, to enter into whatever associations he wishes, and generally to choose his place in society. The central institution of these societies is the economic market in which commodities (including human labour) are bought and sold. Kinship is of small importance and authority is largely the creature of contract.[2]

How can this typology be used to explain variations in men's ideas of justice? The fundamental assumption made here is that a man's sense of justice is strongly affected by the nature of the relationships which he enjoys with other men. The social structure of a particular society generates a certain type of interpersonal relationship, which in turn gives rise to a particular way of assessing and evaluating other men, and of judging how benefits and burdens should be distributed. My aim is to show that there is an intelligible connection between the nature of a man's relationship with other men and his conception of justice. The argument, in other words, takes this form: given that a person's relationships with others are predominantly of this type, it is *rational* or *appropriate* for him to adopt the following conception of justice. . . . Such an argument appeals to common notions of rationality and appropriateness; the existence of such notions is an assumption which cannot here be justified. Furthermore, my general methodology—the view that explanation takes the form, first, of demonstrating

---

[2] In constructing this classification I owe a good deal to the contrast frequently drawn by ninteenth-century writers—e.g. by Maine between societies of status and societies of contract, by Spencer between militant and industrial societies, by Durkheim between mechanical and organic solidarity, by Tönnies between *Gemeinschaft* and *Gesellschaft*. I take these distinctions as alternative ways of expressing the contrast between non-market and market societies. I have, however, found it more illuminating to use a threefold distinction, since among non-market societies there seems to be an important difference between the largely egalitarian primitive societies and the highly stratified hierarchical societies. A somewhat similar tripartite classification is adopted by Hobhouse (*Morals in Evolution* (London, 1915), ch. 2).

a correlation between social structures and certain ideas, and, second, of showing an intelligible connection between the two elements—is taken for granted.[3]

A more specific point of method deserves fuller consideration. While there is little difficulty in obtaining evidence concerning the ideas of men in contemporary societies, it is much more difficult to discover what people in past primitive or hier-archical societies (or, indeed, in earlier forms of market society) actually thought about, for instance, questions of social justice. We have no direct access to their beliefs, and so we have to infer them from other evidence. In the case of primitive societies, this evidence consists mainly in the actual behaviour of the people concerned—for instance, the way in which they operated their property systems, or the criteria they used in dividing up the spoils of a hunting expedition. When we come to feudal societies we have, in addition to such behavioural evidence, an extensive body of literature which deals explicitly with such questions as the nature of justice. In European feudalism the bulk of this literature was furnished by Christian-ity. How far can this be taken as a reliable guide to the beliefs of the population as a whole? It has been suggested to me that Christianity as we find it in the writings of scholarly clerics was very different from Christianity as understood by the com-mon people. I have tried to meet this criticism by considering, alongside the Christian writings of the feudal period, the work of lawyers and social critics, such as popular preachers and balladers. If these different sources show a consensus of opinion on certain fundamental points, I think it is safe to conclude that those beliefs were also accepted by the population as a whole, irrespective of social rank.

This last remark raises a further critical question: granted that in primitive societies an explanation of shared ideas in terms of social relationships may be adequate, when we reach complex class-divided societies must we not regard social ideas as components of class ideologies used to buttress the position of the dominant class? If this is so, can an explanation of the

---

[3] I have found Weber's position of most use; see *The Theory of Social and Economic Organization*, ed. T. Parsons (New York, 1964), pp. 88–115. I have, however, departed from Weber in considering only the influence of social structures on ideas and neglecting the reciprocal influence. This is done solely for reasons of space.

type proposed possibly be adequate? To this I should reply, first, that there need be no inconsistency between regarding ideas as the direct products of interpersonal relationships and recognizing their ideological functions as the supports of a dominant class; second, that it is very doubtful whether the concepts of class and class ideology can be applied with their full meaning to societies prior to capitalism—a point which has been taken by some of the more reflective Marxists.[4] The question of class ideology will therefore only be considered when we come to look at market societies of the capitalist type.

2 *Primitive Societies*

There is one rather obvious sense in which men in primitive societies do not have our concept of social justice. Whether we place the emphasis on the principle of desert or on the principle of need, we have in either case an understanding of social justice as an ideal which stands in contrast to the existing state of affairs; typically, as I have argued throughout Part II, our ideals of social justice form parts of wider views of society which, to a greater or lesser extent, go beyond society as it now is. Such world-views are not to be found in primitive societies. Primitive men do not conceive of the possibility of transforming society so that it comes to match up to a social ideal.[5] If, therefore, we are to find a concept of social justice in these societies, we must look, not for an abstract ideal, but for an idea which is expressed in actual social practices. We should turn our attention, for instance, to the way in which primitive societies allocate parcels of land to their members, or to the manner in which tribesmen share out the spoils of a hunting expedition. Of course, we must examine not only the physical distribution of goods, but the principles which lie behind this distribution, in so far as we can discover what they are.

My thesis, however, will be that primitive societies do not practise social justice as we understand it. Their treatment of individuals and their manner of distributing benefits are guided by principles which do not correspond to the principles

---

[4] See, for example, G. Lukacs, 'Class Consciousness' in *History and Class Consciousness* (London, 1971).

[5] See R. Redfield, *The Primitive World and Its Transformations* (Harmondsworth, 1968), ch. 5.

of social justice found in modern societies. There are points of resemblance, but the divergences are more striking. To show this, I shall focus my attention on those elements of social organization which are common to the great majority of primitive societies. These societies show wide variation in certain respects, but it would be impossible here to give adequate attention to individual differences.

It was commonly held by nineteenth-century investigators of tribal societies that these societies practised communism. No distinction, they said, was made between one man's property and his neighbour's, and each took from the common pool whatever items he needed. (This view was especially strongly maintained by L. H. Morgan, who passed it on to Marx and Engels.) Modern anthropological opinion, however, agrees in regarding this as a serious error.[6] The earlier investigators, failing to find property rights which were the exact analogues of those in market societies, concluded that common ownership must prevail. In fact, private ownership is the norm in primitive societies, but the rights of ownership are different from, and generally more restricted than, the corresponding rights in a society such as our own. At the very least, primitive men own their clothes, items for their personal use, their tools, and weapons. It is also usual for them to own their cattle, their crops, and whatever they have produced, gathered, or killed by their own labour. The ownership of land is a rather more complicated matter: with hunters and gatherers, and with primitive pastoralists, the lands generally belong to the tribe as a whole, private ownership having little point in these cases. With agriculturalists, however, private ownership of farming and gardening land is again the norm, though as we shall see the *sense* in which the land is privately owned must be properly understood.

When we speak of a person owning something, our standard meaning is that he has an absolute and exclusive right to the enjoyment of that thing. His right excludes any other person having an equivalent right to the same object, and he is per-

---

[6] See, for example, A. S. Diamond, *Primitive Law, Past and Present* (London, 1971); R. H. Lowie, *Primitive Society* (London, 1921); M. Gluckman, *The Ideas in Barotse Jurisprudence* (Manchester, 1972); B. K. Malinowski, *Crime and Custom in Savage Society* (London, 1926).

mitted to use the object as he likes within the law, to sell it to whom he pleases, and to destroy it if he wishes. Primitive ownership is rarely of this kind. A man who possesses a personal ornament may be obliged to pass it on to a kinsman at some definite time in the future. A hunter returning with a catch may be under an obligation to distribute some portion of that catch to other persons specified or unspecified. Thus in Samoa 'fishermen on returning to the shore have to give a portion of their catch to anyone they meet in the lagoon or on the shore . . . ',[7] and similar practices are to be found elsewhere, for example among several of the Eskimo peoples.[8] The ways in which primitive rights of property in land differ from their equivalents in modern society deserve fuller examination.

First of all, the rights of ownership of a given piece of land may be divided between several persons. For instance, the person who directly cultivates a patch of ground may have the right to the continued use of that land, but if he leaves his village of residence the right to dispose of the plot passes to the village headman. The headman in turn may have been granted his rights over the land by the tribal chief, who retains a residual right of ownership.[9] Thus the rights of each person are more limited than the rights of the modern property owner. Their continued possession may also be conditional upon the fulfilment of accompanying obligations. As Gluckman says of Barotse landholding:

In practice in these systems persons can maintain rights of tenure only if they fulfill their obligations both to superiors and to subordinates. Tenure of land therefore arises from, and is maintained by, fulfillment of obligations to other persons and not from title to the land itself.[10]

He justifies this claim by showing that in legal disputes the judges' main concern, in reaching a settlement, was to determine 'whether the parties had behaved as reasonable incumbents of the social positions . . . which they occupied in relation to one another'.[11] Thus a dispute between kinsmen over the

---

[7] M. Mead, 'The Samoans' in M. Mead, *Cooperation and Competition among Primitive Peoples* (Boston, 1961), p. 292.

[8] See Lowie, op. cit., p. 199. [9] See Gluckman, op. cit., esp. ch. 5.

[10] Ibid., p. 79. [11] Ibid., p. 14.

rights to a number of gardens was adjudicated by an inquiry into how each of them had carried out his role as village headman, cousin, nephew, etc. A man who had behaved inappropriately was liable to be deprived of his rights. A similar conclusion emerges from Malinowski's study of the Trobriand Islanders, where a man's right to take part in fishing expeditions and receive a share of the catch was correlated with an obligation to join an expedition whenever he was asked.[12] A final point about property in primitive societies is that a man's rights of property are liable to be overridden by the needs of other members of his society or by social need in general. Among the Barotse, hungry travellers have the right to take sufficient food to sustain themselves from the edges of the king's gardens,[13] and similar practices are widespread.[14] In Tikopia, a canoe may be borrowed when it is needed without the owner's permission.[15] Again, among the Eskimos of the Behring Strait and the Greenlanders

. . . if a man borrows an article from another and fails to return it, the owner is not entitled to claim it back, as they consider that when a person has enough property to enable him to lend some of it he has more than he needs.[16]

These limitations which primitive people place on rights of ownership furnish us with important clues about their social thinking. We have seen that the strict protection of individual rights which is demanded by our own conception of social justice reflects the view that justice concerns the proper treatment which is due to each individual, irrespective of general social utility. In this perspective, the just act and the socially useful act may on occasion diverge. By contrast, primitive men naturally think of the welfare of the group and subordinate the welfare of particular persons to that general end. While it may be going too far to say with Maine that the subject of rights and duties in primitive societies is the group, not the individual, it is certainly true that rights are granted in these societies when

---

[12] Malinowski, op. cit., Part I, ch. 2.   [13] Gluckman, op. cit., pp. 146–7.
[14] See E. Westermarck, *The Origin and Development of the Moral Ideas* (London, 1906), vol. ii, pp. 14–15.
[15] M. Gluckman, *Politics, Law and Ritual in Tribal Society* (Oxford, 1965), p. 54.
[16] Westermarck, op. cit., vol. ii, p. 70, f.n.

it serves the common interest to do so, and they are limited or rescinded on the same basis. This thinking underlies the restrictions on property rights which we have observed, and is particularly well illustrated by the borrowing of canoes permitted by the people of Tikopia. Of a similar practice which existed among the Chukchi Eskimos, an observer writes:

It is contrary to the sense of justice of the natives to allow a good boat to lie idle on shore, when near by are hunters in need of one.[17]

I should say of this practice rather that it shows the *weakness* of the Eskimos' sense of justice, and their willingness to allow considerations of common interest to override individual claims. The same tendency can be seen in primitive thinking on questions of distribution: when John Ladd asked a Navaho Indian how he would distribute 500 sheep among his fellows, his informant replied that they should be given to those best able to look after them.[18]

We have so far been looking at property rights in primitive societies as evidence for the claim that ideas of social justice play at most a minor role in those societies. A further source of evidence is the widespread recognition of duties of generosity (although, as we shall see, the term 'generosity' may turn out to be somewhat misleading in this context.) By a duty of generosity, I mean a duty to give goods and services to people who cannot claim them as a matter of justice. This duty appears in several forms in primitive socities.

Firstly, it is widely recognized that people with goods enough for themselves should give help to those in need. We have seen that in some cases people in need have a right to help themselves (for instance, they may take food from the edges of gardens), but more frequently it is left to the possessor of goods to show his generosity. Haimendorf writes of a simple food-gathering people, the Chenchus:

The human qualities most highly valued are helpfulness, generosity, courage, and an amiable temper. The emphasis on helpfulness is understandable in a society where no one keeps a store of food and a person unable to go out collecting food must starve unless other members of the small group of families living in the same locality

[17] Cited in Lowie, op. cit., p. 200.
[18] J. Ladd, *The Structure of a Moral Code* (Cambridge, Mass., 1957), pp. 289–90.

give him a share of the roots they have gathered. Usually this is done as a matter of course. . . . .[19]

The widespread recognition of such duties is shown in the evidence collected by Westermarck.[20]

Secondly, mention should be made of the duties which are acknowledged concerning hospitality to guests. Primitive societies have developed elaborate rules for the treatment of guests, which both demand hospitality for the stranger and limit the extent to which it must be given.[21] The contrast between primitive and market societies in this respect has on occasion been vividly demonstrated when the two cultures have come into contact.[22]

Thirdly, we must take into account the practice of gift-giving, which is found throughout the primitive world. This practice takes several forms. There is first the arrangement whereby useful goods are exchanged between communities, gift-giving here taking the place of barter. For instance, Malinowski observed that in the Trobriand Islands there was a regular exchange of gifts between coastal and inland villages, the coastal villages sending freshly caught fish inland, and the inland communities reciprocating with gifts of vegetables.[23] A similar interchange was recorded by Mead between the beach, plains, and mountain people of New Guinea.[24] But there are also cases in which the goods exchanged have purely symbolic value; for instance, the shell necklaces and armshells which are given by the chief of one Trobriand tribe to the chief of another on the occasion of a ceremonial visit.[25] Finally, the interchange of gifts may take a highly competitive form, as it does in the institution of the potlatch among Indian tribes on the west coast of America. Here the object of each tribe is to crush the other by presenting gifts, or even destroying property, in quantities which the rival tribe cannot match.[26]

---

[19] C. von Fürer-Haimendorf, *Morals and Merit* (London, 1969), p. 19.
[20] Westermarck, op. cit., vol. i, pp. 540–6.   [21] Ibid., vol. i, ch. 24.
[22] See, for example, the remarks made by an eighteenth-century Ononadaga chief to a white man, cited in Hobhouse, op. cit., p. 339.
[23] Malinowski, op. cit., Part I, ch. 3.
[24] M. Mead, 'The Arapesh of New Guinea' in M. Mead, op. cit.
[25] M. Mauss, *The Gift* (London, 1970), ch. 2.
[26] See, for example, I. Goldman, 'The Kwakiutl Indians of Vancouver Island' in M. Mead, op. cit.

I have collected these phenomena under the heading of duties of generosity because I wish to stress the important differences between them and duties of justice. Although the subject of such a duty is bound by custom to perform the expected action (and, as we shall see, may suffer ill consequences if he defaults), the object of the duty has no claim on the giver, and there is no way in which he can compel performance. The type of duty involved is reflected in the way in which practices such as gift-exchange are understood and conducted. Among the Trobriand Islanders, for instance, occasions of gift-exchange are also used for the straightforward exchange of useful goods. But the two activities are conducted in quite different ways. The bartering is conducted in the usual spirit of hard bargaining; whereas in the transfer of gifts each donor behaves as magnanimously as possible, presenting the finest gifts while apologizing for their inadequacy—the whole ceremony being conducted in a solemn manner, accompanied by the blowing of a conch-shell.[27]

Yet there are two reasons why presenting these obligations as duties of generosity might be misleading. First, the duties form part of a network of obligations which bind the parties to each other by relations of reciprocity. Under most circumstances, the transfer of a gift effectively compels the recipient to give one back (sooner or later); so what are apparently 'pure' gifts actually form part of a complex system of give and take. Malinowski comments that gift-giving in primitive society is governed by the norm of reciprocity, and that 'in the long run the mutual services balance'. This seems to be true as a generalization, though one should also observe that, on the one hand, when gift-exchange takes the form of potlatch, the recipient may have to repay with considerable interest,[28] and, on the other hand, that some tribes recognize a 'pure' form of gift alongside repayable ones.[29] The rule of reciprocity is less plainly

[27] Mauss, op. cit., pp. 20–1.

[28] Mauss claims that in potlatches 'the interest is generally between 30 and 100 per cent a year' (op. cit., p. 40).

[29] For instance, among the Dakota Indians three types of gift were recognized: the solicited gift, which required repayment by an article of greater value; the voluntary gift, expressing personal esteem, which might or might not be repaid, and if repaid, not necessarily with an article of similar value; and the charity gift, given in such a way that no return was implied. (J. Mirsky, 'The Dakota' in M. Mead, op. cit., pp. 388–9.)

in evidence when the duty of generosity consists of helping those in need or in showing hospitality to a guest, though even here one should remember that any man may at some time in the future be somebody else's guest, so there is at least potential repayment in these cases, if not always actual repayment. This suggests a further reason why it may be misleading to describe these duties as duties of generosity. To some extent they are performed from self-interest rather than from altruism. Practices such as gift-giving, helping the needy, and showing hospitality to guests have a prudential aspect; the person who is now the benefactor may himself be in need of aid in the future, and so along with everyone else he stands to benefit from the existence of the practice. Furthermore, we must not overlook the religious and magical sanctions which are attached to duties of generosity such as hospitality.[30] These may constitute an important reason for performance. Finally, acts of generosity in primitive societies may bring a good deal of prestige to the person who undertakes them. Indeed, in societies which are largely egalitarian and lack complex structures of authority, lavish displays of generosity may be one of the few ways in which a man can gain status and a measure of authority among his fellows. This feature is common to societies which range, at one extreme, from subsistence economies, such as that of the Chenchus where generosity consists merely in sharing out the roots one has gathered,[31] to wealthy groups such as the Indians of North-West America where the elaborate ritual of the potlatch allows men and tribes to outface one another.[32]

On this account, we must avoid misinterpreting the statement that primitive societies recognize duties of generosity rather than duties of justice. When we describe an act as generous, we mean not only that the act was of a certain kind (i.e. that it benefited others who had no just claim to what they received) but also that it was undertaken from a certain motive (for example, concern for the welfare of others). In primitive societies, men act in generous ways but from motives which represent some blend of altruism and self-interest in varying proportions. One could put the point slightly differently by saying that whereas market societies regard justice as obligatory

---

[30] See Westermarck, op. cit., vol. i, ch. 24.
[31] Haimendorf, op. cit., ch. 1.   [32] Mauss, op. cit., ch. 2., section 3.

and generosity as optional,[33] primitive societies regard generosity as obligatory. They use duties of generosity as a means of
solving distributive problems which in market societies are
solved largely by duties of justice: problems such as how to look
after the destitute, or how to prevent excessive inequalities
of wealth from building up.

Although primitive societies do not recognize the ideal of
social justice to any great extent, they do pay some attention to
the three criteria of social justice which we have previously
distinguished; that is to say, they regard a person's rights,
deserts, and needs as morally relevant to the question of how
he should be treated. I shall, however, try to show that these
criteria are not used by primitive men in the same way as by
ourselves. In the case of the concept of rights, we have already
established the contrast between rights in primitive societies
and rights in modern societies. Among primitive men, rights
are granted to individuals on the grounds of common interest,
and can be nullified on the same grounds. A person's right is not
a sacrosanct claim which holds against society whatever the
consequences. The character of such rights is revealed in the
manner in which disputes over rights are settled. If, say, two
men claim rights which conflict with one another (for instance,
in a case of disputed ownership), those adjudicating the dispute
will be less concerned to look into the past to establish which
man's title is the stronger, and more concerned to find a solution to the quarrel which will allow both men to carry out their
functions in a harmonious manner in the future.

We have also looked at the moral claims of need which are
recognized in primitive societies. On some occasions a person's
needs are thought to give him sufficient justification for taking
another man's property without his permission; but more
usually the person in need has to wait on the generosity of his
benefactor, and can do nothing to enforce his claim. (We have
seen, though, that the benefactor may face sanctions such as
loss of prestige if he defaults.) This, then, is rather different
from the principle that a man's needs give him a just claim to a

[33] Generosity *may* be obligatory for people in particular positions with particular
aims. For instance, wealthy manufacturers with a desire to enter the peerage are
well advised to be actively philanthropic. But in general a member of a market
society can avoid being generous without being held in low regard by his fellows.

sufficient quantity of goods to satisfy them. However, bearing in mind the close connection between needs and the principle of equality,[34] we should also look here at egalitarian practices in primitive societies to see whether these do not constitute a genuine attempt to realize an egalitarian ideal of justice. Such egalitarianism is most characteristically manifested in the division of the spoils of hunting and fishing expeditions. To choose examples from opposite ends of the globe, several Eskimo tribes insist that when large animals such as seals and walruses are taken, the flesh should be shared by all members of the hunter's community;[35] and Australian tribes likewise make an equal division of the game, in some cases even insisting that the hunter himself takes the smallest, worst, or last portion.[36]

If we look more closely at these examples, however, we shall find once again that a concern for the common welfare underlies the apparent egalitarianism of such practices. The aim is not really equal distribution undertaken to implement some ideal of equality, but *wide* distribution of the goods in question. Why is wide distribution useful? Firstly, because these tribes exist more or less at the level of subsistence, threatened frequently by starvation. A practice of sharing out large quantities of food obviously increases everyone's long-term chances of survival. Secondly, we must recognize that food cannot be preserved for more than a limited length of time, so were it to be left in the hands of a single man then (at least in the case of a large animal) it might well decay before it could be eaten—a very wasteful result.[37] We might also note here that other tribes, instead of simply sharing out game equally, have evolved complex rules for allocating different portions of the animal to individuals standing in various relationships to the hunter.[38] This seems to bear out the view that the aim of these distributive practices is to spread the spoils of hunting among as many people as possible, rather than to implement a formal notion of equality.

[34] See chapter 4, section 4.   [35] Lowie, op. cit., p. 199.
[36] Hobhouse, op. cit., p. 323.
[37] 'The American anthropologist, Alfred Louis Kroeber, made the rather sad remark that there is a correlation between how quickly the goods a society produces deteriorate and its practice of hospitality.' M. Ossowska, *The Social Determinants of Moral Ideas*, p. 50.
[38] Hobhouse, op. cit., p. 323.

What, finally, of the concept of desert? A succinct way of summarizing the evidence from primitive societies is to say that these societies recognize personal merit but not personal desert. Primitive men recognize the possession of certain qualities as meritorious, but do not generally believe that merit should be honoured or rewarded by the subject receiving benefits of a tangible or intangible kind. It is of course true that merit naturally brings with it a certain reward: the prestige which the meritorious man will command among his fellows; but in primitive societies it is not thought that such a man deserves to receive further extrinsic benefits, such as a position of power or a larger share of the tribe's wealth.

The sources of merit in primitive societies show a good deal of variation, but by and large conform to Hume's dictum that personal merit consists in those qualities useful or agreeable to the person himself or to others. We have already seen that generosity is regarded as meritorious in a great many societies, but beyond this we must take account of the particular circumstances of each group. Thus among the Hopi Indians, a peace-loving, agricultural people, industry is highly valued;[39] whereas the Kalingas, a warlike tribe of the Philippine Islands, regard aggressiveness and the killing of enemies as meritorious.[40] Again, the Apa Tanis, who have evolved a simple form of village government to settle their disputes, value negotiating skill and the ability to influence the course of a debate.[41] In each case, we see that the quality regarded as meritorious benefits either its possessor or the community to which he belongs. However, it would be an overstatement to say that merit in primitive societies is always based upon such utilitarian considerations. It is hard to see, for instance, how sexual prowess, which is regarded as meritorious by the Nagas, contributes to the well-being either of its possessor or of his society.[42] Furthermore, once we reach peoples with advanced religious beliefs, such as the Buddhist Sherpas of Tibet, we find that acts of religious significance (for example, the reading and reciting of sacred texts) become increasingly important as sources of merit.[43]

[39] R. B. Brandt, *Hopi Ethics* (Chicago, 1954), p. 138.
[40] Haimendorf, op. cit., pp. 105–11.
[41] Ibid., pp. 74–83.   [42] Ibid., pp. 102–3.   [43] Ibid., pp. 182–94.

In some primitive societies merit is given symbolic recognition, the meritorious man being allowed to wear some specified ornament or other mark of success. Among Indian peoples such as the Dakota, bravery in battle entitled a man to adorn himself in specified ways—each mark corresponding to a particular deed.[44] Haimendorf's claim, that such external marks of merit are needed only when communities have grown beyond the size at which every individual is intimately known to every other, seems plausible here. In general, however, primitive men do not think that individuals deserve to enjoy benefits in proportion to their capacities and efforts. This is shown most convincingly in their distributive practices, some of which we have already examined. The readiness with which the products of hunting and fishing are taken from those who have killed the game and are distributed throughout the community shows an indifference to the claims of desert as we would see them. Nor can this conclusion be avoided by arguing that primitive societies regard fish and game as the result of luck rather than of individual skill and effort. For instance, the Samoans who, as noted earlier, required fishermen to distribute some of their catch to everyone they met on return, admired fishing skills and held the skilled man in high regard.[45] Merit was recognized, but there was no implication that the meritorious man deserved to keep all those benefits that his efforts and abilities had brought him. More generally, the practice of distributing produce to needy people (who must in some cases be 'undeserving') shows that any notion that men should have exactly those goods which their actions have produced is alien to primitive thought.

Having shown that the idea of social justice is of little importance in primitive societies, and that although the ideas of right, desert, and need are present in some form in those societies, there is no attempt to make the over-all distribution of benefits fit any one of these three criteria, we must ask what explanation can be given for these facts. In particular, what differences between primitive societies and market societies account for the fact that the idea of social justice plays a much larger role in the latter than in the former? Why should the

[44] J. Mirsky, 'The Dakota' in M. Mead, op. cit., pp. 404–5.
[45] M. Mead, 'The Samoans' in M. Mead, op. cit., pp. 296–7.

practices and institutions of primitive societies be regulated by a concern for the common good, while in market societies this consideration is often felt to be less important than the demands of justice?

I wish to account for this difference by offering two explanatory hypotheses which may be seen as mutually reinforcing. The first concerns the economic basis of primitive societies; the second concerns the social relationships which predominate in those societies. The economic explanation is suggested by Hume's thesis that rules of justice are adopted when material goods are neither too scarce nor too abundant. Most primitive societies exist in conditions of scarcity. Their food-producing techniques do not allow the creation of large surpluses, nor could they preserve such surpluses were they to produce them. They are therefore continually exposed to the risk of famine through drought, movements of game, and other natural occurrences. In these circumstances it is understandable that primitive thinking should be heavily preoccupied with social survival and the avoidance of starvation. Given such preoccupations, it also becomes intelligible that justice should occupy a decidedly minor place in primitive thought. Concern for the proper treatment of each individual taken separately must be subordinated to the demands of social survival and social prosperity. One cannot, for instance, pay strict attention to an individual's property rights if his land could be better used by somebody else, producing more food to be shared by everyone; one cannot give very much weight to the deserts of a hunter returning with a large animal if the animal could be used to feed a hungry village. A tribesman would probably not argue explicitly in these ways, but I am trying to show that the economic circumstances of primitive societies understandably produce a certain ordering of values, which in turn accounts for the relatively low priority given to considerations of justice.

It might seem that the argument of the last paragraph implies a utilitarian theory of justice: principles of justice are adopted because it is socially beneficial to do so, and not adopted otherwise. This is not my view. The argument points rather to a utilitarian account of the circumstances of justice, and in particular to the negative conclusion that where there exist strong utilitarian reasons against adopting principles of justice, such principles will not be taken up. It does not follow that where these reasons are lacking, as in a developed market society, justice must be founded on utility. Justice may instead be an independent moral value, but one which is inevitably overridden by concern for the common good in circumstances where the survival of society itself is at stake.

My second hypothesis concerns the social relationships which prevail in primitive societies. These societies are made up of small numbers of people; they are close-knit; and they are relatively homogenous. These features combine to influence the nature of person-to-person relationships in primitive societies, which differ markedly from the majority of interpersonal relationships in market societies. People encounter one another as familiars, not as strangers, and each is likely to know a good deal about the other. Their relationships will also be emotionally charged, by contrast to the emotional neutrality which prevails, for instance, between partners to an economic exchange in a market society. Primitive men will often feel a responsibility for the welfare of the other, to whom they are bound by ties of kinship, past obligation, and so forth; again, this contrasts with the indifference which is characteristic of interpersonal relationships in market societies. Taking these points together, how do person-to-person relationships in primitive societies affect the moral attitudes which predominate in those societies? I shall try to show that they lead to an emphasis on values such as generosity rather than to a concern for social justice.

Consider a situation typical of market societies: an employer wishing to deal justly with the men he employs, let us say by paying them a wage whose size depends upon the number of hours worked and the type of work performed (skilled work commanding a higher rate). This way of treating other people is entirely congruous with the relationship which exists between employer and employee, assuming that this takes the pure market form. For (a) the employer has no personal knowledge of the employee, other than of the work which the employee performs for him. Thus the calculation of desert is a simple one for the employer to make, since he is ignorant of any additional personal qualities which might put in question his method of measuring desert. (b) He has no emotional relationship with any of his employees, and is therefore not moved to depart from the strict rule of justice by personal animosities or friendships. (c) Neither does he stand in kinship relations to the people he employs, which might otherwise incline him to show special favours to those who are kin to him. (d) He has no obligations to his employees, other than those which he has voluntarily assumed through contract; again, a possible reason for treating some with greater generosity than others has been removed.

In short, the impersonal relationship between employer and worker typical of market society is congruous with the employer's wish to realize distributive justice, by allocating benefits according to a simple and measurable quality possessed by each employee.

In primitive societies employer/employee relationships are largely absent. However, an analogous situation might be that of a man who wishes for help in harvesting his crop, and therefore summons his fellow villagers to assist him. In such cases, it is usual to feast the helpers during and after their work—rewarding them through an act of generosity rather than through an act of justice, since at the feast there is no distinction between those who have worked for long hours and those who have worked for short, there is no attempt at precise remuneration, and so forth. This is intelligible because the relationship between crop-owner and helpers militates against any attempt to implement distributive justice. For (a) the crop-owner knows his helpers well; to reward them according to desert he would have to consider A's laziness, B's natural ineptitude, the sacrifice that C has made in coming to help, and so on. He may be forgiven for not making the attempt. (b) He will be moved by personal likes and dislikes, by kinship ties, and so on, to favour some at the expense of others. (c) He has acquired a multiplicity of rights against, and obligations to, the men who help him, from similar occasions in the past. These rights and obligations are ill defined in extent. It would be impossible to calculate how much should be paid back to each helper for the work he is now doing.

To summarize, the familiar relationship between crop-owner and helper is incongruous with an attempt to realize strict justice by treating each man according to his deserts, whereas it is congruous with an act of generosity on the crop-owner's part which bestows an unmeasured amount of benefit on each helper regardless of desert.

Besides the utilitarian reasons against adopting principles of justice, therefore, the person-to-person relationships which are characteristic of primitive societies make such principles inappropriate. These relationships are on the one hand intimate, and on the other complex and ill defined—one man's relationship with another will be constituted by past transactions, kinship ties, and so forth, as well as by personal feelings of friendship or animosity. In these circumstances, it would be psychologically incongruous to act towards other people on the basis of some impersonally recognized quality, such as their economic deserts. Primitive morality is therefore more concerned to establish what kind of action a person should perform in a given situation than to specify the precise claims which one person has against another. Justice is understandably not a prominent feature of primitive societies, whereas virtues such as generosity and sociability are.

3 *Hierarchical Societies*

My discussion in this section will be restricted to the feudal type of hierarchical society, and more specifically to feudalism in Western Europe between the tenth and the thirteenth centuries. I shall begin by giving a brief outline of the social structure of feudalism before describing the social ideas characteristic of that system.

The two most fundamental relationships in feudal society were that between lord and vassal, and that between lord and serf. Each took the general form of a contract betweeen superior and inferior, in which the inferior party offered to perform certain specified services for the other in return for protection and the opportunity to make a living. In the case of vassalage, the contract was made between two men who were nominally free (the obligations of a vassal did not pass directly to his descendants), the vassal swearing in general to be his lord's 'man' and in particular to give military service of a stated nature and extent; the lord offering protection and a fief, which generally consisted of a landed estate sufficient to support the vassal.[46]

See F. L. Ganshof, *Feudalism* (London, 1964), Part III.

As for serfdom, the contract here was largely tacit since the serf's status was passed on to his descendants without a renewal of the agreement, but the relationship was again a reciprocal one, the serf performing tasks of many kinds for his lord in return for protection and the right to till a share of the estate. The relationship was regulated by the 'custom of the manor'.[47] The difference between these two contracts should not be overstressed since in practice vassalage tended to become heritable, the son of the previous vassal routinely swearing homage to the lord. We may therefore conclude that feudal society was built upon contracts between man and man which differed from the 'free contracts' of market societies in being contracts of allegiance (rather than contracts between equals) whose terms were governed by custom (rather than being chosen by the parties) and which were in practice largely heritable.

An immediate consequence of the feudal relationships was that, as in primitive societies, property rights were divided among a number of men of different status. Apart from a residue of free peasant proprietors (known as 'allodialists'), each piece of land was owned by a number of men, from the tenant who actually worked the land, through the lord to whom he owed service, to the lord of that lord, and so on. Each man had a distinct set of rights over the land, the exercise of which was governed by custom.

Feudal law was likewise fragmented. Each man was subject to the rules of law prevailing in his locality, and little attempt was made to create a uniform legal system. Since a man carried his law with him, there was truth in the remark attributed to the Archbishop of Lyons, that when five men were gathered together it was no surprise if each of them obeyed a different law.[48] Feudal law was also fragmented in another sense: men of different status in the hierarchy were tried by different courts for committing the same crime, and were liable to receive different penalties as well. Manorial lords administered the law among their tenants, while they themselves were judged by a group of their peers.

Within the law, custom was dominant. We may conveniently

---

[47] M. Bloch, *Feudal Society* (London, 1965), Part V.
[48] Bloch, op. cit., p. 111.

consider this under two aspects. First, as far as the content of the law was concerned, custom took precedence over deliberately enacted law. If two laws were found to be in contradiction, the older of the two was thought to possess superior validity.[49] In fact, the feudal period exhibited a decided preference for unwritten custom, handed down by oral tradition, over written law—a preference which, as Bloch points out, was by no means irrational since unwritten law could undergo subtle changes to meet new social needs more easily than could codified law.[50] Second, in deciding particular cases, established practice was almost always the clinching factor. Thus if the right to work a piece of land was in dispute between two men, the one who could prove that he (or his ancestors) had ploughed the field in earlier years was certain to succeed in his suit.[51]

We see that the hierarchical principle contained in the lord–vassal and lord–serf relationships permeated both the system of property and the legal system of feudalism. The social structure, too, was created by the basic contractual relationships. The manorial lord could bring about status differences among his serfs, for instance by elevating some among them to the position of 'serjeants' who were entrusted with the administration of his estate, and correspondingly rewarded. Among the lords themselves, the contract of vassalage produced distinct strata referred to from an early period by different titles—'vavasours', 'barons', etc.[52] Thus the feudal social structure was characterized by a large number of hierarchically arranged statuses which were clearly recognized by the members of feudal society. On the other hand, it should be remembered that since this structure was the product of many individual contracts, it was possible for a man to raise himself in the hierarchy, for instance by increasing the number of vassals dependant upon him. Thus a certain amount of social mobility was possible without the hierarchy itself being significantly altered. It was only during the period of feudalism's decline that the nobility, especially on the continent, sought to form themselves into an exclusive class by preventing any but the sons of nobles from gaining noble status.[53]

[49] F. Kern, *Kingship and Law in the Middle Ages* (Oxford, 1939), Part II, ch. 1.
[50] Bloch, op. cit., ch. 8.   [51] Ibid., p. 115.   [52] Ibid., ch. 25.
[53] Ibid., ch. 24.

A word must be said finally about two groups in feudal society who appear to stand outside the hierarchy as so far described. In the case of the clergy, firstly, we appear to encounter an independent hierarchy which cannot be placed in any definite relationship with the secular pyramid: indeed a common way of viewing society in medieval times was in terms of a threefold distinction between 'those who pray, those who defend the country, and those who toil—the priests, the knightly order and the working people'.[54] In practice, however, the clergy acquired well-defined positions within the secular structure. Parish priests entered into a feudal relationship with the local lord, often swearing homage to him in return for the living which the parish provided. The great bishops and abbots were major landowners who acquired vassals in just the same way as secular nobles. Thus although the separate status of the clergy must be recognized—in particular, the fact that they were subject to their own body of law must not be forgotten—from the point of view of social structure it is equally important to stress the close integration of secular and spiritual hierarchies. With the merchants, on the other hand, we encounter a group who, although economically indispensable to feudal society, formed no real part of the feudal system. They were permanent outsiders who were generally regarded with disapproval and mistrust by the rest of society. More especially, the communal oath which was sometimes taken by the merchants in a particular town aroused the anger of the feudal nobility, for, as Bloch points out, it was an engagement between equals which stood in direct contrast to the feudal oath between superior and inferior, and thereby threatened the basic principle of feudalism.[55]

With this we may conclude our brief survey of the structure of feudal society and turn to look at the social ideas, especially the ideas of justice, which it produced. In a society so thoroughly steeped in religion, our first and most important source of evidence must be Christian thought. It should be borne in mind, however, that Christianity was evolved in quite different circumstances, as the religion of a small persecuted minority, and its social teaching had to be carefully modified to fit its

[54] S. Ossowski, *Class Structure in the Social Consciousness* (London, 1963), pp. 58–9.
[55] Bloch, op. cit., ch. 26.

new role as the established faith of a hierarchically ordered society. We must look first at the social thought of the Church fathers before considering the modifications which were introduced into Christian thought during the feudal period. The general outlook of the early Church was one of indifference towards secular society. Men should continue to perform their lay functions in the normal manner, but salvation was to be sought exclusively through the Church. The main social institutions—the structure of inequality, including the division between free men and slaves, the property system, the system of government—were regarded as conventional remedies for the sinful condition into which men had fallen. By nature men were free and equal, and all goods were enjoyed in common. This equality persisted in men's relation to God, but not elsewhere.[56]

When the Church gained its pre-eminent position in feudal society, a more positive attitude towards secular society had to be adopted in keeping with its general aim of achieving a unified Christian civilization. The theory of the Church fathers was not sharply rejected, but rather subjected to subtle but important changes of emphasis. Although the theory of a primitive condition of man, in which government was absent, men were equal, and property was common, was retained, the existing social institutions were no longer regarded as sinful and contrary to natural law. The division between the primitive state of man and man in his fallen condition was made less clear-cut. The conception of natural law was refined so that different sets of institutions could with equal validity be said to accord with it. The canon lawyer Rufinus, for instance, distinguished between the absolute commands and prohibitions of natural law (which were immutable) and its *demonstrationes*, which could be modified by human custom. Thus under one set of circumstances common property might be one of the *demonstrationes* of natural law while under different circumstances private property might be similarly justified.[57]

[56] R. W. and A. J. Carlyle, *A History of Mediaeval Political Theory in the West*, vol. i (Edinburgh and London, 1903), Part III, chs. 10–12.
[57] See Carlyle and Carlyle, op. cit., vol. ii (Edinburgh and London, 1909), Part II, chs. 3 and 6; R. Schlatter, *Private Property: the History of an Idea* (London, 1951), pp. 42–4.

Under the conditions then existing, private property was not sinful but positively valuable.

In this way, Christian thought came to terms with the existence of social hierarchy, private property, and political authority, and began to regard these institutions as divinely ordained to fit man's earthly condition, without relinquishing entirely the notion of a higher primitive state. Troeltsch maintains that in making this adjustment two ideas taken from early Christianity were particularly important: the idea of the social organism, according to which each man is called to a station and expected to perform the duties attached to it; and the idea of patriarchalism, according to which authority carries with it the obligation to render aid to those over whom it is exercised. These two images combined to give Christian thought a conservative bent:

Society is full of inequalities of every kind, both in the Church and in the world. The equality which does exist is exclusively religious, and even here the position of clergy, monks and laymen is very different. These inequalities, however, are most evident in the relations between master and servant, and in differences in property, official position, and the various secular callings. In this respect it is the duty of every man to remain within his own class, and to serve others gladly.[58]

Against this background we may understand the conception of justice in medieval Christianity. Justice was seen as an important social virtue, and was thought primarily to consist in the observance or enforcement of the law. In terms of our own analysis, justice was interpreted as the protection of a man's legal rights, these rights deriving by custom from his position in the social hierarchy. We have seen that the law in feudal society was fragmented, and this conception of justice therefore contained no notion of the equal treatment of all men: it was thought rather, as one writer has put it, that 'law and justice have as their true purpose the harmonious preservation of the social *status quo* in the interest of common peace and order'.[59]

[58] E. Troeltsch, *The Social Teaching of the Christian Churches* (London, 1931), vol. i, p. 291.
[59] A.-H. Chroust, 'The Function of Law and Justice in the Ancient World and the Middle Ages', *Journal of the History of Ideas*, vii (1946), p. 320.

Besides this primary sense, justice also carried two secondary meanings. Before we examine these, however, an objection to the claims of the last paragraph must be considered. Some pronouncements of the writers we are considering suggest an opposite relationship between law and justice: rather than law being the criterion of justice, it is suggested that law only becomes law when it accords with the principles of justice. This appears to be implicit in the theory of natural law, where human law gains its validity from its correspondence with the law of nature. As the point was summarily stated, an unjust law is no law at all.

To evaluate this objection, we must consider briefly the character of natural law and ask in particular how the *content* of natural law was to be determined. The striking point here is the great flexibility of the law of nature, as understood by medieval Christians. The two main sources of natural law were human reason and scriptural revelation; but these sources required definite interpretation, and also had to be supplemented to deal with many social issues on which they were silent, and these were the tasks of human legislators. Thus, as we have already noted, a wide variety of social institutions might be equally consistent with the law of nature. It seems, therefore, that the only occasion on which natural law might be appealed to in order to condemn a human law would be when the legislator had acted in clear contradiction of an accepted principle of Christian morality. In all other cases, existing law and custom were held to be compatible with (and indeed justified by) natural law. In practice, then, justice was almost always identified with preserving the law as it stood; the notion that human law might lose its legal character by violating natural law was intended as a warning to legislators rather than as a working principle for ordinary men.

Although justice was predominantly identified in the minds of medieval Christian writers with the protection of legally established rights, secondary recognition was given to the claims of need. Here the doctrine that by natural law all property was originally held in common became of practical importance. Because God had in the beginning given the earth to all men to enjoy in common, it followed, first, that no one had a right to take for himself more than he needed, and, second, that a man had only a right to take that of which he made good use.[60] A distinction was drawn between necessities and superfluities, at a level which depended upon a man's station in life. As Tierney puts it, 'medieval canonists took it for granted that different styles of living were appropriate to the different grades in the hierarchy'; superfluities were the goods which a man possessed over and above this accepted standard of living. It was a matter of justice that superfluous goods should be given to those in need, whereas if a man gave away his own necessities to another this was an act of charity or mercy.[61] Aquinas took this doctrine a step further when he argued that a man in need was entitled to avail himself of another man's property;

It is not theft, properly speaking, to take secretly and use another's property in a case of extreme need; because that which he takes for the support of his life becomes his own property by reason of that need.[62]

The final application of the concept of justice in medieval Christianity lay in the doctrine of the just price. This doctrine was intended to govern the buying and selling of goods in the market place; it was held to be morally obligatory to exchange goods at the just price, and indeed legal remedies were available to those who had bought or sold at a price which was afterwards found to diverge considerably from the just price.[63] From our point of view the important question is how the just price of goods was to be determined, and what notion of justice was being invoked in the determination. In particular, was any idea of desert involved, any sense that the producer of goods should be given a fair reward for his skills and efforts? The commentators on this issue can be divided into two schools. The older opinion, represented by, for instance, Weber[64] and Troeltsch,[65] was that the doctrine of the just price expressed a form of economic traditionalism. The just price of

---

[60] Carlyle and Carlyle, op. cit., vol. ii, Part II, ch. 6.

[61] B. Tierney, *Medieval Poor Law* (Berkeley and Los Angeles, 1959), ch. 2.

[62] Aquinas, *Summa Theologica*, ii–ii, qu. 66, art. 7, in D. Bigongiari (ed.), *The Political Ideas of St. Thomas Aquinas*, p. 139.

[63] See J. W. Baldwin, *The Medieval Theories of the Just Price* (Philadelphia, 1959).

[64] M. Weber, *The Protestant Ethic and the Spirit of Capitalism.*

[65] Troeltsch, op. cit., vol. i, ch. II, section 8.

any item was that which permitted its producer to maintain himself at the standard of life appropriate to a person of his social standing. The doctrine therefore fitted neatly into the general view of society as a hierarchically graded organism, and matched the primary belief that the purpose of justice was to sustain each man in his position in the hierarchy. More recently, however, this view has been attacked by American scholars, who maintain that the just price was simply to be identified with the current price of a commodity—usually with the price which it fetched in the open market, occasionally with the price which had been fixed by the authorities.[66] From this standpoint, an object might be sold above its just price, if, for instance, the seller took advantage of the buyer's ignorance to exact a price higher than that which the object would generally fetch at that time and place.

It would require much careful analysis of the original texts to decide between these two interpretations, but fortunately this is unnecessary for our purposes. The important point is that, whichever account of the just price is correct, the doctrine contains no principle of desert which would cause us to modify our general picture of feudal ideas of justice. In neither version is it suggested that the just price is the price which adequately repays the producer for the skills and efforts he has put into making the object. Attempts to find such a 'cost of production' theory in Aquinas are convincingly refuted by Baldwin. It is true that the writers we are considering believed that labour gave a man a title to his profits—profits made in other ways were condemned as usury—but this is quite different from holding that the *amount* of return should correspond to the amount of labour put in. Baldwin summarizes the canonists' view thus:

Merchants who realised their gains because of contributions of cost, labour, and risk were morally free from censure. Although from a modern economist's point of view this Canonist analysis of profit has implications for their theory of the just price, the Canonists themselves did not make the connection between a price computed from these factors and the market price. For the just price in the

---

[66] See Baldwin, op. cit.; R. de Roover, 'The Concept of the Just Price: Theory and Economic Policy', *Journal of Economic History*, xviii (1958).

external forum was simply the current price, and the factors of costs, labour, and risk morally justified merchants' gains in the internal forum.[67]

The evidence from Christianity points to the following general conclusions about feudal ideas of justice. First, by contrast to primitive societies, justice was an important value in feudal society. Second, the chief demand of justice was that legally established rights should be protected; a subsidiary demand was that those with superfluous wealth should give to those in need; while the claims of desert were not thought to be relevant to justice. Third, the function of justice was to preserve the existing hierarchy, rather than to provide criteria for social reform. In short, while we can recognize elements of our own notion of justice in feudal thought, feudal society clearly lacked our idea of social justice as a goal to be achieved. These conclusions are borne out when we examine the alternative sources of evidence, beginning with the civil lawyers.

We need not dwell long on the civilians, since in all important respects their views converge with those of the canonists and theologians. Justice is again thought to be expressed primarily in the law, though it is recognized that the law is in some ways an imperfect expression of natural justice; furthermore, justice is constant, whereas the positive law is found to vary according to circumstances. However, it is not suggested that the idea of justice should be used in a critical fashion to reform the existing body of law; it is rather to be appealed to only in those cases in which the law at present gives no guidance. In practice, then, we again find that justice is primarily to be realized by the constant application of positive law.[68]

It is perhaps more surprising to find that the social critics of feudal society agree with the exponents of the established religion over the questions we have discussed. There is no shortage of vitriolic attacks on nobles, knights, the clergy, and so forth, delivered by popular preachers or expressed in the songs of minstrels. These attacks, however, were aimed at the personal failings of those occupying the privileged positions in the social hierarchy rather than at the hierarchy itself. Indeed, the critics usually pointed out that each class in society

[67] Baldwin, op. cit., p. 58.
[68] Carlyle and Carlyle, op. cit., vol. ii, Part I, chs. 1–3.

exhibited its own distinctive vices, as well as sharing in common faults, such as pride and avarice.[69] The common people were warned against trying to better their place in society, and we find, characteristically, that the German minstrel Freidank 'unsparingly castigates the oppression of the poor by the rich but remarks that if a poor man becomes rich he usually turns into the worst of oppressors'.[70] The metaphor of the body was often used to point out that the different classes in society were necessary to one another, and particularly to remind the privileged that their position was ordained in order that they should serve the needs of the poor. Hertz summarizes the German evidence in the following words:

In spite of the abundance of social criticism, however, almost all authors stood for the maintenance of the existing social order and believed that its faults could be mended if everybody stayed in his class and fulfilled the duties connected with it.[71]

Owst arrives at a similar conclusion on the basis of a survey of English popular preaching:

. . . each man's first duty—be he knight or priest, workman or merchant—is to learn and labour truly in the things of his own particular calling, resting content therewith and not aspiring to meddle with the tasks and mysteries of others. The social ranks and their respective duties, ordained by God for humanity, were intended to remain fixed and immutable. Like the limbs of the Body, they cannot properly exchange either their place or function.[72]

Although we should not expect to find philosophical discussion of justice in these popular writings, it is fairly clear that the same notion of justice is implicit here as was made explicit in the Christian texts: first, the preference for hierarchy over equality; second, the importance of respecting traditional rights and performing traditional duties; third, (perhaps stressed more heavily here) the duty of the rich to satisfy the needs of the poor. This is strong evidence that feudal society was at one in its understanding of justice, and that when the poor attacked the rich, they did so on the grounds

[69] See G. R. Owst, *Literature and Pulpit in Medieval England* (Oxford, 1961).
[70] F. O. Hertz, *The Development of the German Public Mind*, vol. i (London, 1957), p. 146.
[71] Hertz, op. cit., p. 148.   [72] Owst, op. cit., p. 557.

that the rich were failing to carry out commonly recognized duties of justice, rather than in terms of an ideal of social justice which implied fundamental changes in the established order.

A final point of confirmation is to be found in Cohn's study of medieval millenarian movements.[73] These movements represent the most radical form of dissent which can be discovered in the medieval period; yet Cohn points out that demands for radical *social* reform (in particular for the abolition of private property and the creation of an egalitarian society) are only to be found at the close of the Middle Ages, certainly not before the late fourteenth century. At this time feudal society had begun to disintegrate, and a proletariat was beginning to form in the larger European cities. Furthermore, Cohn argues that the advocates of these radical proposals found most of their adherents among socially marginal groups— landless peasants, unskilled workers, beggars, etc. He draws a contrast with traditional peasant political attitudes which were directed towards the preservation of existing rights and, where possible, the winning of better economic conditions, but without any basic challenge to the social hierarchy. Cohn's findings show that, so long as the structure of feudal society remained intact, it was able to generate in its members a conception of justice which supported that structure. The only alternative to accepting society as it stood was to withdraw from society and take up the religious life; the idea of reforming society was foreign to the feudal mind.

What is the connection between the feudal conception of justice and the conditions of life in feudal society? Let us begin by noting that the supply of food and other basic goods was more certain in feudal societies than in most primitive societies. Although poor by comparison to modern market societies, they generally afforded the peasantry a subsistence income and of course allowed privileged groups—the nobility and the clergy—to live off the surplus created by the peasants. In considering primitive societies, I argued that an overriding concern for economic survival militated against the development of a sense of justice; the main preoccupation of feudal society, however, was less economic survival than the preserva-

[73] N. Cohn, *The Pursuit of the Millennium* (London, 1970).

tion of order—what men feared was that society would disintegrate into a congeries of warring platoons, as indeed it did from time to time. To preserve order in the absence of a sovereign power, it was above all necessary that customary rights and obligations should be respected; in such a context it becomes intelligible that justice should become an important value, and that it should be interpreted in a conservative sense, to refer to the protection of established rights. We have repeatedly stressed that in feudal society the function of justice was to stabilize the social hierarchy in the interests of order.

We may turn now to the social relationships characteristic of feudalism. How did men holding different positions in the hierarchy encounter one another? First, it was clear that each man had a single dominant role, determined mainly by the type of work he performed, and these sole differences were made perfectly manifest in differences of dress, speech, etc. Second, there was at the same time sufficient geographical and social mobility to make it clear that the various estates were not occupied by men of different 'breeds': there was a sense of common humanity and an appreciation that the separation of men into estates was conventional, although of course absolutely necessary. Third, the relationship between superior and inferior was a personal one. The serf was not subordinated to the nobility as a collective group but tied to one particular lord, and equally the vassal swore homage either to a single lord or (through a corruption of the institution) to a small number of lords. Writers on feudalism have observed that the system worked best when this personal relationship was preserved through sustained contact between master and man. Now if we take these three points together, what moral ideas are likely to emerge from such a system of relationships? First, the strength of role divisions is such that more emphasis will be laid on maintaining the various roles than on giving each person his due as an individual. Justice will be thought to consist primarily in treating a man according to his station rather than according to his particular personal qualities. In other words, (as I shall argue later) justice as desert can only emerge as a value when the market has rendered role divisions much more fluid, so that we encounter other men as individuals rather than as the occupants of fixed roles. So long as role distinctions

remain strong, the appropriate way of understanding justice is
as the protection of a man's rights which derive from his social
position.

We have also seen, however, that in feudal society the occupants of different roles were linked to one another by ties
of personal dependence. Relationships of this type naturally
created a sense of mutual obligation rather than a sense of
mutual indifference. Although there was no question of the lord
acknowledging the serf as his equal, he did recognize that they
were connected by a personal bond, and that he therefore had a
responsibility for the serf's welfare (no doubt in practice such
responsibilities were often evaded, but we are here considering
the moral responses appropriate to feudal society). This is the
basis of the recognition given to the claims of need in the
feudal conception of justice. A condition of need gave a man
a just claim on the resources of those placed in privileged
positions, and especially of course on the master to whom he
was personally tied. We should again note the contrast with
market society where impersonal market relationships predominate, and men are likely to encounter one another as strangers.

It may be said that a sufficient explanation of the recognition given to the claims of need in feudal society is the influence
of Christian teaching; it is unnecessary to seek for further
reasons in the feudal social structure. But we have seen that the
social teaching of Christianity was adapted to feudalism in
such a way that elements which were radically incompatible
with that system were discarded. If doctrines such as that of
Augustine—'Justice consists in helping the wretched'—
were acceptable to the medieval Church, it was because they
corresponded to moral sentiments which feudalism tended
spontaneously to produce.

It is worth noting that the features of feudalism we have
referred to in our explanation are not present in all types of
hierarchical society. In a caste system, for instance, each person
is strictly confined within the caste of his birth, and contact
between members of different castes is kept to a minimum.
Under these circumstances, the idea that men naturally belong
to different 'breeds', rather than sharing in a common humanity, can more easily take root.[74] This idea will naturally be

[74] Cf. C. Bouglé, *Les Idées égalitaires* (Paris, 1899), esp. Part II, ch. 3.

reflected in beliefs about justice—it would be surprising, for instance, if the claims of need were regarded as a matter of justice in a caste system. Now caste systems are plausibly seen as the purest type of hierarchical society.[75] It is therefore wrong to conclude that our analysis of justice in feudal society can be applied to other kinds of hierarchical society, which may embody different notions of justice or indeed lack any notion of justice at all. On the other hand, we may conjecture that where, as in feudalism, hierarchy is combined with personal dependence and a small degree of mobility, a strong sense of justice will emerge, which is nevertheless different in content from that found in market societies. Under feudalism justice is understood, first, as the obligation to respect established rights, and, second, as the obligation to help the needy, within the limits of one's social position; little or no weight is given to the claims of desert. We shall see that in market societies these priorities are sharply reversed.

4 *Market Societies*

At the beginning of this chapter, I introduced the social typology which I was about to use with the observation that each type of society—primitive, feudal, and market—was distinguished by the prominence of certain features within it, while features characteristic of the other types would be present to a lesser degree. It is particularly important to bear this in mind when discussing market society. I shall describe the early capitalist systems of Western Europe and America as 'market societies', while acknowledging that in real terms these systems superimposed 'non-market' social structures and relationships upon market ones. What are the distinctive social relationships which make up a market society? Its social structure is created out of a series of contracts and exchanges between otherwise free and equal individuals. By contrast to their situation in primitive society, men in market society are not bound by obligations of kinship and traditional status. By contrast to feudalism, they have no fixed place in a hierarchy, and owe no allegiance to any superior. Under a market system, men are

---

[75] See especially C. Bouglé, *Essays on the Caste System* (Cambridge, 1971); L. Dumont, *Homo Hierarchicus* (London, 1972).

equal before the law. They are free to choose their occupations, to join whatever associations they wish, to buy and sell in the market, to make contracts without restriction, to gain wealth and prestige. Any social and economic inequalities arise from these activities. Most of what each man produces is exchanged in the market, rather than consumed directly; this implies a fairly extensive division of labour and a system of mutual inter-dependence centred on the market.

If we compare this market model with the actual conditions of Western capitalism (at any point in its development) we shall see that, although market relations have always been predomi-nant, they have been combined with other elements of social structure, especially with the existence of vertical class divisions. Capitalist societies are not pure market societies, firstly be-cause they typically contain an aristocratic class whose social position is inherited rather than achieved through production and exchange; and secondly, because they contain a working class whose situation is only partly a market one. The worker enters into market relationships with his employer (he freely exchanges his services for a wage) and with the tradesmen from whom he buys his goods, but his relationship with his fellow workers is not basically a market one. It is rather one of mutual assistance and mutual support for security, and for protection against a common opponent—the employer. Trade unions, the chief institutional form through which this class solidarity has been expressed, have rightly been recognized by theorists of the market as incompatible with a pure market system, rather as the communal compact of medieval burgesses was seen by feudal thinkers as alien to that system. We shall later examine what effect its ambiguous position—half in and half out of the market—has had on the social ideas of the work-ing class.

The fact that in the real world market relations only exist in conjunction with vertical class divisions has the unfortunate consequence that we cannot find a homogeneous market society with an appropriate set of shared social ideas. But it may be possible to overcome this difficulty to a certain degree by finding within market societies a group of people for whom market relations are particularly salient. During the earlier period of capitalism, particularly in Britain and the U.S.A., the middle class appear to form such a group. I include among the middle class capitalists, merchants, shopkeepers, and (more arguably) independent artisans and farmers. These men worked for themselves, and their success depended upon their ability to produce and sell in the market. They inherited no fixed position in society, yet the social structure was sufficiently open for them to rise in the world according to their ability and good fortune, at least until they reached the very top of the social scale. In this respect they are of course to be contrasted both with the landed aristocracy and with the working class. The position of the professional class is rather more ambiguous, since in the early capitalist period it had not yet achieved that independence of the market which it was later to acquire—professional men, for example, were usually paid by fees, and lived on an equal footing with urban businessmen.[76] However, the central figures in our investigation must be the entrepreneur, the trader, and the shopkeeper.

The social ideas of these men have often been presented as a class ideology—a distorted set of beliefs which the middle class succeeded in imposing upon the other classes of society in order to achieve a secure position of economic and political dominance. Undoubtedly, middle-class ideas did serve to promote class interests, but I want for present purposes to approach these ideas from another direction, not as a functional weapon of class domination, but as a direct response to the social relationships within which the middle class found itself. (These two approaches are not of course incompatible, unless the class ideology thesis is taken to imply a deliberate attempt on the part of the class to put forward ideas which it knew to be false.) As before, ideas of justice are best understood in the context of broader views of society.

The rise of a 'spirit of capitalism' characteristic of market society was the subject of a famous controversy between Weber, who saw the emergence of Protestantism (particularly in its Calvinist form) as an important cause of the capitalist spirit, and the followers of Marx, who held that the economic conditions of capitalism were of themselves sufficient to invoke the

[76] See H. Perkin, *The Origins of Modern English Society, 1780–1880* (London, 1972), p. 428.

appropriate spirit. Both sides of the debate, however, recognize an important contradiction between the traditional content of Christian social theory and the new social ideas which were necessary to a market society. Christian thought, in both its Catholic and its Lutheran forms, essentially retained the medieval picture of an organic, hierarchically ordered society, in which the various classes of men had been ordained to serve one anothers' needs. In conformity with this picture, a man's social duty was thought to reside primarily in the competent execution of the tasks associated by tradition with his station in life, rather than in bettering his social position or in creating large quantities of material wealth. As market relationships became more prominent, and as the middle class began to exert more social influence, a new theory, which we may refer to as individualism, was developed.[77] This theory abandoned any notion of a natural hierarchy in society, and began instead with the idea that men were born free and equal, possessing sets of rights which derived from their inherent natural capacities. Society was seen as the product of the contracts and associations into which these free individuals had entered for their own advantage. The social order was not a constraint on human ambitions, rather whatever order society possessed was the result of human wants and interests, and ideally at least should be readily modifiable if those wants and interests changed. A man's duty was no longer to remain within his station, but instead to take on whatever tasks, and reap whatever rewards, his abilities would allow him. In religious thought, this meant that the doctrine of the 'calling' was transformed from a recipe for economic traditionalism into the demand that each man should seek out the calling most suited to his capacities.[78] The parable of the talents was cited to show that God had granted each man abilities in order that he should put them to the best use possible, and gain his just reward in the process:

[77] The term 'individualism' has many possible referents. It is here used to refer to the theory of society which is outlined in the remainder of the paragraph. Steven Lukes, in his book *Individualism* (Oxford, 1973), has distinguished between several different doctrines commonly called individualism. The theory of society here described appears to combine at least three of these doctrines: methodological individualism, economic individualism, and the belief in the abstract individual.

[78] See M. Weber, *The Protestant Ethic and the Spirit of Capitalism.*

If God show you a way in which you may lawfully get more than in another way (without wrong to your soul or to any other), if you refuse this, and choose the less gainful way, you cross one of the ends of your calling, and you refuse to be God's steward, and to accept His gifts and use them for Him when He requireth it . . .[79]

The secular equivalent of this view was the argument that each man, in pursuing his private advantage, contributed as much as he could to the common stock of goods, and therefore that the general happiness would be furthest advanced by giving free play to private ambition. This argument was set out most dogmatically in the writings of the lesser political economists. Malthus, for example, maintained:

If no man could hope to rise or fear to fall in society; if industry did not bring its own reward, and indolence its punishment; we could not hope to see that animated activity in bettering our own condition which now forms the master-spring of public prosperity.[80]

Such a view became widely accepted among the entrepreneurial middle class. Beatrice Webb's report of the moral beliefs held by her mother is presented as typical of the period:

. . . it was the bounden duty of every citizen to better his social status; to ignore those beneath him, and to aim steadily at the top rung of the social ladder. Only by this persistent pursuit by each individual of his own and his family's interest would the highest general level of civilization be attained. . . . No one of the present generation realises with what sincerity and fervour these doctrines were held by the representative men and women of the mid-Victorian middle class.[81]

Two further points ought to be made about this individualist theory of society. First, it might be advanced either in a capitalist or in an anti-capitalist form. In its capitalist form, the theory held that the ownership of capital was (at least for some people) an essential part of the development of personal capacities, and that the existence of such ownership was in no way inconsistent with the freedom of contract and association which the model

[79] R. Baxter, cited in Weber, op. cit., p. 162.
[80] Cited in Perkin, op. cit., p. 226.
[81] B. Webb, *My Apprenticeship* (Harmondsworth, 1971), p. 40.

demanded. On the other hand, the theory as developed by critics of capitalism such as Hodgskin and the anarchist Tucker saw the ownership of capital by a few as an obstacle to genuine individualism, and the individualist ideal as realizable only through the free association of labourers (Hodgskin)[82] or independent proprietorship (Tucker).[83] During the period we are considering, the middle class adopted the theory almost exclusively in its capitalist form; land ownership was frequently attacked, but rarely so the ownership of capital. It was only with the growth of monopolies and trusts in the later years of capitalism that anti-capitalist individualism became at all popular in middle-class circles.

Second, an important component of the individualist theory was the belief that every man had the opportunity to climb the social ladder and to achieve the highest rewards that society had to offer. This did not necessarily mean that opportunities were equal (equality of opportunity is a more recent ideal) but rather that no barriers of a legal, social, or economic type would prevent the man with determination to succeed from gaining his rewards. This belief has recently been referred to as 'the myth of the self-made man'.[84] It was particularly stressed by those who wanted to purvey the theory to a working-class audience, since it implied that no working man, however humble his present position, was prevented from bettering his condition except by his personal inadequacies. As Samuel Smiles put it, 'What some men are, all without difficulty might be. Employ the same means, and the same results will follow.'[85] This feature of the theory helps to explain its breadth of appeal, indicated perhaps by the enormous sales which *Self-Help* had achieved by the end of the nineteenth century.[86]

An integral part of individualism was a conception of justice as the requital of desert. This criterion is stressed to the exclusion both of the protection of rights and of the fulfilment of needs. Of course, in individualist theory the rights of property are inviolable, and contracts must be enforced, but the ultimate ground for these views is either utilitarian or else resides in

[82] T. Hodgskin, *Labour Defended Against the Claims of Capital* (London, 1922).

[83] B. R. Tucker, *State Socialism and Anarchism* (London, 1895).

[84] Perkin, op. cit., ch. 7.   [85] Cited in Perkin, op. cit., p. 225.

[86] See A. Briggs, *Victorian People* (Harmondsworth, 1955), ch. 5, pp. 125–6.

the conception of justice referred to. Individualism has no time
for rights as such, when these are neither socially useful nor
necessary to ensure that desert gets its proper reward; it would
not, for instance, acknowledge that the rights traditionally
attached to a particular social position were in any way worthy
of respect. Anything that a man may justly claim he must earn
by exercising his capacities in a socially useful way, in which
case the institutions of property, contract, and exchange will
ensure that he gets a fair return.

This interpretation of justice as the requital of desert was
bolstered by the view that a man's character was made by him,
not for him, so that the various abilities, skills, and efforts
which formed the basis of desert were seen as being within a
person's own control. Conversely, incapacity and failure of
will were seen as the results, not of external circumstances, but
rather of inner weakness. Tawney notes the Puritan origins of
this belief:

Convinced that character is all and circumstances nothing, he
[the Puritan] sees in the poverty of those who fall by the way, not
a misfortune to be pitied and relieved, but a moral failing to be
condemned, and in riches, not an object of suspicion—though like
other gifts they may be abused—but the blessing which rewards the
triumph of energy and will.[87]

Such a conviction was particularly important to those like
Smiles who wanted to explain the deprived condition of large
numbers of men by reference to their personal weakness, and to
convince the populace that it was within their power to remake
their characters and acquire valuable propensities like thrift
and foresight. I have argued in an earlier chapter that desert
need not be understood in this way,[88] but there is no doubt that
the identification of justice with the requital of desert looks
strongest when desert is based upon features of men which are
thought to be within their control. It is interesting to note
here that the Calvinist doctrine of predestination appears to
have strengthened rather than weakened the conviction that a
man had the power to remould his character and capacities.

---

[87] R. H. Tawney, *Religion and the Rise of Capitalism* (Harmondsworth, 1938),
pp. 229–30.
[88] See chapter 3, section 3.

Confident that they belonged to the elect, Calvinist business-men knew that God would give them the strength to live according to the highest moral standards, particularly the standard of hard work in one's daily calling.[89]

Two particular features of the middle-class belief system illustrate the strength of the notion of desert within that system. One is the gospel of work. In sharp contrast to the medieval schema in which each social estate had its own allotted function, the distinction between productive and unproductive classes emerged early in the history of market societies.[90] The productive classes were taken to include both capitalists and labourers, who were compared favourably with the unproductive members of society, such as landlords, who lived idly off their rents. Sometimes, abstinence was added to labour as a justifying condition of reward. Senior put the point succinctly:

Wages and profits are the creation of man. They are the recompense for the sacrifice made, in the one case, of ease; in the other, of immediate enjoyment. But a considerable part of the produce of every country is the recompense of no sacrifice whatever; is received by those who neither labour nor put by, but merely hold out their hands to accept the offerings of the rest of the community.[91]

Among the middle class in Victorian England, work became a primary virtue in itself, and idleness was regarded as an unforgiveable sin. Their sense of justice was revolted by the parasite who consumed what others had produced.[92]

A second illuminating feature of the belief system we are examining is the manner in which the problem of poor relief was treated. It might be thought natural that the claims of the poor should be presented as claims of need, and that the distribution of poor relief should be made to depend on the extent of personal need; we have seen that this is how the problem was treated in feudal thought. But in market societies, an attempt was made to replace need criteria by desert criteria even in this

---

[89] Weber, op. cit., ch. 4.

[90] See, for example, Adam Smith, *The Wealth of Nations*, ed. A. Skinner (Harmondsworth, 1970), Book ii, ch. 3.

[91] Cited in Perkin, op. cit., p. 227.

[92] See W. E. Houghton, *The Victorian Frame of Mind* (New Haven, 1957), ch. 10, pp. 242–62.

area. A distinction was first drawn between the 'deserving' and
the 'undeserving' poor—that is to say, between those who, although displaying meritorious personal qualities, had been
reduced to poverty by accidental circumstances beyond their
control, and those whose poverty could be attributed directly
to personal failings such as drunkenness, idleness, etc. In
England, the Charity Organisation Society used this distinction as a leading principle in its work, attempting to give aid
only to those who could be shown to be deserving, and limiting
the extent of its charity to what was necessary to set the individual back on his feet again.[93] Secondly, when it came to dealing with the undeserving poor, the emphasis was less on helping
the needy than on encouraging the undeserving to become
deserving. This thinking underlay the changes made in the
Poor Law in 1834 which, by establishing the workhouse system,
attempted to ensure that the poor would earn the subsistence
they were receiving, and learn in time to acquire habits of
industry.[94]

The problem of estimating desert was solved in individualist
theory by relying on the institutions of the free market—exchange and contract—to return a fair reward to each producer. We have already seen[95] how Spencer, the paradigm
case of an individualist, refers to the laws of supply and demand
as the guarantee of fairness in a market system. A more formal
way of showing the connection between desert and the market
was to employ the labour theory of value. If the value of an
object is equal to the quantity of labour embodied in it, if the
system of exchange ensures that (in the long run) objects
exchange in proportion to their values, and if, finally, quantity
of labour is an adequate measure of desert, then a market
system must reward producers according to their deserts. Of
course we do not need to suppose that the middle class generally
was familiar with the details of political economy to make this
point; all we need assume is that the doctrines which the political economists set out formally were informally understood and
accepted by the class as a whole. The evidence for this ranges
from the wide sale in England of Harriet Martineau's popu-

[93] See Webb, op. cit., pp. 206–25; Perkin, op. cit., pp. 446–8.
[94] See S. and B. Webb, *English Poor Law Policy* (London, 1910), esp. ch. 1.
[95] Chapter 6, esp. section 3.

larizations of the subject[96] and the success of Spencer and the 'Social Darwinists' in America,[97] to the direct reports by contemporaries such as Beatrice Webb.[98]

Why should individualism, and the theory of justice as the reward of merit that goes with it, have been produced by market society, and especially by the group in that society for whom market relations were particularly salient? One answer is that individualism is simply a correct description of market society; and that the market really does reward people according to their deserts. But this is manifestly too crude an answer, and neither of the claims contained in it is very plausible. We shall do better to look for an intelligible link between the social position of the group we have singled out for examination and the ideas of justice to which it adhered. The relevant features of the social position of the middle-class entrepreneur or tradesman are as follows: first, the lack of a fixed social status such as would be provided by a hierarchical society, but instead the opportunity to make one's way in the world by one's efforts; second, the absence of a traditional set of rights and obligations— whether to kinsmen, etc., as in primitive society, or to superiors and/or inferiors as in hierarchical society; third, social and geographical mobility, with the consequence that many of one's social encounters are with strangers; fourth, the prominence of market relations themselves—particularly the exchange of goods and services, and free entry into contract.

The fourth of these features is perhaps the most important. The intellectual results of the exchange relationship have been classically analysed by Marx and Bouglé.[99] Both see the market as essentially egalitarian in its implications; it undermines hierarchical social and legal relations because market power is solely a function of the amount of exchange value (goods or money) that a person possesses. From the point of view of the market traditional social distinctions are irrelevant, and there is a contradiction between the equality of the market place and, say, the social inequality of a system of estates. As

[96] R. K. Webb, *Harriet Martineau* (New York, 1960), ch. 4.
[97] R. Hofstadter, *Social Darwinism in American Thought* (Philadelphia, 1945).
[98] See B. Webb, op. cit., esp. ch. 1.
[99] K. Marx, *Grundrisse* (Harmondsworth, 1973), esp. pp. 239–50; C. Bouglé, *Les Idées égalitaires*, esp. Part II, ch. 2.

market relations become more dominant, egalitarian demands are made—for equal human rights, equality before the law, political equality, etc. But this egalitarianism stops short of economic equality in the strong sense, for the market requires equality in the exchange of values rather than the equal treatment of individuals. Its principle of operation is that each man should receive back the exact equivalent in value of what he brings to the market; however, the amount brought to the market will depend upon the productive powers of the individual, which differ of course from person to person. What the market achieves is a distribution according to desert (where desert is measured by the creation of exchange value) rather than economic equality. Bouglé is correct when, in setting out the 'egalitarian ideas' which characterize modern (late nineteenth-century) society, he gives the principle 'to each according to his works' as the criterion of economic distribution, and rejects the principle of equal distribution which he believes to enjoy little favour with his contemporaries.

We can thus see how the experience of the market leads people to adopt a conception of justice as the requital of desert. The paradigmatic exchange relationship takes place between two people who are strangers to one another, who owe neither deference nor services to each other, and whose knowledge is limited to the relative values of the goods or services to be exchanged. This relationship allows no foothold either to the notion of protecting rights or to the notion of satisfying needs. Established rights are irrelevant because neither person stands in any fixed role relationship towards the other, there are no standing obligations, and so on. Needs are irrelevant because each party to the exchange is bent solely on making the most favourable bargain possible, and in any case has no knowledge of the needs of the other party. On the other hand, although an exchange relationship does not have as its *direct* object the requital of desert, it does *indirectly* bring about this result provided that desert is defined in such a way that a person's deserts are embodied in the commodity which he brings to the exchange. At the very least, the definition of justice as desert is the only substantive conception which is consistent with the type of interpersonal relationship characteristic of the market.

Our diagnosis of the position of the middle class in the early stages of capitalism showed not only that market relationships were particularly prominent in their experience, but also that other types of relationship were lacking. There were neither the bonds of hierarchy nor the ties of community which might provide the support for alternative conceptions of justice to the desert conception supported by the market. However, this point must not be overstated: obviously, middle-class entrepreneurs had families and circles of friends, and in these relationships different ideas of justice would be appropriate—considerations of need, for example, would clearly be in place within the family. But two further observations qualify this concession. First, it was possible to maintain a clear separation between justice within the family and social justice, and to prevent domestic ideas of justice from modifying social ideas; a separation which would clearly be impossible in, say, a primitive society. (We observed this separation made fully explicit in the writings of Spencer.) Second, the market did not leave the morality of domestic life wholly unaffected. It is significant, for instance, that a compassionate woman such as Beatrice Webb's mother should feel obliged to pay servants at exactly the market rate even when it became obvious that the work demanded was injuring their health.[1] The dominant ideas of social justice were formed by the market system, and the family group did not provide a strong enough countervailing force to modify those ideas significantly.

Again, the market network in England coexisted with a scale of prestige, in which the highest places were reserved, not for the successful entrepreneur, but for the landed aristocracy. This had the consequence that for many members of the middle class the ideally preferred form of life was that of the country gentleman, and it became a common ambition of the entrepreneurial class to acquire enough capital to purchase an estate in the country and retire from business.[2] But this appears in no way to have diminished the influence of market relationships over the ideas of middle-class men for as long as they remained within that class. Presumably those men who aspired to gentlemanly retirement were also those who attacked the traditional landowner as an idle parasite.

[1] B. Webb, op. cit., pp. 39–40.
[2] See Brigges, op. cit., p. 141; Houghton, op. cit., pp. 189–90.

For the middle class in the period we are considering, then, the most salient interpersonal relationships were market ones, and this helps us to understand why a concept of justice centred on the notion of desert should have been adopted by this group. The members of the working class, however, entered into relationships of a different type with one another, which may broadly be described as co-operative. The two classic institutions here were the trade union and the co-operative society. These institutions were based upon mutual aid for common ends rather than upon competition and exchange between individuals. At the same time, the salience of market relationships must not be underestimated. The worker was bound to his employer by a tie no stronger than that of contract, so that he was free at any time to look for better employment. It was also possible for him to cease working for a wage, become self-employed, or even become an employer himself. Of course, this was not a realistic possibility for any but a small minority of the working class; but the fact that it was a possibility at all had the important implication that the ambitious worker was always torn between seeking individual advancement through his own efforts and seeking collective advancement for his class as a whole through bodies such as trade unions and class parties.

The consequence of this ambiguity in its social position was that the members of the working class were torn between two competing images of society, each with its associated ideal of social justice. In so far as they were influenced by market relationships, they developed an individualist theory of society, which might or might not take a capitalist form, and adopted a conception of justice centred on the notion of desert. In so far as they were influenced by co-operative relationships, they developed a collectivist view of society, and adopted a conception of justice centred on the notion of need. This ambiguity is often obscured by those who say that the working class was at this period generally committed to the value of equality, without enquiring carefully into the meaning of this commitment. Leaving aside those working men who wanted only to remain in their traditional station, and those whose ambition was confined to individual advancement without any change in the over-all structure of society, we have firstly those men who wanted merely to redress the balance between capital and labour to ensure that labour got its fair reward, without attacking capital as such. This demand embodies a conception of justice which is only trivially different from the middle-class ideal described earlier. Secondly, there were those who followed Hodgskin in wanting to abolish capital altogether, in order that the working class should receive the full fruits of its labour, while also demanding that each individual worker should then receive the whole product of *his* labour—again a conception of social justice centred on the notion of desert, though here interpreted in a more radical manner. Thirdly, there was the demand that the collective ownership of the means of production should lead to co-operative work and to the division of the product according to need. Here, finally, the market ideal had been abandoned entirely in favour of a new vision of society and a radically different conception of social justice. However, it is impossible to say how widely this latter view was held, or indeed whether it was clearly distinguished from the previous one. Agreement at this level was not necessary for practical political work, which in the short term was concentrated on winning concessions for the worker from the employer. In short, the shared commitment to a diffuse ideal of equality conceals from us the basic equivocation in the working-class belief system which, if my analysis is correct, can be understood by reference to the ambiguous social position of that class, especially in relation to market institutions.[3]

[3] The same data are sometimes given a rather different interpretation. The members of the working class are seen as the victims of an imposed middle class ideology, in the face of which they spasmodically attempt to develop a genuine working-class outlook which forms a 'correct' response to their material situation. In my view, this interpretation must be rejected for two reasons: first, the individualist ideal and the collectivist ideal are equally 'correct' views for the working class to take up, since they correspond to different aspects of their material situation. The middle class did not have to impose an ideal which was in some way fundamentally at odds with the experience of the working class—thought no doubt the work of middle-class ideologists such as Smiles helped to reinforce the individualist elements in working-class thinking. Second, working-class radicalism could be expressed either in terms of the individualist view of society, or in terms of the collectivist view. For instance, the abolition of capital could be seen either as the condition for a genuine market system in which each worker would receive the full fruits of his labour, or as the condition for the abolition of the market, and the establishment of a co-operative system with distribution taking place according to need. For this reason, working-class radicalism does not necessarily imply a sharp break with the dominant belief system, but may instead represent an internal modification of that system.

5 *The Transformation of Market Societies*

This diagnosis of working-class beliefs about justice prepares the way for a discussion of the changes which have taken place in market societies since the mid-nineteenth century. I shall argue that these changes are sufficiently extensive for us to give the current system in the West a new label—'organized capitalism' is the one I shall use—and that this social transformation has produce a marked shift in ideas of social justice. Yet because the economic market remains a prominent feature of this system, I prefer to regard organized capitalism as a variant form of market society, rather than as a radically new social type. The focus of attention will continue to be Britain and the U.S.A.

The first change which has contributed significantly to the transformation of market societies is the growth of large enterprises. The average size of companies has increased, and many areas of production are now dominated by a small number of giant firms. This has had both economic and social consequences. Economically, the system no longer matches the market model, in which many individual producers bring their commodities to the market and the price is fixed by the working of supply and demand. Of course, capitalist economies never fully realized this ideal of perfect competition even at the height of the market period, but the growth of 'stable oligopoly' (as some writers have termed it) among producers marks a further step away from the ideal, with ideological consequences which we shall examine presently. Socially, the change has meant the decline of the entrepreneur. There are certainly still some classical examples of entrepreneurship to be found, of fortunes made from humble beginnings in back-yard workshops, but increasingly the experience of the middle-class industrialist is that of membership of a large organization. He will join as a salaried junior manager, work in various positions within the authority structure of the firm, and perhaps eventually become a member of the board of directors; at no point will he own the company,[4] or be in a position to make independent decisions about what it will do. Even the shop-

---

[4] The *proportion* of the company's shares that he owns is likely to be very small, though their money value may be considerable. See T. Nichols, *Ownership, Control and Ideology* (London, 1969), ch. 6.

keeper, traditionally the pocket edition of the entrepreneur, is now likely to be a salaried employee of a large chain of stores.

Besides an internal evolution within the business sector, market societies have also experienced the growth of non-market institutions in public and professional spheres. In addition to increases in the government bureaucracy, there has been a proliferation of public and semi-public agencies, concerned with such matters as social welfare, the environment, etc. There has also been a steep rise in the proportion of people with professional jobs.[5] I refer to these employments as 'non-market' because they are performed (with variations in detail) by salaried persons who give a service to others without seeking to profit from the undertaking. The recipient may or may not pay a fee for what he gets, but even if he does the exchange is not a market one, since the fee may either be paid directly to the public agency employing the administrator or professional, or, if it is paid to the individual giving the service, it will be estimated according to a fixed scale, not subject to any sort of market haggling. It must be said that there are some areas of professional life which diverge from this standard and approximate to market practice—private medicine, for instance—but generally the principle holds. In the case of professional groups, this insulation from the market is achieved by a code of ethics which is learnt during training and upheld by the professional association; with other groups the standard of service is upheld through bureaucratic control.

Finally, the broadening and strengthening of the trade union movement has altered the position of the working class within capitalism. In some respects, the manual worker's situation still approximates most closely to the market ideal, since he is liable to be hired and fired according to the current demands of production, whereas other employees have achieved a career pattern of employment, with some security of tenure, regular promotions, etc. However, the worker no longer bargains individually with his employer over pay and conditions, but instead these are fixed collectively by the union. I have of course argued that trade unions always acted as an alternative source of experience to the market for the working class, but

[5] See P. Halmos, 'The Personal Service Society', *British Journal of Sociology*, xviii (1967).

since the mid-nineteenth century they have increased both in economic power in the workplace and in political influence. The closed shop, for example, which is the direct antithesis of the free market in labour, was only permitted to develop gradually during the course of this century. Similarly, unions have succeeded in establishing and maintaining pay differentials for the various grades of skilled and unskilled work, which are not necessarily related to the market price of each grade— i.e. to the price which would have to be paid in a free market to secure an adequate supply of any given grade of labour. The long-term growth in union power is too familiar a theme to require further illustration, nor is it necessary to document the political strength of the union movement, achieved mainly through the advent of social-democratic parties.

The over-all trend, therefore, is as follows. Classical market society was characterized by entrepreneurs who owned and managed their own firms, and who made individual contracts with free workers according to the current condition of the labour market. Organized capitalism has substituted collective bargaining between trade unions and large corporations. The worker contracts with management through the intermediary of a collective organization; and the manager himself has to work as a member of an organization, not as an individual decision-maker. Simultaneously with these changes in the economic sphere, there has been a steady increase in professional and administrative work, which does not conform to market principles. We must now ask how these changes in social organization have affected the experience of men in market society, and in turn their ideas about society and social justice.

The chief consequence is that the exchange relationship itself has declined ,in importance, while the new factor of increasing significance is membership of a corporate group. The manager's experience is coloured by his membership of a corporation, the administrator's by belonging to a bureaucracy, the professional's by his membership of an association, and the worker's by belonging to a factory work group organized by a union. The corporate group gives each person an identity and a status, as opposed merely to a market situation. The exchange relationship has not completely disappeared, of course, since each person is placed in such a relationship as a buyer of goods and services, but it no longer dominates personal experience as it did when the market was at its height.

This general thesis holds best of professionals and administrators. It holds with some reservations (to which I shall return) of managers in industry. But in the case of the working class, the evidence points to significant variations from one industrial context to another. For the 'affluent workers' studied by Goldthorpe *et al.*, neither work group, nor firm, nor union acted as an important focus of loyalty and identification, and their membership of these groups was largely 'instrumental'—i.e. used for extracting maximum economic rewards from work. But these workers are contrasted with others—craftsmen, for instance, or miners—for whom work group and union provided a strong sense of corporate identity.[6] Because of these variations, I shall begin by examining changes in middle-class thought and belief, remembering that in this class the ideology of market society was found in its purest form; working-class attitudes will be considered in the following section.

The declining salience of exchange relationships, together with the increasing influence of corporate group membership, has undermined individualism as a theory of society. Individualism took as its starting-point the individual with his innate natural rights, and regarded society as the product of the contracts and associations entered into by such individuals for their own advantage. This picture became increasingly irrelevant to a society dominated by large corporations and national trade unions. In its place a new theory was developed, which I shall call the organized view of society. This depicts society as an 'organization of organizations'; that is to say, society is constituted by the rationally co-ordinated activities of a number of organizations, which themselves co-ordinate the activities of many individuals. Each organization is made up of a number of functionally specific positions, harmonized by a system of authority—authority which, however, is based on managerial ability or professional expertise, rather than on coercive power. Each individual is allotted by a selection procedure to the function for which his skills and capacities best

[6] See J. H. Goldthorpe, D. Lockwood, F. Bechhofer, J. Platt, *The Affluent Worker: Industrial Attitudes and Behaviour* (Cambridge, 1968).

suit him. He works in a spirit of service to society, rather than for economic gain, though he will be paid a salary whose size depends upon his position in the organization. The task of co-ordinating the activities of the various organizations with one another may be assigned to the government, or it may be left to a process of mutual adjustment between the corporate groups themselves.

Intellectual presentations of this view of society are to be found in the writings of Saint-Simon, Durkheim, the Webbs, and Tawney.[7] It is of some interest that, with the partial exception of the first-named, these thinkers are socialists; the organized view is probably most consistent when held in a socialist form. It can, however, be given a capitalist interpreta-tion without undue difficulty, by regarding the capitalist, not as a profit-seeking entrepreneur, but as someone who manages labour and makes decisions about future investment, for which functions he is paid a salary. It is pointed out, correctly enough, that these functions are fulfilled in socialist systems as well. Like individualism, therefore, the organized view of society can be developed in capitalist or anti-capitalist directions.

It may be helpful to indicate what distinguishes this view of society from the others which have been examined in the course of this work. As we have seen, it is distinguished from individualism by its emphasis on organization, and by its assumption that social good results from the rational co-ordination of the activities of altruistic men, rather than from the free play of individual self-interest. It resembles the view of society as a hierarchical order (which we attributed to Hume, and found to be widespread in feudal society) by in-corporating a hierarchy of status, power, and economic reward, but it diverges from that view by its insistence that the social order be rationally planned to promote the common good, and by its belief that the individual should be placed in the hier-archy according to his capacity and talent, rather than by birth or custom. Finally, organized society resembles Kropot-

---

[7] See H. de Saint-Simon, *L'Organisateur* in *Oeuvres de Saint-Simon et d'Enfantin* (Paris, 1865–76), vol. xx; E. Durkheim, *The Divison of Labour in Society*, especially the preface to the second edition; A. M. McBriar, *Fabian Socialism and English Politics, 1884–1918* (Cambridge, 1966); R. H. Tawney, *The Acquisitive Society* (London, 1921); and in general S. S. Wolin, *Politics and Vision* (Boston, 1960), ch. 10.

kin's solidaristic community in relying on the motive of personal altruism to achieve the social good, but departs from it by incorporating inequalities of status, power, and reward, and by making the impersonal organization, rather than the community of familiars, the object of service. Thus the organized view of society appears to borrow elements from each of the ways of looking at society we have earlier contrasted, but to rearrange those elements in a novel way.

It is easy to see why this view of society should appeal to members of the professional class, for it seeks to extend to the whole of society principles which define the professional's own role—the principle of service to others and the professional code of ethics, for example. Indeed, some advocates of the organized model, such as Durkheim and Tawney, saw their proposals explicitly as an attempt to 'professionalize' those sectors of society—especially business—which had hitherto been governed by the disorderly market. Perkin has shown how the professions in Britain, as they became properly established during the nineteenth century, ceased to act as the spokesmen for other classes and began to develop their own 'professional ideal', which matches organized society in its insistence on functional specialization, expertise, and selection by merit.[8] It is understandable, therefore, that the continued growth of the professions in the twentieth century should have strengthened this view of society and helped to diffuse it among other social groups. The disputes which have taken place within and between professions can be seen to be internal to the organized view—for example, the successful attempt by doctors to avoid becoming salaried employees of the state does not constitute a rejection of this view, but involves instead a particular interpretation of it: an interpretation which stresses the independent professional association, as opposed to the co-ordinating role of the state.

The case of the industrial middle class is more complex. Two influences combined to undermine the individualist view of society which this group had traditionally held. First, critics of the capitalist system, who adhered implicitly or explicitly to the professional ideal and the organized view of society, attacked the profit-seeking behaviour of the industrialists as anti-social.

[8] Perkin, op. cit., pp. 252–70.

Since this attack could no longer be met with the dogmatic assertion that private vices were, in the long term, always public benefits, the industrial middle class was obliged to cast about for a new vindication of its role. This could be supplied by finding a place for the industrialist within the organized view of society, by presenting him as a professional with a social function. Second, internal changes in industry itself, which we have outlined above, demanded a similar ideological shift. It was no longer plausible to regard individual firms simply as contractual associations, held together by market bargaining between employer and workers. Such a view was contradicted both by the stronger and more secure position of the worker within the firm, and by the new role of the salaried manager. Instead, the firm had to be seen as an organization, with the managers given the task of leading and supervising the workers, as well as fitting in to a hierarchy of managerial authority.

The shift from individualist to organized view of society among the industrial middle class can be illustrated by two developments in business thinking. The first concerns the role of the businessman himself and the virtues required to carry out that role successfully. The second is the new idea of the social responsibilities of business. We shall examine these developments in turn.

In the individualist theory, the entrepreneur was held to contribute most to the general happiness of society by privately aiming to maximize his profit, and the qualities most valued were those which would help him to realise this end: hard work, perseverance, calculation, thrift, etc. Note that all of these are qualities which characterize individual performance at work; none of them has to do with interpersonal relationships. By the early part of this century, a marked change can be seen in the writings of those who speak on behalf of business. The executive or manager is no longer seen as an independent entrepreneur, but as a leading member of a team, whose qualities are those required to keep others working contentedly under his direction. The emphasis is now put on 'willingness to assume responsibility, self-control, broadmindedness', and similar virtues, which are important for gaining the co-operation of others, rather than for making any direct contribution to production or profit-making.[9] Riesman has incapsulated this change in his distinction between the 'inner-directed' man of traditional capitalism and the 'other-directed' man of managerial society.[10]

While the role of the businessman was being redefined, a new account of the relationship between business and society was in the making. In place of a doctrine of *laissez-faire*, founded on the claim that private profit-making promotes the general happiness, business spokesmen began to speak of service to the community, of the social responsibilities of industry. Managers were represented as professionals, whose authority derived from their expertise, and whose responsibilities were social in nature: they served the community rather than the owners of capital.[11] This general obligation was sometimes broken down into separate obligations—to customers, employees, shareholders, and the general public, for instance.[12] Whatever the precise nature of the list, the intention was the same: to deny that managers were the slaves of profit and to affirm that they were members of a corporation which contributed directly to the common good.

Behind these new lines of thought we can clearly see the general shift from individualist to organized view of society. It is another question how far the new thinking governs the actual behaviour of managers in business, and how far it is merely an attempt to interpret their role in terms of an ideology which has become dominant in society. I shall return to this question later. The present point is that even if the new ideology of business is divorced from actual practice, it nevertheless testifies to the shift in public opinion since the time when individualism was the dominant philosophy. Even if talk of professionalism and corporate responsibilities is spurious, the fact that this language must now be used to vindicate business activities show that the organized view of society has come to be commonly accepted.

Having now traced the change in general ideas which has

[9] See R. Bendix, *Work and Authority in Industry* (New York, 1956), pp. 300–8.

[10] D. Riesman, *The Lonely Crowd* (New Haven and London, 1950).

[11] See M. Heald, 'Management's Responsibility to Society: the growth of an idea', *Business History Review*, xxxi (1957); J. Child, *British Management Thought* (London, 1969).

[12] For an example, see Nichols, op. cit., p. 161.

accompanied the transition from market to organized capitalism, we can turn more specifically to the concept of social justice. Under the market, let us recall, the principle of desert reigned supreme—a man's deserts being estimated by the quantity of goods and services he brought to the market. I shall argue that acceptance of the new image of society has changed this in two ways: first, although desert remains the main element in the idea of social justice, the basis of desert has subtly changed; second, the principle of need has been reintroduced into the idea of social justice.

Let us consider first the change in the basis of desert. In individualist theory each man was seen as an independent producer of goods or supplier of services, and the operation of the market ensured that he reaped his just reward. In the theory of organized society, however, each person is seen as part of a corporate group which collectively supplies goods or services. It is impossible, therefore, to measure individual deserts by the separate value of each man's products. How, then, can desert be estimated and rewarded? This must be done in two stages. First, the various positions in each organization are graded according to the contribution they are deemed to make to the collective product. Each position is then remunerated according to its grade. Second, entrance to the different positions is regulated by competitive examination, or some other method of selection by merit. In this way, the most deserving individual is allotted to the highest position in the organization, and receives the reward which is attached to that position. The same holds of every other position.

We have here, therefore, what Spencer condemned as the 'artificial apportionment of greater rewards to greater merits'. It is artificial in the two-fold sense that the rewards attached to each position are fixed by a human estimate of contribution, and the criterion of merit is also settled by human decision: someone has to decide what qualities the competitive examination is to test. Consequently, there are considerable difficulties in applying this conception of justice, for how can contributions be assessed in practice, and, even supposing this possible, what degree of wage inequality would accurately reflect a given difference in contribution? Furthermore, can we be sure that there is a 'correct' test of merit for any particular occupation? Such difficulties have led one commentator on wage policy to complain that in practice tradition, rather than any rational considerations, seems to be the main factor influencing wage differentials.[13] It might, however, be more accurate to say that status is the decisive factor—the value of jobs is judged by the general aura of prestige that surrounds them, and the 'fair' wage estimated accordingly. But even if the claims of this theory of justice are thus distorted in its practical application, it may fare no worse than the individualist theory. For the assertion that the economic market accurately rewards desert is quite as vulnerable to empirical refutation as the claim that desert will be rewarded in a properly organized society. Indeed, one might add that really gross violations of social justice—vast sums of money received for little or no contribution—are more likely to occur in a market context than in an organization.

The organized view of society also reintroduces the principle of need into the sphere of social justice, after it had been excluded by individualism. We have seen that organized society makes service to the community the dominant motive in work; the justification for rewarding the incumbent of one position more highly than the incumbent of another is that he makes a greater contribution to social well-being. But social well-being must eventually be broken down into individual benefits, and the chief constituent of individual well-being is the satisfaction of needs. Thus the better-off can show their own rewards to be just by meeting the just claims to their services made by those in need. It is important here that the needy have a claim of *justice* to the benefits created by others, otherwise the notion of 'service' degenerates into paternalistic charity.

This reconciliation of the principles of desert and need—desert being manifested in fulfilling a function which helps to satisfy the needs of others—has a strong moral appeal. It is interesting to note that Saint-Simon, who may be regarded as the earliest organization theorist, took as his fundamental principle of morality 'promoting the moral and physical well-being of the poorest class'.[14] The same moral intuition

[13] B. Wootton, *The Social Foundations of Wage Policy* (London, 1958).
[14] H. de Saint-Simon, *Social Organization, The Science of Man and Other Writings* (New York, 1964), p. 86.

may explain the attraction of Rawls's principle that social and economic inequalities should be arranged to the greatest benefit of the least advantaged—though we have seen that Rawls's own understanding of this principle conflicts with our sense of justice, precisely because he interprets the advantages of the better-off as pure incentives, rather than as deserved rewards. Finally the idea reappears in a speech by Edward Heath in which he explains the meaning of 'Tory fairness':

Most people would regard it as fair that the imaginative and energetic in our society should have higher rewards—providing always that the resources they created were used to bring effective help to those in real need.[15]

The growing recognition given to the claims of need in market societies can be traced most easily in the field of social policy. We saw earlier how in nineteenth-century Britain the problem of poverty was approached in terms of 'desert' rather than of 'need'. A decisive change of attitude can be seen when the principles which had governed the Poor Law since 1834 were re-examined by a Royal Commission in 1905–9. It is well known that the members of this Commission were divided in their views, and produced a Majority and a Minority Report. Both Reports had some features in common: they concurred in the view that poverty could not be dealt with merely by a system of deterrence, but that preventative and curative measures must also be taken; they also supported increased state provision for the sick, the aged, and so forth. In these respects, members of both groups showed how considerations of need were coming to replace considerations of desert in the area of poor relief. But whereas the Minority Report pushed this trend to its logical conclusion, and eliminated the notion of desert altogether, the Majority Report wanted to retain it in part. It insisted on seeing the poor as a distinct group in society whose position could be attributed to defects of moral character—they were still the 'undeserving'. For this reason it advocated the continued existence of a separate destitution authority, charged with the care of this group in particular. The Minority Report, on the other hand, wished to see several distinct authorities taking care of special-

ized needs—education, health, old age, etc.—to which everyone would turn when the occasion demanded.[16]

The Majority position can therefore be seen as a half-way
stage between the nineteenth-century attitude to poor relief
and the attitude embodied in the Minority Report (which was,
incidentally, very largely the work of the Webbs). Clearly, it is
the latter position which has prevailed in subsequent social
policy. Both in the particular area of the relief of poverty and
in the general area of the social services, need has become the
principal factor governing the allocation of resources. In some
cases aid has been given as a universal provision, in other
cases it has been given on a selective basis. The choice between
these policies is really a practical matter, rather than a question of principle. On grounds of both justice and efficiency it
might seem that selectivity is to be preferred, since it ensures
that the aid given is concentrated where it is most needed
(for example, it might appear fairer to give state pensions only
to those whose own resources fall below a certain level, rather
than uniformly to everyone); but experience has shown
that where a criterion of selection is used, some people who
are entitled to benefit do not claim what is due to them (whether
through pride or ignorance), so that the outcome may be less
fair than a system of universal provision. Whichever method is
preferred, however, the aim is to distribute a proportion of
society's goods to those in need, a policy which is fundamentally
at odds with the conception of social justice developed by the
original market society.[17]

I have argued so far that as market societies have developed from free market to organized capitalism, a new theory
of society (organized society) and a new conception of social
justice have evolved. Having established the general nature of
the transformation, I want to look briefly at its timing and extent: how far has the trend away from individualism gone,
and is it likely to continue? On the question of the decline of

[16] See S. and B. Webb, op. cit., chs. 5–7; T. H. Marshall, *Social Policy* (London,
1970), ch. 3; P. Ford, *Social Theory and Social Practice* (Shannon, 1968), Part III.

[17] The claim that people in market societies now regard it as fair to redistribute
resources to those in need must be distinguished from the claim that the actual
effect of the welfare state has been to reduce inequalities through redistribution
to the poorer members of society. For a powerful critique of the latter claim, see
J. C. Kincaid, *Poverty and Equality in Britain* (Harmondsworth, 1973).

individualism, Dicey made the celebrated claim that in England the year 1870 marked the transition from the period of individualism to the period of collectivism;[18] and although there has been much detailed dispute about how far either ideal was realized in public policy during the respective periods, the broad claim appears still to stand. A recent survey concludes that policy-making ceased to be dominated by *laissez-faire* principles at some time during the period 1865–85.[19] In America the decline of individualism took place later and more slowly; individualism appears to have remained dominant at least until the end of the nineteenth century. In the case of both countries, if we were to follow Dicey in taking legislation as a symptom of public opinion, we should have to conclude that the shift away from individualism took place in fits and starts. As far as Britain is concerned, the periods when social welfare policies were most vigorously advanced were the years following 1906 and 1945. The reforms of the latter period are commonly seen in relation to the increased sense of national solidarity produced by the war years. But although dramatic events may in this way accelerate or retard the change in ideological outlook, the shift from individualistic to organized view of society has clearly been a gradual one, with periods of reformist legislation crystallizing the cumulative change in public opinion over a number of years.

The main obstacle to the continued transformation of market societies is the economic market itself. Despite the changes in the economic and social system outlined earlier, these societies are still centred on the institutions of exchange, contract, and production for profit. For this reason the organized view of society must be regarded as an ideological distortion of social reality, rather than as an accurate description—just as individualism was an ideological view of the older form of market society. The incompatibility between image and reality can be seen most clearly by examining the position of business managers and executives. The claims that business has become a profession, and that it acknowledges its social responsibilities, conflict with the hard fact that a businessman's actions are still

---

[18] A. V. Dicey, *Law and Public Opinion in England* (London, 1905).

[19] A. J. Taylor, *Laissez-faire and State Intervention in Nineteenth Century Britain* (London, 1972).

constrained by the need to make a sufficiently large profit. Because business is not directly oriented to serving the community, and because it lacks any agreed code of professional ethics, its claims to professional status must be largely discounted.[20] Such a conflict is reflected in the thinking of managers and executives themselves. Not all of them have embraced the new conception of the businessman's role which we outlined above. Bendix reports that 'managerial collectivism', as we may term it, has greater appeal to the younger men at the bottom and middle levels of management than to the top executives, who often retain an individualistic outlook.[21] A further study casts some doubt on the meaning of the 'social responsibilities' which businessmen acknowledge. Nichols asked company directors and senior managers to choose among sets of alternative statements about the role of business in society. One group of statements, labelled *'Laissez-faire'*, corresponded to the traditional individualist view of the businessman's role. A second group, labelled 'Social Responsibility', represented the businessman as having an ethical concern for the welfare of society—the view required by the 'professionalization of business' thesis. A third group of statements, labelled 'Long-Term-Company-Interest', portrayed the businessman's concern with welfare and related issues as prudential in nature—that is to say, it was suggested that businessmen should concern themselves with such non-profit matters because this would serve the long-term interest of their firms.[22] Faced with this

[20] See B. Barber, 'Is American Business Becoming Professionalised?' in E. Tiryakian (ed.), *Sociological Theory, Values and Sociocultural Change* (London, 1963).
[21] Bendix, op. cit., pp. 331–4.
[22] For example, the respondents were asked to choose between the following three statements:
'1. (*Laissez-faire*) A firm exists for one purpose only: to satisfy a need at a profit. Managers should not, and cannot, be concerned with social and moral consequence; if they were, the country's economic position would be undermined and with it the welfare of us all.
'2. (Social Responsibility) A business conducted solely for the profit of shareholders is unethical. A firm is a social institution; it exists to further the social welfare. The management is an arbiter with responsibilities to serve the social and economic needs of employees, customers, shareholders and the local and national communities.
'3. (Long-Term-Company-Interest) Profit is the one absolute in business and it is to the nation's benefit that this be so. But in the interests of long-term survival every firm must gain the sympathetic understanding and co-operation of all people directly or indirectly within its sphere of interest.'

choice, most respondents (57 per cent) opted for the 'Long-Term-Company-Interest' statements, with 'Social Responsibility' coming second (33 per cent). While this result clearly signals the passing of *laissez-faire* attitudes in business, it also gives little support to those who claim that businessmen are now public servants with the welfare of the community at heart. It is interesting to note, however, that those businessmen who had participated in the affairs of professional management bodies, and thus came closer to the ideal of the 'professional manager', were much more inclined to take the 'Social Responsibility' view than those who had not, and this might suggest that the transformation of outlook is still continuing.

A further noteworthy point is that when Nichols probed his respondents for the reasons behind their choices, it emerged that they could see little difference between the 'Long-Term-Company-Interest' statements and the 'Social Responsibility' statements. He finds this perfectly explicable:

If a businessman really believed that there was a fundamental difference between advancing the long-term interests of his company and pursuing socially responsible policies he would have to recognize that he had placed himself in a virtually insoluble conflict situation. [23]

In other words, the businessman lives in a world in which the ideology of social responsibility is pervasive; he himself is obliged to pursue the private interests of his firm. He can cope with this contradiction by identifying the company's interests with the interests of society.

To conclude on the professionalization of business (which, I have argued, corresponds to a shift from individualistic to organized conceptions of society): internal changes in the structure of firms and external changes in society have combined to push businessmen towards accepting the new ideology of professionalism; but their real situation as producers in a competitive market means that they cannot conform to the canons of the ideology. On the one hand, the divergence between behaviour and ideals must be recognized; on the other, the ideals themselves must be taken seriously as evidence of a changing view of society and a new conception of social justice. Halmos's formulation of this point cannot be bettered:

[23] Nichols, op. cit., p. 184.

I agree with Bernard Barber that professionalism in business remains more an ideological aspiration than a social fact but I must stress that the widespread hankering after the dignity and honour of a professional status among businessmen is itself also a socio-cultural fact which clearly signifies a profound discontent with a mercenary role-definition in the world of business, and a nostalgic longing to amend that role-definition. I do not assume that business has already become professionalized but rather that the fact of its growing aspiration to become professionalized has a powerful contribution to make to a general moral change which is accelerated by a more realistic professionalization in other sectors of life.[24]

We have so far examined the way in which the market inhibits the emergence of the organized view of society and its accompanying ideal of social justice. I want finally to look at a source of tension within the ideal itself. Social justice means here, first, the reward of desert (as determined by the organizational status of the individual) and, second, the distribution of goods and services according to need. Now the two parts of this ideal conflict with one another. Some decision has to be made as to what proportion of society's resources will be used to reward desert, and what proportion will be used to satisfy needs—in concrete terms, how much will be paid out in wage differentials, and how much provided as social services, according to need. But this policy-conflict only conceals a deeper moral conflict. For the idea of rewarding desert presupposes human inequality—differences of reward correspond to inequalities of status within the organization, and these in turn correspond to inequalities of skill and talent, whereas the idea of distributing according to need, when this is seen as a matter of justice, presupposes a sense of human equality.[25] Within the organized model of society, either egalitarian or inegalitarian elements can become dominant. For instance, it is possible for inequalities of reward to become increasingly symbolic in nature, with a growing proportion of resources distributed as free services, according to the standard of equality. Speaking in 1949, Marshall predicted such a development.[26] But he also noted the contrary possibility—that the inegalitarian elements in the current view of society would oust the

[24] Halmos, loc. cit., p. 25.   [25] See above, pp. 146–7.
[26] T. H. Marshall, 'Citizenship and Social Class' reprinted in *Sociology at the Crossroads* (London, 1963), pp. 125–7.

egalitarian, or, as he put it, that citizenship instead of producing equality would come to legitimate differences in social
status.[27] This would happen if status differences began to
influence the provision of services. Those in the higher positions
would receive a better standard of treatment than those below
them. The distribution of services would be governed partly
by need and partly by the status of the recipient. This seems
to me a more likely development than Marshall's main prediction. It may be discerned in recent changes in the pension
system, by which pensions, instead of being uniform, are to be
graduated according to the previous earnings of each person.

What factors encourage such a development, and what factors hinder it? On the favourable side, we should note that
until everyone has been brought up to an acceptable minimum standard of life, egalitarian ideas are reinforced by
considerations of humanity. But provided everyone has achieved
the minimum, why should not some people receive a higher
quality of service than others? For instance, if everyone is
guaranteed an adequate standard of medical care, why
should not the more deserving receive better treatment than
the less deserving? Objections to this proposal cannot be
humanitarian, but only egalitarian. On the other side, such a
system of graduated provision conflicts with the basic notion of
service, which is supposed to consider only the needs of the
client. But perhaps the notion can be modified to take account
of differences of status. Doctors, for example, seem able to
reconcile their medical ethics with the practice of private
medicine, which gives superior treatment to those able to
afford it.

To diagnose the current state of the idea of social justice, we
must therefore take account of two conflicts. There is first the
incomplete shift from individualistic to organized view of
society, each of which underwrites a different conception of
justice as desert. Thus we find a tendency to believe that all
rewards gained in the open market are fair, because rewards
can only be gained by those supplying socially useful goods
and services; and a contrary tendency to believe that desert
must be socially estimated, and that from this point of view
many of the rewards actually gained are unjust—the earnings

[27] Ibid., pp. 110–15.

of film stars, pop singers, and property speculators, for instance. Second, there is the unresolved tension between desert, in either of its interpretations, and considerations of need. Clearly the idea of social justice is continuing to change under the impact of social forces, and it would be presumptuous to predict what direction this will take in the future.

6 *Egalitarian Justice*

My investigation up to this point has centred on the three-fold social typology which I introduced in the first section of this chapter. Taking each social type in turn, I have sought to show an intelligible connection between its social structure and the ideas of social justice which are found in it (or in the case of primitive societies, between their social structure and the *absence* of ideas of social justice). In this final section, I want to reverse the method of investigation and ask: what social conditions, if any, produce a belief in social justice as equality? Our examination of social types has uncovered none in which social justice means equality, understood as the principle that each member of society should enjoy the same level of well-being as every other. We have found, it is true, that primitive societies, hierarchical societies, and market societies in their modified form, each give some weight to considerations of need in their social thinking. But equally, in each case, distribution according to need serves as a minor modification to another principle (in primitive societies, the common good; in hierarchical societies, justice as the protection of rights; in organized market societies, justice as desert). It is safe to generalize that in no society has distribution according to need become the main element in a shared conception of social justice. Yet we have also seen that political theorists such as Kropotkin have put forward interpretations of justice as equality and as distribution according to need (two interpretations which are philosophically distinct, but in practice amalgamated[28]). Is this merely an aberration of intellectuals, or are there identifiable circumstances which lead ordinary people to conceive of justice in this way? In what follows, I shall be looking mainly at the occurrence of egalitarian ideas in market societies, which appear to be peculiarly prone to produce ideas that

[28] See above, ch. 4, section 4.

deviate from the normal response to their social structure. The first part of the argument will be negative. Having already claimed, with reference to earlier market society, that the working class does not generally adhere to an egalitarian creed, I wish now to reinforce this claim by examining some more recent empirical evidence on the subject, and thus to dispose of the view that the working class is the natural locus of egalitarianism. Having removed this preconception, the way will be open for a positive account of the circumstances which produce egalitarian beliefs.

Recent research into the beliefs and attitudes of working-class people points to the following two general conclusions: first, the working class does not hold a social outlook that is radically opposed to the middle-class view of society, but instead the working class is rather less firmly committed to the common set of beliefs than is the middle class. Second, the working-class outlook is less internally consistent than that of the middle class, more liable to be composed of heterogeneous elements.[29] In particular, it is claimed that members of the working class are more liable to take up radical positions on concrete issues that are seen to bear directly on their daily lives, but more likely to take up conservative positions on general questions of political philosophy. Mann suggests that people in this position do not generally need to develop a coherent outlook on society for themselves, so that they are ready to accept the prevailing outlook without serious question. Whether this explanation is correct or not, the picture that emerges is of a working-class view of society which contains conflicting elements, but which does not depart radically from the middle-class view as a whole.

This broad picture is confirmed when we look at beliefs about social justice. Like the middle class, the working class in organized capitalism believes that society's resources should mainly be distributed according to merit, but that welfare state measures should ensure the satisfaction of basic needs.[30] Working-class opposition to equality in any stronger sense

[29] See M. Mann, 'The Social Cohesion of Liberal Democracy', *American Sociological Review*, xxxv (1970).
[30] For the high level of agreement on welfare state measures even in the U.S.A., see R. F. Hamilton, *Class and Politics in the United States* (New York, 1972), ch. 3. The data on this issue are not, however, broken down by class.

than this comes out clearly in a depth study of political ideology carried out by Lane.[31] His subjects (from the American working class) believed that social rewards should be unequal, and that by and large the better-off deserved their success on the basis of effort and ability. When the ideal of equal incomes was put to him, each person in Lane's sample rejected it.

This finding has to be modified to take account of another piece of research in which the attitudes of the rich and the poor to the opportunity structure of American society were compared.[32] The relevant findings here were that while almost everyone (excluding Negroes) thought that there was 'plenty of opportunity' for the average person to get ahead in America, when they were asked whether opportunities for rich and poor actually were equal, the consensus broke down. The wealthier respondents were more likely to believe that equality of opportunity currently existed than the poorer ones; they were also more likely to attribute material success to the personal merit of the individual, while the poor tended to think that the social structure was responsible for a person's success or failure. Now these findings do not directly undermine Lane's claim that the working class believes in equality of opportunity and distribution according to merit as ideals; there is obviously a difference between holding something as an ideal and believing it to be realized in practice. But if Rytina *et al.* are correct in suggesting that the members of the working class are less likely to see equality of opportunity as a reality, then we may infer that they will also be less strongly committed to it as a value. Their perceptions are confused: America is 'the land of opportunity', yet in real terms the rich and the poor do not have equal chances. If a society which proclaims equality of opportunity is seen not to realize it, then it is likely that one's commitment *to the ideal* will be weakened—without necessarily being replaced by anything else.

A similar pattern of beliefs was discovered by Goldthorpe *et al.* in their study of 'affluent workers' in Britain.[33] These men

[31] R. E. Lane, *Political Ideology* (New York and London, 1962).

[32] J. H. Rytina, W. Form, and J. Pease, 'Income and Stratification Ideology: Beliefs about the American Opportunity Structure', *American Journal of Sociology*, lxxv (1969–70).

[33] J. H. Goldthorpe, D. Lockwood, F. Bechhofer, and J. Platt, *The Affluent Worker in the Class Structure* (Cambridge, 1969), ch. 5.

did not see society as divided by class barriers which could not be crossed; indeed, they tended to place most members of society within a single large class, differentiated by money incomes rather than any other feature. At the same time, success or failure was not put down to personal qualities, but to 'structural' factors such as a person's family background, education, and so forth. This implies that for these 'affluent workers' equality of opportunity had not been realized; but they did not seem inclined to replace it by the ideal of an egalitarian society. When asked whether a classless society was possible, most of the sample (69 per cent) replied that, for various reasons, social inequalities were necessary. Although no positive conclusion concerning working-class beliefs about justice can be derived from this evidence, it accords with our previous view that the working class holds much the same ideas of fairness as does the middle class; but because it is less likely to see the current system as realizing the shared ideas of justice, its commitment to those ideas is weaker.

I have so far been talking as though the working class were a homogeneous entity, and it is now time to question that assumption. The most important differences within the class, for the purposes of our analysis, are between workers in different occupational situations, and between workers in different countries. To take occupational differences first, it has long been known that workers in industries such as mining and dockwork hold more radical views than (to take examples from the other end of the scale) shop assistants or farm labourers. The most ambitious attempt to systematize this observation has been made by Lockwood.[34] His claim is that working-class images of society can be arranged into three pure types, each corresponding to a different work situation. The 'traditional proletarian' worker lives in an 'occupational community' with his fellows. He forms close ties with his work-mates, which carry over into leisure activities. His image of society is a dichotomous one—a large class of working people being set against a small group of bosses and managers, the relationship between the two classes being seen as largely antagonistic. By contrast, the 'traditional deferential' worker has weak ties with his fellow

[34] D. Lockwood, 'Sources of Variation in Working Class Images of Society', *Sociological Review*, xiv (1966).

workers, but a close personal relationship with his employer. He is likely to be found in small businesses or agriculture, and in a community with a well-established status system. The resulting image of society is hierarchical: a definite ordering of social status, in which each person has a place. The working man ought to keep to his position, and show proper respect to his betters. Finally, the third work situation is that of the 'privatized' worker, whose involvement with his job and his work-mates is low, and who does not belong to any well-defined community. His life is centred on the home, and his activities are directed towards consumption. We have already encountered his characteristic image of society (the affluent workers of the Goldthorpe *et al.* study are interpreted as 'privatized'): it is a 'money model', in which class divisions are absent or unimportant.

Lockwood does not directly discuss the attitudes towards social justice held by his three types of workers, but it is permissible to suggest some inferences. The workers most likely to hold egalitarian attitudes are the 'traditional proletarians'. The dichotomous view of society which they espouse can lead to the privileges of the managing class being seen as illegitimate, and their strong commitment to the working-class community implies mutual aid and equality within it. It would be over-stating the point to say that the dichotomous image implies an egalitarian interpretation of social justice, but it is the image which is most likely to foster such an interpretation, since it can be developed into the radical demand that the managing class be removed, and the working-class community become society itself. By contrast, the image of the 'traditional deferential' worker suggests an interpretation of justice as the maintenance of rights—Lockwood includes in this image the belief that the natural leaders of society have 'hereditary or quasi-hereditary credentials'. The 'privatized' worker appears to approach most closely to the middle-class conception of justice as the reward of desert (modified to some extent by need)—though, as we have seen, he is less likely than his middle-class counterpart to think that society already matches this conception.

The significance of Lockwood's theory depends on the proportion of the working class which falls into each of his categories.

His contention is that most workers are becoming increasingly 'privatized', and this is borne out by the evidence. The occupational situation which produces the 'proletarian' worker is getting rarer, as industries such as mining decline, geographical mobility increases, and the old working-class communities are broken up by modern town planning. Equally, the 'deferential' worker has proved harder to find in practice than one would expect from Lockwood's initial description. Two recent pieces of research, taking Lockwood as their starting-point, have failed to find a consistent 'deferential' image of society among workers whose occupational situation corresponds to Lockwood's stipulations.[35] In both instances, the researchers found that deferential elements were combined with individualistic elements in their respondents' outlook: for instance, if respect was paid to those who held key positions in society, the reason was that these men were thought to have earned their position, rather than to have inherited it as Lockwood's notion of deference would suggest. We can conclude that, although some account must be taken of occupational differences when we talk of working-class beliefs about social justice, there is no need to modify in any fundamental way the conclusion we reached earlier: that the working class does not adhere to a value system which is radically different from that of the middle class, and in particular that it does not typically interpret social justice in an egalitarian fashion.

It might appear, however, that even if this conclusion holds good for the working class in countries such as Britain and the U.S.A., it will have to be modified to take account of the different patterns of belief in countries such as France and Germany. The most obvious contrast between the two groups of countries lies in the differing political allegiances of the workers. In France and Germany, a large proportion of the working class has supported Marxist parties, whose ultimate aim is apparently to bring into existence a communist society. In Britain and the U.S.A., on the other hand, mass support has always gone to moderate reformist parties, whose egalitarian aims have gone little further than the creation of a welfare

[35] E. V. Batstone, 'Organizational Size and Class Imagery' (duplicated); R. H. Fryer and R. Martin, 'The Deferential Worker: persistence and disintegration in paternalist capitalism' (duplicated).

state.[36] A further strand of evidence pointing in the same direction is Lipset's observation that American trade unions have not been at all concerned with removing wage differentials between skilled and unskilled workers, whereas in many European countries this has been an important objective of the union movement.[37]

The first piece of evidence has to be treated with some caution, since a man may support an anti-capitalist party for a number of reasons other than that he shares its theoretical outlook; and it is fairly safe to say that many Communist party supporters in present-day France or pre-Fascist Germany did not have as their ultimate goal Marx's 'true' communism, where goods are distributed according to need. Nevertheless we have still to explain why the pattern of support is different here than in Britain or the U.S.A.; and although a complete explanation would have to include many historical contingencies, social differences between the two groups of countries seem to supply part of the answer.

Lipset argues that the lack of concern about wage differentials in the U.S.A. can be attributed to the egalitarian nature of American society. What he means by this is that the U.S.A. lacks a traditional status system which would hold the working class in a position of subordination. Instead, the working class is fully integrated into the social structure, and status is largely a function of income. In our terms, the U.S.A. corresponds more closely to a true market society than do the other countries which Lipset considers. In France, the preservation of an aristocratic social system has meant that working-class advances have been strongly resisted, and trade unionism has been bitterly opposed by employers, who have tried to preserve the paternalistic stance of the traditional aristocrat towards their workers. In Germany, according to Lipset, the situation is rather different: trade unions were recognized at an early stage, but here the *political* ambitions of the workers were frustrated by the undemocratic nature of the constitution. In so far as

[36] The British Labour party was of course committed to nationalization plans for many years, but its social ideal has always been Fabian rather than communist —it has aimed at what I have called the socialist variant of 'organized society', not at an egalitarian form of socialism.

[37] S. M. Lipset, *The First New Nation* (London, 1964), ch. 5.

workers' parties gained admission to the political system, Lipset claims, they exchanged their Marxist beliefs for reformist ones. The general contrast, then, between France/ Germany and the U.S.A. is that in the former countries the working class was kept in a position of subordination—either economically or politically—while in the latter it was admitted to full membership of the larger society; and this accounts for the spread of radical socialist views in the former countries, and their absence in the latter. (Britain stands somewhere in between, according to Lipset.)

From a different perspective, Mann reaches an essentially similar conclusion.[38] A fully developed capitalist system creates a common (moderate and reformist) set of attitudes among both middle and working class. Working-class radicalism occurs in the initial stages of industrialism, before market relationships have become dominant, and where the employing class tries to preserve feudalistic relations with the work force. As he concludes, 'the more employers behave as true capitalists, the securer will they rest in their beds!'[39]

We may sum up this part of the argument by saying that in a market society, of either a pure or an organized type, the working class does not hold an egalitarian conception of social justice, but instead a conception which is essentially similar to the middle-class idea. In special circumstances—when market relationships for one reason or another become less salient— part of the working class may come to hold egalitarian beliefs. But this discovery ought to be integrated into a more general account of the social conditions which produce egalitarianism, which I shall now try to provide.

I have already suggested that support for Marxist parties is not a particularly reliable indicator of belief in egalitarian justice. Although Marxist theory holds that communism is the eventual goal of the social revolution, it is predominantly concerned with the critique of capitalist society; and people may support a Marxist party because they share its opposition to capitalism, without necessarily believing that a fully equal society is either feasible or desirable. For this reason, I have

[38] M. Mann, *Consciousness and Action among the Western Working Class* (London, 1973), chs. 4–5.
[39] Ibid., p. 42.

chosen to concentrate on a different phenomenon as a manifestation of the belief in equality—namely the many attempts that have been made to set up egalitarian communities within existing society. People who actually try to live as egalitarians clearly believe that equality is the proper interpretation of social justice. Admittedly, equality is only practised within the community itself; but nearly all the founders of these miniature societies have believed that their model is one which could and should be generally adopted. (Some of them believed, more optimistically, that the example they were setting would have precisely this result.) So, while support for Communist parties may sometimes show a belief in equality, attempts to live communistically do so less ambiguously.

Egalitarian communities have been established throughout the modern period in Europe and North America, but certain periods stand out as particularly fertile in this respect. The first wave of communities originated with the dissenting sects in fifteenth- and sixteenth-century Germany. Groups such as the Taborites, the followers of Thomas Müntzer, and the Anabaptists developed their religious dissent into a belief that the millennium was at hand. To prepare for it, they formed themselves into communities, and instituted a system of common property—this being seen as the highest form of life for a Christian. None of these communities lasted for very long, since their inhabitants soon found themselves at war with the local princes.[40]

The second large wave of egalitarian communities fared rather better. These were the communities set up in Britain and the U.S.A. during the nineteenth century—the peak period for community-founding being between 1820 and 1850. The most notable of the British communities were the Owenite settlements at Orbiston, Ralahine, and elsewhere;[41] in America, we find the Owenite colony at New Harmony, several other communities inspired by the writings of Cabet and Fourier, and many communistic settlements with a religious basis—the most famous being the Shaker colonies, the Amana society,

[40] See N. Cohn, *The Pursuit of the Millennium*, chs. 11–13; K. Kautsky, *Communism in Central Europe in the Time of the Reformation* (London, 1897).
[41] See W. H. G. Armytage, *Heavens Below* (London, 1961); R. G. Garnett, *Co-operation and the Owenite socialist communities in Britain, 1825–1845* (Manchester, 1972).

and the Perfectionists of Oneida.[42] The duration of these communities varied a great deal: New Harmony dissolved after only two years, while some of the religious societies lasted for up to a century. In most cases, however, the cause of dissolution was internal difficulty of one sort or another, rather than outside interference.

The third wave of community-founding occurred throughout the West in the 1960s (though our attention will be confined to Britain and the U.S.A.). This wave was more heterogeneous than its predecessors: an extraordinarily varied range of communities was set up, most of them extremely short-lived. What binds them together, however, is their founders' common rejection of conventional society. Not all of these communities were strictly egalitarian in their distributive practices, but they generally embodied some communistic elements.[43]

Finally, we should also consider the kibbutzim in Israel, since they furnish the best examples of long-lived communities with a secular basis; it is, however, more difficult to place their founders in time and space, since they have drawn recruits from a number of different societies and over an extended period of time. We can nevertheless make some observations about the social origins of the early members of the kibbutz movement.

It would plainly be wrong to treat these 'waves' of communities as if they were identical in all respects. The earliest wave was composed of people obsessed by certain religious phantasies, which they imbibed from heretical preachers. The second wave was more sober and realistic, concerned with the gradual regeneration of society according to the particular standards of each group. The most recent wave seems by comparison rather frivolous, laying much more stress on the gratification of the individuals concerned and much less on the renovation of society. The kibbutzim must clearly be considered as part of the Zionist movement, as well as from a communist standpoint. Yet although these differences must be plainly acknowledged, I think we can generalize in a limited way from the evidence available.

[42] See J. H. Noyes, *History of American Socialisms* (London, 1870); C. Nordhoff, *The Communistic Societies of the United States* (New York, 1961).
[43] See A. Rigby, *Alternative Realities* (London, 1974); R. M. Kanter, *Commitment and Community* (Cambridge, Mass., 1972).

First, whether or not individuals held egalitarian beliefs before entering communistic societies, this was not their prime motive for joining. Rather, their initial desire was for community itself: these men and women wished to live in a closer association with one another than was possible in conventional society, whether for religious reasons or from a secular belief in the virtues of community. As they formed themselves into communities, they saw that their desire for fellowship would not be fully satisfied while distinctions of property were allowed to remain; treating other people as brothers meant sharing goods according to need. Thus the belief in egalitarian justice grew out of the conception of interpersonal relationships implied by the ideal of community. This interpretation can be backed up by observing that very often common property was introduced into these communities some time after their foundation. For instance, the Anabaptists only adopted common ownership as their regime in Münster moved towards its climax.[44] In America, the Amana society and the Perfectionists were not originally founded on a communistic basis, but introduced this principle during their development.[45] Even those communities based explicitly on a socialist philosophy did not immediately institute an egalitarian system of distribution—Owen did not intend to introduce communism into New Harmony until three years after its foundation, though in the event the time scale was compressed;[46] and neither Orbiston nor Ralahine ever became fully communistic.[47]

Given that the belief in complete equality is derived from the ideal of a close-knit community—and we may recall here that we gave a similar analysis of the intellectual background to Kropotkin's conception of social justice—we have two further questions to ask. First, what causes people to reject the kind of social relationships which conventional society offers, and to seek to form themselves into solidaristic communities? Second, once a community is founded, what determines whether its members continue to espouse the communal ideal? Our theory of equality will, in other words, have

[44] Cohn, op. cit., pp. 264–6.
[45] Nordhoff, op. cit., pp. 29–30, 260.
[46] Noyes, op. cit., pp. 36–7.
[47] Garnett, op. cit., chs. 3–4.

two parts to it: an account of how people come to reject the conventional ideas of social justice, and to adopt instead an egalitarian conception; and an account of the factors which support, or conversely erode, that conception once it is embodied in the practice of a community.

To begin with the first question, we must at once reject the notion that any social class is particularly predisposed to the search for community and the accompanying belief in equality. The members of the early German communities were predominantly poor peasants and artisans. The German peasantry also provided the stock for several of the American communities, including the one at Amana. The Owenite communities, on the other hand, were mainly recruited from the working class (the recruits to Orbiston included weavers, joiners, and shoemakers). Finally, the recent commune movement has drawn its members mainly from the young, well-educated section of the middle class.[48] Thus if we are to find a general explanation of the phenomenon we are considering, it must refer to experiences which each of these groups shared, despite their very different class backgrounds. The explanation which seems most plausible is that each of these groups suffered a process of social dislocation, in which established patterns of social relationships were sharply disrupted. Instead of being integrated into a stable social structure, where reasonable expectations could be formed about the future, these groups found themselves in a state of *anomie* with no preformed pattern of life to follow. The precise nature of the dislocation differs from case to case; yet it is interesting that several of the authors we have cited offer explanations of communalism which conform to this general hypothesis.

Cohn has this to say of medieval millenarian movements (which include the German communistic sects):

Revolutionary millenarianism drew its strength from a population living on the margin of society—peasants without land or with too little land even for subsistence; journeymen and unskilled workers living under the continuous threat of unemployment; beggars and vagabonds—in fact from the amorphous mass of people who were not simply poor but who could find no assured and recognized place

[48] Rigby, op. cit., esp. ch. 7.

in society at all. These people lacked the material and emotional support afforded by traditional social groups; their kinship-groups had disintegrated and they were not effectively organized in village communities or in guilds; for them there existed no regular, institutionalized methods of voicing their grievances or pressing their claims.[49]

He adds that millenarian beliefs gained currency when such groups were exposed to natural disasters (such as famine or plague) or to man-made disasters (such as warfare). Under these circumstances their dislocation was intensified.

Garnett's analysis of the Owenite movement in Britain stresses that the socialist colonies were the first response of the working class to its experience of industrialism. The early years of capitalism clearly placed exceptional strains on many working people: it was a period of rapidly changing price and wage levels;[50] the shift from country to town proved disruptive for many; and new, unfamiliar patterns of work had to be learnt.[51] In the light of these difficulties, Garnett's claim seems plausible:

The Owenite experiments provided a first secular alternative to the milieu of industrial society. The ranks of the Owenites included world-makers but possibly some escapists who were attracted to the communities because such settlements were a protective framework within which an individual could at least survive and then begin to adapt to communal patterns.[52]

He adds that working-class enthusiasm for Owenism later gave way to the co-operative and trade union movements, as the class achieved a more stable position within capitalism.

Rigby's study of modern communes contains no single explanation of why individuals are led to join them. Nevertheless, observing that most members are young, well educated, and middle-class, he makes some relevant points about this social group. The transition from adolescence to adulthood has become particularly problematic for them. The young person is

[49] Cohn, op. cit., p. 282.
[50] See G. D. H. Cole and R. Postage, *The Common People, 1746–1946* (London, 1956), esp. chs. 17 and 24.
[51] For an account of this from the employers' point of view, see A. Ure, *The Philosophy of Manufactures* (London, 1835), Book iii, ch. 1.
[52] Garnett, op. cit., p. 230.

invited to choose between various possible social roles, and is allowed to experiment by adopting them temporarily. But it is possible that none of the available roles will meet the expectations which the middle-class youth, in particular, has been given by his upbringing. According to Rigby, this is partly because most work roles are seen to give insufficient freedom and autonomy to the individual, and partly because the speed of technological change makes adult patterns of life seem irrelevant. The young person, therefore, has to find a satisfying identity in a situation where no ready-made identity is available. Rigby does not explain why some young people manage to resolve this problem in a conventional way, while others adopt 'deviant' solutions (including commune membership), any more than Garnett shows why some working-class people were satisfied with capitalist employment at the same time as others were embracing Owenism. Nevertheless, both may be seen as indicating a set of conditions which predisposes a large number of people to adopt the egalitarian ideal, to which an account of individual case-histories would have to be added in a complete explanation.

Finally, Spiro's account of the Jewish community in Poland which provided most of the membership of the kibbutz that he studied shows once again a condition of social dislocation.[53] The Jews hoped to become fully integrated into Polish society, and some even became Polish patriots; however, their hopes were soon frustrated, particularly by their experiences in the education system, where they suffered painfully from discrimination. Later, there were anti-Semitic pogroms in Poland. Taken together, these experiences led many young Jews to give up their aspirations for integration into Polish society and to join a youth organization known simply as The Movement. Originally devoted to country hikes and scouting activities, The Movement gave its members a sense of intense comradeship and emotional unity, as well as a disgust for conventional society. When The Movement later became Zionist, its principles were translated into the organization of the kibbutz.

Each of these examples, then, shows a common pattern: the members of a group suffering from social dislocation seek for a new form of community in which they can live in

[53] M. E. Spiro, *Kibbutz: Venture in Utopia* (New York, 1963), ch. 3.

close harmony with one another and realize certain moral or spiritual values. As their relationship becomes more intensely communal, they discard received notions of social justice, and adopt an egalitarian ideal as an expression of their new-found community with one another. We should not pretend that this explanation is a particularly rigorous one. The idea of 'social dislocation' cannot be given a precise definition. Furthermore, we have seen that only *some* members of groups suffering dislocation respond by adopting communal patterns of life, and this leaves open the question of how these people are distinguished from the rest. Finally, some writers have suggested that the same general conditions which produce radical movements of the left may also produce radical movements of the right (such as fascism), and this seems intuitively plausible. Thus we can only claim to have identified, in a general way, one important necessary condition for the production of egalitarian ideas of justice. But, assuming that in the long term social dislocation is the exception rather than the rule, even this limited discovery may be a helpful beginning.

Another condition for egalitarianism is worth noting briefly. Whereas the ideas of justice we have examined grew more or less directly out of people's experiences in society, the belief in egalitarian justice has to be promulgated consciously by intellectuals. If social dislocation is a necessary condition of egalitarianism, another condition is that an intellectual leader shall direct the search of the dislocated group in this particular direction. The German communities were inspired by heretical preachers; the socialist colonies by Owen, Cabet, Fourier, or one of their disciples. The religious communities in America were usually controlled by a spiritual leader, such as Noyes at Oneida, or Rapp at Economy.[54] Even in the more loosely organized contemporary communes, Rigby generally found one or two intellectual leaders who were older, better read in the history of communal ideas, and possessed of a more consistent schema for interpreting the world—these individuals, Rigby says, help to mould the ideas of their fellow members into the communitarian pattern.[55]

[54] For the authority of Noyes and Rapp, see the sections on the Perfectionists and the Harmonists in Nordhoff, op. cit.

[55] Rigby, op. cit., pp. 40–2.

Having looked at the factors which cause men to break with conventional society and to form egalitarian communities, let us turn now to the second question: what forces within the community tend to preserve the egalitarian ideal, and what forces tend to erode it? In the light of the discussion so far, the answer should be fairly clear: to the extent that relationships within the community maintain their solidaristic character, equality will be preserved; but if the community begins to degenerate into an association for mutual advantage alone, more conventional ideas of justice (distribution according to desert) will begin to reappear. How far is this hypothesis born out in experience?

The founding of a community is often accompanied by intense feelings of comradeship among the members. But this initial enthusiasm cannot be sustained, and so communities which survive for any length of time have to develop what Kanter calls 'commitment mechanisms' to strengthen the allegiance of the individual to the community and its ideals.[56] These mechanisms may be of various types, but they include routines for ensuring a high degree of contact between members of the group (for example, all meals are taken in common), and also an organization of work which reduces the division of labour by instituting job rotation and/or communal work. However, such mechanisms bring with them certain costs: in particular, the members may come to feel the need for greater privacy, and the reduction of the division of labour may conflict with the demands of efficient production. Such consequences often lead to a gradual weakening of the close bonds of community and to a reversion to a more conventional form of organization, which allows members to have private rooms and private belongings, for instance, and permits individuals to specialize in the type of work for which they are most suited. But these developments undermine equality and distribution according to need: individuals come to have rights in their own possessions, which can no longer be commandeered by the community; different levels of skill and effort at work become apparent, giving some members a higher status in the eyes of their fellows than others, which in turn can lead to a belief that their deserts should be materially rewarded.

[56] Kanter, op. cit., Part II.

These processes can be seen at work in the nineteenth-century communities. The successful communities prospered, became more specialized internally, and lost some of their religious or moral fervour. Eventually many of them ceased to distribute their goods according to need, and became, by common consent, joint-stock companies.[57] Some of the same tendencies can be seen at the present time in the kibbutzim. Cohen points out the dilemma inherent in the kibbutz's original commitment to the two values of communality and progress.[58] 'Communality' implies close, spontaneous relationships between people, with a minimum of formal roles and institutionalized planning. 'Progress', however, implies that relationships should be governed by considerations of economic efficiency, which in turn entails that work roles should be specialized, and that an organization for controlling production should be established. Cohen charts the 'circle of progressive rationalization' whereby the values and institutions associated with the idea of progress have come to oust the communal values and relationships from the kibbutz. The argument is taken a step further in a paper by Yuchtman which explores the relative attractiveness of the work roles of managers and workers in the kibbutz.[59] It is found that managers are generally less satisfied with their roles than workers, despite the fact that they enjoy a higher level of 'non-material' rewards (such as the opportunity to put their ideas into practice, to exert influence in their branch of production, and so forth). Yuchtman offers the following explanation: although the kibbutz is officially committed to equality as a mode of distribution, changes in the mode of organization (exemplified by the emergence of a distinct managerial stratum) make 'equity'—in our terms, a distribution according to desert[60]—a more

---

[57] Ibid., ch. 6.

[58] E. Cohen, 'Progress and Communality: Value Dilemmas in the Collective Movement', *International Review of Community Development*, xv–xvi (1966).

[59] E. Yuchtman, 'Reward Distribution and Work-role Attractiveness in the Kibbutz—Reflections on Equity Theory', *American Sociological Review*, xxxvii (1972).

[60] Yuchtman's concept of equity is derived from Sampson ('Studies of Status Congruence' in L. Berkowitz (ed.), *Advances in Experimental Social Psychology*, vol. iv (New York and London, 1969)) who in turn obtained it by running together Adams's idea of equity ('Inequity in Social Exchange' in L. Berkowitz (ed.), *Advances in Experimental Social Psychology*, vol. ii (New York and London, 1965)) and Homans's idea of distributive justice (*Social Behaviour: Its Elementary Forms*).

appropriate norm. The managers are aware that their job requires more skill than the worker's and ought therefore, in accordance with the rule of equity, to get higher rewards. Because it does not (Yuchtman assumes that the 'non-material' rewards are insufficient) the managers feel dissatisfied. The implication, which Yuchtman does not draw, is that at some point the managers will press for the explicit adoption of the equity rule by asking for a wage differential between themselves and the workers. At this point the transition in ideas of justice would be complete.

We cannot yet say whether this prediction will be fulfilled in the case of the kibbutzim, and other communities have rarely lasted for long enough to allow the transformation I have sketched to occur. Nevertheless, the limited evidence available supports my contention that an egalitarian conception of justice will be preserved in a community in so far as it manages to maintain close, solidaristic relationships among its members; to the extent that impersonal relationships emerge, and the community turns into a mere association, justice as the reward of desert will reappear.

This concludes the discussion of egalitarian justice. I have not sought to discover the causes which may lead individual people —intellectuals, for instance—to adopt equality as an abstract ideal.[61] Instead I have focused my inquiry on the processes

---

Sampson defines the concept of equity in the following way: 'A condition of justice obtains when the person gets what he deserves, when, to be more specific, his outcomes (i.e. what P gets) relative to the outcomes of other (O) are in proportion to their respective investments or inputs.' (Op. cit., p. 259.) Equity, then, is initially defined in terms of desert; however, when the list of possible 'investments' is spelt out, it includes 'education, age, experience, training, skill, sex, ethnic background, social status, effort, and seniority'. Some of these clearly have nothing to do with desert, so Sampson's position is rather confused. I think we can deal with the problem by saying that the concept of equity is *meant* to refer to a distribution of rewards according to desert, but the concept's users fail to distinguish between legitimate bases of desert, and features (such as ethnic background) which may in practice be used as a basis for reward differentials, without thereby becoming legitimate. People may actually treat black men in a different way from white men, but they are unlikely to say that this is fair, simply on the basis of the difference in skin colour. For a similar critical point about Homans's idea of justice, see W. G. Runciman, 'Justice, Congruence and Professor Homans', *European Journal of Sociology*, viii (1967).

[61] Such people may in fact possess a 'split' conception of justice. As an ideal, they would like to see everyone treated according to his needs. In practice, they have to act and judge in a situation where the ideal is not generally applied. They

whereby large numbers of men become sufficiently committed
to equality to practise it in their daily lives. I believe this is the
more important investigation, besides being closest to the mode
of inquiry adopted in the earlier sections of this chapter.

---

are therefore likely to appeal to considerations of desert, etc., to back up their
practical judgements of justice, even while believing that justice 'really' means
distribution according to need.

CONCLUSION

There are three tasks reserved for this final section of the book: first, to clear away certain residual difficulties arising from the sociological analysis in chapter eight; second, to examine how the sociological analysis stands in relation to the earlier parts of the work; and third, to consider what kind of political theory is compatible with the method of treating political concepts that has been adopted here.

The argument of the last chapter, reduced to its simplest terms, is that our concept of social justice has grown out of the specific arrangements of market society, and that while other types of society may embody concepts which are in certain respects analogous to ours, they do not have any single concept with the same range of uses. Furthermore, some of the conflicts which are inherent in our concept can be understood by reference to its historical development under the impact of social change—for instance, the rather uncertain place occupied by the idea of need in our thinking about justice may be explained by reference to the changes in social thought accompanying the transition from free market to organized capitalism. Now if this argument is to be fully successful, it should eventually give a complete sociological account of the structure of the concept which was originally revealed by philosophical analysis. If the philosophical and sociological parts of this inquiry are compared, however, it will be seen that one of the three constituent elements of our concept of justice—the principle of rights—has been omitted from the sociological account of market society; and the reasons for this omission must now be explained.

From our point of view the cardinal feature of market societies, not shared by primitive or hierarchical societies, is that their members characteristically evaluate the social distribution of benefits by reference to certain ideal standards of distribution—namely criteria of desert and need. This is above all what we have in mind when we talk about the idea of social justice. The point I was concerned to make was that although other kinds of society clearly have fixed rules of distribution, etc., they do not have an idea of social justice in the sense just explained. Having said this, and having looked at various differences between market and other societies which may serve to explain it, we may now go on to say that the general criteria of social justice can only be implemented by establishing fixed institutions and rules, and thus by conferring certain positive rights upon individuals. Because such implementation is always imperfect, there must arise the conflicts between established rights and deserts or needs which we analysed in chapter one. Once a right has been established, it gains its own intrinsic value because individuals come to govern their actions by reference to it, and so any interference with rights will affect the security and freedom of action of some people. But in market societies rights are open to criticism as they are not in, say, feudal societies. The question of whether an individual ought to have the rights that he does may always be raised, and if a given distribution of rights is seen to be sufficiently unjust (by a desert or need criterion) we may decide to alter it. Thus what is distinctive about the social thinking of market societies is their assessment of existing rights by ideal standards of social justice, and it is these ideal standards which stand most in need of sociological explanation. This accounts for the direction of the argument in the last chapter.

Finally, we should note that actual market societies still contain some remnants of 'feudal' thinking, in which rights are accepted even though they have no foundation in one of the ideal standards of justice. For instance, a few people will be found to accept the notion of a 'natural aristocracy'—of a class of people with an inherited right to govern their inferiors. This should serve to remind us that our social classification was a classification of ideal types, and that real societies will always contain elements drawn from each type; thus market societies contain some hierarchical elements, and so forth.

The view that our concept of social justice grows out of the specific arrangements of market societies can also help us to interpret the argument about communities and egalitarian justice. At first glance it appears that communistic settlements share some of the features of primitive societies—both are cases of small, close-knit societies with a high level of co-operation among their members. Given this resemblance, it may seem surprising that their social thinking should be so different, primitive societies being chiefly concerned with the collective good (rather than with the claims of individuals), communities being concerned with social justice in the sense of a distribution according to need. But this difference becomes intelligible when we take account of two characteristics of modern communities which are not shared by primitive societies. First, communistic settlements are intentional groups, in the sense that they are deliberately set up to realize certain ideals, such as religious fellowship or co-operative living. Second, they are composed of people who have been brought up under the conditions of market society, and therefore have many of the attitudes characteristic of that society; in particular they think of themselves as individuals with just claims to various goods and services. When they enter a community, these individuals do not wish to lose their individuality in the group, but rather to develop that individuality in association with others. When questions of distribution are discussed, therefore, it is understandable that they should seek an arrangement which gives full weight to individual claims: i.e. one governed by an ideal of social justice. Primitive tribesmen, on the other hand, neither see themselves as individuals in the relevant sense nor conceive of deliberately arranging society to realize a distributive ideal. We should therefore mistrust accounts which emphasize the similarity between tribal societies and modern experiments in communal living; and indeed, we saw that one pertinent criticism of Kropotkin's theory was that he illegitimately used examples drawn from tribal societies to support his theory of anarchist communism. Although the founders of communities reject some of the dominant values of market societies, in other respects their thinking betrays their social origins; and this is true of their concern for the moral claims of the individual, which forms the basis of their egalitarian notion of social justice.

Let us now summarize our sociological analysis of conceptions of social justice. In primitive societies a traditional network of close personal relationships produces a commitment to values such as generosity rather than to any concept of social justice.

In hierarchical societies of the feudal type the combination of firmly established social ranking and a degree of personal contact across ranks leads to a primary emphasis on justice as the protection of established rights and a secondary emphasis on justice as the relief of the needy. In market societies the predominance of impersonal exchange relationships leads to a new interpretation of justice as the requital of desert, though the transformation of these societies brought about chiefly by the rise of corporate groups has changed the basis of desert and reintroduced the principle of need as a subsidiary criterion of justice. Finally, within market societies various groups suffering from social dislocation have responded by establishing egalitarian communities embodying a 'deviant' conception of justice as distribution according to need.

How do these findings stand in relation to Part II of the book? There we were concerned to show how different principles of justice were connected to wider views of society, and to do this we examined the models of society contained in the writings of three political thinkers. Each of the models examined—the stable order in the case of Hume, the competitive market in the case of Spencer, the solidaristic community in the case of Kropotkin—was shown to support a separate principle of social justice. Now these models of society, although in their full detail unique to each thinker, have in a more diffuse form been shared by large numbers of people, and the relative popularity of the different models is related to the actual nature of the society in which they are living. In our sociological investigation we often found it necessary to refer to views of society as a prolegomenon to examining conceptions of social justice. Thus in feudal society we found a conception of social order which bore a close resemblance to Hume's more explicit view of society, and this helped to account for the idea of justice as the protection of established rights which was predominant in that society. The individualistic theory typical of early market society resembled Spencer's view of society as a competitive market, and it was therefore understandable that justice should there be interpreted as the requital of desert. The attempts made to form egalitarian communities were reminiscent of Kropotkin's anarchist communist social ideal, and we were thereby better able to understand the distinctive conception of justice as distribution according to need adopted by these communities. To account for the notion of justice in contemporary market societies, we had to introduce a fourth view of society, which I called the organized view, and again it was useful to draw upon explicit formulations of this model in writers such as Durkheim and Tawney. In this way our exploration of the theoretical relationship between views of society and conceptions of social justice has helped us to put social justice into sociological perspective. But clearly there are dangers in an approach of this kind. In imputing general views of society to ordinary people in various social contexts, we run the risk of imposing a consistency upon their thinking and judgement which does not really exist. Yet despite this risk, the imputation will be justified if it enables us to link together and make sense of a number of attitudes which would otherwise seem arbitrary. For instance, if we find that a member of the middle class in mid-nineteenth century Britain was disposed to attack wealthy landowners, praise hard work, and believe that the poor should not be given relief without earning it, we can connect these attitudes together by supposing that he held an individualistic view of society, from which each attitude follows as an implication. It will be difficult to find direct evidence for our imputation, since views of society are likely to remain tacit rather than to be openly expressed. If, however, we can find reliable indicators for each of the views we have discussed,[1] and if the use of these images of society turns out to have genuine explanatory value, we will have sufficient justification for this approach. I hope that the use I have made of views of society in explaining variations in men's conceptions of social justice shows that the second condition can be fulfilled.

Our final question must be whether the kind of analysis advocated here leaves any room for political theory, particularly for political theory which is prescriptive as well as analytical. In order to answer this question, it is useful to begin by drawing an explicit contrast between the approach to social

[1] There has been some useful progress in finding empirical indicators for working-class images of society, mainly inspired by the theoretical framework set out in Lockwood's 'Sources of Variation in Working Class Images of Society'. I believe that if the argument of Part III of this book is to be advanced any further, it must be through a more rigorous use of empirical evidence in ascribing views of society than has been possible here.

justice adopted here and that adopted by Rawls in *A Theory of Justice*. Rawls believes that there is a single conception of justice which can be rationally defended—the conception contained in his two principles of justice.[2] The defence consists partly in showing that the conception corresponds to our considered judgements of justice, partly in showing that it represents the rational choice of individuals placed in a hypothetical situation in which they are ignorant of their personal qualities and their place in society. Leaving aside the technical difficulties involved in Rawls's deduction of the principles of justice from the hypothetical situation, it should be clear where Rawls's argument diverges from my own. Rather than assuming that there is a single conception of justice upon which everyone's judgements of justice will eventually converge, I have stressed that the concept is made up of several conflicting principles, and furthermore, that the relative weights attached to each principle vary sharply from one type of society to another. Moreover, Rawls's enterprise of deducing principles of justice from the choices made by rational individuals in the 'hypothetical situation' seems, from the perspective adopted here, completely misguided. For how are these rational individuals supposed to arrive at their decision? What kinds of reasoning are they allowed to employ, what sorts of consideration will weigh with them? Much criticism of Rawls has been directed against his list of 'primary goods'—the goods of which, it is supposed, each individual will try to obtain the largest amount possible—and against his attempt to establish priorities among the primary goods (for instance his claim that liberty will be preferred to material wealth).[3] It is said that to reach these conclusions Rawls has to build certain specific preferences into the psychological make-up of his individuals. This point is perfectly correct, but it ought to be taken further. The whole enterprise of constructing a theory of justice on the basis of the choices hypothetically made by individuals abstracted from society is mistaken, because these abstract ciphers lack the prerequisites for developing conceptions of justice. Or if such a derivation is possible, the choosers must have been left

[2] See above, p. 41.
[3] The definitive criticism is B. Barry, *The Liberal Theory of Justice* (Oxford, 1973). See also R. Keat and D. Miller, 'Understanding Justice'.

with certain culturally acquired attitudes and modes of reasoning. This follows from our thesis that men hold conceptions of social justice as part of more general views of society, and that they acquire these views through their experience of living in actual societies with definite structures and embodying particular kinds of interpersonal relationship. In fact, Rawls's individuals are given the attitudes and beliefs of men in modern market societies, and it is therefore not surprising that the conception of justice they are supposed to adopt should approximate to the conception which is dominant in those societies.

Yet when all this has been said, Rawls can still point out that his theory contains a fairly specific conception of social justice which could be used, for instance, to evaluate a government's social policy, and to many people this has seemed a cardinal virtue of the theory. By contrast, my own account appears to point to the relativist conclusion that no single conception of justice can be preferred to any other, and that consequently no definite prescriptions about the justice or injustice of a policy can be made (except perhaps where a policy satisfies all the relevant principles or none of them). More generally, whereas Rawls's approach gives political theory a prescriptive role, mine appears to confine it largely to analysing the different meanings which a concept such as justice may possess, in preparation for a sociological investigation of conceptual change. Is there any way in which a more positive role for political theory can be retrieved from my analysis?

One way to combine awareness of cultural diversity and conceptual change with a prescriptive form of political theory is to adopt a doctrine of historical progress. Here one assumes that the concepts and principles of one's own society, although different from those found elsewhere, are 'higher' or 'more adequate', and can therefore be justified on rational grounds. This was roughly Hegel's position. Unfortunately it is only too obviously circular, since the criterion of a 'higher' or 'more adequate' principle will be culturally specific. Only if we could find a universally accepted criterion (such as a criterion of logic) for judging between concepts or principles could we escape from relativism in this way, and it seems impossible that such a criterion could be found.

If we abandon doctrines of historical progress, we shall have to start by admitting that our political theory is specific to a particular time and place, and that our concepts and arguments will only be accepted within the framework of our own culture. Our object in political theory will then be to explicate the ideas and principles found in that culture, and to find out whether there are any decisive arguments for taking up particular prescriptive standpoints, using the criteria that are available. To illustrate by our own example, we found that in contemporary thinking the concept of social justice is made up of three distinct principles, and that these principles can be defended by appeal to different views of society. But when it came to adjudicating between views of society, matters were less straightforward. On the one hand, there was an agreed method of assessing each view—namely by appeal to sociological evidence (rather than, for example, by theological argument, as might be the case in other forms of society). On the other hand, the fact that people appear to hold irreducibly different value priorities (itself a characteristic phenomenon of contemporary society) made it seem unlikely that a decisive argument could be produced in favour of any single social perspective. Thus in this particular case, the political theorist could not, using agreed criteria, argue conclusively in favour of one principle of justice at the expense of others. He could, however, *defend* such a perspective if he thought that the evidence was strongly in its favour. The issue, therefore, is not whether political theory can be prescriptive, but whether the political theorist's prescriptions differ in status from those of any other member of society. Our study suggests that there *is* a difference in status, but it does not consist in the political theorist's prescriptions having a logically watertight backing where the ordinary man's are based on intuition. Rather, the political theorist makes a more systematic use of shared criteria of logic and empirical evidence, and the superior strength of his position will lie in its internal consistency and the weight of evidence he can marshall behind it.

Readers with a yearning for Rawlsian 'moral geometry' may still find this disappointing. Can there be no conclusive arguments in political theory, and, moreover, arguments of universal validity that hold good across social and historical barriers?

This is indeed a pleasant prospect, but since there seems little hope of its being realized, I conclude that we shall have to make do with more modest results.

BIBLIOGRAPHY

ACTON, HARRY B., 'Prejudice', *Revue internationale de philosophie*, vi (1952), pp. 323–36.

ADAMS, J. STACY, 'Inequity in Social Exchange' in L. Berkowitz (ed.), *Advances in Experimental Social Psychology*, vol. ii (New York and London, 1965).

AQUINAS, THOMAS, *Summa Theologica* (excerpts) in D. Bigongiari (ed.), *The Political Ideas of St. Thomas Aquinas* (New York, 1953).

ARISTOTLE, *Ethica Nichomachea* in *The Works of Aristotle*, ed. W. D. Ross, vol. ix (Oxford, 1915).

ARMYTAGE, WALTER H. G., *Heavens Below: Utopian Experiments in England 1560–1960* (London, 1961).

AYER, ALFRED J., 'Freedom and Necessity' in A. J. Ayer, *Philosophical Essays* (London, 1954).

BALDWIN, JOHN W., *The Medieval Theories of the Just Price: Romanists, Canonists and Theologians in the Twelfth and Thirteenth Centuries* (Philadelphia, 1959) in *Transactions of the American Philosophical Society*, vol. xlix.

BARBER, BERNARD, 'Is American Business becoming Professionalised?' in E. Tiryakian (ed.), *Sociological Theory, Values and Socio-cultural Change* (London, 1963).

BARRY, BRIAN M., *Political Argument* (London, 1965).

—— 'On Social Justice', *Oxford Review*, v (Trinity, 1967), pp. 29–52.

—— *The Liberal Theory of Justice* (Oxford, 1973).

BATSTONE, ERIC V., 'Organizational Size and Class Imagery: A Case Study in Banbury' (duplicated).

BENDIX, REINHARD, *Work and Authority in Industry* (New York, 1956).

BENN, STANLEY I. and PETERS, RICHARD S., *Social Principles and the Democratic State* (London, 1959).

BENTHAM, JEREMY, *A Fragment on Government and An Introduction to the Principles of Morals and Legislation*, ed. W. Harrison (Oxford, 1948).

BERLIN, ISAIAH, 'Equality', *Proceedings of the Aristotelian Society*, lvi (1955–6), pp. 301–26.

—— 'Does Political Theory Still Exist?' in P. Laslett and W. G. Runciman (eds.), *Philosophy, Politics and Society*, 2nd Ser. (Oxford 1962).

346 *Bibliography*

—— 'Two Concepts of Liberty' in I. Berlin, *Four Essays on Liberty* (Oxford, 1969).

BLOCH, MARC, *Feudal Society*, 2 vols., trans. L. Manyon (London, 1965).

BONAR, JAMES, *Philosophy and Political Economy* (London, 1968).

BOUGLÉ, CÉLESTIN, *Les Idées égalitaires: étude sociologique* (Paris, 1899).

—— *Essays on the Caste System*, trans. D. F. Pocock (Cambridge, 1971).

BRANDT, RICHARD B., *Hopi Ethics: a theoretical analysis* (Chicago, 1954).

—— 'The Concepts of Obligation and Duty', *Mind*, lxxiii (1964), pp. 374–93.

—— 'Some Merits of One Form of Rule-Utilitarianism' in K. Pahel and M. Schiller (eds.), *Readings in Contemporary Ethical Theory* (Englewood Cliffs, N.J., 1970).

BRAYBROOKE, DAVID, 'Let Needs Diminish that Preferences may Prosper', *American Philosophical Quarterly Monograph Series*, No. 1 (Oxford, 1968), pp. 86–107.

BRIGGS, ASA, *Victorian People: a reassessment of persons and themes, 1851–67* (Harmondsworth, 1955).

BROAD, CHARLES D., *Five Types of Ethical Theory* (London, 1930).

BURROW, JOHN W., *Evolution and Society: a study in Victorian Social Theory* (Cambridge, 1970).

CALVEZ, JEAN Y. and PERRIN, JACQUES, *The Church and Social Justice: the Social Teaching of the Popes from Leo XIII to Pius XIII, 1878–1958* trans. J. Kirwan (London, 1961).

CAMBELL, CHARLES A., 'Is 'Freewill' a Pseudo-problem?', *Mind*, lx (1951), pp. 441–65.

CARLYLE, ROBERT W. and CARLYLE, ALEXANDER J., *A History of Mediaeval Political Theory in the West*, 6 vols. (Edinburgh and London, 1903–36).

CARTER, APRIL, *The Political Theory of Anarchism* (London, 1971).

CHILD, JOHN, *British Management Thought: a critical analysis* (London, 1969).

CHROUST, ANTON-HERMAN, 'The Function of Law and Justice in the Ancient World and the Middle Ages', *Journal of the History of Ideas*, vii (1946), pp. 298–320.

COHEN, ERIK, 'Progress and Communality: Value Dilemmas in the Collective Movement', *International Review of Community Development*, xv–xvi (1966), pp. 3–18.

COHN, NORMAN, *The Pursuit of the Millennium: Revolutionary Millenarians and Mystical Anarchists of the Middle Ages* (London, 1970).

COLE, GEORGE D. H. and POSTGATE, RAYMOND, *The Common People*, *1746–1946* (London, 1956).

CRANSTON, MAURICE, 'Human Rights, Real and Supposed'; 'Human Rights: A Reply to Professor Raphael', in D. D. Raphael (ed.), *Political Theory and the Rights of Man* (London, 1967).

DIAMOND, ARTHUR S., *Primitive Law, Past and Present* (London, 1971).

DICEY, ALBERT V., *Lectures on the Relation Between Law and Public Opinion in England During the Nineteenth Century* (London, 1905).

DUMONT, LOUIS, *Homo Hierarchicus: the Caste System and Its Implications*, trans. M. Sainsbury (London, 1972).

DURKHEIM, EMILE, *The Division of Labour in Society*, trans. G. Simpson (New York, 1964).

DWORKIN, RONALD, 'Is Law a System of Rules?' in R. S. Summers (ed.), *Essays in Legal Philosophy* (Oxford, 1968).

FEINBERG, JOEL, 'Duties, Rights and Claims', *American Philosophical Quarterly*, iii (1966), pp. 137–44, reprinted in E. A. Kent (ed.), *Law and Philosophy* (New York, 1970).

— — 'Justice and Personal Desert' in J. Feinberg, *Doing and Deserving: Essays in the Theory of Responsibility* (Princeton, 1970).

— — 'The Nature and Value of Rights', *Journal of Value Enquiry*, iv (1970), pp. 243–57.

FEYERABEND, PAUL K., 'Problems of Empiricism' in R. Colodny (ed.), *Beyond the Edge of Certainty: essays in contemporary science and philosophy* (New York, 1965).

FLEW, ANTONY G. N., 'Divine Omnipotence and Human Freedom' in A. Flew and A. MacIntyre (eds.), *New Essays in Philosophical Theology* (London, 1955).

— — *Evolutionary Ethics* (London, 1967).

FORD, PERCY, *Social Theory and Social Practice: An Exploration of Experience* (Shannon, 1968).

FRANKENA, WILLIAM K., 'The Concept of Social Justice' in R. B. Brandt (ed.), *Social Justice* (Englewood Cliffs, N.J., 1962).

FRANKLIN, BENJAMIN, *Autobiography*, ed. W. MacDonald (London, 1948).

— — *The Way to Wealth* (London, n.d.).

FRYER, ROBERT H. and MARTIN, RODERICK, 'The Deferential Worker: persistence and disintegration in paternalist capitalism' (duplicated).

FÜRER-HAIMENDORF, CHRISTOPH VON, *Morals and Merit: a Study of Values and Social Controls in South Asian Societies* (London, 1969).

GANSHOF, FRANCOIS L., *Feudalism*, trans. P. Grierson (London, 1964).

GARNETT, RONALD G., *Co-operation and the Owenite socialist communities in Britain, 1825–45* (Manchester, 1972).

GLUCKMAN, MAX, *Politics, Law and Ritual in Tribal Society: Some Problems in Social Anthropology* (Oxford, 1965).

—— *The Ideas in Barotse Jurisprudence* (Manchester, 1972).

GODWIN, WILLIAM, *Enquiry Concerning Political Justice*, ed. K. Codell Carter (Oxford, 1971).

GOLDMAN, IRVING, 'The Kwakiutl Indians of Vancouver Island' in M. Mead (ed.), *Cooperation and Competition Among Primitive Peoples* (Boston, 1961).

GOLDTHORPE, JOHN H., LOCKWOOD, DAVID, BECHHOFER, FRANK, and PLATT, JENNIFER, *The Affluent Worker: Industrial Attitudes and Behaviour* (Cambridge, 1968).

—— *The Affluent Worker in the Class Structure* (Cambridge, 1969).

GUARDIAN, 30 March 1972.

HALBWACHS, MAURICE, *L'Évolution des besoins dans les classes ouvrières* (Paris, 1933).

HALÉVY, ELIE, *The Growth of Philosophic Radicalism*, trans. M. Morris, pref. J. Plamenatz (London, 1972).

HALMOS, PAUL, 'The Personal Service Society', *British Journal of Sociology*, xviii (1967), pp. 13–28.

HAMILTON, RICHARD F., *Class and Politics in the United States* (New York, 1972).

HANSON, NORWOOD R., *Patterns of Discovery* (Cambridge, 1958).

HARDIE, WILLIAM F. R., *Aristotle's Ethical Theory* (Oxford, 1968).

HART, HERBERT L. A., *Definition and Theory in Jurisprudence* (Oxford, 1953).

—— 'Bentham: Lecture on a Master Mind', *Proceedings of the British Academy*, xlviii (1962), pp. 297–320, reprinted in R. S. Summers (ed.), *More Essays in Legal Philosophy* (Oxford, 1971).

—— 'Are there any Natural Rights?' in A. Quinton (ed.), *Political Philosophy* (Oxford, 1967).

HEALD, MORREL, 'Management's Responsibility to Society: the growth of an idea', *Business History Review*, xxxi (1957), pp. 376–84.

HERTZ, FRIEDRICH O., *The Development of the German Public Mind*, vol. i (London, 1957).

HIMMELFARB, GERTRUDE, 'Darwinism, Religion and Morality: Politics and Society' in L. M. Marsak (ed.), *The Rise of Science in Relation to Society* (New York, 1964).

HOBHOUSE, LEONARD T., *Morals in Evolution* (London, 1915).

HODGSKIN, THOMAS, *Labour Defended against the Claims of Capital*, ed. G. D. H. Cole (London, 1922).

HOFSTADTER, RICHARD, *Social Darwinism in American Thought, 1860–1915* (Philadelphia, 1945).

HOHFELD, WESLEY, N., *Fundamental Legal Conceptions as Applied in Judicial Reasoning* (New Haven and London, 1964).

HOMANS, GEORGE C., *Social Behaviour: Its Elementary Forms* (London, 1961).

HONORÉ, ANTHONY M., 'Social Justice' in R. S. Summers (ed.), *Essays in Legal Philosophy* (Oxford, 1968).

HOSPERS, JOHN, *Human Conduct: an introduction to the problem of ethics* (New York, 1961).

HOUGHTON, WALTER E., *The Victorian Frame of Mind, 1830–1870* (New Haven, 1957).

HUME, DAVID, *The History of England* (Oxford, 1826), vol. vii.

—— *An Enquiry Concerning the Principles of Morals* in *Enquiries Concerning the Human Understanding and Concerning the Principles of Morals*, ed. L. A. Selby-Bigge (Oxford, 1902).

—— *A Treatise of Human Nature*, ed. A. D. Lindsay, 2 vols. (London 1911).

—— *Essays Literary, Moral and Political* (London, n.d.).

HUXLEY, THOMAS H., 'Evolution and Ethics'; 'The Struggle for Existence in Human Society' in T. H. Huxley, *Collected Essays*, vol. ix: *Evolution and Ethics and other essays* (London, 1894).

KANTER, ROSABETH M., *Commitment and Community: Communes and Utopias in Sociological Perspective* (Cambridge, Mass., 1972).

KAUFMANN, WALTER, 'Doubts about Justice' in H. E. Kiefer and M. K. Munitz (eds.), *Contemporary Philosophic Thought, IV: Ethics and Social Justice* (New York, 1970).

KAUTSKY, KARL, *Communism in Central Europe in the Time of the Reformation*, trans. J. L. and E. G. Mulliken (London, 1897).

KEAT, RUSSELL and MILLER, DAVID, 'Understanding Justice', *Political Theory*, ii (1974), pp. 3–31.

KELSEN, HANS, 'What is Justice?' in H. Kelsen, *What is Justice?* (Berkeley and Los Angeles, 1957).

KEMP-SMITH, NORMAN, *The Philosophy of David Hume* (London, 1941).

KERN, FRITZ, *Kingship and Law in the Middle Ages*, trans. S. B. Chrimes (Oxford, 1939).

KINCAID, J. C., *Poverty and Equality in Britain: A Study of Social Security and Taxation* (Harmondsworth, 1973).

KLEINIG, JOHN, 'The Concept of Desert', *American Philosophical Quarterly*, viii (1971), pp. 71–8.

KOHLBERG, LAWRENCE, 'From Is to Ought: How to Commit the Naturalistic Fallacy and Get Away with It in the Study of Moral Development' in T. Mischel (ed.), *Cognitive Development and Epistemology* (New York and London, 1971).

KROPOTKIN, PETER, 'Co-operation: a reply to Herbert Spencer', *Freedom* (Dec. 1896–Jan. 1897).

—— —— *Fields, Factories and Workshops* (London, 1899).

—— —— *Mutual Aid: a factor of evolution* (London, 1907).

—— —— *Herbert Spencer: Sa Philosophie* in P. Kropotkin, *La Science moderne et l'anarchie* (Paris, 1913).

—— —— *Modern Science and Anarchism*, 2nd ed. (London, 1923).

—— —— *Ethics: Origin and Development*, trans. L. S. Friedland and J. R. Piroshnikoff (London, 1924).

—— —— *The Conquest of Bread* (New York, 1926).

—— —— *Modern Science and Anarchism; Anarchist Morality; Law and Authority* in *Kropotkin's Revolutionary Pamphlets*, ed. R. N. Baldwin (New York, 1970).

—— —— 'Must we Occupy Ourselves with an examination of the Ideal of a Future System?'; Letter to Nettlau, in *Selected Writings on Anarchism and Revolution*, ed. M. A. Miller (Cambridge, Mass., 1970).

LADD, JOHN, *The Structure of a Moral Code* (Cambridge, Mass., 1957).

LAMONT, WILLIAM D., 'Rights', *Proceedings of the Aristotelian Society*, Supp. vol. xxiv (1950), pp. 83–94.

LANE, ROBERT E., *Political Ideology: Why the American Common Man Believes What He Does* (New York and London, 1962).

LIPSET, SEYMOUR M., *The First New Nation: The United States in Historical And Comparative Perspective* (London, 1964).

LOCKWOOD, DAVID, 'Sources of Variation in Working Class Images of Society', *Sociological Review*, xiv (1966), pp. 249–67.

LOWIE, ROBERT H., *Primitive Society* (London, 1921).

LUCAS, JOHN R., 'Justice', *Philosophy*, xlvii (1972), pp. 229–48.

LUKACS, GEORG, 'Class Consciousness' in G. Lukacs, *History and Class Consciousness*, trans. R. Livingstone (London, 1971).

LUKES, STEVEN, *Individualism* (Oxford, 1973).

LYONS, DAVID, *The Forms and Limits of Utilitarianism* (Oxford, 1965).

—— —— 'Rights, Claimants and Beneficiaries', *American Philosophical Quarterly*, vi (1969), pp. 173–85.

MCBRIAR, ALAN M., *Fabian Socialism and English Politics, 1884–1918* (Cambridge, 1966).

MCCLOSKEY, HERBERT J., 'Egalitarianism, Equality and Justice', *Australasian Journal of Philosophy*. xliv (1966), pp. 50–69.

MALINOWSKI, BRONISLAW K., *Crime and Custom in Savage Society* (London, 1926).

MANN, MICHAEL, 'The Social Cohesion of Liberal Democracy', *American Sociological Review*, xxxv (1970), pp. 423–39.

—— —— *Consciousness and Action Among the Western Working Class* (London, 1973).

MARCUSE, HERBERT, *One-dimensional Man* (London, 1968).

MARSHALL, THOMAS H., 'Citizenship and Social Class' in T. H. Marshall, *Sociology at the Crossroads and other essays* (London, 1963).

—— *Social Policy* (London, 1970).

MARX, KARL, *Economic and Philosophical Manuscripts* in *Karl Marx: Early Writings*, ed. T. B. Bottomore (London, 1963).

—— *Grundrisse: Foundations of the Critique of Political Economy (Rough Draft)*, trans. M. Nicholas (Harmondsworth, 1973).

MAUSS, MARCEL, *The Gift: Forms and Functions of Exchange in Archaic Societies*, trans. I. Cunnison (London, 1970).

MEAD, MARGARET, 'The Arapesh of New Guinea'; 'The Samoans' in M. Mead (ed.), *Cooperation and Competition among Primitive Peoples* (Boston, 1961).

MELDEN, ABRAHAM I., *Rights and Right Conduct* (Oxford, 1959).

MENGER, ANTON, *The Right to the Whole Product of Labour*, trans. M. E. Tanner (London, 1899).

MILL, JOHN STUART, *Utilitarianism; On Liberty; Representative Government*, ed. A. D. Lindsay (London, 1964).

MILLER, DAVID, 'Ideology and the Problem of False Consciousness', *Political Studies*, xx (1972), 432–47.

MIRSKY, JEANETTE, 'The Dakota' in M. Mead (ed.), *Cooperation and Competition Among Primitive Peoples* (Boston, 1961).

MOORE, GEORGE E., *Principia Ethica* (Cambridge, 1903).

MOSSNER, ERNEST C., *The Life of David Hume* (London, 1954).

NATHAN, N. M. L., *The Concept of Justice* (London, 1971).

NICHOLS, THEO., *Ownership, Control and Ideology: an Enquiry into Certain Aspects of Modern Business Ideology* (London, 1969).

NORDHOFF, CHARLES, *The Communistic Societies of the United States* (New York, 1961).

NOWELL-SMITH, PATRICK, *Ethics* (Harmondsworth, 1954).

NOYES, JOHN H., *History of American Socialisms* (London, 1870).

OGDEN, CHARLES K., *Bentham's Theory of Fictions* (London, 1932).

OSSOWSKA, MARIA, *The Social Determinants of Moral Ideas* (London, 1971).

OSSOWSKI, STANISLAW, *Class Structure in the Social Consciousness*, trans. S. Patterson (London, 1963).

OWST, GERALD R., *Literature and Pulpit in Medieval England* (Oxford, 1961).

PARENT, WILLIAM A., 'Some Recent Work on the Concept of Liberty', *American Philosophical Quarterly*, xi (1974), 149–67.

PEEL, JOHN D. Y., *Herbert Spencer: the evolution of a sociologist* (London, 1971).

PERELMAN, CHAIM, *The Idea of Justice and the Problem of Argument*, trans. J. Petrie, intro. H. L. A. Hart (London, 1963).

PERKIN, HAROLD, *The Origins of Modern English Society, 1780–1880* (London, 1972).

PETERS, RICHARD S., *The Concept of Motivation* (London, 1958).

PHILLIPS, D. Z. and MOUNCE, H. O., 'On Morality's having a Point', *Philosophy*, xl (1965), pp. 308–19.

PIAGET, JEAN, *The Moral Judgement of the Child* (London, 1932).

PLAMENATZ, JOHN P., *Man and Society* (London, 1963), vol. i.

PROUDHON, PIERRE J., *What is Property? An Inquiry into the Principles of Right and of Government*, trans. B. R. Tucker (New York, 1970).

RAPHAEL, D. DAICHES, 'Conservative and Prosthetic Justice', *Political Studies*, xii (1964), 149–62.

—— 'Human Rights, Old and New'; 'The Rights of Man and the Rights of the Citizen' in D. D. Raphael (ed.), *Political Theory and the Rights of Man* (London, 1967).

—— 'Hume and Adam Smith on Justice and Utility', *Proceedings of the Aristotelian Society*, lxiii (1972–3), pp. 87–103.

RAWLS, JOHN, 'Distributive Justice' in P. Laslett and W. G. Runciman (eds.), *Philosophy, Politics and Society*, 3rd Ser. (Oxford, 1967).

—— *A Theory of Justice* (Oxford, 1972).

REDFIELD, ROBERT, *The Primitive World and Its Transformations* (Harmondsworth, 1968).

REID, THOMAS, *Essays on the Active Powers of the Human Mind*, ed. B. A. Brody (Cambridge and London, 1969).

RESCHER, NICHOLAS, *Distributive Justice* (New York, 1966).

RIESMAN, DAVID, *The Lonely Crowd: A Study of the Changing American Character* (New Haven and London, 1950).

RIGBY, ANDREW, *Alternative Realities: a study of Communes and their Members* (London, 1974).

RITCHIE, DAVID G., 'On Aristotle's Subdivisions of Particular Justice', *Classical Review*, viii (1894), pp. 185–92.

ROOVER, RAYMOND DE, 'The Concept of the Just Price: Theory and Economic Policy', *Journal of Economic History*, xviii (1958), pp. 418–34.

ROSS, WILLIAM D., *The Right and the Good* (Oxford, 1930).

RUNCIMAN, WALTER G., 'Sociological Evidence and Political Theory' in P. Laslett and W. G. Runciman (eds.), *Philosophy Politics and Society*, 2nd Ser. (Oxford, 1962).

—— *Relative Deprivation and Social Justice: a study of attitudes to social inequality in twentieth-century England* (London, 1966).

— — 'Justice, Congruence and Professor Homans', *European Journal of Sociology*, viii (1967), pp. 115–28.

— — *Social Science and Political Theory* (Cambridge, 1969).

RYAN, JOHN A., *Distributive Justice* (New York, 1916).

RYTINA, JOAN H., FORM, WILLIAM, and PEASE, JOHN, 'Income and Stratification Ideology: Beliefs about the American Opportunity Structure', *American Journal of Sociology*, lxxv (1969–70), pp. 703–16.

SAINT-SIMON, HENRI DE, *L'Organisateur* in *Oeuvres de Saint-Simon et d'Enfantin* (Paris, 1865–76), vol. xx.

— — *Social Organization, The Science of Man and Other Writings*, ed. and trans. F. M. Markham (New York, 1964).

SAMPSON, EDWARD E., 'Studies of Status Congruence' in L. Berkowitz (ed.), *Advances in Experimental Social Psychology*, vol. iv (New York and London, 1969).

SCHLATTER, RICHARD, *Private Property: The History of an Idea* (London, 1951).

SCHUMPETER, JOSEPH A., *Capitalism, Socialism and Democracy* (London, 1954).

SHELTON, H. S., 'The Spencerian Formula of Justice', *International Journal of Ethics*, xxi (1910–11), pp. 298–313.

SIDGWICK, HENRY, *The Principles of Political Economy* (London, 1883).

— — *Lectures on the Ethics of T. H. Green, Mr. Herbert Spencer, and J. Martineau* (London, 1902).

— — *The Methods of Ethics* (London, 1907).

SMART, JOHN J. C., 'Extreme and Restricted Utilitarianism' in P. Foot (ed.), *Theories of Ethics* (Oxford, 1967).

SMITH, ADAM, *The Wealth of Nations*, ed. A. Skinner (Harmondsworth, 1970).

SPENCER, HERBERT, *Social Statics* (London, 1851).

— — *The Principles of Sociology*, 3 vols. (London, 1876–96).

— — 'The Factors of Organic Evolution'; 'Railway Morals and Railway Policy'; 'Parliamentary Reform: The Dangers and the Safeguards' in H. Spencer, *Essays Scientific, Political and Speculative*, 3 vols. (London, 1891).

— — *The Principles of Ethics*, 2 vols. (London, 1893).

— — *The Study of Sociology*, intro. T. Parsons (Ann Arbor, 1961).

— — *The Man versus the State*, ed. D. Macrae (Harmondsworth, 1969).

SPIRO, MELFORD E., *Kibbutz: Venture in Utopia* (New York, 1963).

SPRIGGE, TIMOTHY L. S., 'A Utilitarian Reply to Dr. McCloskey', *Inquiry*, viii (1965), 264–91.

STEWART, JOHN B., *The Moral and Political Philosophy of David Hume* (New York and London, 1963).

STRAWSON, PETER F., 'Freedom and Resentment', *Proceedings of the British Academy*, xlviii (1962), pp. 187–211.

TAWNEY, RICHARD H., *The Acquisitive Society* (London, 1921).

—— *Religion and the Rise of Capitalism* (Harmondsworth, 1938).

—— *Equality*, intro. R. M. Titmuss (London, 1964).

TAYLOR, ARTHUR J., *Laissez-faire and State Intervention in Nineteenth Century Britain* (London, 1972).

TAYLOR, CHARLES, 'Interpretation and the Sciences of Man', *Review of Metaphysics*, xxv (1971–2), pp. 3–51.

THRUPP, SYLVIA L., 'The Gilds' in *Cambridge Economic History of Europe*, vol. iii, ed. M. M. Postan, E. E. Rich, and E. Miller (Cambridge, 1963).

—— 'Gilds' in *International Encyclopaedia of the Social Sciences* (New York, 1968), vol. vi.

TIERNEY, BRIAN, *Medieval Poor Law: a Sketch of Canonical Theory and its Application in England* (Berkeley and Los Angeles, 1959).

TROELTSCH, ERNST, *The Social Teaching of the Christian Churches*, 2 vols., trans. O. Wyon (London, 1931).

TUCKER, BENJAMIN R., *State Socialism and Anarchism: how far they agree, and wherein they disagree* (London, 1895).

Universal Declaration of Human Rights in D. D. Raphael (ed.), *Political Theory and the Rights of Man* (London, 1967).

URE, ANDREW, *The Philosophy of Manufactures* (London, 1835).

URMSON, JAMES O., 'Saints and Heroes' in A. I. Melden (ed.), *Essays in Moral Philosophy* (Seattle, Washington, 1958).

VECCHIO, GIORGIO DEL, *Justice, an historical and philosophical essay*, trans. E. M. Guthrie, ed. A. H. Campbell (Edinburgh, 1952).

VLASTOS, GREGORY, 'Justice and Equality' in R. B. Brandt (ed.), *Social Justice* (Englewood Cliffs, N.J., 1962).

WATT, A. J., 'The Intelligibility of Wants', *Mind*, lxxxi (1972), pp. 553–61.

WEBB, BEATRICE, *My Apprenticeship*, intro. B. Jackson (Harmondsworth, 1971).

WEBB, ROBERT K., *Harriet Martineau: a radical Victorian* (New York, 1960).

WEBB, SIDNEY and WEBB, BEATRICE, *English Poor Law Policy* (London, 1910).

WEBER, MAX, *The Protestant Ethic and the Spirit of Capitalism*, trans. T. Parsons (London, 1930).

—— *The Theory of Social and Economic Organization*, trans. A. Henderson and T. Parsons, ed. T. Parsons (New York, 1964).

WELDON, THOMAS D., *The Vocabulary of Politics* (Harmondsworth, 1953).

WESTERMARCK, EDWARD, *The Origin and Development of the Moral Ideas*, 2 vols. (London, 1906).

WILLEY, BASIL, *The Eighteenth Century Background* (London, 1940).

WILLIAMS, BERNARD, 'The Idea of Equality' in P. Laslett and W. G. Runciman (eds.), *Philosophy, Politics and Society*, 2nd Ser. (Oxford, 1962).

WOLIN, SHELDON S., *Politics and Vision: Continuity and Innovation in Western Political Thought* (Boston, 1960).

WOODCOCK, GEORGE and AVAKUMOVIĆ, IVAN, *The Anarchist Prince, a biographical study of P. Kropotkin* (London, 1950).

WOOTTON, BARBARA, *The Social Foundations of Wage Policy* (London, 1958).

YUCHTMAN, EPHRAIM, 'Reward Distribution and Work-Role Attractiveness in the Kibbutz—Reflections on Equity Theory', *American Sociological Review*, xxxvii (1972), pp. 581–95.

INDEX